COMMONWEALTH CARIBBEAN CONTRACT LAW

The first textbook on Commonwealth Caribbean Contract law for undergraduate and sixth form students, *Commonwealth Caribbean Contract Law* is a new and unrivalled resource on the subject. This textbook utilises Caribbean case law and statutory provisions to provide a clear and immersive path into the study of contract law from a Caribbean perspective. Encompassing topics that include misrepresentation, privity, and remedies, this book expertly introduces and explains the many aspects of contract law in the Caribbean.

Written by a well-established textbook author who is a professor of law at the University of the West Indies, and a solicitor at a leading international law firm based in London, the textbook comprehensively covers all key principles of contractual obligations studied by undergraduate students, and is relevant to practitioners in a modern and accessible way. An invaluable reference, this book is essential reading for those with an academic or professional interest in Caribbean contract law.

Gilbert Kodilinye MA (Oxon), LLM (Lond), TEP, of the Inner Temple, Barrister, Barrister of the Eastern Caribbean Supreme Court, British Virgin Islands, is Professor at the Faculty of Law, UWI Mona. He is the author of four well established textbooks in the Routledge Commonwealth Caribbean Law Series.

Maria Kodilinye LLB (UWI), BCL (Oxon), Solicitor of the Senior Courts of England and Wales, is a solicitor qualified in England and Wales and is an associate at a leading international law firm based in London.

Commonwealth Caribbean Law Series

The Commonwealth Caribbean Law Series is the only series of law books that covers the jurisdictions of the English-speaking Caribbean nations. The titles in the series were first published in 1995, to acclaim from academics, practitioners and the judiciary in the region. Several editions followed, and they have now become essential reading for those learning and practising Caribbean law.

This must have series is required holdings for any law library specialising in Caribbean legal information.

Titles in this series include:

Alternative Dispute Resolution
Albert Fiadjoe

Commonwealth Caribbean Business Law 2/e
Rajendra Ramlogan and Natalie Persadie

Commonwealth Caribbean Company Law
Andrew Burgess

Commonwealth Caribbean Civil Procedure 2/e
Gilbert Kodilinye and Vanessa Kodilinye

Commonwealth Caribbean Constitutional Law
Sir Fred Phillips

Commonwealth Caribbean Criminal Practice and Procedure 3/e
Dana S. Seetahal

Commonwealth Caribbean Law and Legal Systems 2/e
Rose-Marie Belle Antoine

Commonwealth Caribbean Property Law 3/e
Gilbert Kodilinye

Commonwealth Caribbean Public Law 3/e
Albert Fiadjoe

Commonwealth Caribbean Tort Law 4/e
Gilbert Kodilinye

Commonwealth Caribbean Law of Trusts 3/e
Gilbert Kodilinye and Trevor Carmichael

Judicial Review in the Commonwealth Caribbean
Rajendra Ramlogan

Commonwealth Caribbean Administrative Law
Eddy Ventose

Commonwealth Caribbean Contract Law
Gilbert Kodilinye and Maria Kodilinye

Forthcoming titles:

Commonwealth Caribbean Employment and Labour Law
Natalie Corthésy and Carla-Anne Harris-Roper

Commonwealth Caribbean Practice and Procedure 4/e
Dana S. Seetahal

Commonwealth Caribbean Tort Law 5/e
Gilbert Kodilinye

COMMONWEALTH CARIBBEAN CONTRACT LAW

Gilbert Kodilinye and Maria Kodilinye

Routledge
Taylor & Francis Group
LONDON AND NEW YORK

First published 2014
by Routledge
2 Park Square, Milton Park, Abingdon, Oxon, OX14 4RN

Simultaneously published in the USA and Canada
by Routledge
711 Third Avenue, New York, NY 10017

Routledge is an imprint of the Taylor & Francis Group, an informa business

British Library Cataloguing in Publication Data
A catalogue record for this book is available from the British Library

Library of Congress Cataloging-in-Publication Data
A catalog record has been requested for this book

ISBN: 978–0–415–53871–8 (hbk)
ISBN: 978–0–415–53872–5 (pbk)
ISBN: 978–0–203–48864–5 (ebk)

Typeset in Palatino by
RefineCatch Limited, Bungay, Suffolk

CONTENTS

PREFACE

Contract law is an important and dynamic area of law, impacting on a broad spectrum of relationships. This spectrum ranges from complex commercial transactions, to everyday interactions between individual consumers and retailers. Not only is contract law pervasive in everyday life, it is also a compulsory topic of study for law students, including those reading for the LLB degrees in Caribbean universities and those following paralegal courses in the various colleges of further education in the region. It is also an area which most legal practitioners will encounter at some point in their careers, and one which is of major importance in the business sector.

In producing this text, we have endeavoured to fill a gap in the field by providing students with an accessible analysis of the basic principles of contract law. To this end, this first edition collates and analyses selected Commonwealth Caribbean and English cases on contract law, including both reported and unreported Caribbean judgments, which demonstrate the application of key contractual principles in the context of issues most relevant to the region. It is hoped that practitioners and students will find the collection of unreported Caribbean judgments in the text to be a useful resource.

The text deals with the following concepts in turn, focusing on the principles which are most relevant for students and which are applicable in the specific context of the Commonwealth Caribbean: contracts as distinguished from other types of legal relationship; formation of contracts; capacity to enter into contracts; contractual terms; contracts for the sale of goods, including unfair terms; instances where contracts are void or voidable; privity of contract and agency; the discharge of contractual obligations; and remedies for breach.

Gilbert Kodilinye
Maria Kodilinye
20 June 2013

TABLE OF CASES

TABLE OF STATUTES

CHAPTER 1

INTRODUCTION

NATURE AND FUNCTIONS OF CONTRACT LAW

The law of contract may be defined as that branch of the law which determines the circumstances in which a promise will be legally binding on the person making the promise (the 'promisor') and enforceable in a court of law by the person to whom the promise was made (the 'promisee'). A well-accepted definition is that contained in section 1 of the American Law Institute's Second Restatement of the Law of Contracts: 'A contract is a promise or a set of promises for the breach of which the law gives a remedy, or the performance of which the law in some way recognizes as a duty.'

The rationale for the enforceability of contracts is essentially the promotion of trade and commerce, which would be seriously hampered if contracting parties could not be held to their bargains. Accordingly, a party which enters into a valid contract can be assured that it will be able to recover compensation from the other party in the event of the latter's repudiation of the agreement or failure to perform its obligations, and the 'measure' (i.e. the amount) of damages recoverable in contract law is intended to compensate the innocent party not only for any material or financial damage sustained on account of the other party's breach, but also for any loss of profits or other benefits which it would have received if the contract had been performed by that other party.

Enforceable contracts appear in a great variety of forms, ranging from, on the one hand, 'everyday' contracts entered into by consumers, such as those for the sale of goods in a supermarket, or for transportation of a passenger in a bus, train or plane, or for professional services to be rendered by a dentist, plumber or hairdresser to, on the other, complex commercial agreements such as large-scale building and civil engineering contracts affecting several corporate parties, any breach of which could inflict serious financial damage on one or more of the parties. An example of such complex relationships in the Caribbean might occur in the context of the construction of a resort complex involving the following parties and transactions:

(a) A property developer purchases a site for building, with money obtained by way of a loan on mortgage from a bank.
(b) The developer appoints an architect to design the buildings, a landscape artist to design the gardens, a quantity surveyor to draw up bills of quantities, and an attorney to do the conveyancing work.
(c) Tenders are invited for the building work, and the contractor whose tender is accepted is appointed as 'main contractor' under the contract between him/it and the developer.
(d) The main contractor subcontracts various parts of the building work to specialist subcontractors, thereby creating contractual relations between the main contractor and the subcontractors.

In such a scenario, each of the parties will depend on the others to carry out their contractual obligations and, in the event of a breach by a promisor, the innocent promisee under the particular contract will have a right of action for breach of contract against the defaulting promisor. Thus, for example, an architect who produces defective drawings may be liable to the developer, as will a main contractor who uses materials which do not comply with the specifications for the work, or who fails to complete within the period specified by the contract. Similarly, a subcontractor who is in default may be liable to the main contractor, and a developer will be liable to the main contractor for failure to pay him promptly at the stages provided by the contract. In short, it may be said that 'contract is, in effect, the instrument by which the separate and conflicting interests of the participants can be reconciled and brought to a common goal'.[1]

Freedom of contract

The concept of 'freedom of contract' became a basic tenet of jurists, philosophers and economists in the nineteenth century, and it persisted in mainstream legal thinking until comparatively recently. At the heart of this principle is the notion that a party to a contract is expected to decide what is in his own best interests, and the law's function is simply to enforce agreements and not to interfere with them on grounds of 'unfairness' or 'unreasonableness'. This is the essence of *laissez-faire* economics. However, according to some contemporary jurists, the *laissez-faire* approach is acceptable only where the parties to a contract have 'equal bargaining power', which would be the case where a contract is concluded between two corporate entities of equal economic 'muscle', but not where an individual consumer enters into a contract with, for instance, a utility company for the supply of electricity or telephone service, where the terms of the contract are standardised and not subject to bargaining, and where the consumer has no alternative but to accept those terms.[2] Accordingly, limited protection for contracting parties having little or no bargaining power is afforded by statutory provisions in many jurisdictions,[3] and the courts, in some instances, have refused to enforce contractual exemption clauses imposed by a stronger party on the weaker.[4] Nevertheless, in 1967, Lord Reid, commenting on the effect of the so-called 'doctrine of fundamental breach',[5] deprecated the idea of restricting 'the general principle of English Law that parties are free to contract as they may think fit', and in 1980, Lord Diplock reiterated the 'basic principle of the common law of contract . . . that the parties are free to determine for themselves what primary obligations they will accept'.[6]

Sanctity of contracts

The principle of sanctity of contracts means that a contract, once made, must be observed and promises must be kept. The principle serves the requirements of the commercial community by giving security and certainty to contractual relations and

1 *Anson's Law of Contract*, 29th edn, p 3.
2 These are known as 'contracts of adhesion'.
3 See, for example, Consumer Protection Act, Cap 326D (Barbados); Consumer Protection Act, 2006 (Jamaica).
4 See pp 87–90 below.
5 *Suisse Atlantique Société d'Armement Maritime SA v MV Rotterdamsche Kolen Centrale* [1967] 1 AC 361, at 399.
6 *Photo Production Ltd v Securicor Transport Ltd* [1980] AC 827, at 843.

providing assurance that transactions involving financial commitments on the part of the contracting parties will be enforced by the courts. The strictness of the principle is exemplified by the courts' refusal, before 1863, to allow a party to be freed of his contractual obligations on the ground of frustration. Before the case of *Taylor v Caldwell*[7] it was a strict rule that a party could not escape his obligations under a contract by pleading that a fundamental change in the circumstances since the date of the agreement had 'frustrated' the contract. Today, frustration is accepted as a ground for discharging a contract, but the circumstances in which the courts will allow the plea to succeed remain severely limited, and the current position is that frustration will discharge a contract only where the frustrating event 'strikes at the root of the contract', so that the agreement, after the event, becomes fundamentally different in character from that originally contemplated by the parties.[8]

Contract distinguished from tort

Owing to the manner in which tortious and contractual obligations developed simultaneously throughout the history of the common law, the precise relationship between the two areas of law is a matter of debate, and there is a school of thought which argues that tort and contract should be subsumed under a 'law of civil obligations'.

The traditional distinction made between tort and contract is that, in tort, the duties of the parties are primarily fixed by law, whereas in contract they are fixed by the parties themselves. Put another way, contractual duties arise from agreement between the parties, whereas tortious duties exist by operation of law, independently of the consent of the parties. This distinction may be misleading, however, for, in the first place, although contractual obligations are certainly created by agreement, the parties are nonetheless subjected to the underlying principles of contract law developed by the courts. Second, the duties owed by contracting parties towards one another are frequently not duties which they expressly agreed upon but obligations which the law implies, such as the terms implied under sale of goods and hire purchase legislation.[9] Conversely, some duties in tort can be varied by agreement, for example, the duties owed by an occupier of premises to his lawful visitors; and liability in tort can be excluded altogether by consent.

Other points of distinction between contract and tort are:

(a) Damages for purely economic loss are recoverable in contract, whereas such loss is generally not recoverable in the tort of negligence.[10]

(b) A contractual right, such as a debt, can generally be assigned, whereas a right to sue in tort generally cannot.[11]

---

7 (1863) 122 ER 309.

8 See pp 243–252 below.

9 See Chapter 6, below.

10 *Spartan Steel and Alloys Ltd v Martin & Co Ltd* [1973] 1 QB 27. Recovery of damages for negligent misstatements under the rule in *Hedley Byrne & Co v Heller & Partners Ltd* [1963] 2 All ER 575, is a notable exception to the rule of non-recoverability for purely financial loss in tort.

11 See Winfield & Jolowicz, *Tort*, 18th edn, pp 1204–7.

(c) Exemplary (punitive) damages can be recovered in tort in certain limited circumstances, but they are not recoverable in actions for breach of contract.
(d) A minor is fully liable for his torts but he is liable in contract only in very limited circumstances.[12]

There are situations where a claimant may have alternative causes of action in contract and tort against a defaulting defendant. For example:

(a) If D has agreed to transport C's goods and, owing to D's negligence, the goods are damaged or destroyed, D will be liable to C both for the tort of negligence and for breach of the contract of carriage.
(b) A dentist who negligently causes injury in the course of extracting a tooth may be liable to the patient both for the tort of negligence and for breach of an implied term in his contract with the patient that he will take reasonable care.
(c) If C enters D's premises under a contract with D and is injured owing to the defective condition of the premises, D may be liable both in the tort of negligence (or under the Occupiers' Liability Acts[13]), and for breach of contract.
(d) If C is induced to enter into a contract with D by a misrepresentation negligently made by D, and suffers loss thereby, he may recover damages in the tort of negligence (as an exception to the rule that damages for purely economic loss are not recoverable in tort) as well as in contract under the Misrepresentation Acts.[14]

In addition to those cases where the same set of facts can give rise to claims in both contract and tort (as in the cases of the carrier and the dentist), there are areas where there is an overlap between the principles of contract and tort, and it is here that the argument that contract and tort are part of one law of obligations is at its most persuasive. Such areas include: fraudulent misrepresentation in contract, which is the *alter ego* of the tort of deceit; negligent misrepresentation, a concept developed in the law of tort but equally applicable to contract law; the principle of remoteness of damage, a concept common to both contract and tort, though not applied in exactly the same way;[15] and agency, another concept recognised in both contract and tort, though applied in rather different circumstances.[16]

One of the most significant distinctions between tort and contract law concerns the object of an award of damages. Tort law is designed to preserve the status quo, in that the claimant's position should not be made worse by the defendant's act or omission. This objective is expressed in the principle that, in awarding damages in tort, the court should attempt to place the claimant as far as possible in the position in which he would have been if the tort had not been committed. In contract, on the other hand, the defendant is liable to pay such compensation as would put the claimant into the position in which he would have been if the contract had been carried out; in other words, contract damages are intended not merely to preserve the status quo but to fulfill the claimant's expectation of benefit from the contract.[17]

12 See Chapter 5, below.
13 See the Occupier's Liability Acts of Jamaica, Barbados and Bermuda.
14 See pp 150 *et seq* below. Misrepresentation Acts have been enacted in Trinidad & Tobago and Bermuda.
15 See pp 264–266 below.
16 See Chapter 12 below.
17 See Chapter 14 below.

Contract distinguished from trusts

A contract differs from a trust in the following respects:

(a) A contract is essentially a common law obligation, whereas trusts were created and enforced in equity.

(b) A contract arises from agreement or *consensus ad idem* between the parties. A trust *may* arise by agreement – for instance, where a settlor covenants with trustees to settle property in the future or where a company or organisation establishes a pension scheme for the benefit of its employees – but most often it will not arise from agreement but will take effect by way of gift, such as where a testator sets up a trust in his will or executes a voluntary trust deed *inter vivos*.

(c) The right to enforce a contract is a right *in personam* since, as a general rule, action can be brought only against the other contracting party. The right to enforce a trust, on the other hand, is almost, though not quite, a right *in rem* since, in the event of a breach of trust, the trust property or its proceeds can be recovered by means of the tracing remedy, not only from the trustee but also from any other person to whom the trustee has transferred the property, other than a *bona fide* purchaser of the property for value having no notice of the trust.

(d) 'Valuable consideration' in the law of trusts has a wider meaning than in contract, for it includes not only money or money's worth (the contractual definition) but also the consideration notionally given in a marriage settlement by the spouses and issue of the marriage.

RECEPTION OF THE LAW OF CONTRACT IN COMMONWEALTH CARIBBEAN JURISDICTIONS

The law of contract has been received into Commonwealth Caribbean jurisdictions as a part of the common law of England. Historically, the method of reception has varied from one territory to another, principally according to whether the particular territory was subject to settlement (such as Barbados, Antigua, St Kitts/Nevis) or to conquest or cession (such as Jamaica, Trinidad & Tobago, Dominica, Grenada).[18] In the case of settled colonies, the British subjects who settled there were deemed to have taken English law with them, and there was no need for statutory provisions expressly receiving the common law into those territories. In the case of conquered or ceded colonies, on the other hand, the law in force at the time of cession or conquest remained in force until altered by or under the authority of the Sovereign. In the latter class of territory, English law would not generally apply without statutory reception provisions.[19]

Although the distinction between settled colonies on the one hand and conquered and ceded colonies on the other is a useful guide to the method of reception of

18 See Roberts-Wray, *Commonwealth and Colonial Law* (London: Stevens, 1966), pp 539–43; Patchett, 'Reception of Laws in the West Indies' (1972) JLJ 17, p 55; Wylie, *Land Law of Trinidad and Tobago* (Port of Spain: Government of Trinidad and Tobago, 1981), p 5.

19 *Ibid*, Roberts-Wray, pp 540–1.

English law, it has been rightly pointed out that 'the story of the reception of English law in the various parts of the Caribbean is a tangled one',[20] and it is by no means easy to identify the precise method of reception in all the territories. Be that as it may, the current position is that the courts in all jurisdictions in the region are enjoined by statute[21] to apply the doctrines of common law and equity, which includes principles of the law of contract.

20 Wylie, *Land Law of Trinidad and Tobago* (Port of Spain: (Government of Trinidad and Tobago, 1981), p 5.

21 See for example, s 31, Supreme Court of Judicature Act, Cap 117 (Barbados); s 48, Judicature (Supreme Court) Act (Jamaica); s 12, Supreme Court of Judicature Act, Ch 4:01 (Trinidad and Tobago); s 15, Supreme Court Act, Ch 53 (The Bahamas).

CHAPTER 2

OFFER AND ACCEPTANCE

The first requirement of a binding contract is that the parties should have reached agreement (a '*consensus ad idem*'). Normally, an agreement is made when one party (the 'offeror') makes an offer to another (the 'offeree') which the offeree accepts. For example, if R says to E in the presence of witnesses: 'Will you buy my Suzuki car reg no XF 2244 for $10,000?', and E replies, 'Yes, I will', a contract comes into being. In such a simple example, there is no difficulty in identifying the offer and the acceptance, but where the alleged agreement is preceded by protracted negotiations conducted in lengthy correspondence, it may be difficult to discover a precise offer and acceptance. In such a case, it would be necessary for the court to scrutinise the correspondence carefully in order to decide whether or not there was a concluded agreement.[1]

THE OFFER

An offer has been described as 'an expression of willingness to contract on certain terms made with the intention (actual or apparent) that it shall become binding as soon as it is accepted by the person to whom it is addressed'.[2]

An offer may be made to a particular individual or corporation, or to the world at large. In the above example, the offer to sell a Suzuki car was clearly addressed to an individual person, E, whereas an instance of an offer addressed to the world at large is the well-known case of *Carlill v Carbolic Smoke Ball Co*,[3] where the defendants offered by advertisement to pay £100 to any person who, having used their 'smoke ball' in the prescribed manner, nevertheless caught influenza.

An offer may be made by express words (as in the above two examples), or it may be implied from conduct; for example, where a bus travels along a certain route there is an implied offer on the part of the bus company to carry passengers at the published fares, and a contract is formed when a passenger boards the bus.[4]

Supply of information

An offer must be distinguished from a mere supply of information, which is incapable of being 'accepted' so as to ripen into a contract. The classic example is *Harvey v Facey*,[5] a Jamaican case which eventually reached the Privy Council. In this case,

---

1 *Perry v Suffields Ltd* [1916] 2 Ch 187; *A Mahabir and Sons Ltd v Caroni (1975) Ltd* (2002) High Court, Trinidad and Tobago, No S781 of 1997, unreported, *per* Tam J [Carilaw TT 2002 HC 35]. *Speedy Service Liquors Ltd v Airports Authority of Trinidad and Tobago* (2002) High Court, Trinidad and Tobago, Nos 586 and 936 of 1984, unreported [Carilaw TT 2002 HC 105] is an example of offer and acceptance arising from an exchange of letters between the parties.

2 Treitel, *Law of Contract*, 12th edn (London: Sweet and Maxwell, 2007), para 2-002.

3 [1893] 1 QB 256

4 *Wilkie v London Passenger Transport Board* [1947] 1 All ER 258.

5 [1893] AC 552.

the respondent was travelling on a train between Kingston and Porus when he received a telegram from the appellant in the following terms: 'Will you sell us Bumper Hall Pen? Telegraph lowest cash price.' The respondent replied by telegram: 'Lowest price for Bumper Hall Pen £900.' The appellant replied: 'We agree to buy Bumper Hall Pen for £900 asked by you. Please send us your title deeds.' Bumper Hall Pen was a plot of land, and the appellant claimed that a contract of sale had been created by the exchange of telegrams. The Privy Council rejected the appellant's claim, reasoning that the first telegram had asked two questions, (i) whether the respondent was willing to sell, and (ii) as to the lowest price, and that the words 'Telegraph lowest cash price' referred only to the second question. Accordingly, the respondent's telegram in reply was not making an offer but merely supplying information, and the third telegram constituted an offer by the appellant (notwithstanding that the appellant had called it an 'acceptance') which had not been accepted by the respondent. Lord Morris said:[6]

> The third telegram ... treats the answer of LM Facey stating his lowest price as an unconditional offer to sell to [the appellants] at the price named. Their Lordships cannot treat the telegram from LM Facey stating his lowest price as binding him in any respect, except to the extent it does by its terms, viz, the lowest price. Everything else is left open, and the reply telegram from the appellants cannot be treated as an acceptance of an offer to sell to them; it is an offer that required to be accepted by LM Facey. The contract could only be completed if LM Facey had accepted the appellants' last telegram.

Another example where the court found that there was no offer to sell but rather a preliminary statement as to price is *Clifton v Palumbo*.[7] In this case, in which the parties were negotiating the sale of an extensive area of land, C wrote to P: 'I am prepared to offer you or your nominee my Lytham estate for £600,000. I also agree that a reasonable and sufficient time shall be granted to you for the examination and consideration of all the data and details necessary for the preparation of the Schedule of Completion.' It was held that these words did not amount to a definite offer to sell but, especially in view of the large size of the estate, were to be interpreted as an intimation of the price at which C was prepared to consider selling. Lord Greene said:[8]

> There is nothing in the world to prevent an owner of an estate of this kind contracting to sell it to a purchaser, who is prepared to spend so large a sum of money, on terms written out on half a sheet of notepaper of the most informal description and even, if he likes, on unfavourable conditions. But I think it legitimate, in approaching construction of a document of this kind, containing phrases and expressions of doubtful significance, to bear in mind that the probability of parties entering into so large a transaction, and binding themselves to a contract of this description couched in such terms, is remote. If they have done it, they have done it, however unwise and however unbusinesslike it may be. The question is, have they done it?

Harvey v Facey and *Clifton v Palumbo* were followed by the Jamaican Court of Appeal in *Barnett Ltd v Olasemo*,[9] where, following discussions between the parties regarding

---

6 At 554.
7 [1944] 2 All ER 497.
8 At 499.
9 (1995) 32 JLR 284.

the sale of the appellant's land, the appellant wrote a letter to the respondent enclosing a draft agreement of sale 'for the [respondent's] perusal and comments'. Downer JA held[10] that 'the words "draft agreement" and the request for comments made it plain that there was no definite offer', and that 'the reality was that negotiations continued'.

Another recent Caribbean example is *Select Properties Ltd v Texaco (Trinidad) Ltd*.[11] Here, D, a sales representative of N Ltd, who were agents of T Co, wrote to P, a director of S Ltd, offering a property for sale at the price of $4,500,000. P visited the property the same day the letter was received and immediately wrote to D, purporting to accept D's 'offer in respect of the Gulf View Property at the asking price of $4,500,000' and further stating: 'We hereby tender a deposit of ten per cent and will complete payment within ninety days. This acceptance is based on your representation that the property is freehold and there are no restrictive covenants.' Alexander J, in the Trinidad and Tobago High Court, stated that: 'a court should only find a binding contract for sale when there is offer and acceptance; whether there is, depends on the construction of the documents'. In this case, the letter from D was not an offer to sell but only an indication of the price at which T Co were prepared to sell, and there was therefore no concluded contract.

Invitation to treat

An offer must be distinguished from an invitation to treat, which is an invitation to make offers and to do business. An invitation to treat is of no effect in law and cannot ripen into a contract by 'acceptance'. It is sometimes difficult to determine whether a particular communication is to be regarded as an offer, or as a mere invitation to treat: the answer depends essentially on the intention of the parties, taking into account the circumstances surrounding the case. The following instances are to be found in the case law.

Advertisements

An advertisement in a newspaper or periodical that the advertiser has goods or services for sale will generally be regarded as an invitation to treat and not an offer; and the same applies to advertised catalogues and price lists.[12] Thus, for example, an advertisement in a periodical stating that the advertiser had 'Bramblefinch cocks and hens for sale' was held not to be an offer to sell the birds, but an invitation to treat. Readers were free to make offers, which could be accepted or rejected by the advertiser.[13]

10 At 288.

11 (2009) High Court, Trinidad and Tobago, No S 765 of 2003, unreported [Carilaw TT 2009 HC 85].

12 *Grainger & Son v Gough* [1896] AC 325.

13 *Partridge v Crittenden* [1968] 2 All ER 421. The result was that the advertiser was not guilty of offering a wild bird for sale contrary to a statutory prohibition.

Displays of goods in shops and supermarkets

Where the proprietor of a shop displays goods in the shop window or on the shelves inside, marked with their prices, he does not thereby bind himself to sell at that price, or to sell at all. In so doing, he is merely inviting customers to treat. It is the customer who makes an offer by asking to buy the goods or by taking them to the cashier or checkout, and the proprietor or his employee may accept the customer's offer by receiving the purchase price and handing over the goods.[14]

Vending machines

Vending machine sales are treated differently from ordinary shop or supermarket sales, as there is no opportunity for the vendor to decline the sale once the buyer has put his money into or otherwise activated the machine. Accordingly, the display on a food or drinks vending machine will be regarded as an offer which is accepted when the purchaser inserts his money. It has also been held that, at a self-service gas station, an open offer to sell at pump prices is accepted by a motorist putting fuel into his tank,[15] and that, where the entry to a car park is machine-controlled, the proprietor makes an offer to provide parking for a customer, which is accepted by the customer activating the machine.[16] On the other hand, it has been held that the indication of the price at which petrol was to be sold at a gas station where customers were served by attendants was not an offer, but an invitation to treat.[17]

Invitations to tender

Where a public authority or other organisation advertises in a newspaper inviting tenders for, for instance, the carrying out of building works or the supply of goods, it makes not an offer but an invitation to treat. An offer is made by each firm that submits a tender in answer to the advertisement, the advertiser being free to accept or reject any tender, though it is otherwise if the advertisement is accompanied by words which indicate that the highest or lowest tender will be accepted.[18]

Company prospectuses

A prospectus issued by a company in order to invite the public to subscribe for its shares is an invitation to treat; members of the public make offers to buy the shares when they apply for them, and the company accepts each offer by allotting shares to the subscriber.[19]

---

14 *Fisher v Bell* [1961] 1 QB 394; *Pharmaceutical Society of Great Britain v Boots Cash Chemists (Southern) Ltd* [1952] 2 QB; affd [1953] 1 QB 401. On the other hand, in *Chapelton v Barry UDC* [1940] 1 All ER 356, it was held that the display of deck chairs at a beach was an offer to hire.

15 *Re Charge Card Services* [1989] Ch 497.

16 *Thornton v Shoe Lane Parking Ltd* [1971] 1 All ER 686.

17 *Esso Petroleum Ltd v Customs and Excise Comrs* [1976] 1 All ER 117.

18 *Spencer v Harding* (1870) LR 5 CP 561.

19 *Harvela Investments Ltd v Royal Trust of Canada (CI) Ltd* [1986] AC 207.

Auctions

An advertisement to the effect that an auction of various articles will be held on a certain day is an invitation to treat only, and in the event that the auction does not take place, the auctioneer will not be contractually liable to indemnify any person who has incurred expenditure in travelling to the venue in order to attend the sale.[20]

At an auction, the auctioneer's request for bids is an invitation to treat. A bid from the floor is an offer which may be accepted by the fall of the auctioneer's hammer, so no contract is concluded if, after a bid has been made, the auctioneer declines to accept it. On the other hand, it is now established that in the case of an advertisement that certain goods are to be sold at an auction 'without reserve', the auctioneer is bound to sell to the highest bona fide bidder for the goods, and is not entitled to refuse to accept the bid and withdraw the goods from sale, as he will be taken to be bound under a collateral contract with the highest bidder.[21]

Communication of offer

An offer is not effective unless it is communicated to the offeree. One manifestation of this rule is that two identical cross-offers do not create a contract. In *Tinn v Hoffman & Co*,[22] the defendant, on 28 November, wrote to the claimant offering to sell him 800 tons of iron at 69 shillings per ton. On the same day, the claimant wrote to the defendant offering to buy the same quantity of iron at the same price. The letters crossed in the post. The claimant argued that there was a binding contract on those terms. It was held that the defendant was not bound as a result of the simultaneous offers, as each offer was made in ignorance of the other and there was no true *consensus ad idem*.

Another instance of the application of the rule requiring communication of an offer is that where X does work for Y, without the request or knowledge of Y, X cannot sue for the value of the work unless Y is shown to have positively recognised or accepted the work. As Pollock CB commented:[23]

> Suppose I clean your property without your knowledge, have I a claim on you for payment? How can you help it? One cleans another's shoes; what can the other do but put them on? Is that evidence of a contract to pay for the cleaning?

The principle that there must be communication of an offer certainly applies where the offer is made to an individual, and it seems it also applies to offers made to the world at large; for example, where X offers to pay a reward to any person who finds and returns his lost dog and Y, who has not heard of the offer, happens to find and return the dog to X, it has been suggested that Y cannot claim the reward since the offer was never communicated to him.[24] If, however, Y does know of the offer but

---

20 *Harris v Nickerson* (1873) LR 8 QB 286.

21 *Barry v Davies* [2001] 1 All ER 944, applying *dicta* to that effect in *Warlow v Harrison* (1859) 120 ER 309.

22 (1873) 29 LT 271.

23 *Taylor v Laird* (1856) 25 LJ Ex 329, at 332.

24 *Fitch v Snedaker* (1868) 38 NY 248.

performs the act with a motive other than that of claiming the reward, such motive will be irrelevant. Thus, where a claimant, knowing of the offer of a reward for information leading to the conviction of a murderer, supplied the information in order to 'ease her conscience', she was held to be entitled to claim the reward.[25]

THE ACCEPTANCE

In order for a contract to be concluded, the offeree must accept the offeror's offer by words or conduct. 'Acceptance' is 'the expression . . . of assent to the terms of the offer in the manner prescribed or indicated by the offeror.'[26] Thus, once the existence of an offer has been proved, the court must be satisfied that the offeree has accepted the offer in the above sense, and, if such acceptance is established, there will be a contract. Where the parties conduct protracted negotiations, it may be difficult to determine exactly when the offer and acceptance took place; the court will scrutinise the whole correspondence between the parties in order to decide whether they have reached agreement. It is for the parties themselves to agree as to the terms of their contract, and the court will not by construction create new terms and conditions which would have the effect of imposing a new contract on the parties.

Under the 'mirror image' principle, the acceptance must be absolute and must correspond with the terms of the offer. Accordingly, there will be no contract where (i) there is a counter-offer from the offeree; (ii) the 'acceptance' contains terms at variance with those in the offer; or (iii) the 'acceptance' is equivocal or qualified.

Counter-offer

There will be no contract where the 'acceptance' amounts to a counter-offer, which is treated as a rejection of the offer and so brings the offer to an end. The counter-offer is itself open to acceptance or rejection by the original offeror. In *Hyde v Wrench*,[27] V offered to sell a farm to P for £1,000. P replied that he would give £950 for it. V refused to sell at that price. P then said he would pay £1,000, but V withdrew his offer and declined to proceed. It was held that there was no contract and V was not bound to sell. P's counter-offer had destroyed V's offer, and the counter-offer had not been accepted by V.

Where the offeree's purported acceptance contains new terms which are at variance with those of the offer, there will be no contract, the variations being treated as a counter-offer. Thus in one case,[28] P offered £1,450 for V's property. In accepting the offer, V enclosed with his letter of acceptance a contractual document containing terms regarding payment of deposit, stipulations as to title, and completion date which had never been suggested in the offer. It was held that there was no contract. V's response amounted to a counter-offer which had never been accepted by P.

25 *Williams v Carwardine* (1833) 110 ER 590.
26 *Auson's Law of Contract*, 28th edn, p 37.
27 (1840) 49 ER 132.
28 *Jones v Daniel* [1894] 2 Ch 332.

In *Sousa v Marketing Board,*[29] the Board offered to sell bananas to S until 31 December 1955. S replied by letter, stating: 'I am agreeable to the conditions [put forward by the Board], but feel that the time allowed me is very short . . . Consequently, I am asking the Board to grant me an extension into 1956.' Before the Board had time to reply to S's letter, S again wrote to the Board purporting to accept the Board's offer unequivocally. The Trinidad and Tobago Court of Appeal held unanimously that S's first letter amounted to a counter-offer which, on the authority of *Hyde v Wrench,*[30] destroyed the Board's original offer, so that S's second letter containing a purported unequivocal acceptance was, in the words of Hyatali JA, 'a futile exercise, because the offer was already dead'. Wooding CJ also refused to construe S's first letter as 'an inquiry put forward in the hope of inducing better terms', so that, following *Stevenson v McClean,*[31] it would not amount to a rejection of the Board's offer. In his Lordship's view, the first letter could not be regarded as a mere inquiry, and it seemed 'reasonably certain that, either realising this or being so advised, [S] sought to remedy the error by writing [the second letter] which, quite apart from its attempted acceptance of the destroyed offer, [was] in markedly different terms'.

Similarly, in *Barnett Ltd v Olasemo,*[32] as we have seen,[33] the appellant wrote to the respondent enclosing a 'draft agreement' for the sale of the appellant's land. The Jamaican Court of Appeal held that this letter was not an offer capable of acceptance but that, even if it could be construed as an offer, the respondent's letter in reply, enclosing 'an amended draft agreement' for the appellant's 'perusal and comments', amounted to a counter-offer which would have destroyed the original offer, and was not a mere request for information.

In practice, as far as contracts for the sale of land are concerned, there will be no binding contract until the attorneys for vendor and purchaser are in agreement as to all the terms of the sale and after due investigations as to the title and other matters which, particularly from the purchaser's point of view, must be settled before the parties will agree to be bound.

Qualified or equivocal acceptance

To result in a contract, an offer must be accepted unequivocally and without qualifications or conditions. Where, as is common in contracts concerning land, an agreement is stated to be 'Subject to Contract', the effect is that the agreement is regarded as incomplete and will become binding only when a formal document has been drawn up by the parties' attorneys and signed by the contracting parties.

There will be no contract if the 'acceptance' is conditional or qualified. For example, L offered to let two apartments to T for an annual rent of $24,000 per apartment. T 'accepted' L's offer on condition that L fitted two air conditioning units in each apartment. It was held that T's 'acceptance' was conditional, and so no binding

29 (1962) 5 WIR 158 (Court of Appeal, Trinidad and Tobago).
30 (1840) 49 ER 132.
31 (1880) 5 QBD 346.
32 (1995) 32 JLR 284. See also *Chang v Salmon* (1993) 30 JLR 383.
33 P 8, above.

contract came into existence at that stage. But T's 'acceptance' was treated by the court as a counter-offer which L accepted (by conduct) in installing the air conditioners. Ultimately, therefore, there was a binding contract.[34]

Acceptance of tenders

The effect of the acceptance of a tender for the supply of goods depends on the language of the original invitation to tender. Where B's advertisement or invitation to tradesmen to submit tenders states that B will definitely require a certain quantity of goods during a particular period, and S's tender is accepted by B, a binding contract to supply and to pay for the goods will have been created between S and B. S's tender will be regarded as an offer to supply the goods, and B's acceptance of the tender will be an acceptance creating a legal obligation.

On the other hand, it may be clear from the advertisement or invitation to tender that tenders are being sought not for the supply of a definite quantity of goods, but rather for the supply of goods 'if and when demanded'. Accordingly, where a tender is submitted for the supply of goods 'in such quantities as you may order', the offeree does not incur any legal liability by 'accepting' the tender. He becomes liable only if he places an actual order for goods, and he is not bound to place any order at all, unless he has expressly or impliedly undertaken to do so. Such an arrangement is known as a 'standing offer', which can be revoked by S at any time before B makes a requisition for goods, and each requisition by B is regarded as an acceptance creating a separate contract to supply and to pay for the goods requisitioned. The leading case on standing offers is *Great Northern Railway Co v Witham*.[35] Here, in answer to an advertisement for tenders for the supply of goods, W tendered as follows: 'I undertake to supply the company for twelve months with such quantities of [specified goods] as the company may order from time to time.' The company accepted the tender in writing and subsequently made several orders which were satisfied by W. Eventually, the company made an order for goods within the terms of the undertaking which W failed to supply. It was held that W was in breach of contract. W's tender was a standing offer which had been converted into a series of separate contracts each time the company ordered goods, and W was liable to the company for his failure to satisfy the ultimate order. W was free to withdraw from the arrangement with respect to future orders, but he was bound to satisfy existing ones.

The principle in the *Witham* case was applied by the Court of Appeal of Trinidad and Tobago in *Sousa v Marketing Board*.[36] In this case, the Marketing Board had agreed to sell bananas to the appellant until 30 April 1956, setting out the terms and conditions under which it was prepared to do so. Thereafter, the Board supplied the appellant with bananas, as and when he ordered them. Then, on 10 October 1955, the Board gave the appellant one month's notice of its decision to terminate the agreement. The Trinidad and Tobago Court of Appeal took the view that the agreement between the Board was a mere 'gentleman's agreement', not intended to create legal

34 *Oni v Communications Associates of Nigeria* (1973) LD/625/71, High Court, Lagos State, unreported.

35 (1873) LR 9 CP 16.

36 (1962) 5 WIR 158 (Court of Appeal, Trinidad and Tobago).

relations; but, if legal relations were intended, the agreement would be construed as a standing offer which could be revoked at any time, save in respect of orders previously given by the appellant. Wooding CJ said:

> The [Board's] promise of March 25, 1955, if intended to be effectual in law as an offer, which I doubt, amounted in law merely to a standing offer which might be and, indeed, as the parties contemplated, would be converted into a series of contracts by the appellant giving weekly orders for fruit and, at the same time, depositing with the [Board] the price, including the commission charge, but which could be revoked at any time save in respect of orders, if any, theretofore given . . . As Atkin J said: 'The contractor offers to supply goods at a price, and, if the purchasing body chooses to give him an order for goods during the stipulated time, then he is under an obligation to supply the goods in accordance with the order; but, apart from that, nobody is bound.'

Acceptance by conduct

An offer may be accepted by conduct, without express words of acceptance, provided the offeree did the act or acts with the intention of accepting the offer. For example, where B offers to buy goods, S may accept B's offer by sending the goods to B; and where S offers to supply goods and sends them to B, B may accept S's offer by using them. In *Brogden v Metropolitan Railway*,[37] B sent a draft agreement for the supply of coal to S, who made a number of alterations to it and returned it to B, marked 'Approved'. B did not expressly agree to these alterations but for two years accepted delivery of coal under the agreement. It was held that the acceptance of the coal by B meant that there was a binding contract on the terms of the draft.

Communication of acceptance

In general, an acceptance has no effect unless and until it is communicated to the offeror, either by the offeree himself or by his agent.[38] An acceptance is communicated when it is actually brought to the notice of the offeror; so if, for example, an oral acceptance is drowned by the noise of a passing vehicle, or is spoken into a telephone after the line has gone dead, there will be no contract. However, there are some important exceptions to the rule, as follows:

(1) ***Communication to agent.*** An acceptance is valid if communicated to an agent of the offeror having authority to receive it.
(2) ***Default of offeror.*** An offeror may be estopped from denying that he received an acceptance if it was his own fault that he did not receive it, for example where the acceptance is sent by email to the offeror, but the offeror does not bother to read his email messages.
(3) ***Waiver of communication.*** Since the rule that acceptance must be communicated exists for the benefit of the offeror, the offeror can waive the requirement. Waiver is most likely to arise in the following two circumstances:

37 (1877) 2 App Cas 666.

38 *Powell v Lee* (1908) 99 LT 284. It seems from this case that communication of the acceptance by a third party does not suffice.

(i) *In unilateral contracts.* Normally, where the offeror makes an offer to the world at large, for example where he offers a reward to any person who finds and returns the offeror's lost property, he impliedly waives the need for communication of acceptance, and the performance of the act (i.e. the finding and return of the property) is sufficient to make the contract binding on the offeror.[39]

(ii) *Waiver in contracts of sale.* Where S offers to supply goods to B by sending them to him, B can accept the offer simply by using the goods, without communicating this fact to S. And where B offers to buy goods from S, and asks S to supply them, the offer may be accepted by S's despatching the goods to B, without previously informing him that the offer has been accepted. One feature of these cases is that, although no acceptance is communicated to the offeror, the offeree shows by his conduct that he has accepted the offer.

Silence is not acceptance. Although the offeror can waive communication of acceptance, he cannot *impose* a contract upon the offeree by stipulating that silence on the part of the offeree will be deemed to be acceptance. For instance, where F offered to buy his nephew's horse for £30, saying, 'If I hear no more about it, I shall consider the horse to be mine', and the nephew made no reply, it was held that there was no acceptance and therefore no contract because 'the uncle had no right to impose upon the nephew a sale of this horse unless he chose to comply with the condition of writing to repudiate the offer'.[40]

(4) ***Acceptance by post.*** Wherever it is reasonable to use the mail as a means of communicating acceptance, the rule is that the acceptance is complete as soon as the letter of acceptance is posted,[41] that is, when it is placed under the control of the post office staff. Similarly, acceptance by telegram takes effect when the telegram is handed in at the telegraph office. The postal acceptance rule is one of commercial convenience, and it has been held that, where the letter of acceptance is lost or delayed in the post, the contract will nevertheless be completed and the offeror bound. In *Household Fire and Carriage Accident Insurance Co v Grant*,[42] G offered to buy shares in the claimant company. The company's letter of acceptance was posted but it was lost in the mail and never reached G. The company's liquidator sued G for the price of the shares, and the claim succeeded. The contract for the purchase of the shares became binding on G as soon as the acceptance letter was put in the post.

The posting rule can be excluded by the terms of the offer, which may expressly or implicitly provide that acceptance is to take effect only when actually received by the offeror. Thus, where an offer to sell a house was made in the form of an option to purchase 'exercisable by notice in writing to the intending vendor', and a written notice was posted but never reached the offeror, it was held that there was no contract, as the terms of the offer required actual communication of the acceptance.[43]

39 *Carlill v Carbolic Smoke Ball Co* [1893] 1 QB 256.
40 *Felthouse v Bindley* (1862) 11 CB (NS) 869.
41 *Adams v Lindsell* (1818) 106 ER 250; *Henthorn v Fraser* [1892] 2 Ch 27.
42 (1879) 4 Ex D 216.
43 *Holwell Securities Ltd v Hughes* [1974] 1 WLR 155.

The posting rule for communication of acceptance has clearly been reduced in importance owing to the availability today of more modern methods of communication, such as fax, email, and electronic document exchange, as well as courier services and private messenger delivery. There is no consensus regarding the point of time at which an acceptance takes effect with respect to these modern forms of communication, but there seems to be no justification for not applying the normal rule that acceptance takes effect when actually received by the offeror.

Method of communication specified by offeror

An offer which requires the acceptance to be expressed or communicated in a particular way can normally be accepted only in that way.[44] In *Locke v Bellingdon Ltd*,[45] the offer took the form of a 'letter of intent' relating to the proposed purchase of shares in a private company, which was to 'terminate and be of no further force or effect if it has not been accepted by you and returned to us on or before 5pm, March 19, 1999'. By its terms, therefore, the offer could be accepted only by the offeree not only signing but also returning the letter to the offeror. The Barbados Court of Appeal held that since the letter was never returned, there was no acceptance and no contract. Simmons CJ explained:

> The rules governing communication of acceptance mark down that point in time when both parties become aware that each of them is now relying upon the existence of an agreement between them. In our judgment, the fact that the letter prescribed a method of communicating acceptance, that is by signature and return, observance of that mode of communications acceptance was essential to complete the agreement. See *Holwell Securities Ltd v Hughes*.[46] *Eliason v Henshaw*[47] is cited in some books as authority for the proposition that acceptance must be communicated in the manner required by the offeror. Washington J expressed the rule thus: 'It is an undeniable principle of the law of contracts that an offer of a bargain by one person to another imposes no obligation upon the former until it is accepted by the latter, according to the terms in which the offer was made. Any qualification of, or departure from, those terms invalidates the offer, unless the same be agreed by the person who made it.'

Termination of offer

Until an offer is accepted, it creates no legal rights and it can be terminated at any time. Termination may occur in any of the following ways.

(1) ***Revocation (withdrawal).*** An offer may be revoked by the offeror at any time before it is accepted, unless the offeror, by a separate agreement supported by consideration, has bound himself to keep the offer open for a certain time, in which case he may not revoke before expiry of the period. Notice of revocation must be actually communicated to the offeree. This applies equally where revocation is by post, so that if the offeree posts an acceptance before he receives the

---

44 *Chitty on Contracts*, 28th edn, para 2-058.

45 (2002) High Court, Barbados, Civ App No 19 of 2001, unreported [Carilaw BB 2002 CA 42].

46 [1974] 1 WLR 155.

47 (1819) 4 Wheaton 225 (USA).

offeror's letter of revocation, there will be a binding contract, despite the fact that the revocation letter was posted before the letter of acceptance. In *Byrne v Van Tienhoven*,[48] the defendants (in the UK), on 1 October, posted a letter to the claimants (in the USA), offering to sell some tin plate. On 8 October, the defendants posted a letter revoking their offer. On 11 October, the claimants received the defendants' offer and immediately telegraphed their acceptance. On 15 October, the claimants confirmed their acceptance by letter. On 20 October, the defendants' letter of revocation reached the claimants. It was held that the defendants were bound by a contract which had come into being on 11 October, since (a) revocation of an offer is not effective until communicated to the offeree, and (b) the mere posting of a letter of revocation is not communication to the offeree; the rule regarding revocation of an offer is not the same as in the case of acceptance.

Although revocation of an offer must be communicated to the offeree, it need not be communicated by the offeror. It is effective if the offeree learns from any reliable source that the offeror no longer intends to contract with him.[49]

In a unilateral contract, where the offeror makes an offer to the world at large (such as where he offers a reward to any person who finds and returns the offeror's lost property), the question may arise as to when the acceptance of the offer is complete, so as to preclude the possibility of revocation of the offer. The traditional view is that acceptance of such an offer is not complete until the required act has been performed, so that the offeror can revoke at any time before then. This approach could cause hardship to a person who had performed most, but not all, of the act by the time of the revocation. An alternative view, therefore, is that acceptance is complete as soon as the offeree begins to perform the act, and thereafter the offeror cannot revoke, though the offeree cannot claim the reward until he has completed performance of the act required

(2) ***Rejection.*** An offer is brought to an end if the offeree rejects it. Rejection may be expressed or it may be implied, in circumstances where the offeror is justified in inferring that the offeree does not intend to accept the offer. Rejection may also take the form of a counter-offer.

Notice of rejection must be communicated to the offeror; unless and until that happens, it will be of no effect. Thus, for example, if D makes an offer to C by letter, and C, immediately on receiving the letter, posts a letter rejecting the offer, but, before the rejection reaches D, C changes his mind and telephones his acceptance, there will be a binding contract.

(3) ***Lapse of time.*** An offer which is expressly stated to last for a fixed time cannot be accepted after that time, and will lapse on the expiration of the period. Thus, for example, an offer that requires acceptance 'by return of post' will lapse if not accepted by a return postal communication or by some equally prompt method, such as by telephone, fax or email; and an offer which is stated to be 'left open until 5pm on Friday, May 11, 2012' will lapse if not accepted by that time. An offer which does not stipulate any time limit for acceptance will lapse if not accepted within a reasonable time. What is a reasonable time depends on such

48 (1880) 5 CPD 344.
49 *Dickinson v Dodds* (1876) 2 Ch D 563.

circumstances as the nature of the subject-matter, or the means used to communicate the offer. Thus, for instance, an offer to sell perishable goods, or an offer made by telegram or fax would lapse after a short time, whilst an offer to sell land or shares would remain open for a longer time.

(4) ***Death.*** An offer terminates if the offeree dies before accepting it; his personal representatives cannot accept on behalf of his estate. Where it is the offeror who dies before the offeree has accepted, the offer is terminated if the offeree knows of the death; but where the offeree accepts in ignorance of the offeror's death, the position is uncertain. According to one view, an acceptance in such circumstances should be valid, unless the proposed agreement is one in which the personality of the offeror is important, as, for example, in the case of an offer to write a book or to perform at a concert. Another view is that an offer can in no circumstances be accepted after the death of the offeror.

Incomplete agreements

Even where there is a proper offer and acceptance, there will be no binding contract if the terms of the agreement are uncertain or if the agreement is made 'subject to contract'.

Uncertainty

The law requires that the parties should fashion their own contract, and the court will not construct a contract for them out of terms which are vague, indefinite or unsettled. In *Scammell v Ouston*,[50] for instance, O wished to acquire a new van on hire-purchase terms. After lengthy correspondence, O gave a written order for a particular type of vehicle on the understanding that 'the balance of purchase price can be had on hire purchase terms over a period of two years'. The order was accepted by S in general terms, but the hire-purchase terms were never settled. There was a wide variety of such terms, and there was nothing to indicate which of them was favoured by the parties. S later declined to supply the van, and O sued for damages for non-delivery. It was held that no contract had been concluded. The language used by the parties was too vague and obscure to attribute to the parties any particular contractual intention. The 'agreement was inchoate and never got beyond the negotiation stage'. Lord Wright approached the question of whether a purported contract should be held void for uncertainty, as follows:

> There are, in my opinion, two grounds on which the court ought to hold that there never was a contract. The first is that the language used was so obscure and so incapable of any definite or precise meaning that the court is unable to attribute to the parties any particular contractual intention. The object of the court is to do justice between the parties, and the court will do its best, if satisfied that there was an ascertainable and determinate intention to contract, to give effect to that intention, looking at substance, and not mere form. It will not be deterred by mere difficulties of interpretation. Difficulty is not synonymous with ambiguity, so long as any definite meaning can be extracted. The test of intention, however, is to be found in the words used. If these words, considered however

50 [1941] 1 All ER 14.

> broadly and technically, and with due regard to all the just implications, fail to evince any definite meaning on which the court can safely act, the court has no choice but to say that there is no contract.

Liverpool JA further articulated these principles in the Belize Court of Appeal in *Boggess v Hassan:*[51]

> It is a well-established rule that the parties must make their own contract, and this means that they must agree on its terms. If, therefore, the terms are unsettled or indefinite, the contract cannot be upheld. For, although the courts always seek to implement the intention of the parties, they will not make a contract for them in order to do so. On the other hand, it must be emphasised that the courts seek to uphold bargains wherever possible; and the principles which govern their approach were succinctly stated by Lord Wright in *Hillas & Co Ltd v Arcos Ltd,*[52] in the following words: 'Businessmen often record the most important agreements in crude and summary fashion; modes of expression sufficient and clear to them in the court of their business may appear to those unfamiliar with the business far from complete or precise. It is accordingly the duty of the court to construe such documents fairly and broadly, without being too astute or subtle in finding defects; but, on the contrary, the court should seek to apply the old maxim of English law, *verba ita sunt intelligenda, ut res magis valeat quam pereat.* That maxim, however, does not mean that the court is to make a contract for the parties, or to go outside the words they have used, except in so far as there are appropriate implications of law.'

In a Jamaican case, *Negril Holdings Ltd v Century National Bank,*[53] one of the issues was whether an agreement on the part of a customer of the defendant bank to pay interest on an overdraft 'at the bank's usual rate of interest on overdrafts' was too vague and uncertain to be enforceable. Ellis J took the view that the present case was similar to *Scammell* in that the aforementioned clause 'attracted the description of vagueness as did "the usual hire purchase terms" '. Further, 'that vagueness and lack of precision in the meaning of the clause is not curable by a recourse to any prior dealing between the parties.' The earlier case of *Hillas & Co Ltd v Arcos Ltd,*[54] where the vague phrase 'goods of fair specification' had been used in an option to purchase timber, was distinguishable, since in *Hillas* there had been a previous course of dealing between the parties, from which their intentions in the case in dispute could be deduced and, in addition, any uncertainty could be cured by reference to the customary practice in the timber trade. In the present case, as in *Scammell*, there was an absence of accepted business practice that could assist the interpretation of the phrase, 'the usual rate of interest on overdrafts'.

Although a contract cannot be upheld if any of its essential terms are so vague that the court is unable to discern the intention of the parties, the courts do not necessarily expect commercial documents to be drafted with strict precision, and they will try to make sense of them wherever possible. The courts prefer to uphold bargains (as in *Hillas & Co Ltd v Arcos Ltd*) rather than to strike them down (as in *Scammell v Ouston*). Further, the court will not allow an unscrupulous party to escape his obligations under a contract by inserting some meaningless phrase into the

51 (1991) 46 WIR 72 (Court of Appeal, Belize), at 85.

52 (1932) 147 LT 503.

53 (1997) Supreme Court, Jamaica, No 88 of 1991, unreported [Carilaw JM 1997 SC 59].

54 (1932) 147 LT 503.

agreement and subsequently pleading uncertainty on the basis of it. Thus, in *Nicolene v Simmonds*,[55] where the contractual document contained the statement, 'we are in agreement that the usual conditions of acceptance apply', it was held that, since there were no 'usual conditions' of acceptance, this was nothing more than a meaningless phrase which could be ignored, so the validity of the contract was not affected.

A similar situation arose in a Barbadian case, *Niblock v Apthorp*,[56] where a clause in the contractual document relating to a proposed sale of shares stipulated that: 'the usual warranties and indemnities customary on a sale of shares will be given by the shareholders and directors.' Johnson J held that, in the absence of proof that there were any such customary warranties and indemnities in Barbados, the clause was not so essential that it could not be ignored. As Denning LJ had stated in *Nicolene*: 'It would be strange indeed if a party could escape from every one of his obligations by inserting a meaningless exception to some of them . . . You would find defaulters all scanning their contracts to find some meaningless clause on which to ride free.'[57]

Agreements 'subject to contract'

Documents evidencing an initial agreement, such as a letter addressed by one party or his attorney to the other party or his attorney, may be headed with the words 'Subject to Contract', or 'Subject to Formal Contract'. These words, which create a 'strong presumption that the parties do not intend an immediate binding contract',[58] are particularly common in negotiations for the sale or lease of land, but they are not confined to such cases.[59] The effect is to postpone contractual liability until a formal document has been drawn up by the parties' legal advisers and signed by the parties; until such a document has been executed, the parties are not legally bound and either can withdraw from the transaction.[60]

On the other hand, if, on a proper construction of the agreement, the court finds that the parties intended to be bound from the outset, notwithstanding that they contemplated the drawing up of a more formal document, there will be a binding contract. Thus, where V agreed to sell the lease and goodwill of a farm on the terms of a written

---

55 [1953] 1 All ER 822.

56 (1975) High Court, Barbados, No 375 of 1975, unreported [Carilaw BB 1975 HC 15].

57 [1953] 1 All ER 822, at 824–825.

58 Cheshire and Fifoot, *Law of Contract*, 13th edn, p 40.

59 As, for example, in *Apthorp v Niblock* (1976) Court of Appeal, Barbados, Civ App No 9 of 1976, unreported [Carilaw BB 1976 CA 4] (sale of shares); *International Risk Management Ltd v Barwick Industries* (1976) Court of Appeal, Bermuda, Civ App No 8 of 1975, unreported [Carilaw BM 1975 CA 8] (sale of aircraft).

60 *Winn v Bull* (1877) 7 Ch D 29; *Chillingworth v Esche* [1924] 1 Ch 97; *International Risk Management Ltd v Barwick Industries* (1976) Court of Appeal, Bermuda, Civ App No 8 of 1975, unreported [Carilaw BM 1975 CA 8] (agreement 'subject to satisfactory sales agreement'); *Apthorp v Niblock* (1976) Court of Appeal, Barbados, Civ App No 9 of 1976, unreported [Carilaw BB 1976 CA 4]; *Carey v Townsend* (1985) Supreme Court, The Bahamas, No 1268 of 1983, unreported [Carilaw BS 1985 SC 73]; *Knowles v Bank Lane Ltd* (1986) Supreme Court, The Bahamas, No 1141 of 1985, unreported [Carilaw BS 1986 SC 3]; *Brown v Cromarty Investments Ltd* (2000) Supreme Court, The Bahamas, No 723 of 1997, unreported [Carilaw BS 2000 SC 45].

document which was declared to be 'a provisional agreement until a fully legalised agreement' was drawn up and signed, there was held to be a binding contract.[61]

INTENTION TO CREATE LEGAL RELATIONS

An agreement will not be legally binding if the parties did not *intend* it to be binding in law. For example, agreements to play a game of tennis, to attend a social function or to share the cost of petrol on a journey in a private car, are clearly not intended to give rise to legal action in the event of breach. Most social, domestic and family agreements fall into this category. Thus, in *Balfour v Balfour*,[62] where a husband accepted a government post overseas and promised his wife that he would give her an allowance of £30 a month until he returned, it was held that the wife could not sue for the money, as the promise was not intended to be legally binding. Exceptionally, however, a domestic agreement may be binding. In *Simpkins v Pays*,[63] for example, three ladies who lived in the same house took part in a competition in a newspaper, the entry being sent in the name of one of them, D. When the entry won, D refused to share the prize as agreed. It was held that there was an intention to create legal relations, and D was bound to share the money.

In some cases, it is not easy to determine whether or not legal relations were intended. In *Jones v Padavatton*,[64] P, who lived in Trinidad, promised her daughter, who was working in the USA, that if the daughter would go to England to study for the Bar, P would pay her $200 per month. The daughter agreed to this arrangement, which began in 1962. In 1964, P bought a house in England for the daughter to live in, and she let some of the rooms to tenants in order to provide the daughter with an income, in place of the previous monthly payments. In 1967, with the daughter still not having succeeded in passing the Bar examinations, P sought possession of the house. The daughter argued that there was a contract between her and P whereby, in consideration of the daughter giving up her employment in the USA and going to London to study, P would provide the agreed financial support. All three judges of the English Court of Appeal came to the conclusion that P was entitled to recover possession of the house, but by diverse reasoning. Salmon LJ was of the view that the parties did intend to create legal relations, as neither could have 'intended that if, after the daughter had been in London, say, for 6 months, the mother dishonoured her promise and left her daughter destitute, the daughter would have no legal redress', but the contract could not have been intended to last for more than five years, and so the mother was entitled to recover possession of her house. Fenton Atkinson LJ, on the other hand, noting the vagueness of the arrangements, took the view that there was never any contract between the parties, and P was entitled to succeed. He said:[65]

---

61 *Branca v Cobarro* [1947] KB 854.

62 [1919] 2 KB 571.

63 [1955] 3 All ER 10.

64 [1969] 2 All ER 616.

65 At 625.

> At the time when the first arrangements were made, the mother and daughter were, and always had been, to use the daughter's own words, 'very close'. I am satisfied that neither party at that time intended to enter into a legally binding contract, either then or later when the house was bought. The daughter was prepared to trust the mother to honour her promise of support, just as the mother no doubt trusted the daughter to study for the Bar with diligence, and to get through her examinations as early as she could.

Commercial agreements

Whereas, in the case of domestic or family agreements, there is a presumption that they are not intended to create legal relations, in the case of commercial agreements (such as contracts of sale, hire-purchase, agency, insurance, and employment), the opposite presumption applies, and it will be for the party who denies the existence of a binding contract to establish the lack of such intention, the burden of proof being a heavy one.[66] The leading case in this area of the law is *Rose and Frank Co v Crompton (JR) and Bros Ltd*,[67] in which the court had to consider a written agreement between an English company and an American firm, which had, for seven years previously, maintained profitable commercial dealings with each other. In the agreement, the parties expressed their 'willingness that the present arrangements . . . shall be continued on the same lines as at present for a period of three years', provided that 'this arrangement is not entered into . . . as a formal or legal agreement, and shall not be subject to legal jurisdiction in the law courts either of the United States or of England'. It was held that the document was not legally binding, and the claimants were not entitled to damages for breach of its terms. Scrutton LJ expressed the principle thus:[68]

> Now it is quite possible for parties to come to an agreement by excepting legal relations . . . This intention may be implied from the subject-matter of the agreement, but it may also be expressed by the parties. In social and family relations, such an intention is readily implied, while in business matters the opposite result would ordinarily follow. But I can see no reason why, even in business matters, the parties should not intend to rely on each other's good faith and honour, and to exclude all idea of settling disputes by any outside intervention, with the accompanying necessity of expressing themselves so precisely that outsiders may have no difficulty in understanding what they mean. If they clearly express such an intention, I can see no reason in public policy why effect should not be given to their intention.

In *Sousa v Marketing Board*[69] (the facts of which have been given above[70]), as Hyatali JA pointed out:[71]

---

66 *Edwards v Skyways Ltd* [1964] 1 All ER 494; *Collins v Air Jamaica Ltd* (2007) Supreme Court, Jamaica, No CLC-203 of 1995, unreported [Carilaw JM 2007 SC 25].

67 [1925] AC 445.

68 [1923] 2 KB 261, at 288.

69 (1962) 5 WIR 15.

70 See p 14, above.

71 At 170. See also at 165, *per* McShine JA.

> the Board made it abundantly clear [in its letter of 2 May 1955] that it did not propose to enter into any contract with the appellant, and that the agreement to sell him bananas must be construed purely as a 'gentleman's agreement' . . . The appellant, in my view, must be taken, in the absence of any protest, to have accepted or at least impliedly assented to this relationship; and *Rose and Frank Co v Crompton (JR) and Bros Ltd* is one of a line of well-known cases which has clearly established that an agreement binding in honour only, as a gentleman's agreement undoubtedly is, cannot be made the subject of an action in a court of law.

In a Jamaican case, *Nicholas v Okwesa*,[72] the defendant volunteered to help the claimant, with whom he was on friendly terms, to sell her car. The claimant argued that the defendant, in acting as her agent for the purpose of finding a buyer, was in breach of contract, in that he had sold the car for $2,500 less than the price at which he had been instructed to sell. One of the defendant's arguments was that there was no intention to create legal relations as between himself and the claimant, in view of the fact that he was not a car dealer and that he had merely been 'doing the claimant a favour'. In the Supreme Court, Smith J (Ag) held that, notwithstanding the nature of the relationship between the parties, the agreement between them was a commercial one, and the presumption of an intention to create legal relations had not been rebutted. He said:

> Here there is no evidence of an expressed intention that the agreement should not give rise to legal relations; nor is the agreement a social or domestic one, as in *Balfour v Balfour*. This is clearly a business agreement, and it will be presumed that the parties intended to create legal relations and to make a contract. The burden of rebutting this presumption of legal relations lay upon the defendant, and it is a heavy burden. I find that he has not discharged it.

In the Barbadian case of *Headley v Clarke*,[73] the claimant had entered into an arrangement with the defendant whereby the claimant undertook to sell the defendant's house for an agreed commission of 5 per cent of the selling price. In an action by the claimant to recover $185 allegedly due as commission, one of the issues was whether the parties intended that the agreement should create legal relations. The magistrate held that, in the light of several factors, including the fact that the claimant never set himself up as a professional house agent whose usual business was the selling of houses for commission, the parties did not have any intention to create legal relations and so there was no contract of agency between them. On appeal to the Divisional Court, Stoby J overturned the decision of the magistrate. In his view, the magistrate 'was entitled to take into account the fact that the claimant was not a licensed house agent and all other relevant circumstances before deciding whether he accepted the claimant's evidence that the defendant agreed to pay a commission of 5% but, having accepted that evidence, there was no material for the finding that no legal relationship was intended'. There was therefore a contract of agency. The agent had performed his part of the contract by introducing a purchaser who was ready, able and willing to buy, and who did buy the house. He was accordingly entitled to his commission.

---

72 (1986) Supreme Court, Jamaica, No N-174 of 1984, unreported [Carilaw JM 1986 SC 16].
73 (1965) Divisional Court, Barbados, unreported [Carilaw BB 1965 DC 1].

An instance of appellate court judges not being in agreement on the issue of whether the parties intended to create legal relations is the case of *Esso Petroleum Ltd v Commissioners of Customs and Excise*.[74] Here, garage proprietors had offered a free 'World Cup' coin to any person who purchased at least four gallons of petrol. The conventional view was that such an offer was a 'mere puff', not intended to be legally binding, but a majority of their Lordships in the House of Lords, considering this to be a commercial agreement, held that the offer was intended to create legal relations and gave rise to a unilateral contract (much as in the *Carlill v Carbolic Smoke Ball* case), under which the garage proprietor was in effect saying: 'If you buy four gallons of my gasoline, I will give you one of these coins.' The minority, on the other hand, denied that there was an intention to create legal relations, suggesting that if such an arrangement were to create a contract, 'it would seem to exclude the possibility of any dealer ever making a free gift to any of his customers, however negligible its value, to promote his sales.'[75]

Finally, it is well established that where a commercial agreement contains a clause stating that the agreement is to be 'binding in honour only', it will have no legal effect. Such 'honour clauses' are commonly found in football pool coupons, and their effect is to prevent a staker from maintaining an action against the pools company for any money he alleges he has won on the coupon.[76]

74 [1976] 1 All ER 117.

75 At 120, 121.

76 *Jones v Vernon's Pools Ltd* [1938] 2 All ER 626; *Appleson v H Littlewood Ltd* [1939] 1 All ER 464; *Amadi v Pool House Group (Nigeria) Ltd* [1966] 2 All NLR 254.

CHAPTER 3

FORMALITIES

Certain contracts, though not void or voidable, cannot be enforced in a court of law unless the claimant who seeks to enforce the particular contract can produce a sufficient *written note or memorandum* of the agreement signed by the defendant or his agent.

The requirement of writing was first introduced by section 4 of the Statute of Frauds 1677, and Commonwealth Caribbean jurisdictions either apply the original section 4 or have reproduced its provisions in their local enactments, such as the Property and Conveyancing statutes.[1] The contracts affected by section 4 and its equivalents are:

(i) contracts of guarantee;

(ii) contracts for the sale, lease or other disposition of an interest in land.

CONTRACTS OF GUARANTEE (SURETYSHIP)

A contract of guarantee is made where one party (the guarantor, or surety) promises the other (the creditor) that he will answer for the contractual or tortious liability of a third person (the debtor): for example, where G guarantees D's bank overdraft by promising the bank that if D does not repay the loan, G will do so;[2] or where G guarantees the fidelity of a prospective employee (D), such as a produce buyer, by promising the employer that if D defaults or commits a fraud, G will make good the loss to the employer.[3]

Nature of guarantee

In a contract of guarantee or suretyship there are three parties: a principal creditor (C) a principal debtor (D), and a guarantor (G). Thus, where G guarantees D's debt to C, there are three collateral contracts:

(i) the contract between C and D out of which the guaranteed debt arose;

(ii) the contract between G and C whereby G makes himself *secondarily* liable to pay D's debt in the event of D's default; and

(iii) the contract between D and G whereby D promises that if G satisfies D's debt to C, D will reimburse G.

---

1 See, for example, s, 47, Property Act, Cap 236 (Barbados); s 43(1), Property Act, Cap 190 (Belize); and s 4(1) Conveyancing and Law of Property Act, Ch 56:01 (Trinidad and Tobago).

2 *National Bank of Nigeria Ltd v Awolesi* [1964] 1 WLR 1311; *Ikomi v Bank of West Africa Ltd* (1965) ALR Comm 25.

3 *United Africa Co Ltd v Jazzar* (1940) 6 WACA 208.

Guarantee distinguished from indemnity

Whether a contract is one of *indemnity* (which is not subject to the requirements of the Statute of Frauds), or one of *guarantee* depends on the intention of the parties. The main distinction is that a guarantor makes himself *secondarily* liable for the amount of the debt, whereas a person giving an indemnity makes himself *primarily* liable for the amount. In a contract of guarantee, G promises to discharge the debtor's (D's) liability to C, in the event that D fails to do so; in a contract of indemnity, P agrees, either alone or jointly with D, to discharge D's liability to C *in any event*, whether or not D fails to pay the debt.

Guarantee must be supported by consideration

The requirement of consideration in contracts of guarantee was exhaustively examined by Awich J in the Belize Supreme Court in *Bank of Nova Scotia v Liu*.[4] On the basis that a guarantee is an accessory or collateral contract by which the promisor undertakes to answer for the debt, default or miscarriage of another, whose primary liability to the promise must exist or be contemplated, such a contract, to be enforceable, must either be made by deed under seal or be supported by consideration. Awich J also pointed out that the mere existence of an antecedent debt was not valuable consideration sufficient to support the promise of the guarantor made to the creditor. The learned judge continued:

> In a guarantee, the guarantor's promise must be founded on a new consideration, such as a promise to give a loan to another; forbearance to sue the debtor; a promise to reschedule the debtor's loan; or a promise not to close the debtor customer's bank account.[5] The consideration must move from the creditor to the guarantor, not to the debtor; however, it it need not be of any direct benefit to the promisor, the guarantor. A banker's forbearance to sue on a debt already incurred is not a past consideration; it is good consideration to a guarantor. The consideration is the forbearance. It directly benefits the debtor, not the guarantor. There may be a reason or motive by which the guarantor benefits, but that is only indirectly beneficial to the guarantor. A banker usually offers a promise to lend money to one person, the debtor, as consideration to another, the guarantor, for his guarantee, because the banker has more confidence in the guarantor than in the debtor, and usually when the debtor does not have sufficient property to secure the loan.

Guarantor discharged where loan agreement varied

Before the creditor and debtor agree to a variation of the primary loan agreement, the guarantor should be consulted and his approval obtained, otherwise the guarantor may be discharged from further obligation. In *Holme v Brunskill*,[6] Brett LJ said:

4 (2004) Supreme Court, Belize, No 126 of 2000, unreported [Carilaw BZ 2004 SC 2].
5 *National Bank of Nigeria Ltd v Awolesi* [1964] 1 WLR 1311.
6 (1878) QBD 495, at 508.

> If there is a material alteration of the relation in a contract, the observance of which is necessary, the surety is released, and if a man makes himself surety in an instrument reciting the principal relation or contract in such specific terms as to make the observance of specific terms the condition of his liability, then any alteration which happens is material; but where the surety makes himself responsible in general terms for the observance of certain relations between the parties in a certain contract between two parties, he is not released by an immaterial alteration in that relation or contract.

The principle that a surety will be discharged where there is a material alteration in the loan agreement between creditor and debtor was applied by the Privy Council in *National Bank of Nigeria Ltd v Awolesi*.[7] Here, G guaranteed D's overdrawn bank account, which the bank allowed to continue so that D's rejected cheques were met. Later, unknown to G, the bank allowed D to open a new account. Several payments were made into the new account and into a third account at another branch of the same bank. If these payments had been credited to the account guaranteed, the latter account would occasionally have had credit balances. Subsequently, since D operated a large overdraft on the account guaranteed, the bank demanded a reduction of the overdraft and that security be provided. D was unable to meet the demand, and the bank sued both D and G. The lower court entered judgment against G for £9,600, which was the sum determined by combining the three accounts. On appeal to the Privy Council, it was held that, by permitting the opening of the second account, the bank had agreed a substantial variation of the terms of the contract without G's knowledge and to his detriment; further, that the three accounts had been operated in such a manner as to increase the burden on G. Accordingly, G was not liable under the guarantee.

Requirement of writing

Section 4(i) of the Statute of Frauds 1677, which is still in force in England and in Commonwealth Caribbean jurisdictions, provides that a contract of guarantee is unenforceable in a court of law 'unless the agreement upon which such action shall be brought or some memorandum or note thereof shall be in writing and signed by the party to be charged therewith or some other person . . . by him lawfully authorised'. It will be seen that this provision requires either that the guarantee agreement itself should be in writing or that, if the agreement is oral, there must be some written evidence of it.

As Lord Hoffmann explained:[8]

> [The purpose of the statute was] to avoid the need to decide which side was telling the truth about whether or not an oral promise had been made, and exactly what had been promised . . . The terms of the statute . . . show that Parliament, although obviously conscious that it would allow some people to break their promises, thought that this injustice was outweighed by the need to protect people from being held liable on the basis of oral utterances which were ill-considered, ambiguous or completely fictitious.

7 [1964] 1 WLR 1311.

8 *Actionstrength Ltd v International Glass Engineering SPA* [2003] 2 AC 541, at 549.

And, according to Lord Bingham,[9] there was:

> A real danger of inexperienced people being led into undertaking obligations which they did not fully understand, and that opportunities would be given to the unscrupulous to assert that credit was given on the faith of a guarantee which the alleged surety had had no intention of giving.

Form and content required

The formalities required in contracts of guarantee are similar to those required in contracts for the sale of land. Thus:

(a) The guarantee need not be signed by both parties; it is sufficient if it is signed by the 'party to be charged', that is, the defendant (the guarantor) or his agent.

(b) The signature need not be an actual subscription of the party's name: it may be a mark, and it may be printed or stamped. In the recent case of *Golden Ocean Group Ltd v Salgaocar Mining Industries PVT Ltd*[10] it was held to be sufficient that an email concluding the guarantee contained the name 'Guy', the agent of the guarantor. An argument that this was not a signature but a mere salutation delivered in a 'matey' or familiar fashion was rejected, Tomlinson LJ pointing out that 'an electronic signature is sufficient, and a first name, initials or perhaps a nickname will suffice'. The court had no doubt that this constituted an authentication of the contents of the guarantee, sufficient to satisfy the underlying requirements of the Statute of Frauds.

(c) All the material terms of the guarantee must be accurately stated in the memorandum.

(d) The terms of the guarantee need not all be contained in one document, and a note or memorandum may consist of several letters or other communications which can be joined together to make up the memorandum. In the *Golden Ocean Group* case (above), it was held that the exchange of several emails had led to the conclusion of a guarantee in writing sufficient to satisfy the Statute of Frauds; it was not necessary that all the material terms of the guarantee should be contained within a single document.

CONTRACTS FOR THE SALE OR LEASE OF LAND

The effect of sections 2 and 4 of the Statute of Frauds 1677, which is in force in most Commonwealth Caribbean jurisdictions, and its modern equivalents, such as section 47 of the Property Act, Cap 236 (Barbados), section 43(1) of the Property Act, Cap 190 (Belize), section 4(1) of the Conveyancing and Law of Property Act, Ch 10:04 (St Kitts and Nevis) and section 4(1) of the Conveyancing and Law of Property Act, Cap 56:01 (Trinidad and Tobago), is that a contract for the sale of land will be unenforceable if it is not *in writing* or *evidenced by a sufficient written note or memorandum* of the oral agreement, signed by 'the party to be charged' (that is, the defendant against whom the contract is to be enforced) or his agent. The memorandum must contain

9 *Ibid*, at 546.

10 [2012] EWCA Civ 265.

(a) a description of the parties; (b) a description of the property; (c) the price; and (d) any other terms agreed between the parties,[11] such as the completion date (if it has been fixed), any term relating to stages of payment of the purchase money, and any term regarding payment of a deposit by the purchaser. For the memorandum to be effective, all relevant terms should be included; however, terms that will be implied into the contract (such as the term that an unencumbered freehold interest is being sold) need not be included.[12]

In an agreement for a lease, the essential terms to be evidenced in the memorandum were stated in the Jamaican Court of Appeal in *Singer Sewing Machine Co v Montego Bay Co-operative Credit Union Ltd*[13] to be: (a) identities of lessor and lessee; (b) identity of the property; (c) rent to be paid; (d) commencement date; and (e) duration of the lease.[14]

The note or memorandum must be signed by 'the party to be charged', that is the party against whom the agreement is being enforced, or by his agent. An auctioneer has implied authority from both vendor and purchaser to sign a memorandum, but signature on behalf of the purchaser must be contemporaneous with the sale,[15] and it has been held by the Privy Council that where the vendor's attorney or solicitor receives a deposit from the purchaser as stakeholder, he is not precluded from subsequently signing a memorandum of the agreement on behalf of the vendor.[16]

Character and joinder of documents

The memorandum need not be in any special form. Any written evidence, such as a letter (or series of letters) or a purchase receipt, will suffice, provided that it is signed by the defendant[17] or his agent; nor is it necessary for the requisite evidence to be contained in one document; it can be collected from several documents which can be joined together to make one complete memorandum, provided that the document signed by the defendant expressly or impliedly refers to the other document(s) or to

11 See *Seepersad v Mackhan* (1982) High Court, Trinidad and Tobago, No 533 of 1977, unreported [Carilaw TT 1982 HC 27].

12 *Timmins v Moreland Street Property Co Ltd* [1957] 3 All ER 265, CA, *per* Romer LJ.

13 (1997) 34 JLR 251, 257, 275.

14 See *Exotic Fruits and Flowers Ltd v Agricultural Development Corp* (1999) Court of Appeal, Jamaica, Civ App No 110 of 1998, unreported [Carilaw JM 1999 CA 78], in which it was held that the memorandum was not sufficient as it did not state the duration of the lease, nor was the deficiency cured by reference in a newspaper advertisement to the proposed duration of the lease, since an advertisement inviting applications could not be used to determine what was contained in any subsequent agreement between the parties.

15 *Bell v Balls* [1897] 1 Ch 663.

16 *Elias v George Sahely & Co (Barbados) Ltd* [1982] 3 WLR 956, followed in *Taylor v Cox & Co Ltd* (2004) Supreme Court, The Bahamas, No 1396 of 2002, unreported [Carilaw BS 2004 SC 10], *per* Davis J.

17 In *Retese v Harewood* (1983) High Court, Trinidad and Tobago, No 139 of 1975, unreported [Carilaw TT 1983 HC 63], it was held that a letter signed by the defendant vendors and addressed to the National Housing Authority, stating that they were willing to convey to the plaintiff purchaser a named parcel of land, constituted written evidence of an oral agreement to sell the land sufficient to satisfy s 4(1) of the Conveyancing and Law of Property Act. Persaud J pointed out that it was established by several authorities that a letter or other written communication from the 'party to be charged' to a third party could be a sufficient note or memorandum to satisfy the statutory requirement.

some other transaction.[18] If there is such reference, parol evidence is admissible to identify the other document(s) referred to, or to explain the other transaction and identify any document relating to it. Further, it was pointed out by Murphy J in a Cayman case, *Strada Investments Ltd v Temora Investments Ltd*,[19] that the requirement that the document signed by the defendant must contain some reference to some other document or transaction 'effectively means that the incorporated document must pre-date or be contemporaneous with' the signed document.

The principles relating to joinder of documents were applied by the Privy Council in *Elias v George Sahely & Co (Barbados) Ltd*.[20] Here, the claimant had, for several years, been a tenant of the defendant, occupying commercial premises in Bridgetown in which he operated a retail store. The defendant agreed orally to sell the freehold to the claimant, and on the same day the claimant's attorney wrote a letter to the defendant's attorney confirming the oral agreement and setting out its terms. He also enclosed a cheque for the deposit, 'payable to you as stakeholder pending completion of the contract of sale'. As requested, the defendant's attorney signed and sent back a receipt, which stated that the money had been received as a deposit on the property 'agreed to be sold' by the defendant to the claimant. Lord Scarman, delivering the judgment of the Privy Council, held that the trial judge had rightly admitted in evidence: (a) the letter from the claimant's attorney; (b) the receipt; and (c) parol evidence from the claimant's attorney that the receipt had been given in response to the letter. The letter contained all the terms of the concluded oral contract; it could be read together with the receipt; and since the two documents together constituted a sufficient signed memorandum, the contract was specifically enforceable.

Absence of sufficient memorandum

If there is no sufficient memorandum, the contract is *unenforceable* but not void. This means that:

(a) no action can be brought for damages at common law for breach of the agreement;

(b) no action can be brought for specific performance of the agreement in equity, unless there is a sufficient act of part-performance; and

(c) rights that do not require action in court remain valid; thus, if the purchaser unjustifiably refuses to complete, the vendor may retain any deposit paid.

Part-performance

In equity, an oral contract for the sale of land may be specifically enforced despite the absence of a written memorandum, if the claimant (that is, the party seeking to

18 *Timmins v Moreland Street Property Co Ltd*, above; *Martin v Vaughan* (1971) High Court, Barbados, No 236 of 1970, unreported [Carilaw BB 1971 HC 2]; and *RPL (1991) Ltd v Texaco (Trinidad) Ltd* (2009) High Court, Trinidad and Tobago, No S 807 of 2003, unreported [Carilaw TT 2009 HC 84], where the following documents were read together by the court to make a complete memorandum: letter from P to V expressing desire to purchase property from V; cheque issued and tendered by P as deposit; letter from V to P stating that V was unable to sell the property, and returning deposit.

19 [1996] CILR 246, at 261.

20 [1982] 3 WLR 956. Followed in *Smatt v Lyons* (1987) 24 JLR 530 (Court of Appeal, Jamaica).

enforce the agreement) has done *a sufficient act of part-performance of the contract*. The principle underlying the doctrine of part-performance is that: 'if one party to an agreement stands by and lets the other party incur expense or prejudice his position on the faith of the agreement being valid, he will not then be allowed to turn round and assert that the agreement is unenforceable. Using fraud in its older and less precise sense, that would be fraudulent on his part, and it has become proverbial that courts of equity will not permit the statute to be made an instrument of fraud.'[21]

In order to amount to a sufficient part-performance, the acts of the claimant:

> must be such that they point unmistakably and can only point to the existence of some contract such as the oral contract alleged. But of course the acts of part-performance need not show the precise terms of the oral contract . . . The terms of the oral contract must be proved by acceptable evidence, but effect to them can only be given if and when acts of part-performance establish that there must have been some such contract. Until then, the door is, so to speak, closed against them.[22]

Thus, to amount to part-performance, the acts must be capable of explanation only by the existence of a contract, and they must be consistent with the particular contract which is alleged to exist.

The most common acts of part-performance in the context of sale of land are the vendor's giving up possession, or the purchaser's taking possession.[23] Carrying out repairs to the property may also be a sufficient act of part-performance.[24] On the other hand, the payment of money will not, by itself, usually amount to part-performance, as a party who merely pays money has not 'altered his position to a point where the court cannot undo what has been done', since the court can order repayment of the money. However, in *Steadman v Steadman*,[25] it was held that the payment of arrears of maintenance did constitute part-performance of an agreement between husband and wife concerning maintenance and the transfer of the matrimonial home, so that the part of the agreement relating to the transfer of the matrimonial home was rendered enforceable; and although payment of a deposit will not normally be considered to be a sufficient act of part-performance, there are at least two Caribbean cases in which such a payment was held to be sufficient.[26]

On the other hand, in *Crevelle v Affoon*,[27] the Court of Appeal of Trinidad and Tobago held that the purchaser's giving instructions to his solicitor to draft a conveyance, payment for the draft, and the passing of the draft to the vendor, did not constitute part-performance of an oral agreement to sell land. Distinguishing *Steadman v Steadman* on the facts, Narine pointed out, first of all,[28] that it was well established

21 *Steadman v Steadman* [1976] AC 536, at 540, *per* Lord Reid.

22 *Ibid*, at 546, *per* Lord Morris. See also *Daulia Ltd v Four Millbank Nominees Ltd* [1978] 2 All ER 557; *McCook v Hammond* (1988) 25 JLR 296 (Court of Appeal, Jamaica).

23 *Jackman v Jones* (1987) 22 Barb LR 54 (High Court, Barbados); *Phillips v Bisnott* (1965) 8 WIR 299 (Court of Appeal, Jamaica); *Francis v Mines* (2001) Court of Appeal, Jamaica, Civ App No 94 of 1998, unreported [Carilaw JM 2001 CA 7], *per* Langrin JA (entry into possession coupled with a receipt for payment).

24 *Eldemire v Honiball* (1991) 28 JLR 577, PC.

25 [1976] AC 536.

26 *Medford v Cumberbatch* (1987) 22 Barb LR 54; *Abrakian v Wright* (2005) Supreme Court, Jamaica, No A083 of 1994, unreported [Carilaw JM 2005 SC 63].

27 (1987) 42 WIR 339.

28 *Ibid*, at 344.

that preparatory acts such as instructing a solicitor to prepare a lease or conveyance did not constitute sufficient part-performance of a contract to lease or sell land, but in the present case matters had gone beyond the mere preparation of the conveyance, as, in the absence of conditions, it was the purchaser's duty to send the transfer for execution by the vendor, and that obligation had been fulfilled by the purchaser in this case. However, if the sending of the conveyance for execution was sufficient to raise the inference that there must have been some prior agreement to sell the land, and if such a conclusion were 'to be taken in isolation and as a statement of the law and of general application', Narine JA 'shuddered to think of the extent of fraud that could be perpetrated' in the context of the 'loose' conveyancing practice in Trinidad and Tobago.[29] In particular, as Sykes J pointed out in a recent Jamaican case, *Abrikian v Wright*,[30] the Court of Appeal was concerned that unilateral acts by a claimant which were not brought to the attention of the 'party to be charged' could be relied on as acts of part-performance. There was a danger that a claimant could do 'secret' acts, then claim that those acts amounted to part-performance.

In conclusion, all three judges in the Trinidad and Tobago Court of Appeal declined to follow *Steadman*, in so far as it may be taken to have relaxed the requirements for part-performance, and preferred 'the traditional equity jurisprudence . . . that the act of part-performance must be *referable to some contract concerning land*',[31] rather than the *Steadman* approach which required merely that the acts should prove the existence of *some contract*, and be consistent with the contract as alleged.

29 *Ibid*, at 345.

30 (2005) Supreme Court, Jamaica, No A083 of 1994, unreported [Carilaw JM 2005 SC 63].

31 (1987) 42 WIR 339, at 352. Emphasis supplied.

CHAPTER 4

CONSIDERATION

DEFINITION AND NATURE OF THE DOCTRINE

The classic definition of consideration was given in *Currie v Misa*[1] by Lush J, who said:

> A valuable consideration, in the sense of the law, may consist either in some right, interest profit or benefit accruing to the one party [the promisor], or some forebearance, detriment, loss or responsibility given, suffered or undertaken by the other [the promisee]. In short, consideration is either a benefit to the promisor or a detriment to the promisee or, in Pollock's words, 'the price for which the promise of the other is bought, and the promise thus given for value is enforceable'.[2]

Consideration is necessary for all contracts, except contracts made by deed under seal. The essence of the requirement is that gratuitous promises cannot be enforced. Thus, for example, if D promises to give $1,000 to C but subsequently changes his mind, C has no cause of action against D for breach of contract, since C gave no consideration for D's promise; but if D's promise to pay the $1,000 had been given in return for C's promise to look after D's pets while D was away on holiday, then C could succeed against D.

The nature and rationale of the doctrine of consideration are explained in *Chitty on Contracts*[3] thus:

> The basic feature of the doctrine is that 'something of value in the eye of the law' must be given for a promise in order to make it enforceable as a contract. It follows that an informal gratuitous promise does not amount to a contract. A person or body to whom a promise of a gift is made from purely charitable or sentimental motives gives nothing to the promisee, and the claims of such a promisee are regarded as less compelling than those of a person who has provided (or promised) some return for the promise. The invalidity of informal gratuitous promises of this kind can also be supported on the ground that their enforcement could prejudice third parties such as creditors of the promisor. Such promises, too, may be rashly made; and the requirements of executing a deed or giving value provide at least some protection against this danger.

In the 2007 case of *Collins v Air Jamaica Ltd*,[4] C, who had been an employee of the airline for over 20 years, was made redundant. The letter terminating C's employment set out his entitlements to severance pay and other benefits, and continued: 'Because of your years of service, a decision has been taken to extend privilege travel benefits to you and your registered eligible dependants . . . You will be entitled to a total of eight trips per annum on Air Jamaica's services', at the reduced rate which he had enjoyed as an employee. The ownership of the airline subsequently changed, and the travel benefit was withdrawn. C sued

---

1 (1875) LR 10 Ex 153.

2 *Principles of Contract* , 13th edn, 1950, p 133.

3 28th edn, Vol 1, Ch 3.

4 (2007) Supreme Court, Jamaica, Claim No 1995 CLC 00203, unreported.

the airline for the value of the benefit, contending, *inter alia*, that he had given consideration for the benefit by forbearing to challenge his redundancy in the courts. Mangatal J rejected C's contention, holding that C had furnished no consideration for the travel benefit and therefore could not recover its value. She said: 'It may well be that the transport benefit offered was a promise gratuitously made, from sentimental motives or rash motivation. I can find no evidence to suggest that Mr Collins has "given something of value in the eye of the law" in exchange for the defendant's travel benefit promise ... There is no evidence of forbearance to sue.'

EXECUTORY AND EXECUTED CONSIDERATION

Consideration is *executory* where D's promise is made in return for a counter-promise from C: for example, in a contract of sale, where D promises to deliver a quantity of goods in return for C's promise to pay an agreed price for them.

Consideration is *executed* where D's promise is made in return for the performance of an act, and where C makes no promise to perform the act but in fact goes ahead and does the act. In such a case, the performance of the act constitutes both the acceptance of D's offer and the consideration necessary to support an action by C. For example, in the example of the advertisement by D that he will pay a reward to any person who finds and returns his lost dog, C's act in finding and returning the dog is executed consideration.

PAST CONSIDERATION

Where the act on which the promisee relies as consideration was performed by him *before the promisor made his promise*, the consideration is said to be 'past' and is treated as no consideration at all. For example, C offers to drive D from Kingston to Montego Bay in C's car. On arrival at Montego Bay, D promises to pay C $5,000(J) for his trouble and expense. D's promise is not binding on him because the consideration provided by C, namely the act of driving D to Montego Bay, is 'past', as it occurred before D made his promise. Similarly, where R bought T's horse for £30 and, after the sale, T promised R that the horse was 'sound and free from vice', but the horse turned out to be vicious, it was held that there was no consideration to support T's promise and he was not liable. The sale itself could not be valuable consideration because it had been completed by the time the promise was given.[5]

On the other hand, it has been held that past consideration will be effective where (a) it was given at the request of the promisor, and (b) it was assumed by the parties at the time it was given that the act or service was ultimately to be paid for. Thus, where D and E, the joint owners of certain patent rights, wrote to C, 'In consideration of your [past] services as the practical manager in working our patents, we hereby agree to give you a one-third share of the patents', it was held that although the consideration was past in time, it was effective. The court would infer that when

5 *Roscorla v Thomas* (1842) 3 QB 234.

C assumed his duties as manager, there was a tacit understanding that his services were to be paid for.[6]

CONSIDERATION MUST MOVE FROM THE PROMISEE

A party to a contract can enforce it only if he can show that *he* has provided consideration for the other party's promise. It is not sufficient for him to show that some other person has provided consideration. For example, X,Y and Z all sign an agreement whereby Z promises X and Y that he will pay $100,000 if Y builds a house for Z. Y builds the house. Although Y can sue, X cannot sue Z for the money since, though he was a party to the agreement, no consideration 'moved' from him.

Although consideration must move from the promisee, it need not move to the promisor. Thus, for example, if Y guarantee's Z's overdraft at the bank, Y becomes liable on the guarantee as soon as the bank advances money to Z; it is immaterial that Y gets no benefit from the advance. Similarly, consideration is supplied by a promisee who gives up a job or surrenders the tenancy of an apartment, even though no direct benefit results to the promisor from those acts.

An important exception to the rule that consideration must move from the promisee is provided by the Bills of Exchange legislation,[7] which provides that it is not necessary that a person who seeks to enforce a negotiable instrument, such as a bill of exchange, cheque or promissory note, should himself have furnished consideration for it, provided that consideration has been given at some time during the history of the instrument.

ADEQUACY OF CONSIDERATION

A promise cannot be enforced unless the promisee has given *some value* for it, whether the value consists of a benefit to the promisor or a detriment to the promisee; but the court will not question whether *adequate or fair value* was given. In the absence of fraud or undue influence, the court will not interfere with the bargain struck by the parties, and it is no defence to an action on the contract for the promisor to plead that the consideration provided by the promisee was 'too small' or 'inadequate'. Thus, in *Haigh v Brooks*,[8] where the consideration for a promise to pay certain bills was the surrender of a document that purported to be a guarantee but which turned out to be of doubtful validity, it was held that the virtual worthlessness of the consideration was no defence to an action on the promise. In the words of Lord Denman CJ, 'the plaintiffs were induced by the defendant's promise to part with something which they might have kept, and the defendant obtained what he desired by means of that promise.'[9]

---

6 *Re Casey's Patents* [1892] 1 Ch 104; applied in *Pao On v Lau Yiu Long* [1980] AC 614, p 629, *per* Lord Scarman.

7 See, for example, s 27, Bills of Exchange Act (The Bahamas), Ch 335; s 27, Bills of Exchange Act, 1893 (Jamaica); and s 27, Bills of Exchange Act (Trinidad & Tobago), Ch 82:31.

8 (1839) 113 ER 119.

9 At 123.

Similarly, a 'token' or 'nominal' consideration suffices, as where a tenant under a lease agrees to pay a 'peppercorn' rent, or a rent of '£1 a year',[10] for, in the colourful words of Lord Somervell, at common law 'a contracting party can stipulate for what consideration he chooses. A peppercorn does not cease to be good consideration if it is established that the promisee does not like pepper and will throw away the corn.'[11] Thus, where chocolate manufacturers sold gramophone records for 1s 6d each, plus three wrappers from their 6d bars of chocolate, it was held that the delivery of the wrappers formed part of the consideration, though the wrappers were of little value and were in fact thrown away.[12]

Qualifications to the principle

(1) Although nominal consideration suffices at common law, equity will not grant specific performance of a contract which is not supported by *substantial* consideration. This is a manifestation of the maxim that 'Equity will not aid a volunteer'.
(2) A sale supported by nominal consideration must be distinguished from a conditional gift. For example, where D promises C that he will give C the contents of a parcel if C will collect the parcel from the post office, there is a gift of the parcel, subject to a condition precedent. But where D promises to give C the contents of the parcel if C will give D $5, there is a sale supported by nominal consideration.
(3) A promise made 'in consideration of natural love and affection' is not binding, as such consideration is not regarded as 'valuable' in law.
(4) A promise which is too vague and insubstantial will not amount to valuable consideration; for example, where a son, in return for his father's promise to discharge him from liability on a promissory note, agreed to cease boring his father with complaints.[13]

Forebearance to sue

A forebearance to sue, even for a short time, may be valuable consideration for a promise, even if there is no actual waiver or compromise of the right of action, provided that some liability existed or was reasonably supposed to exist by the parties. In *Alliance Bank Ltd v Broom*,[14] for instance, the defendants were asked by their bankers to give security for money owed to the bank. They promised to assign certain documents of title to the bank, but failed to do so. The bank sought specific performance of the promise. It was held that the bank's claim succeeded. It had provided consideration for the defendants' promise by forebearing to sue for the money owed.

---

10 *Thomas v Thomas* (1842) 2 QB 851.

11 *Ibid.*

12 *Chappell & Co Ltd v Nestle Co Ltd* [1960] AC 87, at 114.

13 *White v Bluett* (1853) 23 LJ Ex 36.

14 (1864) 2 Drew & Sm 289. In *Strachan v Jamaican Redevelopment Foundation Inc* (2007) Supreme Court, Jamaica, No 3381 of 2006, unreported [Carilaw JM 2007 SC 104], Sykes J held that a forbearance to pursue an appeal to the Court of Appeal was sufficient consideration.

SUFFICIENCY OF CONSIDERATION

Although consideration need not be 'adequate', it must be 'sufficient' or 'real'. Consideration will be 'insufficient' and therefore ineffective if it consists of (a) something the promisee was already bound to do by law, or (b) something he was already bound to do under an existing contract with the promisor.

Promisee already bound by law

An example of a promisee being already bound by law is where C was under a subpoena to attend court to give evidence; his attendance at court to give evidence on behalf of D could not be consideration for a promise made by D, as C was already bound by law to attend.[15] But where the party who is under a legal duty to provide a service provides more than he is legally bound to do, then consideration will be sufficient, even though it is an act of the same kind as that which he is legally bound to do. Thus, for example, where a police force, which was under a legal duty to provide mobile police to protect a coal mine during a miners' strike, at the request of the mine owners provided a stationary force, consideration was sufficient, and the police force was held entitled to the payment promised by the mine owners.[16]

Promisee already bound under existing contract with promisor

The classic example of this type of case is *Stilk v Myrick*.[17] Here, on a voyage from London to the Baltic and back, two seamen deserted. The captain, being unable to replace the deserters, promised the rest of the crew that if they worked the ship back to London, he would divide the wages of the deserters amongst them. It was held that the crew members could not enforce this promise. They had provided no consideration for it, as they were already bound under their contracts of employment to work the ship back to London. On the other hand, it has been held that if the desertion so depletes the crew that completion of the voyage involves hazards of a kind not originally contemplated, and if the crew are induced to continue by a promise of extra pay, they will be doing something they were not already bound to do, and will be entitled to recover the extra pay.[18] It seems also that a promise to perform or the actual performance of something which the promisor is already bound to do under an existing contract with a *third party* may be sufficient consideration.[19]

Discharge of an existing duty

The principle that performance of a duty already owed to the promisor is insufficient consideration applies not only to the *creation of new obligations* (as in *Stilk v Myrick*,

15 *Collins v Godefroy* (1831) 109 ER 1040.

16 *Glasbrook v Glamorgan CC* [1925] AC 270.

17 (1809) 170 ER 1168.

18 *Hartley v Ponsonby* (1857) 119 ER 1471.

19 *New Zealand Shipping Co Ltd v Satterthwaite (The Eurymedon)* [1975] AC 154; *Pao On v Lau Yiu Long* [1979] 3 All ER 65; *Burnet v Bank of Nova Scotia Jamaica Ltd* (1986) 23 JLR 262.

above) but also to the *discharge of an existing duty*. For example, Y owes a debt of $15,000 to X. Y pays or promises to pay $10,000 in return for X's promise to forgo the balance. Is X bound by his promise? This is a case where Y has offered *partial* performance of his existing contractual duty in return for X's promise to accept the partial performance as full satisfaction of Y's duty. Applying the principle that performance (*a fortiori* partial performance) of an existing contractual duty owed to the promisor is not sufficient consideration for his promise, X is not bound; he may 'go back on his word' and sue for the full amount owed. This principle was established in *Pinnel's Case*,[20] where it was decided that if D owes a debt of, say, $20,000 and C agrees to accept $15,000 'in full satisfaction' of the debt, C is not bound by his promise and may subsequently sue for the full amount; however, it was also held in the same case that there will be sufficient consideration for the promise to discharge if:

(a) the promisee gives *something different* from that originally owed (for example, 'a horse, a hawk or a robe'), which may be good satisfaction for a debt of money; or
(b) the promisee pays part of the sum owed *on an earlier date or at a different place* from that originally stipulated.

The rule in *Pinnel's Case* was confirmed nearly three centuries later by the House of Lords in *Foakes v Beer*.[21] Here, Dr Foakes was a judgment debtor of Mrs Beer in the sum of £2,090. Mrs Beer agreed that if Foakes paid her £500 in cash and the balance of the debt by instalments, she would not take 'any proceedings whatever on the judgment.' Dr Foakes paid the amount of the judgment debt exactly as required, but Mrs Beer then claimed an additional amount as interest (on the basis that a judgment debt bears interest as from the date of the judgment). When sued, Dr Foakes pleaded that his obligation to pay interest had been discharged by Mrs Beer's promise not to take any proceedings on the judgment. The House of Lords, applying the rule in *Pinnel's Case* which, as Lord Selborne pointed out, 'may have been criticised as questionable in principle', but 'has never been judicially overruled' and, 'on the contrary, has always, since the sixteenth century, been accepted as law', held that Mrs Beer's claim succeeded. There was no sufficient consideration for her promise not to sue.

The principle in *Pinnel's Case* and *Foakes v Beer* was applied by the Jamaican Court of Appeal in *Manhertz v Island Life Insurance Co Ltd*.[22] In this case, the appellants had borrowed $4.8 million from the respondent insurance company on the security of a mortgage of their property. The instrument of mortgage contained the usual mortgagee's power of sale and provided that the loan was to be repayable by monthly instalments over a period of five years. The appellants fell behind in their payments and, after attempts to secure payment of the arrears proved fruitless, the respondent proceeded to exercise its power of sale. The property was put up for sale by auction, but no bids were received. Subsequently, the appellants offered to pay $3.6 million 'in full and final settlement' of the debt, which by then amounted to over $7 million. The respondent by letter agreed to accept the appellant's offer. The $3.6 million was never paid, and a further attempt to sell the property by auction was

20 (1602) 5 Co Rep 117a.
21 (1884) 9 App Cas 605.
22 (2008) Court of Appeal, Jamaica, Civ App No 24 of 2006, unreported [Carilaw JM 2008 CA 46]. See also *Advanced Tyre Systems Ltd v KR Contractors Ltd* (2008) High Court, Trinidad and Tobago, No S-1163 of 2005, unreported [Carilaw TT 2008 HC 84].

unsuccessful. The matter eventually came to court and the trial judge gave judgment for the respondent for $7.7 million. On appeal to the Jamaican Court of Appeal, one of the appellants' arguments was that, by accepting their offer to pay $3.6 million, the respondent had waived its right to claim under the terms of the mortgage agreement. The Court of Appeal upheld the decision of the trial judge that the agreement to accept the lower amount in full satisfaction was unenforceable because of the lack of consideration to support it. Smith JA said:

> By virtue of the rule in *Foakes v Beer*,[23] at common law a creditor is not bound by a promise to accept part payment in full settlement of a debt. An accrued debt can be discharged by the creditor's promise only if the promise gives rise to an effective accord and satisfaction. According to the rule in *Foakes v Beer*, the payment of a lesser sum than the amount due cannot be a satisfaction of the debt unless there is some 'added' benefit to the creditor, so that there is an accord and satisfaction . . . The rule in *Foakes v Beer* was followed and applied by this court in *Adams v R Hanna and Sons Ltd*.[24] In that case, a writ of seizure and sale was issued against a judgment debtor for the amount of a judgment debt and costs. Subsequently, the judgment creditor agreed to accept a smaller sum in settlement of the judgment debt. The judgment debtor paid the smaller sum, which was accepted by the judgment creditor 'in settlement of suit'. There was a subsequent seizure and sale of the judgment debtor's goods. This Court held that the payment of the lesser sum was not a satisfaction of the greater sum which was owed . . . In the instant case, [there was] clearly an agreement to accept a lesser sum than the amount due. There is absolutely no mention of any 'additional benefit' to the respondent. The respondent is not bound by such an agreement. There is no consideration and consequently no accord and satisfaction. Further, even if there was a valid consideration, the appellants were unable to perform their promise to pay the smaller amount.

PROMISSORY ESTOPPEL

The rule in *Pinnel's Case* and *Foakes v Beer* may be circumvented by applying the equitable doctrine of promissory estoppel, which has been defined thus:

> Where, by words or conduct, a person makes an unambiguous representation as to his future conduct, intending the representation to be relied on, and to affect the legal relations between the parties, and the representee alters his position in reliance on it, the representor will be unable to act inconsistently with the representation if, by doing so, the representee would be prejudiced.[25]

This doctrine came to the fore in *Central London Property Trust Ltd v High Trees House Ltd* (known as the *'High Trees Case'*).[26] Here, the landlord company granted a 99-year lease of a block of flats to the defendants at an annual rent of £2,500. Following the outbreak of the Second World War in 1939, the defendants were unable to find sufficient sub-tenants for the flats, and were consequently unable to pay their rent. In the circumstances, the landlord agreed to reduce the rent by half, to £1,250. After the war

---

23 (1884) 9 App Cas 605.

24 (1967) 11 WIR 245.

25 Hanbury and Martin, *Modern Equity*, 18th edn (London: Sweet & Maxwell), para 27-021.

26 [1947] KB 130. The *High Trees* principle was applied to a waiver of rent in *Curtis v Hotel Corporation of the Bahamas* (1998) Supreme Court, The Bahamas, No FP/14 of 1996, unreported [Carilaw BS 1998 SC 87].

ended in 1945, there was no longer any difficulty in subletting the flats. Denning J held that the landlord was entitled to claim the full rent as from that year, but he also stated that the landlord would have been estopped from recovering the full rent for the war years since, although at common law the landlord was not bound by its promise to accept a reduced rent on account of the lack of consideration for the promise, in equity it would have been estopped from claiming the full rent for those years, because 'a promise intended to be binding, intended to be acted upon, and in fact acted on, is binding so far as its terms properly apply'.

Denning J's application of the equitable doctrine was justified by reference to the following statement of principle by Lord Cairns in *Hughes v Metropolitan Railway Co*:[27]

> If parties who have entered into definite and distinct terms involving certain legal results . . . afterwards by their own act or with their own consent enter upon a course of negotiation which has the effect of leading one of the parties to suppose that the strict legal rights arising under the contract will not be enforced, or will be kept in suspense, or held in abeyance, the person who otherwise might have enforced those rights will not be allowed to enforce them where it would be inequitable, having regard to the dealings which have thus taken place between the parties.

The principle in *Hughes* and *High Trees* was applied in a Trinidadian case, *Point Lisas Industrial Port Development Corporation Ltd v KP's Transport Ltd*.[28] Here, the applicant owed the respondent $760,585. The respondent agreed to accept $650,000 'in full and final settlement of all claims, costs, interest and other charges whatsoever'. Blackman J conceded that *Foakes v Beer*[29] was clear authority that, at common law, an agreement for the payment of a lesser sum than that actually owed was not valid, in the absence of consideration moving from the promisee. However, he noted that although *Hughes v Metropolitan Railway Co* had been decided seven years before *Foakes*, there was no reference to it and no principle of equity invoked in *Foakes*, and that it was 'now beyond dispute that principles of equity prevail over the common law since they have been fused'. Further, he could find no evidence that the respondent had been put under pressure to accept the lesser amount, nor intimidated, nor taken advantage of in any way. Accordingly, in his view, 'it would be wholly inequitable for the respondent to renege on the accord reached between it and the applicant who acted in good faith.'

Scope of promissory estoppel

Although the application of the doctrine of promissory has not been free from controversy and there remain a number of uncertainties regarding its proper scope, the following principles have emerged from the case law:

1. *The promise must be clear and unequivocal.* There will be no estoppel if the language of the promise was indefinite or imprecise.[30] Such promise may be express or implied from words or conduct.

---

27 (1877) 2 App Cas 439.

28 (1991) High Court, Trinidad and Tobago, No 5261 of 1985, unreported [Carilaw TT 1991 HC 128].

29 Above, n 23.

30 *Woodhouse AC Israel Cocoa Ltd v Nigerian Produce Marketing Co Ltd* [1972] AC 741.

2. *It must be inequitable for the promisor to go back on his promise.* If, for instance, the promise to accept a lesser sum than the amount owed was extracted by threats or coercion, it would not be inequitable to allow the promisor to go back on his promise and claim the full amount, pleading the lack of consideration for the promise. An example of such a situation is *D&C Builders Ltd v Rees.*[31] Here, the defendants owed £482 to the claimant, a small company, for building work done for them. After delaying payment for several months, and knowing that the clamant was in severe financial difficulties, the defendants offered the claimant £300, saying, in effect, that if the claimant did not accept this amount, it would get nothing. The claimant agreed to accept the £300, but later went back on its promise and sued to recover the balance of the debt. Lord Denning held that although there was a promise of a type that was within the doctrine of promissory estoppel, it would not in this case be inequitable to allow the claimant to go back on its promise, since the defendants had improperly taken advantage of the claimant's precarious financial position. The defendants were accordingly liable for the balance of the debt.

   Again, in *Manhertz v Island Life Insurance Co Ltd,*[32] the facts of which are set out above, the Jamaican Court of Appeal held that it would not be inequitable to allow the promisor to resile from its promise, since the promisees had failed to honour their own obligations under the settlement agreement. The Court referred to *Adams v Hanna and Sons Ltd,*[33] where Duffus P stated that, 'for a debtor to obtain the benefit of the principle of equitable estoppel, he must not only show that the creditor's conduct was inequitable but that his own conduct was such that he ought to be given the helping hand of equity.'

3. *The doctrine does not create new contractual rights.* Promissory estoppel (unlike proprietary estoppel) does not create new legal rights; it merely prevents the promisor from enforcing his strict legal rights. In the absence of consideration, a promise cannot be enforced, and equitable estoppel cannot be used as the basis of an action against the promisor. 'The doctrine can be used as a shield, but not as a sword.' Thus, where a husband, on divorce, promised to pay his ex-wife an allowance of £100 a year, and failed to make the payments, it was held that the wife could not enforce the promise, since (a) there was no consideration for it, and (b) promissory estoppel could be used only as a defence and not to found a cause of action.[34]

4. *The doctrine does not extinguish existing obligations but merely suspends them.* The promisor may, on giving reasonable notice, resume the right he has waived, and revert to the original terms of the contract. The promise becomes irrevocable only where the promisee cannot resume his position.[35]

5. *The promisee must have altered his position in reliance on the promise.*[36] This requirement is in accordance with the general principle of equity regarding estoppel,

---

31 [1965] 3 All ER 837.

32 Above, n 22.

33 (1967) 11 WIR 245.

34 *Combe v Combe* [1951] All ER 767.

35 *Tool Metal Manufacturing Co Ltd v Tungsten Electric Co Ltd* [1955] 2 All ER 657.

36 *Ajayi v RT Briscoe (Nigeria) Ltd* [1964] 3 All ER 556; *Jamaica Telephone Co Ltd v Robinson* (1970) 16 WIR 174, at 179, *per* Luckhoo JA.

which is that it would be unfair and unconscionable if 'a man who had indicated that he is not going to insist upon his strict legal rights, as a result of which the other party has altered his position, should be able to turn around at a minute's notice and insist upon his rights, however inconvenient it may be to the party who thought he was temporarily relieved.'[37] In such circumstances, an estoppel will arise against the party who has waived his rights.

Promissory estoppel and waiver

The close relationship between promissory estoppel and waiver can be seen in *Jamaica Telephone Co Ltd v Robinson*.[38] Here, R was in default in the payment of just over £4, owed for telephone services supplied by the appellant company. On 8 March 1969, the company issued R with a 'disconnect notice' reminding him of the amount owed on his phone bill and informing him that, unless payment were received, or suitable arrangements made for the settling of the account by 20 March, the telephone service would be disconnected. On 19 March, R paid the amount stated in the disconnect notice, but the company nonetheless disconnected R's phone on 21 March. Upon realising that R had in fact paid the amount stated in the disconnect notice, the company restored the phone connection after a lapse of about eight hours. R sued the company, claiming that disconnecting the phone was a breach of contract.

All three judges of the Jamaican Court of Appeal were in agreement that R had a good claim, but they used widely divergent reasoning in reaching that conclusion, such reasoning including a discussion of promissory estoppel and waiver. Luckhoo JA emphasised the requirement that, for promissory estoppel to apply, R would have to show that he had altered his position. He said:[39]

> Can it be said that that in the instant case the respondent altered his position in reliance upon the promise contained in the disconnect notice not to disconnect before March 20, 1969, if the amount stated therein were earlier paid? I am unable to see that he did so. While it is true that he made the payment in consequence of the receipt of the disconnect notice, he only did after default what he was bound to do in any event. There was not a tittle of evidence that he altered his position by reason of the receipt of the disconnect notice. He could not therefore rely upon the principle of promissory estoppel had the appellants sought to enforce the strict terms of the contract, and it follows that he can invoke no such principle to bar the appellants from raising a defence which they could otherwise have raised to his claim.

Smith JA pointed out that the £4 became due and payable on 13 February 1969, under cl 1(b) of the telephone subscriber service contract between R and the company, and that under cl 5 of that contract, R became liable to have his telephone service disconnected without notice from 14 February. However, the disconnect notice constituted a waiver of the company's strict rights under cl 5 of the contract. He explained:[40]

---

37 *Tool Metal Manufacturing Co Ltd v Tungsten Electric Co Ltd* [1955] 2 All ER 657.

38 (1970) 16 WIR 174.

39 At 179.

40 At 183.

> The defendant company waived its right to disconnect the plaintiff's telephone . . . on condition that that the plaintiff pay the amount due by March 20, 1969. The plaintiff fulfilled the condition by payment by that date. The defendant company's right to disconnect the telephone, which was postponed by the terms of the 'disconnect notice', was therefore extinguished from the moment of payment.

Finally, the approach of Fox JA combines elements of, and shows the close relationship between the common law concept of waiver and the equitable principle of promissory estoppel. In Fox JA's view, the company was entitled to disconnect R's phone under cl 5 of the service contract without notice, for default in payment of any money due under the agreement, but it was 'estopped by the system which it had introduced for the collection of amounts due under the agreement'. That system entailed first sending a bill to the subscriber, informing him of the amount due up to a certain date. If payment was not forthcoming, the company would then send a disconnection notice, warning of disconnection on failure to settle the bill by a certain date. Fox JA continued:[41]

> In effect, the company promised not to insist on its strict legal rights under cl 5, and assured the subscriber that disconnection of his telephone for default in the payment of moneys due under the agreement would occur as a final step in a series of steps designed to inform him of the amount due and to give him a reasonable time to make payment. Counsel for the company contends that this promise is without consideration and therefore unenforceable. It is true that absence of consideration for a promise of this kind created theoretical difficulties over which the common law stumbled for centuries. But within the past century, as a result of increasing recourse to a principle of equity, these difficulties have all been swept away, and the fact that, as in this case, there is no consideration to support a promise to vary the agreement does not necessarily have the effect of nullifying the promise. The company intended its promise to be acted upon. The plaintiff acted upon its promise. He waited to be informed by a bill of the amount due and owing under the agreement, and took advantage of the time for making payment which was allowed by the system of sending a 'disconnect notice.' The company will not be allowed to go back on that promise.

A comparison between the respective approaches of Smith JA and Fox JA in the *Jamaica Telephone* case shows the similarity between the ingredients of waiver and those of promissory estoppel. This similarity was noted by Denning LJ in *Charles Rickards Ltd v Oppenheim.*[42] In this case, the defendant, having ordered a car chassis from the claimants, twice waived the delivery date and, when the claimants still did not deliver after expiry of the extended time period, treated the contract as repudiated. It was held that the defendant was entitled to do so since, although he would have been prevented from going back on his waiver of the time stipulation, he was entitled to reimpose a new time limit (of which the claimants had received reasonable notice), which the claimants had failed to keep. Denning LJ explained:[43]

> Whether it be called waiver or forbearance on his part, or an agreed variation or substituted performance, does not matter. It is a kind of estoppel. By his conduct, [the

41 At 181–183.

42 [1950] 1 KB 616.

43 At 623.

> defendant] evinced an intention to affect their legal relations. He made, in effect, a promise not to insist on his strict legal rights. That promise was intended to be acted on, and was in fact acted on. He cannot afterwards go back on it.

It has been pointed out, however, that the analogy between waiver and promissory estoppel is 'not completely exact'[44] for, as the judgment of Luckhoo JA in *Jamaica Telephone* emphasises, for a promissory estoppel to be binding, the promisee must have altered his position in reliance on the promise, whereas in waiver, being a common law rather than an equitable principle, no reliance on the part of the person requesting the waiver is required; it is sufficient that he acted on the waiver. The concept may accordingly be defined as an indulgence given by one party to the other, which does not need consideration to support it, and which may be withdrawn by giving reasonable notice.

44 *Anson's Law of Contract*, 29th edn (Oxford, 2010), p 469.

CHAPTER 5

CAPACITY

In general, all natural persons have full legal personality, and, therefore, contractual capacity; that is, they are fully capable of entering into contractual relations with other persons. However, certain classes of natural person lack full contractual capacity: minors, drunken persons, insane persons and illiterates.

MINORS

The age of adulthood or majority, 18 years, is set by legislation[1], and is the age at which natural persons generally become legally capable of entering into contracts. Minors thus generally lack contractual capacity; however, in some circumstances, contracts made or purported to be entered into by minors are binding; the validity and enforceability of such contracts are governed by common law principles as amended by legislation.

When considering the capacity of minors to enter into contracts for the sale of goods, regard must be had to relevant sale of goods legislation, which largely codifies the common law position. The legislation itself states simply that, except in the case of contracts for 'necessaries', the capacity of minors to enter into contracts for the sale of goods is regulated by the general common law principles concerning capacity to contract and to transfer and acquire property.[2]

Under general common law principles, contracts entered into by minors can be grouped into three categories, as follows:

a. contracts rendered void by the Minors Act;[3]
b. contracts voidable at common law; and
c. contracts binding on the minor.

Void contracts

Pursuant to section 19 of the Minors Act 1985 (Barbados), each of the following types of contract entered into by minors (whether by specialty or simple contract) is absolutely void:

(a) contracts for the repayment of money lent or to be lent (including loan contracts);

---

1 See s 3, Minors Act, Cap 215 (Barbados); s 2, Age of Majority Act, Ch 46:06 (Trinidad and Tobago); and s 3, Age of Majority Act 2001 (Bermuda).

2 See s 4, Sale of Goods Act, Cap 318 (Barbados); s 4, Sale of Goods Act, Cap 393 (Antigua and Barbuda); and s 4, Sale of Goods Act, Cap 261 (Belize).

3 See s 19, Minors Act Cap 215 (Barbados). See also Infants Act, Ch 46:02 (Trinidad and Tobago); Law of Minors Act, Cap 169 (St Vincent and the Grenadines); Infants' Relief Act, Ch 134 (The Bahamas); and Infancy Act, Ch 46:01 (Guyana).

(b) contracts for goods supplied or to be supplied (other than contracts for necessaries); and
(c) all accounts stated with minors.[4]

The effect of the Minors Act is that a minor cannot be sued on any of these types of contract. Thus, for example, a minor cannot be sued to recover money owed by him on an overdraft at the bank, nor can an adult who guarantees the minor's overdraft be sued on the guarantee;[5] and a minor cannot be sued for the price of non-necessary goods supplied to him. Under the same principle, it has been held[6] that a power of attorney granted by a minor aged 17 was void and that all transactions entered into by the grantee of the power as agent of the minor were also void.

Voidable contracts

Voidable contracts are contracts which remain binding on the minor unless he repudiates them before becoming an adult, or within a reasonable time after attaining the age of adulthood. This category of contract is limited to those under which the minor acquires an interest in something permanent in nature, that is, out of which arise continuing obligations that are binding on the minor, such as agreements to take leases of land, partnership agreements, and agreements to take shares which are not fully paid up.

As stated above, when a minor enters into such a contract, it is voidable by the minor before or within a reasonable time of attaining the age of majority. What is a reasonable time will depend on the circumstances. In one case, it was held that the repudiation by a minor of a covenant in a marriage settlement four and a half years after the minor had attained his majority was unreasonably late and therefore ineffective.[7]

Until the minor decides to repudiate, he is fully liable to perform his obligations under the contract. Thus, for instance, a minor who takes a lease of property must perform the covenants in the lease, including the covenant to pay rent,[8] and a minor who takes up shares in a company is liable to pay calls on the shares.[9] Following repudiation, it is clear that the minor ceases to be liable for future obligations under the contract, such as rent due after that date; but there is some doubt as to whether he is liable to satisfy existing obligations, such as payment of rent falling due before the repudiation.[10] It seems the better view is that the minor is bound by obligations accruing before repudiation. Thus, in *Blake v Concannon*,[11] it was held that a minor who repudiated a tenancy on attaining his majority, having occupied the premises

4 An account stated is an agreed balance payable between the parties and resulting from a series of transactions.
5 *Coutts & Co v Brown-Lecky* [1947] KB 104.
6 *Onyiliofor v Nkwocha* [1978] NCLR 354.
7 *Edwards v Carter* [1893] AC 360.
8 *Davies v Beynon-Harris* (1931) 47 TLR 424.
9 *North Western Railway Co v McMichael* (1851) 5 Ex 114.
10 See Cheshire, Fifoot and Furmston, *Law of Contract*, 13th edn, p 448.
11 (1870) IR 4 CL 323.

for several months, was liable to pay half a year's rent accruing while he was in possession.

Where the minor repudiates the contract, he may recover any money paid or property transferred, but only where there has been a total failure of consideration. The test for 'total failure of consideration' is not whether the minor received any real advantage from the contract, but whether he obtained the very consideration which he had bargained for. In *Steinberg v Scala (Leeds) Ltd*,[12] a minor applied for and was allotted shares in a company; she received no dividends, and the value of the shares remained low. 18 months after allotment, while she was still a minor, she repudiated the contract and sought to recover the amount she had paid on allotment and on the first call. It was held that she could not recover the money; there had been no total failure of consideration, since, by allotting the shares to her, the company had done all that it had bargained to do under the agreement.

Contracts binding on minors

A minor is fully bound if he enters into a contract for necessaries. 'Necessaries' are defined by the sale of goods legislation as 'goods suitable to the condition in life of such [minor] . . . and to his actual requirements at the time of sale and delivery'. Furthermore, 'where necessaries are sold and delivered to a [minor] . . . he must pay a reasonable price therefor.'[13]

Case law is instructive in fleshing out the meaning of the term 'necessaries'. Precedents show that necessaries include not only necessary goods but also such essentials as board and lodging, medical care,[14] legal advice,[15] and food and clothing for the minor's wife or children.[16] Instruction in art or trade, or intellectual, moral and religious training may also be deemed necessary, since 'the proper cultivation of the mind is as expedient as the support of the body'.[17] Goods which are of mere luxury are always excluded, but luxurious articles of utility are in some cases allowed. The question of necessity or otherwise is a mixed question of both law and fact.[18]

For a minor to be liable for necessaries, the onus is on the seller to prove not only that the items sold to the minor were suitable to his station in life but also that he was not adequately supplied with goods of that nature at the time of the sale. A classic example is *Nash v Inman*,[19] where a tailor brought an action against a Cambridge undergraduate (a minor) to recover £122, being the price of 11 fancy waistcoats supplied to him. The action was dismissed, on the ground that the defendant was already sufficiently supplied with clothes suitable to his position. Again, in the case of luxury goods, it may be obvious that the items in question cannot be necessaries

12 [1923] 2 Ch 452.

13 See s 4, Sale of Goods Act, Cap 318 (Barbados); s 4, Sale of Goods Act, Ch 82:30 (Trinidad and Tobago); and s 3, Sale of Goods Act (Jamaica).

14 *Peters v Fleming* (1840) 6 M & W 42.

15 *Helps v Clayton* (1864) 17 CBNS 553.

16 *Chapple v Cooper* (1844) 13 M & W 252.

17 *Ibid.*

18 *Ryder v Wombwell* (1868) LR 4 Exch 32.

19 [1908] 2 KB 1.

for the particular minor, as where a pair of crystal, ruby, and diamond solitaires and an antique goblet worth nearly £50 in total were sold to a minor having an annual income of £500.[20] It is thus clear that the seller of 'necessary' goods to a minor acts at his peril, in the sense that he takes the risk that the minor may be less well off than he imagined, or that, unknown to the seller, the minor was already adequately supplied with such goods, so that in either case the price would be irrecoverable.

Even where a contract with a minor concerns the sale or supply of necessaries, it will be void if it contains harsh or onerous terms which are disadvantageous to the minor; as, for example, where a car rental agreement provided that the minor was to be absolutely liable for damage to the vehicle, whether or not caused by his fault or neglect.[21] Further, the Sale of Goods Acts provide that a minor's obligation is to pay *a reasonable price* for goods sold to him.[22]

It seems clear that a minor's liability to pay a reasonable price for necessaries is quasi-contractual; he is liable only for necessaries actually supplied to him and is not liable on executory contracts for necessaries. Thus, until goods have been actually delivered to him, he is under no liability,[23] and it seems he may even refuse to accept them when tendered.[24] On the other hand, where the subject-matter of the contract is not goods but, for example, training or education, it seems that the contract may be binding on the minor even where it has not been executed. In *Roberts v Gray*,[25] G, a minor, entered into a contract with R, a professional billiard player, whereby G was to accompany R on a world tour and gain training and experience as a match player of billiards. R incurred considerable expenditure in preparation for the tour, but, following a dispute, G repudiated the agreement and the tour had to be cancelled. R sued G for breach of contract, and the agreement was treated as one for necessaries. G argued that since the contract had been repudiated while still executory, in that he had not received any training or experience, he should not be liable. It was held, however, that G was liable. Hamilton LJ was 'unable to appreciate why a contract which is in itself binding, because it is a contract for necessaries not qualified by unreasonable terms, can cease to be binding merely because it is executory':[26] a statement which directly contradicts the rule relating to contracts for necessary goods. However, the approach in *Roberts v Gray* can be rationalised by treating such agreements not as contracts for necessaries but as beneficial contracts of service which are regarded as binding even where not completely executed.[27]

20 *Ryder v Wombwell*, above.

21 *Fawcett v Smethurst* (1914) 84 LJKB 473.

22 Section 4(1), Sale of Goods Act, Cap 318 (Barbados); s 4(1), Sale of Goods Act, Ch 337 (The Bahamas); s 4(1), Sale of Goods Act, Cap 261 (Belize); s 3, Sale of Goods Act (Jamaica); s 3, Sale of Goods Act, Cap 393 (Antigua and Barbuda); s 4, Sale of Goods Act, Ch 82:30 (Trinidad and Tobago); s 3, Sale of Goods Act 1978 (Bermuda).

23 *Nash v Inman* [1908] 2 KB 1, at 8.

24 Cheshire, Fifoot and Furmston, *Law of Contract*, 13th edn, p 443.

25 *Roberts v Gray* [1913] 1 KB 520.

26 *Ibid*, at 530.

27 See below.

Beneficial contracts of service

Minors are bound by beneficial contracts of service, that is, contracts under which the minor obtains education or training for a trade or profession. The contract, in order to be valid, must be an employment or apprenticeship contract, or must be at least analogous to such a contract.[28] Contracts under this heading are binding on the minor only if they are proved to be substantially for his benefit.

A case in which there was a contract of service which was not beneficial is *De Francesco v Barnum*.[29] Here, B, a 14-year-old girl, entered into a contract of apprenticeship with DF for a 7-year period, during which she was to be taught stage dancing. Under the terms of the contract, B agreed not to marry during the apprenticeship, and not to accept any professional engagements without DF's consent; her pay was set at a very low level, and DF was not bound to provide her with engagements or to support her while she was unemployed; finally, DF could terminate the apprenticeship if B was found to be unfit for stage dancing. It was held that the provisions of the contract were unreasonable and not beneficial to B, and the contract was therefore unenforceable. According to Fry J, the court had to 'look at the whole contract, having regard to the circumstances of the case, and determine . . . whether the contract is or is not beneficial'.[30]

On the other hand, there are cases in which minors have been held bound by service contracts which were found to be substantially beneficial to the minor; for example, where a minor, in taking up employment with a railway company as a porter, agreed to join the company's own accident insurance scheme and to forgo his statutory right of action for personal injuries,[31] and where, in a contract between a minor and the British Boxing Board of Control, whereby the minor received a licence to box which enabled him to acquire experience in his profession, a clause enabled the Board to withhold earnings on account of his being disqualified for a foul committed during a bout.[32] In both of these cases, the contracts were held binding on the minor.

A service contract will thus be binding on a minor provided it is shown to be beneficial to him; on the other hand, other types of contract will not be binding merely because they are beneficial to the minor. It is well established, for instance, that a trading contract is not binding on a minor, however beneficial it may be for him. Thus, for instance, a haulage contractor (a minor) was held not liable to pay instalments under a hire-purchase agreement in respect of a vehicle which he had hired for use in his business;[33] and where a minor hay and straw dealer contracted to sell and deliver a consignment of hay, but failed to deliver, it was held that he was not liable to repay the price to the buyer.[34]

---

28 *Cowern v Nield* [1912] 2 KB 419.
29 (1890) 45 Ch D 430.
30 *Ibid*, at 439.
31 *Clements v London and North Western Rly Co* [1894] 2 QB 482.
32 *Doyle v White City Stadium Ltd* [1935] I KB 110.
33 *Mercantile Union Guarantee Corporation Ltd v Ball* [1937] 3 All ER 1.
34 *Cowern v Nield* [1912] 2 KB 419.

Liability of minors in tort and contract

A minor is generally liable in tort to the same extent as an adult, but he is not liable for a tort which is directly connected with a contract which is not binding on him. Thus, for instance, where a minor obtains a loan by falsely misrepresenting that he is over 18, he cannot be liable for the tort of deceit, since the action in tort is directly connected with the void loan contract.[35] Similarly, where a minor buys non-necessary goods on credit, he cannot be sued for conversion or detinue if he fails to pay for them or return them to the seller.[36]

In some cases, it may be difficult to determine whether an action in tort is or is not directly connected with a contract for which the minor is not liable. The position seems to be that where the act complained of was *of a kind contemplated by the contract*, then the minor cannot be liable in tort, because of the connection with the contract; but where the wrongful act was not contemplated by the contract, and external to it, the minor can be held liable in tort. Thus, where a minor hired a horse and injured the animal by excessive riding, the minor was not liable in the tort of negligence because the act complained of was of a type contemplated by the contract;[37] and it has been held that where a minor rents a car to transport his luggage from the railway station and, while using the car to drive to another place several miles beyond the station, injures a person through his careless driving, he cannot be liable in negligence, because of the close connection between the act of careless driving and the rental contract.[38] On the other hand, where a minor hired a horse for riding, under strict instructions that he was 'not to jump or lark with' it, and he lent the animal to a friend who jumped and killed it, the minor was held liable in tort, as the wrongful act was not contemplated by the contract.[39] Similarly, a minor who hired a microphone and amplifier and improperly handed it over to a friend was liable in tort for the return of the items. As Lord Greene explained:[40]

> The terms of the bailment of these articles to the defendant did not permit him to part with their possession at all. If it was the bargain that he might part with them, it was for him to establish that fact and he has failed to do so. On that basis, the action of the defendant in parting with the goods fell outside the contract altogether, and that fact brings the case within *Burnard v Haggis*.[41]

Restitution in equity

At common law, as we have seen, a minor who obtains property under a contract induced by his fraud, as where he misrepresents that he is of full age, cannot be held liable for the tort of deceit, nor can he be compelled to pay for the property (unless it consists of necessaries), as that would amount to enforcing a void contract. Under

35 *R Leslie Ltd v Sheill* [1914] 3 KB 607.
36 *Ibid.*
37 *Jennings v Rundall* (1799) 8 TR 335.
38 *Fawcett v Smethurst* (1914) LJ KB 473.
39 *Burnard v Haggis* (1863) 143 ER 360.
40 *Ballett v Mingay* [1943] 1 All ER 143, at 145.
41 (1863) 143 ER 360.

the equitable doctrine of restitution, however, where a minor obtains goods by fraud and *remains in possession of them*, he may be compelled to restore them to the other contracting party.[42]

Where, on the other hand, the minor is no longer in possession of the goods, an order of restitution would obviously be fruitless, and the court will not order the minor to pay the monetary value of the goods, as that would amount to enforcing a contract declared void by the statutes.[43]

Equally, a minor who obtains a loan of money by fraudulently misrepresenting that he is of full age cannot be compelled to repay the loan at common law, as contracts of loan are declared void by the statutes; nor would restitution be available in equity, as the essence of a loan is that it is not the identical notes or coins that are to be repaid, but other notes and coins of equal value.[44]

But what is the position where a minor obtains goods from C by fraud, then sells them for value? Will C be entitled to recover from the minor the proceeds of sale in the minor's hands? The authorities on this question are conflicting. It was held in *Stocks v Wilson*[45] that a minor who had obtained non-necessary goods on credit from S by falsely representing that he was of full age, and later sold the goods, was accountable to S for the proceeds of sale; but this decision was later disapproved, though not overruled, by the English Court of Appeal in *R Leslie Ltd v Sheill*.[46] The *Stocks v Wilson* approach to the equitable doctrine of restitution can perhaps be justified by analogy with the equitable remedy of tracing, whereby a beneficiary can trace into the hands of a trustee not only the original trust property in the trustee's hands, but also the proceeds of sale of such property, on the ground that there is an identifiable fund in existence against which the beneficiary's right *in rem* can be enforced.

MENTALLY DISORDERED PERSONS

Under the sale of goods legislation, a mentally disordered person is bound by contracts for necessaries.[47] As in the case of minors, the definition of 'necessaries' is set by the legislation as goods which are suitable (a) to the condition in life of the mentally incapable, and (b) to his actual requirements at the time of sale and delivery. A mentally disordered person must pay a reasonable price for necessary goods provided under a contract which he purported to make.[48]

As in the case of minors, the liability to pay is quasi-contractual, so that it arises only where the goods are actually delivered to the mentally disordered person. There must have been some element of consent on the part of the mentally

42 *Lempriere v Lange* (1879) 12 Ch D 675.

43 *R Leslie Ltd v Sheill* [1914] 3 KB 607.

44 *Ibid.*

45 [1913] 2 KB 235.

46 [1914] 3 KB 607.

47 See s 4(1), Sale of Goods Act, Cap 318 (Barbados); s 4, Sale of Goods Act, Cap 393 (Antigua and Barbuda); and s 3, Sale of Goods Act (Jamaica).

48 See s 4, Sale of Goods Act, Cap 318 (Barbados); s 4, Sale of Goods Act, Cap 393 (Antigua and Barbuda); and s 3, Sale of Goods Act (Jamaica).

disordered person, since the seller cannot force the goods on him and then claim payment.

In the case of non-necessary goods, the mentally disordered person is bound by his contracts unless he can show (1) that, owing to his mental condition, he did not understand what he was doing,[49] and (2) that the other party was aware of his incapacity.[50] Where these two requirements are shown, the contract is voidable, not void.[51] Lord Esher MR articulated the rule as follows:

> When a person enters into a contract, and afterwards alleges that he was so insane at the time that he did not know what he was doing, and proves the allegation, the contract is as binding on him in every respect, whether it is executory or executed, as if he had been sane when he made it, unless he can prove further that the person with whom he had contracted knew him to be so insane as not to be capable of understanding what he was about.

Contracts made by a mentally disordered person during a lucid interval, and those made before but ratified during a lucid interval, are binding on him.[52]

The rules governing capacity of the mentally ill may, by analogy, be applied to the senile or to persons suffering from 'mental infirmity'. In a Barbadian case, *Wiltshire v Cain*,[53] the court drew such an analogy. In this case, the plaintiff brought an action for specific performance of an agreement for the sale of land. Counsel for the defendant, an elderly gentleman, argued *inter alia* that at the time of making the agreement and for at least one year prior thereto, the defendant was suffering from general loss of memory, mental debility and senile decay and was incapable of understanding the meaning and effect of the agreement. It was further argued that the plaintiff was aware of this mental infirmity at the time of the agreement. While, on the facts, the court did consider the defendant sufficiently mentally competent to enter into a valid contract, Field CJ commented:

> A person may be or become of unsound mind because he has lost the ability to reason by disease, grief or other accident. Where a person in such a condition can be shown not to have understood, because of his mental condition, what he was doing and further that the other party was aware of this incapacity, then any contract, other than a contract for necessaries, made by such a person is not binding on him.

DRUNKEN PERSONS

Under the sale of goods legislation, a drunken person is bound to pay a reasonable price for necessaries sold to him.[54]

Where a person enters into a contract in such a state of intoxication that he did not understand what he was doing, and the other party was aware of that fact, the

---

49 *Boughton v Knight* (1873) LR 3 PD 64.

50 *Molton v Camroux* (1948) 4 Exch 487.

51 *Imperial Loan Co Ltd v Stone* [1982] 1 QB 599, at 601.

52 *Hall v Warren* (1804) 9 Ves 605.

53 (1960) Supreme Court, Barbados, writ dated 30 December, 1958, unreported [Carilaw BB 1960 HC 3].

54 Section 4(1), Sale of Goods Act, Cap 318 (Barbados). See also s 4, Sale of Goods Act, Cap 393 (Antigua and Barbuda); s 4, Sale of Goods Act, Ch 82:30 (Trinidad and Tobago); and s 3, Sale of Goods Act (Jamaica).

contract is voidable at the drunkard's option,[55] but may be ratified by the latter when the intoxication ceases.[56]

ILLITERATES

At common law, the defence of *non est factum* may be available to an illiterate person who signs a document under a fundamental mistake as to its nature or contents. (See Chapter 8, below).

COMPANIES

Formation

Companies may be formed by statute under companies legislation or by royal charter.

The ability of a company, formed pursuant to statute, to exercise its capacity to contract, and its capacity to act generally, is subject to any restrictions set out in its constitutional documents.

Companies incorporated under older companies legislation generally have constitutional documents comprising (1) memorandum of association, and (2) articles of association. The memorandum of association of such a company will set out a list of the company's purposes and permitted actions. The capacity of the company to contract will be limited to the contents of this list, which is called the company's 'objects'. Any acts exceeding the limits set by the objects clause are *ultra vires* and void.[57] As explained by Lord Cairns in *Ashbury Railway Carriage & Iron Co v Riche*, the rationale for the *ultra vires* rule was that (1) it followed naturally from statutory incorporation and (2) it would protect the company's investors and creditors.

Companies under this regime will tend to have their objects drafted very widely to allow for the widest capacity possible.

Companies incorporated under updated companies legislation[58] are generally not bound by the objects set out in their memorandum of association, and their capacity is not dependent on permitted objects set out in the constitutional documents. Within the boundaries of applicable laws and regulations, the only restrictions on these companies' capacity will be those restrictions expressly included in the articles of association.

55 *Manches v Trimborn* (1946) 115 LJKB, cf *In the Estate of Park* [1954] P 112; and see Fridman (1963) 79 LQR 502, 518–519; *Re Beaney* [1978] 1 WLR 770.

56 *Gore v Gibson* (1845) 13 M & W 623, *Matthews v Baxter* (1873) LR 8 Exch 132.

57 *Ashbury Rly Carriage & Iron Co v Riche* (1875) LR 7 HL 653.

58 See for example ss 21–23, Companies Act, Ch 81:01 (Trinidad & Tobago); ss 4–5, Companies Act (Jamaica); ss 17–19, Companies Act, 1995 (Antigua and Barbuda); ss 17–19, Companies Act, Cap 308 (Barbados); and ss 17–19, Companies Act, 1994 (St Vincent).

The rules of attribution

A company, being an artificial person (a *persona ficta*), must act, and enter into contracts, through its employees, agents, officers or members (its shareholders). The defining feature of a company is that it has legal personality which is separate and distinct from the natural person(s) of which it is made up. The principles governing what a company can or cannot do, or has or has not done, are called the rules of attribution.

Lord Hoffmann explained in *Meridian Global Funds Management Ltd v Securities Commission*[59] that the rules of attribution are divided into primary rules, consisting of those set out in the company constitution (its memorandum and articles of association), and secondary rules, encompassing general principles of, for instance, agency and vicarious liability.

In situations where neither the primary nor secondary rules of attribution can resolve a question of attribution, the court will determine (1) to whom, in the circumstances, the acts or omissions are to be attributed and/or (2) which acts or omissions are attributable to the company.[60]

Pre-incorporation contracts

Generally, at common law, contracts purported to be entered into by a company before the registration of that company will personally bind the persons purporting to agree the contract on the company's behalf.[61]

Courts have tended to find in favour of enforceability of pre-incorporation contracts where possible, particularly where the parties involved were aware of the non-existence of the company.[62] Not all pre-incorporation contracts will bind the signatory. Whether the company or its agent is ultimately bound by the contract depends on the intention of the parties.[63]

Directors

Once the company is registered, the directors will usually undertake the day-to-day management of the company. Directors should act within the limits of both their authority (whether actual or ostensible) and the company's capacity; in the event that a director, contracting on behalf of a company, exceeds his/her authority in doing so, the contract will be binding provided that the third party entering into the contract believed in good faith that the director had the authority to make the contract on the company's behalf.[64]

---

59 [1995] UKPC 5.

60 *Chitty on Contracts*, Volume 1, 9-007.

61 See Chapter 12, below.

62 *Kelner v Baxter* (1866) LR 2 CP 174.

63 *Hawkes Bay Milk Corp v Watson* [1974] 2 NZLR 236.

64 See Chapter 12, below.

LIMITED LIABILITY PARTNERSHIPS

Limited liability partnerships are formed by statute, and have legal personality in the same way as companies. They can contract and be sued in their own name.

ARTIFICIAL PERSONS LACKING CAPACITY

Certain classes of artificial person lack full contractual capacity. They are: limited partnerships; partnerships; and unincorporated associations.

Limited partnerships

Limited partnerships are formed under relevant legislation,[65] and must be registered in accordance with the legislation.[66] These are unincorporated entities which must act through their general partners acting on behalf of the partnership.

Partnerships

A partnership is the relation which subsists between persons carrying on a business in common with a view of profit. Partnership legislation sets out certain rules which must be used in determining whether a partnership does or does not exist.[67]

Partnerships are formed pursuant to statute.[68] They are unincorporated entities and do not have legal personality. They cannot enter into contracts and cannot sue and be sued in their own name.

Every partner is an agent of the partnership. The acts of partners carried out in the business of the partnership in the usual way will bind the partners. The business in question must, however, be the kind which is carried on by the particular partnership.[69]

Where restrictions on the capacity of the partners to act for the partnership have been agreed, acts exceeding the partners' powers will not be binding on third parties having no notice of the agreement.[70]

Partners are personally, and jointly and severally, liable for losses suffered by third parties due to a partner's wrongful acts or omissions. They are also jointly liable for debts and obligations arising out of the partnership's business in their lifetime. After death, a deceased partner's estate is also severally liable in the due course of administration for such debts and obligations, in so far as they remain unsatisfied, but subject to the prior payment of his/her separate debts.[71]

---

65 See Partnerships (Limited) Act (Jamaica).

66 Section 10 and s 12, Partnerships (Limited) Act (Jamaica).

67 Section 3, Partnership Act, Ch 310 (The Bahamas).

68 See, for example, Partnership Act, Ch 310 (The Bahamas); and Partnership Act, Ch 81:02 (Trinidad and Tobago).

69 Section 6, Partnership Act, Ch 310 (The Bahamas).

70 Section 8.

71 Section 10.

Other unincorporated associations

Other unincorporated associations, such as trade unions, clubs or societies, do not have legal personality and cannot contract, sue or be sued in their own name,[72] except pursuant to express statutory authorisation, as in the case of trade unions.[73]

If the persons making a contract on behalf of an unincorporated association had no authority to do so, they may be personally liable under the contract.[74]

72 *London Association for Protection of Trade v Greenlands Ltd* [1916] 2 AC 15.

73 *British Association of Advisers and Lecturers in Physical Education v National Union of Teachers* [1986] IRLR 497.

74 *Bradley Egg Farm v Clifford* [1943] 2 All ER 378.

CHAPTER 6

TERMS

CONTRACTUAL TERMS

The terms of a contract are its contents, and they define the rights and obligations arising from the contract. Contractual terms may be *express* or *implied*.

Express terms are those specifically laid down by the contract, and they consist of express oral or written statements made by the parties.

Implied terms are those which are not specified in the contract but which are implied either (i) by statute, or (ii) by custom, or (iii) by the court.

EXPRESS TERMS

A contract may be (i) purely written, (ii) purely oral, or (iii) partly written and partly oral. Generally, no formality is required for a term, whether oral or in writing (or partly orally or partly in writing), to form part of a contract. If the terms of a contract are in dispute, a court will determine what terms were decided on by the parties. The object of the court in this exercise is to do justice to the parties, and the court should not be 'deterred by difficulties of interpretation, as difficulty is not synonymous with ambiguity'.[1] This is a question of fact, and, in respect of oral contracts, precise evidence may be required in order to clarify exactly what the terms of the agreement were, as the dispute may turn on very fine details.[2]

PROOF OF TERMS

Oral contracts

Terms and representations

Statements made by parties can be categorised as (1) promises or (2) mere representations. Except in the case of the simplest transactions, there will generally be a period of negotiation before the final terms of the contract are agreed. Promises (sometimes called 'warranties') made during negotiations and not withdrawn will form part of an oral contract and are therefore binding. An action for damages will lie for breach of these terms.[3] By contrast, there are some statements (often referred to as 'mere puffs') which cannot be relied upon as terms of the contract because they are imprecise or were not meant to be taken literally. The court must determine the category into which a statement fits.

---

1 *Hardman v Meister* BS 1993 SC 64.

2 For example, in *Smith v Hughes* (1871) LR 6 QB 597, the dispute centred on whether goods were described as 'good oats' or 'good old oats'.

3 *J Evans & Son (Portmouth) Ltd v Andrea Merzario Ltd* [1976] 2 All ER 930.

A statement made during negotiations may be either (a) a contractual term which constitutes a binding obligation (unless held to be a mere puff), or (b) a mere representation, which is an inducement to enter into a contract.

The distinction between each type of statement is important as, on the one hand, the breach of a promise (which is a binding term), gives rise to the usual remedies for breach of contract (that is, damages, rescission). On the other hand, failure to conform to a mere representation, though in some circumstances giving the right to rescind the contract, will not be remediable by damages unless the representation was deliberately false (i.e. fraudulent) or made negligently, in which case actions in tort for damages for deceit or negligence respectively will lie. Further, in Trinidad and Tobago and Bermuda, as well as in the UK, damages can be recovered under the Misrepresentation Acts.[4]

Since the question of whether a statement is a contractual term (warranty) or a mere representation is a question of law, and not fact, the issue is one for the court to decide.[5] The court's task in deciding whether a representation is a binding term is a difficult one. In making this determination a court will take various factors into account, including the importance of the truth of the statement,[6] the length of time which passed between the making of the statement and the final agreement,[7] whether the party making the statement was better placed than the recipient of the statement to verify its truth,[8] and, where the contractual terms are later put into writing, whether the statement was included in the written agreement.[9] It should be noted that none of these tests is conclusive.[10]

The key determining factor in whether or not a statement is a term (and therefore gives rise to contractual liability) was laid down in *Heilbut, Symons & Co v Buckleton*[11] The test is whether there is evidence of an intention (that is, *animus contrahendi*) by one or both parties that there should be contractual liability in respect of the accuracy of the statement. In *Heilbut*, B said to J, HS's broker, 'I understand you are bringing out a rubber company.' The reply was, 'We are.' B then asked whether J had any prospectuses, and his reply was that he did not. B then asked 'if it was all right', and replied: 'We are bringing it out', to which the respondent said, 'That is good enough for me.'

B took a large number of shares which were allotted to him. He gave evidence that his reason for being willing to do this was that the position the appellants

4 See, for example: Misrepresentation Act, Ch 82:35 (Trinidad and Tobago); and Law Reform (Misrepresentation and Frustrated Contracts) Act 1977 (Bermuda).

5 *Heilbut, Symons & Co v Buckleton* [1913] AC 30.

6 *Bannerman v White* (1861) 10 CB NS 844.

7 *Routledge v McKay* [1954] 1 WLR 615. See also *Pasley v Freeman* (1789) 3 Term Rep 51, 57; *Schawel v Read* [1913] 2 IR 64; *Mahon v Ainscough* [1952] 1 All ER 337; *Inntrepreneur Pub Co v East Crown Ltd* [2000] 2 Lloyd's Rep 611.

8 *Dick Bentley Productions Ltd v Harold Smith (Motors) Ltd* [1965] 1 WLR 623; *Esso Petroleum Co Ltd v Mardon* [1976] QB 801. Cf *Heilbut, Symons & Co v Buckleton* [1913] AC 30; *Gilchester Properties Ltd v Gomm* [1948] 1 All ER 493.

9 *Heilbut, Symons & Co v Buckleton* [1913] AC 30, 50; *Gilchester Properties Ltd v Gomm* [1948] 1 All ER 493; cf *Miller v Cannon Hill Estates Ltd* [1931] 2 KB 113; *Inntrepreneur Pub Co v East Crown Ltd* [2000] 2 Lloyd's Rep 611.

10 *Heilbut, Symons & Co v Buckleton* [1913] AC 30, 50.

11 [1913] AC 30.

occupied in the rubber trade was of such high standing that 'any company they should see fit to bring out was a sufficient warranty' to him 'that it was all right in every respect'.

At that time, the rubber industry was booming, and so the rubber company's shares remained at a high value. It was later discovered that, contrary to the prospectus, the rubber estate owned by the company was deficient in rubber trees and the company's shares fell in value.

The House of Lords held that there was no breach of contract, on the basis that J's statement about the rubber company was a mere representation and not a binding warranty. This was because it had not been shown that the parties had intended for contractual liability to arise in respect of the accuracy or otherwise of the statement.

In *Oscar Chess Ltd v Williams*,[12] a car salesman sold a second-hand Morris car to a purchaser, in the honest belief, based on reasonable grounds, that it was a 1948 model. This belief was based on the fact that the date of the car included in the vehicle registration book was 1948. It was held that in producing the registration book, the salesman did not intend to bind himself so as to warrant the accuracy of the statement that it was a 1948 model.

By contrast, in *Dick Bentley Productions Ltd v Harold Smith (Motors) Ltd*,[13] a car salesman who sold a car on the basis of a milometer showing that the vehicle had driven 20,000 miles, when in fact it had driven 100,000 miles, was held to have warranted the truth of the statement, thereby binding himself contractually. The court found that the salesman had 'stated a fact that should be within his own knowledge. . .[that] he had jumped to a conclusion and stated it as a fact'. The court distinguished *Oscar Chess* on the basis that there the salesman had held an honest belief, based on reasonable grounds, that the car was a 1948 model. This was contrasted with the position in the *Dick Bentley* case where the representation, tested by what the intelligent bystander would infer from the conduct of the parties, was a statement made by a seller in a position to find out, but not having found out, the facts.

Thus, a statement will only be a term of the contract if the party making it intended to make himself contractually liable for the truth of the statement. In determining whether this intention exists, the court will consider the totality of the evidence showing the specific circumstances of the agreement (such as the knowledge, and access to knowledge, of the seller in the *Dick Bentley* case).

These cases show that distinguishing between binding and non-binding statements is a difficult task, particularly where there is a complex matrix of fact.

Denning LJ's judgment in the *Oscar Chess* case is instructive on the court's attitude towards determining whether a statement is a promise or a mere representation. He explained:

> I entirely agree with the Judge that both parties assumed that the Morris was a 1948 model and that this assumption was fundamental to the contract. But this does not prove that the representation was a term of the contract. The assumption was based by both of them on the date given in the registration book as the date of first registration.

12 [1957] 1 WLR 370.
13 [1965] 1 WLR 623.

They both believed it was a 1948 model, whereas it was only a 1939 one. They were both mistaken and their mistake was of fundamental importance . . .

In saying that he must prove a warranty, I use the word 'warranty' in its ordinary English meaning to denote a binding promise . . . During the last fifty years, however, some lawyers have come to use the word 'warranty' in another sense. They use it to denote a subsidiary term in a contract as distinct from a vital term which they call a 'condition'. In so doing they depart from the ordinary meaning, not only of the word 'warranty', but also of the word 'condition'. There is no harm in their doing this, so long as they confine this technical use to its proper sphere, namely to distinguish between a vital term, the breach of which gives the right to treat the contract as at an end, and a subsidiary term which does not . . . The crucial question is: was it a binding promise or only an innocent misrepresentation? The technical distinction between a 'condition' and a 'warranty' is quite immaterial in the case, because it is far too late for the buyer to reject the car. He can at best only claim damages. The material distinction here is between a statement which is a term of the contract and a statement which is only an innocent misrepresentation. This distinction is best expressed by the ruling of Lord Holt, 'Was it intended as a warranty or not?', using the word warranty there in its ordinary English meaning: because it gives the exact shade of meaning that is required. It is something to which a man must be taken to bind himself.

In applying Lord Holt's test, however, some misunderstanding has arisen by the use of the word 'intended'. It is sometimes supposed that the tribunal must look into the minds of the parties to see what they themselves intended. That is a mistake.

Lord Moulton made it quite clear that 'The intention of the parties can only be deduced from the totality of the evidence.' The question whether a warranty was intended depends on the conduct of the parties, on their words and behaviour, rather than on their thoughts. If an intelligent bystander would reasonably infer that a warranty was intended, that will suffice. And this, when the facts are not in dispute, is a question of law. That is shown by *Heilbut v Buckleton* itself, where the House of Lords upset the finding by a jury of a warranty . . .

If an oral representation is afterwards recorded in writing, it is good evidence that it was intended as a warranty.

If it is not put into writing, it is evidence against a warranty being intended. But it is by no means decisive . . .

One final word: it seems to me clear that the motor dealers who bought the car relied on the year stated in the log-book. If they had wished to make sure of it, they could have checked it then and there, by taking the engine number and chassis number and writing to the makers. They did not do so at the time, but only eight months later. They are experts, and not having made that check at the time I do not think they should now be allowed to recover against the innocent seller who produced to them all the evidence he had, namely the registration book.

Written contracts

In the case of contracts in writing, it is the duty of courts to interpret their terms. This is a matter of law for the court,[14] and the court will therefore not be obliged to incorporate into its interpretation, for example, concessions made by the parties about the meaning of the contract.[15]

14 *Bentsen v Taylor, Sons & Co (No 2)* [1893] 2 QB 274.

15 *Bahamas International Trust Co Ltd v Threadgold* [1974] 3 All ER 881.

Signature

It is a fundamental principle that the parties are bound by the content of a written contract and cannot seek to amend or add to its terms after the fact. Once an agreement is signed, a party cannot use the fact that he or she did not read the terms, to avoid liability under the contract. In *L'Estrange v Graucob Ltd*,[16] the plaintiff purchased a slot machine from the defendants, and in doing so signed an order form. The order form contained fine print, including the following term:

> This agreement contains all the terms and conditions under which I agree to purchase the machine specified above, and any express or implied condition, statement, or warranty, statutory or otherwise not stated herein is hereby excluded.

When the slot machine was delivered, the plaintiff found that it did not function correctly. She brought an action against the defendants on the basis that the machine was not fit for the purpose for which it was sold. The defendants sought to rely on the printed exclusion clause, and the plaintiff argued that she had not read the form and did not know what it contained. The court held that since the plaintiff had signed the agreement, the disputed term was valid. It was immaterial that the plaintiff had not read the terms. Scrutton LJ described the court's decision thus:

> A clause of [this] sort has been before the courts for some time. The first reported case in which it made its appearance seems to be *Wallis, Son & Wells v Pratt & Haynes*, where the exclusion clause mentioned only 'warranty' and it was held that it did not exclude conditions. In the more recent case of *Andrews Bros (Bournemouth) Ltd v Singer & Co Ltd*, where the draftsman had put into the contract of sale a clause which excluded only implied conditions, warranties and liabilities, it was held that the clause did not apply to an express term describing the article, and did not exempt the seller from liability where he delivered an article of a different description. The clause here in question would seem to have been intended to go further than any of the previous clauses and to include all terms denoting collateral stipulations in order to avoid the result of these decisions.
>
> The main question raised in the present case is whether that clause formed part of the contract. If it did, it clearly excluded any condition or warranty.
>
> In the course of the argument in the county court, reference was made to the railway passenger and cloak-room ticket cases . . .
>
> These cases have no application when the document has been signed. When a document containing contractual terms is signed, then, in the absence of fraud, or, I will add, misrepresentation, the party signing it is bound, and it is wholly immaterial whether he has read the document or not.

Authorities as to the effect of signature must be considered in light of consumer protection legislation which affects the enforceability of terms which are unfair.[17]

It has also been suggested by commentators, although no authority is cited for this proposition, that a party's signature will bind him not only with respect to the contents of the document signed, but also with respect to other documents which are referred to, or incorporated by reference, in the agreement.[18]

---

16 [1934] 2 KB 394. See also *Potter v Port Services Limited* AG 2003 PC 1 (some or all of the terms of an unsigned agreement may be enforceable if the parties act and rely on those terms).

17 See, for example, s 9, Consumer Protection Act, Cap 326D (Barbados).

18 Beale, Bishop and Furmston, *Contract Cases & Materials*, 4th edn (Butterworths, 2001) p 349.

Notably, following the decision in *Interfoto Picture Library Ltd v Stiletto Visual Programmes Ltd*,[19] where a contract contains particularly onerous or unusual printed terms, the party seeking to enforce such terms must prove that they were brought to the other party's attention.

Parol evidence rule

There is a presumption that a written document contains all the terms of the contract, but the presumption is rebuttable by evidence that the parties did not intend the written document to be exclusive, but wished it to be read in conjunction with their oral statements. This is known as the parol evidence rule. The rule has been described in the following terms:

> It is firmly established as a rule of law that parol evidence cannot be admitted to add to, vary or contradict a deed or other written instrument ... Parol evidence will not be admitted to prove that some particular term, which has been verbally agreed upon, had been omitted (by design or otherwise) from a written instrument constituting a valid and operative contract.[20]

The name of the rule may be misleading; it is not a rule of evidence at all, but is a rule of substantive law. This is because it does not describe *how* evidence of contractual terms may be adduced, but rather the rule *prevents* a party from adducing evidence which is extrinsic to a written contract.[21]

Thus, in *Hawrish v Bank of Montreal*,[22] a lawyer acting for a company agreed to guarantee 'all present and future debts' of the client company, up to £6,000. The lawyer then later adduced evidence to show that the parties had intended for the guarantee to apply to an overdraft facility of the company, and not to all of its debts. The amount of the overdraft was £6,000. It was held that the lawyer's evidence was inadmissible.

Parol evidence and the rebuttable presumption

It should be emphasised that the parol evidence rule creates a presumption which can be rebutted. This principle was demonstrated in *Jacobs v Batavia and General Plantations Trust Ltd*.[23] There, the plaintiff, in reliance on a prospectus, purchased bonds issued by the defendant company. Both the bonds themselves and the prospectus contained terms relating to the bonds. The key difference between the two documents was that an obligation of the company to make early repayment of the bonds in the event that the company sold certain estates was only included in the prospectus terms and not in the bond terms. The defendant company sold the estates and failed to make early repayment of the bonds in contravention of the terms in the prospectus. The plaintiff brought an action against the defendant company for an injunction preventing it from using the proceeds of sale of the estates.

---

19 [1989] QB 433.

20 *Jacobs v Batavia and General Plantations Trust Ltd* [1924] 1 Ch 287.

21 Beale, Bishop and Furmston, *Contract Cases & Materials*, 4th edn (Butterworths, 2001), p 352.

22 (1969) 2 DLR (3d) 600.

23 [1924] 1 Ch 287. See also *Ehrmann v Groome* (1971) High Court, Grenada, No 284 of 1969, unreported [Carilaw GD 1971 HC 14].

In *Jacobs*, the court held that the bond documents did not comprise the entire contract, but had to be considered together with the prospectus. According to Wedderburn J:

> What the parol evidence rule has bequeathed to modern law is a presumption – namely that a document which *looks* like a contract is to be treated as the whole contract.

Similarly, the court in *Gillespie Bros & Co v Cheney, Eggar & Co*[24] described the rule as follows:

> Although when the parties arrive at a definite written contract the implication or presumption is very strong that such contract is intended to contain all the terms of their bargain, it is a presumption only, and it is open to either of the parties to allege that there was, in addition to what appears in the written agreement, an antecedent express stipulation not intended by the parties to be excluded, but intended to continue in force with the express written agreement.

Thus, for example, it has been held that an overdraft facility granted orally should be read together with a written loan agreement.[25]

Where a document which does not contain all of the terms of the agreement refers to another document, it is possible to admit extrinsic evidence to show what those other terms are. The two documents will then be read together. This principle was affirmed in the Barbadian case of *Elias v George Sahely & Co (Barbados) Ltd*.[26] There, Lord Scarman said:

> The first inquiry must, therefore, be whether the document signed by or on behalf of the person to be charged on the contract contains some reference to some other document or transaction . . . If . . . a document . . . refers to a transaction of sale, parol evidence is admissible both to explain the reference and to identify any document relating to it. Once identified, the document may be placed alongside the signed document. If the two contain all the terms of a concluded contract, the statute is satisfied.

Where it is found that the presumption in the parol evidence rule has been rebutted, terms which are extrinsic to the written contract, but which nevertheless form part of the binding agreement, will be deemed to have been included in the agreement. This is called rectification. Rectification is also available to amend a written contract where it was executed under a common mistake.[27] It should be noted that rectification of a contract to incorporate extrinsic terms does not exclude oral terms found to be enforceable as a collateral contract.

Collateral contracts

Collateral contracts are secondary contracts which are enforceable as independent agreements, separately from a primary contract. They tend to be invoked to enforce promises made in exchange for the entry into the primary contract.

Collateral contracts may be used to remedy the strictures of the parol evidence rule, because that rule prevents the admission of extrinsic terms except where it can

24 [1896] 2 QB 59.
25 *African Continental Bank Ltd v Adewuyi* 1967(1) ALR Comm 195.
26 (1982) Privy council, Barbados, No 2 of 1982, unreported [Carilaw BB 1982 PC 1].
27 See Chapter 14 below

be shown that such a term was intended to form part of the primary contract. Instead, the enforcing party can argue the existence of a parallel, independent contract, the terms of which are enforceable notwithstanding that those terms were not intended to vary the terms of the primary contract.

In order to be binding, a purported collateral contract must not only be independent of the primary or previous contract, but it must also satisfy the requisite ingredients for the existence of a contract including, notably, that of consideration.

The principle was described in *Heilbut, Symons & Co v Buckleton*[28] in the following terms:

> It is evident, both on principle and on authority, that there may be a contract the consideration for which is the making of some other contract. 'If you will make such and such a contract I will give you one hundred pounds,' is in every sense of the word a complete legal contract. It is collateral to the main contract, but each has an independent existence, and they do not differ in respect of their possessing to the full the character and status of a contract.

In the *Heilbut Symons* case, Lord Moulton stated that collateral contracts are 'viewed with suspicion by the law. They must be proved strictly.' He went on to say that they 'must from their very nature be rare'.[29] However, this has not deterred the courts from finding in favour of the existence of collateral contracts.

In *Esso Petroleum Co Ltd v Mardon*,[30] Esso leased a petrol station site to M. Before the lease had been concluded, an employee of Esso had overestimated by more than 100 per cent the capacity of the petrol station. He stated that the capacity would reach 200,000 gallons of petrol. The planning authority then declined to give permission to Esso to have the pumps at the front of the site, and they were instead placed at the rear. It turned out that the site could not produce more than 60,000 to 70,000 gallons. M had relied on the employee's estimate in entering into the lease. Esso sued M for possession of the site and monies for petrol supplied to M, and M counterclaimed for, *inter alia*, breach of a collateral term.

The English Court of Appeal held that the estimate provided by Esso's employee gave rise to a collateral warranty, not as to the accuracy of the opinion, but that the estimate had been prepared with reasonable care and skill. This was particularly the case as Esso had not revised the estimate even after the configuration of the petrol station had to be changed due to failure to obtain the relevant planning permissions. The change in configuration would have meant that the station was less visible to passing drivers.

The decision was based on two factors. First, it was intended that M would rely on the estimate and that Esso would be liable as to its accuracy. Secondly, Esso's special knowledge and skill meant that it owed M a duty of care to use reasonable care and skill in making the estimate.[31] Esso were liable for the incorrect opinion and M was awarded damages for breach of contract by Esso. Lord Denning MR captured the Court's decision as follows:

---

28 [1913] AC 30.

29 [1913] AC 30, *per* Lord Moulton.

30 [1976] QB 801.

31 *Hedley Byrne & Co Ltd v Heller & Partners Ltd* [1963] 2 All ER 575.

> it is plain that Esso professed to have – and did in fact have – special knowledge or skill in estimating the throughput of a filling station. They made the representation – they forecast a throughput of 200,000 gallons – intending to induce Mr Mardon to enter into a tenancy on the faith of it. They made it negligently. It was a 'fatal error'. They thereby induced Mr Mardon to enter into a contract of tenancy that was disastrous to him. For this misrepresentation they are liable in damages.

Similarly, where A contracted with B to paint a pier, and B induced A to choose a paint made by B, it was held that there were two contracts. In addition to the contract in accordance with which B agreed to paint the pier, there was a collateral contract according to which A agreed to use B's paint, in exchange for a guarantee that the paint was suitable for the job.[32]

In *United Insurance Co v Barbados Packers & Canners Ltd,*[33] the Barbados Court of Appeal held that, between the parties to a contract for the insurance of frozen meat, there was no collateral contract for the inspection of the meat by the plaintiff, Barbados Packers & Canners Ltd. The parties had not intended for there to be an independent contract collateral to the main contract and so, by virtue of the parol evidence rule, the defendant was barred from adducing extrinsic evidence as to any purported obligation to inspect the meat. Williams JA summarised the court's decision in the following terms:

> This reinforces the view which I hold, based on the evidence, that the parties in their discussions were negotiating one contract and one contract only, that is, the one incorporated in the policy, and that it was never in their minds to enter into another agreement independent of that contract. When Mr. Worme said that the insurance would only be accepted if the temperatures were inspected daily, he was at the time contemplating making inspection an obligation of the plaintiff under the policy. It appears that he subsequently changed his mind and did not refer to it in the policy but it certainly does not appear from the evidence that the parties ever negotiated or intended to negotiate a contract independent of the main policy.
>
> In the premises, my judgment is that the defendant has raised no ground absolving it from liability under the policy; and even if the question of a collateral contract can on the pleadings be raised to enable it to make a counterclaim against the plaintiff for its breach of another contract, the evidence does not support the finding that any such contract ever came into existence.

A court may find that a collateral contract exists on the basis of the parties' actions or statements during negotiations.[34]

However, in *BL Securities v Wheatington Investments Limited,*[35] the Bahamian Supreme Court held that an addendum to an agreement was excluded from being a collateral contract on the basis that it merely reflected the pre-contractual negotiations, and was not intended to be an independent agreement. This was in light of an 'entire agreement' clause in the main agreement which stated that the agreement encompassed the entire agreement between the parties and superseded all other agreements or understandings, whether written or oral.

32 *Shanklin Pier Ltd v Detel Products Ltd* [1951] 2 KB 854, [1951] 2 All ER 471.

33 (1984) Court of Appeal, Barbados, No 7 of 1981, unreported [Carilaw BB 1984 CA 6].

34 *City and Westminster Properties (1934) Ltd v Mudd* [1959] Ch 129, [1959] 2 All ER 733.

35 (1998) Supreme Court, The Bahamas, No 1048 of 1996, unreported [Carilaw BS 1998 SC 41].

CLASSIFICATION OF TERMS

The classification of terms is an important question when determining what remedies are available upon the breach of a contractual term. Terms may be classified as conditions, warranties or intermediate terms. The classification of terms as any one of these categories generally depends on the intention of the parties and the relative importance of that term (or of the breach of that term) in the context of the transaction. In some cases, as with terms implied under the Sale of Goods legislation, statutory provisions may classify terms as either conditions or warranties.[36]

Conditions

A condition is a term of a contract which the parties regarded as essential, in respect of which one party either promises to perform an obligation, or promises the accuracy of a statement. In the event of a breach of a condition, the innocent party is entitled to rescind the contract, treating himself as discharged from further performance. This is so, even if the innocent party has not suffered any loss because of the breach. The innocent party may also affirm the contract if he so chooses. In addition to the right to rescind or affirm the agreement, the innocent party may in either case claim damages for any losses suffered.

The rationale for the ability of the innocent party to rescind for breach of a condition was set out by Fletcher Moulton LJ in his dissenting judgment in *Wallis, Son & Wells v Pratt & Haynes*.[37] There, he said:

> There are some [obligations] which go so directly to the substance of the contract or, in other words, are so essential to its very nature that their non-performance may fairly be considered by the other party as a substantial failure to perform the contract at all. On the other hand there are other obligations which, though they must be performed, are not so vital that a failure to perform them goes to the substance of the contract . . . later usage has consecrated the term 'condition' to describe an obligation of the former class and 'warranty' to describe an obligation of the latter class.

In *Locke (JR) v Bellingdon Limited*[38] the Barbados Court of Appeal held that the failure by the plaintiff, Locke, to pay a deposit for the purchase of commercial property formerly occupied by Paradise Beach Hotel, amounted to a repudiatory breach entitling the defendants to treat the contract as being at an end.[39] Simmons CJ stated the Court's ruling and explained the decision as follows:

---

36 See, for example, s 11 Sale of Goods Act, Cap 318 (Barbados); s 11 Sale of Goods Act, (Jamaica); s 12 Sale of Goods Act, Ch 337 (The Bahamas) and ss 12–17, Sale of Goods Act, Cap 261 (Belize).

37 [1960] 2 KB 1003 at 1012.

38 (2002) Court of Appeal, Barbados, No 19 of 2001, unreported [Carilaw BB 2002 CA 42].

39 See also *Walker v Anderson* (2000) Court of Appeal, Jamaica, No 42 of 1999, unreported [Carilaw JM 2000 CA 35] (failure to build a house which is fit for human habitation will amount to a repudiatory and fundamental breach entitling the innocent party to rescind the building contract); *Harbour Cold Stores Ltd v Chase Ramson Ltd* (1982) Court of Appeal, Jamaica, No 57 of 1978, unreported [Carilaw JM 1982 CA 5]; *Bidaisee v Sampath* (1985) High Court, Trinidad and Tobago, No 1079 of 1979, unreported [Carilaw TT 1985 HC 154].

Repudiation is a drastic action which should only be held to arise in clear cases of a refusal to perform contractual obligations, where the matter goes to the root of the contract. In considering whether there has been a repudiation of a contract by one party, which is a question of fact, it is necessary to examine that party's conduct as a whole and ask the question: 'does that conduct indicate an intention to refuse performance of the contract or abandon the contract?' Clearly, the conduct of the repudiating party must be evaluated objectively. The guiding principle is that enunciated by Lord Coleridge CJ in *Freeth v Burr*.[40] The Lord Chief Justice said, and it is still the law: 'In cases of this sort, where the question is whether the one party is set free by the action of the other, the real matter for consideration is whether the acts or conduct of the one do or do not amount to an intimation of an intention to abandon and altogether to refuse performance of the contract.'

It is all a matter of construction. The Court must construe the language used by the light of the contract and the circumstances of the case to see whether there was a renunciation of the contract. The entire circumstances must be looked at – Lord Selborne LC in *Mersey Steel and Iron Co Ltd v Naylor, Benzon & Co.*[41]

For conduct to be characterised as repudiatory, the breach or threatened breach must go to the root or core of the contract and it follows that a threatened or anticipatory breach will amount to repudiation if it relates to a fundamental term going to the root or core of the contract.

Counsel for Locke submits that the payment of the initial deposit was not a fundamental term. It did not go to the root or core of the contract. Mr Mahfood argues the converse proposition.

In *Bunge Corporation v Tradax SA*, Lord Scarman said:[42]

> The first question is always, therefore, whether, on the true stipulation and the contract of which it is part, it is a condition, an innominate term, or only a warranty. If the stipulation is one which on the true construction of the contract the parties have not made a condition, and breach of which may be attended by trivial, minor or grave consequences, it is innominate, and the Court (or an arbitrator) will, in the event of dispute, have the task of deciding whether the breach that has arisen is such as the parties would have said, had they been asked at the time they made their contract, 'It goes without saying that, if that happens, the contract is at an end'!

In this appeal, in order to determine whether the deposit was a fundamental term going to the root of the contract, the starting point must surely be to assess the nature of the deposit. It seems to us that a deposit is the security for completion of the contract and a guarantee of its performance. If that is so, it would seem axiomatic that it is an essential stipulation going to the root of the contract and breach of it would entitle the innocent party to treat the contract as at an end . . .

What were the consequences of failure to pay the initial deposit? Under Clause (4) of the Letter of Intent the initial deposit was refundable only if the respondents refused to enter into the Stock Purchase Agreement or were unable to convey ownership of the companies. But the Letter was silent as to the consequences of default by Locke. So, applying Lord Wilberforce's second question in *Bunge Corporation v Tradax* (*supra*) we think that the parties must have contemplated the end of the deal if Locke failed to show the colour of his money. We have to apply an objective test and ask whether Locke's

40 LRG 208, at 213.

41 9 App Cas 434.

42 [1981] 2 All ER 513, at 543.

conduct, objectively determined, showed an intention not to perform the contract. This issue being one of fact, citation of other decided cases on other facts is hardly helpful or, indeed, necessary.

Nevertheless, the appellant placed great reliance upon *Afovos Shipping Co v Pagnan*.[43] There, the first part of clause 5 imposed upon the respondent charterers a primary obligation to pay the 'said hire' (which by clause 4 had been fixed at a monthly rate and pro rata for any part of a month) punctually and regularly in advance by semi-monthly instalments in the manner specified, which involved a minimum of 42 and a maximum of 54 instalments during the period of the charter. Lord Diplock held that failure to comply with the primary obligation by delay in paying one instalment was incapable in law of amounting to a 'fundamental breach' of contract by the charterers. The reason for Lord Diplock's decision was that such delay in payment of one half-monthly instalment would not have the effect of depriving the owners of substantially the whole benefit which the parties intended the owners to obtain. His Lordship explained that even though failure to pay punctually was made a breach of condition, it was not thereby converted into a fundamental breach and the doctrine of anticipatory breach applied only to fundamental breaches.

This case does not avail the appellant Locke. Dr Cheltenham also cited two others – *Woodar Investment Development Ltd v Wimpey Construction UK Ltd*[44] and *Forslind v Bechely Crundall*.[45]

In *Woodar*, the plaintiffs agreed to sell 14 acres of land to the defendants. The completion date of the sale was set at 2 months after the granting of outline planning permission or February 21, 1980, whichever was earlier. The defendants were to pay a price of £850,000 and, on completion, a further £150,000 to third parties who had no legal connection to the plaintiffs. The market became unfavourable to the defendants and they sought to rescind the agreement which was a right allowed for by the agreement but in circumstances which did not exist. The defendants honestly believed that they were entitled to rescind. The plaintiffs claimed that the conduct of the defendants amounted to repudiation. By a majority of 3:2 the House of Lords held that the defendants' conduct did not amount to repudiatory breach because a party who took action relying simply on the terms of the contract in question and not manifesting by his conduct an ulterior intention to abandon it was not to be treated as repudiating it.

Woodar in fact shows the kind of good faith conduct that does not amount to repudiation. In that case there was no finding of fact as to repudiation. What the parties did was to bring an action for interpretation of the contract – see the judgment of Lord Wilberforce.

In *Afovos Shipping* (*supra*), the Court reasoned that the breach was not an actual breach going to the root of the contract. Anticipatory breach did not apply since this doctrine only applies to breach of a fundamental term. And all that *Forslind* decides is that where the conduct of one of the parties to a contract has been such as would lead a reasonable person to the conclusion that he does not intend to perform his part of the obligation, the other party to the contract, whatever in fact may have been the actual intention of the former, may treat such conduct as an intimation that the contract has been repudiated.

We think that Locke's conduct, objectively determined, did evince an intention not to perform the contract.

43 [1983] 1 WLR 195.

44 [1980] 1 WLR 277.

45 (1922) SCHL 173.

Similarly, in *Oncology Association Ltd v AG*,[46] the Supreme Court of the Bahamas held that the defendant Ministry of Health was entitled to rescind an agreement with Oncology Association Ltd, the plaintiff, for the provision by the latter of radiotherapy services for cancer patients. This was on the basis that the Oncology Association had failed to provide an adequate standard of care contrary to the following provision of the agreement, leading to excessive and unnecessary patient morbidity:

> OAL shall provide all patients referred by the Minister a standard of skill, quality and care as would be reasonably expected of a comparable institution in the United States of America.

The court, in holding that breach of this term was a fundamental breach, considered not only the wording of the term, but also the context of the agreement; namely, that the contract was for the preservation of public health. This lent weight to the proposition that the parties must have intended that a breach of this term would go to the very core of the agreement.

The parties may agree expressly that a term of a contract is a condition.[47] Legislation may also imply that a term is a condition.[48] A court may also find that a particular term is a condition in light of the nature, purpose and circumstances surrounding the agreement. As to how a court will come to this finding, it was stated in *Bentsen v Taylor, Sons & Co (No 2)*:[49]

> There is no way of deciding that question except by looking at the contract in the light of the surrounding circumstances, and then making up one's mind whether the intention of the parties, as gathered from the instrument itself, will best be carried out by treating the promise as a warranty sounding only in damages, or as a condition precedent by the failure to perform which the other party is relieved of his liability.

Stipulations as to time are not ordinarily construed so as to make time of the essence, and so breach of a contractual deadline will not generally be a fundamental breach.[50] However, where time is specified in the contract as being of the essence,[51] or where the court considers the parties must have intended time to be of the essence,[52] such a failure to meet a deadline will amount to a fundamental breach.

---

46 (2005) Supreme Court, The Bahamas, No 395 of 1999, unreported [Carilaw BS 2005 SC 37].

47 *Dawsons Ltd v Bonnin* [1922] 2 AC 413; *Lombard North Central Plc v Butterworth* [1987] QB 527.

48 See ss 11–16, Sale of Goods Act, Cap 318 (Barbados); ss 11–16, Sale of Goods Act (Jamaica); ss 12–17, Sale of Goods Act, Ch 337 (The Bahamas) and ss 12–17, Sale of Goods Act, Cap 261 (Belize).

49 [1893] 2 QB 274.

50 This position is reflected in sale of goods legislation. See for example, s 11 Sale of Goods Act, Cap 318 (Barbados); Sale of Goods Act (Jamaica); s 12, Sale of Goods Act, Ch 337 (The Bahamas) and ss 12–17, s 11 Sale of Goods Act, Cap 261 (Belize).

51 *Steadman v Drunkle* [1916] 1 AC 275, 279; *Financings Ltd v Baldock* [1963] 2 QB 104, 120; *Bunge Corp v Tradax Export SA* [1980] 1 Lloyd's Rep 294, 305, 307, 309, 310 (affirmed [1981] 1 WLR 711); *Lombard North Central Plc v Butterworth* [1987] QB 527. Cf *Canadian Imperial Bank of Commerce v Owners of and all parties interested in the motor vessel 'New Light'* (1997) Supreme Court, The Bahamas, No 1217 of 1994, unreported [Carilaw BS 1997 SC 87] (a party failing to complete cannot then insist that time had been of the essence. In the case of an extension to a contract making time of the essence, if no time for completion is set, then time will be at large).

52 [1978] AC 904, 937, 941, 944, 950, 958; *Bunge Corp v Tradax Export SA* [1981] 1 WLR 711, 728–729; *Universal Bulk Carriers Ltd v André et Cie SA* [2000] 1 Lloyd's Rep 459, 464; *BS & N Ltd v Micado Shipping Ltd (The Seaflower)* [2001] 1 Lloyd's Rep 348, 350, 354; *MSAS Global Logistics Ltd v Power Packaging Inc* [2003] EWHC 1393 (Ch).

An example of this rule is to be found in the case of *Maya Island Resort Properties Ltd v Curry*,[53] where a failure of three days to pay the outstanding balance on a contract for the sale of land was held by the Belize Supreme Court not to have amounted to a fundamental breach. There, although a deadline for payment of the purchase price had been set, there had been no date set for the passing of title. As time had not been made of the essence in the contract, there was no fundamental breach arising from the three-day delay in paying the purchase price.

A party may serve notice making time of the essence after entering into the contract, where the other party is in default. However, he cannot do so if he himself is in default. Thus, in *Chaitlal v Ramlal*,[54] a Trinidadian case which went on appeal to the Privy Council, it was held that M, the vendor in a contract for the sale of land, could not serve notice on the prospective purchaser, R, because he was in default of an obligation to supply R with certain information. In this case, the parties had entered into a contract for the sale of land, with no date specified for completion. After entering into the contract, M purported to serve notice on R, making time of the essence under the contract. After a delay of more than three years, and several attempts to progress the sale, M sold the land to a third party. R brought an action for specific performance of the original contract for sale, and a declaration that the deed of conveyance of land to the third party was void. In giving the court's decision in favour of R, Sir Martin Nourse said:

> The question is whether, in that state of affairs, Mr Mahase was entitled to give Mr Ramlal a notice making time of the essence of the contract.
>
> On either or both of two related but distinct grounds that question must be answered in the negative. The first ground, the ground preferred by Mr Dingemans, is that when time is not originally made of the essence of the contract one of the parties is not entitled by notice to make it so unless the other party is in default. In the case of an open contract, where it is implied that completion or the performance of any intermediate obligation will take place within a reasonable time, it is only after the passage of such a time that a notice can be given because, until then, there has been no default in the performance of the contract. Thus in *Green v Sevin*,[55] Fry J said, at p 599:
>
>> It is to be observed that the contract for purchase had limited no time for completion, and that, therefore, according to the rule in this country, each party was entitled to a reasonable time for doing the various acts which he had to do. What right then had one party to limit a particular time within which an act was to be done by the other? It appears to me that he had no right so to do, unless there had been such delay on the part of the other contracting party as to render it fair that, if steps were not immediately taken to complete, the person giving the notice should be relieved from his contract.
>
> In the present case, as at 4th April 1974 there had been no delay, and therefore no default, on the part of Mr Ramlal. Not until Mr Mahase had supplied him with the appropriate information as to title could he have come under any obligation to complete.
>
> The related but distinct ground is that the party serving the notice purporting to make time of the essence must himself be ready, able and willing to complete at the date when the notice is served. This is an express requirement of the conditions commonly

---

53 (2010) Supreme Court, Belize, No 216 of 2009, unreported [Carilaw BZ 2010 SC 55]; see *also Carter v Pleasure Island Limited* (2006) Supreme Court, Belize, No 384 of 2001, unreported [Carilaw BZ 2006 SC 16].

54 (2003) Privy Council, Trinidad and Tobago, No 36 of 2001, unreported [Carilaw TT 2003 PC 4].

55 (1879) 13 Ch D 589.

> incorporated in contracts for the sale of land in this country, but it does no more than express what would in any event be implied by law; see Halsbury's Laws of England, 4th edition, vol 42 (1999 reissue), para 121, note 7 and the cases there cited. It is evident that the requirement cannot be satisfied where the party serving the notice is himself in default. In the present case, on 4th April 1974, Mr Mahase was in default through not having supplied Mr Ramlal with the appropriate information as to title.
>
> For these reasons, their Lordships are of the opinion that the letter of 4th April 1974, whatever its terms may have been, could not have made time of the essence of the contract. Nor was there anything in the subsequent correspondence to make it so. In their letter of 1st August 1974 Wilsons informed Capildeos that Mr Mahase had decided 'to stand firm on the deadline communicated in ours of the 4th April, last', but that he would be prepared to compromise on two conditions: first, that Mr Ramlal should make payment for the excess land; second, that completion should take place by 21st August 1974. While it could perhaps be argued that the final paragraph of Capildeos' reply of 16th August constituted a recognition of the revised completion date, no agreement was ever reached as to the amount to be paid for the excess land. In the circumstances, there was never any concluded agreement for a compromise as proposed in Wilsons' letter of 1st August and time was never made of the essence of the contract. Accordingly, Mr Ramlal, not having been in default on 5th November 1974 when Mr Mahase conveyed the land to the Jaglals, thereupon became entitled to relief against Mr Mahase . . .
>
> Their Lordships are of the opinion, though for somewhat different reasons, that the decision of the Court of Appeal was correct and ought to be affirmed. The Court of Appeal's order does not specify the relief to be granted to Mr Ramlal. It appears that he is entitled to a declaration that the agreement of 13th October 1971 ought to be specifically performed and an order that the two surviving Jaglals should convey the disputed land to him.

The determining factor in a court's classification of a term as being either a condition or a warranty is whether the parties' intention, as objectively ascertained based on an assessment of the evidence, will be best promoted by classifying the term as the one or the other. In a Bermudian case, *Hamiltonian Hotel & Island Club Ltd v Daulphin*,[56] the Court of Appeal considered two terms which had been breached by the plaintiff, and which the defendant argued were fundamental breaches. There, the plaintiff, a professional tennis player, had lent money to the defendant, the Hamiltonian Hotel, for the building and renovation of tennis courts. Under the terms of the agreement, the plaintiff was also to construct a shop and provide tennis lessons to patrons of the hotel using its courts. Another term required the plaintiff to audit the company books annually. The defendant argued that the plaintiff's failure to comply with this term was a fundamental breach entitling it to treat the contract as being at an end. The court, finding that this was not a repudiatory breach, said:

> The lender shall keep a set of books relating to his said operation which shall be available to the hotel at any time and audited annually at his expense by the hotel auditors.

There was no evidence that the plaintiff was ever asked by the hotel to present either audited books for review by the hotel or unaudited books for auditing as well as for review by the hotel. The court's decision – that this breach was not a fundamental one – was primarily based on the defendant's apparent lack of interest in the plaintiff's breach of the term during their business relationship:

56 (1990) Court of Appeal, Bermuda, No 10 of 1989, unreported [Carilaw BM 1990 CA 2].

> even assuming that it was the duty of the respondent to have the books audited and that he was in breach of that obligation, the appellant having attached precious little importance to the obligation during the currency of the agreement could hardly be heart at this stage to assert that such failure constituted a repudiators breach of the agreement.

The second condition to be considered by the court related to the shop constructed by the plaintiff. A term in the contract provided for the plaintiff to credit 10 per cent of the costs he incurred in building to the hotel in lieu of rent. This was to be done over the 10-year term of the agreement. The term read:

> The lender [the plaintiff] shall construct the pro shop in the hotel premises to be used in conjunction with the said tennis courts, and shall credit the hotel annually with ten per cent of the cost of construction thereof in lieu of rent for the said pro shop.

The defendant argued that this provision required the plaintiff to make payments to the hotel, equivalent to 10 per cent of the costs of building the shop. The Court of Appeal agreed with the decision in the lower court that, in light of the entirety of the agreement, the proper construction of the clause was that the plaintiff did not have to make payments to the hotel for rent. The expenses he had already incurred, which were to be allocated at a rate of 10 per cent each year as a substitute for rent, were sufficient. Da Costa JA explained the decision on the basis that commercial reality, the understanding of the original parties to the agreement, and the relevant clauses in the contract, all seemed to indicate the true intention of the parties.

Promissory conditions

A condition may be 'promissory' in the sense that it is a promise by one party to perform (or procure the performance) of an obligation. Failure to do so will entitle the innocent party to treat the contract as being at an end and, if he has suffered loss, to sue for damages for such loss.

Contingent conditions

Contingent conditions may be contrasted with promissory conditions. These are obligations that do not arise until the occurrence of a particular event. Until that event has taken place, the obligation of one or all parties will remain suspended.[57] In *Trans Trust SPRL v Danubian Trading Co Ltd*,[58] Denning LJ considered a condition in a contract for the sale of goods in which the buyer had agreed to open a line of credit for the seller. Denning LJ said:

> What is the legal position of such a stipulation? Sometimes it is a condition precedent to the formation of a contract, that is, it is a condition which must be fulfilled before any contract is concluded at all. In those cases the stipulation 'subject to the opening of a credit' is rather like a stipulation 'subject to contract'. If no credit is provided, there is no contract between the parties. In other cases, a contract is concluded and the stipulation for a credit is a condition which is an essential term of the contract. In those cases the provision of the credit is a condition precedent, not to the formation of the contract, but

57 See *Trans Trust SPRL v Danubian Trading Co Ltd* [1952] 2 QB 297.
58 [1952] 2 QB 297, 304.

to the obligation of the seller to deliver the goods. If the buyer fails to provide the credit, the seller can treat himself as discharged from any further performance of the contract and can sue the buyer for damages for not providing the credit.

Conditions precedent

Generally, a condition precedent is a condition, the fulfilment of which is required in order for the agreement to come into effect.[59] Examples of typical conditions precedent are the receipt of shareholder approval of a transaction or receipt of regulatory consent.

Where a condition precedent fails to be satisfied, (1) it may suspend the parties' rights and obligations under the agreement;[60] (2) one party may be bound unilaterally to perform an obligation, subject to a condition, although the agreement is not yet bilaterally binding until the condition is satisfied;[61] or (3), the contract may become binding, but rights and obligations under the contract are suspended until a specified condition is met.[62]

The parties are at liberty to draft (or, if oral, to finalise) their agreement to provide that a condition precedent has a particular effect. For example, they may wish for ancillary obligations under the agreement to be effective notwithstanding the transaction contemplated by the agreement cannot proceed for failure to satisfy the condition precedent. Typical examples of this type of provision are confidentiality provisions and further assurance clauses. Further assurance clauses are clauses requiring one or both parties to go beyond the precise obligations laid out in the agreement and to take all steps required to make the contract effective. This could include procuring that third parties take certain actions to this effect.

Conditions precedent are usually contingent, in which case no liability arises if the condition in question fails to be satisfied.

Conditions subsequent

A contract that becomes immediately binding on agreement of the final terms may provide for (1) termination of the agreement (or termination of some or all of the parties' obligations), or (2) the ability of the parties to treat the agreement as being at an end, if certain conditions are met, or fail to be met, after the contract has come into effect. These provisions are conditions subsequent.

---

59 See, for example, *Property and Bloodstock Ltd v Emerton* [1967] 2 All ER 839, affirmed [1968] Ch 94; *United Dominions Trust (Commercial) Ltd v Eagle Aircraft Services Ltd* [1968] 1 WLR 74, 82; *Wood Preservation Ltd v Prior* [1969] 1 WLR 1077; *LG Schuler AG v Wickman Machine Tool Sales Ltd* [1972] 1 WLR 840, 850, 854, 859 CA; affirmed [1974] AC 235, 250–251, 256 HL; *North Sea Energy Holdings NV v Petroleum Authority of Thailand* [1997] 2 Lloyd's Rep 418, 429.

60 *Pym v Campbell* (1856) 6 E & B 370; *Aberfoyle Plantations Ltd v Cheng* [1960] AC 115; *William Cory & Son Ltd v IRC* [1965] AC 1088; *Haslemere Estates Ltd v Baker* [1982] 1 WLR 1109.

61 *Smith v Butler* [1900] 1 QB 694; *United Dominions Trust (Commercial) Ltd v Eagle Aircraft Services Ltd* [1968] 1 WLR 74; *Wood Preservation Ltd v Prior* [1969] 1 WLR 1077; cf *Eastham v Leigh, London & Provincial Properties Ltd* [1971] Ch 871.

62 *Worsley v Wood* (1796) 6 Term Rep 710; *Clarke v Watson* (1865) 18 CB(NS) 278; *Re Sandwell Park Colliery Co* [1929] 1 Ch 277; *Parway Estates Ltd v IRC* (1958) 45 TC 135; *Smallman v Smallman* [1972] Fam 25; *North Sea Energy Holdings NV v Petroleum Authority of Thailand* [1907] 2 Lloyd's Rep 418.

Thus, where X agreed to buy a horse from Y, it was a term of the contract that the horse had been in the Bicester Hunt, and if this condition turned out to be untrue, X would have until a specified day to return the horse. It was found after completion of the contract and delivery of the horse that the horse had not in fact been in the Bicester Hunt and it was held that X was entitled to return the horse and recover the purchase price. This was notwithstanding that the horse had sustained an injury while in X's possession (through no fault of X).[63]

The Belizean case, *Gegg v Belize International Insurance Co Limited*,[64] lends support to the importance of carefully drafted conditions precedent. There, it was held that an insurance contract did not contain a condition precedent requiring the premium to be paid before the contract came into force. The facts of the case were as follows:

> G, the plaintiff, and B, the defendant insurance company, had entered into a contract for marine insurance in respect of G's boat, the 'Don Pedro'. The Don Pedro ran aground on the reef at Ambergris Cay where it suffered severe damage, and B claimed under the insurance policy. B refused to indemnify G on the basis that G had failed to make all of the required payments under the policy.
>
> It was held that, on a reading of the terms of the insurance policy, it had been brought into force when the boat was launched. The drafting of the contract did not specify that payment by B of all premiums due was a condition precedent required to bring the policy into force. Consequently, B was liable to indemnify G under the policy even though B had failed to keep up with payments.

On the other hand, in the Barbadian case of *Pillersdorf v Denny*,[65] it was held that P could not enforce against D's estate an agreement for the sale by D to P of a parcel of land, since the agreement was subject to an unsatisfied condition precedent. By the terms of a written contract, D had agreed to sell a parcel of land to P, who paid a deposit to D in respect of the sale. The contract was conditional on the purchaser's obtaining planning permission for residential development of the site. P did obtain planning permission, but not until over two years after the agreement was made.

It was held that, in order for the agreement to take effect, P would have to have satisfied the condition precedent that planning permission was to be obtained within a reasonable time. P had failed to obtain the permission within a reasonable time, and the condition precedent had not been satisfied. Consequently, the obligations under the agreement for the sale of the land had not come into effect, and P's claim for specific performance of the contract was dismissed.

Conditions to be satisfied concurrently

Concurrent conditions are conditions which are to be performed at the same time or conditions each of which is dependent on the other. An example of concurrent conditions is to be found in contracts for the sale of goods, where (1) the delivery of goods and (2) the payment for those goods are concurrent conditions.

---

63 *Head v Tattersall* (1871) LR 7 Ex 7.

64 (1977) Supreme Court, Belize, No 40 of 1977, unreported [Carilaw BZ 1977 SC 10].

65 (1975) High Court, Barbados, No 555 of 1973, unreported [Carilaw BB 1975 HC 4].

Warranties

The word 'warranty' is used in a wide variety of circumstances, including (as discussed above) in the context of proof of terms, where it is intended to connote a binding contractual term (which is generally contrasted with a mere representation which is non-binding). On the other hand, the word 'warranty' in its technical sense relates to *classification* of terms rather than proof. It is used to distinguish one type of binding term (warranties) from another (conditions or intermediate terms).

The essential feature of a warranty is that it is a subsidiary, non-essential term, breach of which gives rise only to an action for damages by the innocent party. In insurance law, 'warranty' sometimes means an essential term. Breach of a warranty entitles the innocent party to damages only.[66]

It has been noted that the introduction of a new category of 'intermediate' terms has meant that terms will now rarely be classified as warranties except where designated as such and implied by legislation.[67]

Intermediate terms

The strict classifications of conditions and warranties would allow a non-defaulting party to a contract to treat a contract as being at an end, even where that party had not suffered significant losses. This was perceived as an abuse of the classification, which had been developed in furtherance of contractual certainty. The courts therefore developed a more flexible approach to the classification of terms, encouraging performance[68] by limiting the circumstances in which a non-defaulting party can treat the contract as being at an end.

Unless specifically agreed by the parties or determined by legislation, breach of an intermediate term entitles the innocent party to treat the contract as being at an end only if the breach has caused the innocent party to be substantially deprived of the whole benefit intended for him under the contract.[69] Thus in *Hong Kong Fir Shipping Co Ltd v Kawasaki Kisen Kaisha Ltd*,[70] it was held that the provision of a ship that was unseaworthy owing to the incompetence of its crew was not a breach of a contract for the charter of a ship, sufficient to entitle the charterers to treat the contract as being at an end. This was notwithstanding the inclusion of terms requiring the ship to be 'fitted for ordinary cargo service' and to be maintained by the owners in 'a thoroughly efficient state'.

Diplock LJ explained the rationale for finding in favour of a third category of term:[71]

---

66 *Hong Kong Fir Shipping Co Ltd v Kawasaki Kisen Kaisha Ltd* [1962] 2 QB 26.

67 *Chitty on Contracts: Volume 1 – General Principles*, 30th edn (Sweet & Maxwell, 2012) 12-031. See also ss 11–16, Sale of Goods Act, Cap 318 (Barbados); ss 11–16, Sale of Goods Act, (Jamaica); ss 12–17, Sale of Goods Act, Ch 337 (The Bahamas); and ss 12–17, Sale of Goods Act, Cap 261 (Belize).

68 *Cehave NV v Bremer Handelsgesellschaft mbH* [1976] QB 44; *Reardon Smith Line Ltd v Hansen-Tangen* [1976] 1 WLR 989.

69 *Hong Kong Fir Shipping Co Ltd v Kawasaki Kisen Kaisha, Ltd* [1962] 1 All ER 474.

70 *Ibid.*

71 *Ibid*, at 485.

Every synallagmatic contract contains in it the seeds of the problem: in what event will a party be relieved of his undertaking to do that which he has agreed to do but has not yet done? The contract may itself expressly define some of these events, as in the cancellation clause in a charterparty, but, human prescience being limited, it seldom does so exhaustively and often fails to do so at all . . . where an event occurs the occurrence of which neither the parties nor Parliament have expressly stated will discharge one of the parties from further performance of his undertakings, it is for the court to determine whether the event has this effect or not. The test whether an event has this effect or not has been stated in a number of metaphors all of which I think amount to the same thing: does the occurrence of the event deprive the party who has further undertakings still to perform of substantially the whole benefit which it was the intention of the parties as expressed in the contract that he should obtain as the consideration for performing those undertakings? This test is applicable whether or not the event occurs as a result of the default of one of the parties to the contract, but the consequences of the event are different in the two cases. Where the event occurs as a result of the default of one party, the party in default cannot rely on it as relieving himself of the performance of any further undertakings on his part and the innocent party, although entitled to, need not treat the event as relieving him of the performance of his own undertakings. This is only a specific application of the fundamental legal and moral rule that a man should not be allowed to take advantage of his own wrong . . .

The common law evolves not merely by breeding new principles but also, when they are fully grown, by burying their ancestors.

As my brethren have already pointed out, the shipowner's undertaking to tender a seaworthy ship has, as a result of numerous decisions as to what can amount to 'unseaworthiness', become one of the most complex of contractual undertakings. It embraces obligations with respect to every part of the hull and machinery, stores and equipment and the crew itself. It can be broken by the presence of trivial defects easily and rapidly remediable as well as by defects which must inevitably result in a total loss of the vessel. Consequently, the problem in this case is, in my view, neither solved nor soluble by debating whether the owners' express or implied undertaking to tender a seaworthy ship is a 'condition' or a 'warranty'. It is, like so many other contractual terms, an undertaking one breach of which may give rise to an event which relieves the charterer of further performance of his undertakings if he so elects, and another breach of which may not give rise to such an event but entitle him only to monetary compensation in the form of damages. It is, with all deference to counsel for the charterers' skilful argument, by no means surprising that, among the many hundreds of previous cases about the shipowner's undertaking to deliver a seaworthy ship, there is none where it was found profitable to discuss in the judgments the question whether that undertaking is a 'condition' or a 'warranty'; for the true answer, as I have already indicated, is that it is neither, but one of that large class of contractual undertakings, one breach of which may have the same effect as that ascribed to a breach of 'condition' under the Sale of Goods Act, 1893, and a different breach of which may have only the same effect as that ascribed to a breach of 'warranty' under that Act. The cases referred to by Sellers LJ illustrate this, and I would only add that, in the dictum which he cites from *Kish v Taylor*,[72] it seems to me from the sentence which immediately follows it as from the actual decision in the case and the whole tenor of Lord Atkinson's speech itself that the word 'will' was intended to be 'may'.[73]

72 [1912] AC, at 617; 12 Asp MLC at 22.

73 There, Lord Atkinson had said: 'The fact that a ship is not in a fit condition to receive her cargo, or is from any cause unseaworthy when about to start on her voyage, *will* justify the charterer or holder of the bill of lading in repudiating his contract and refusing to be bound by it' [emphasis added].

> What the learned judge had to do in the present case as in any other case where one party to a contract relies on a breach by the other party as giving him a right to elect to rescind the contract, was to look at the events which had occurred as a result of the breach at the time at which the charterers purported to rescind the charterparty, and to decide whether the occurrence of those events deprived the charterers of substantially the whole benefit which it was the intention of the parties as expressed in the charterparty that the charterers should obtain from the further performance of their own contractual undertakings . . .
>
> The question which the learned judge had to ask himself was, as he rightly decided, whether or not, at the date when the charterers purported to rescind the contract, namely 6 June 1957, or when the owners purported to accept such rescission, namely 8 August 1957, the delay which had already occurred as a result of the incompetence of the engine-room staff, and the delay which was likely to occur in repairing the engines of the vessel and the conduct of the owners by that date in taking steps to remedy these two matters, were, when taken together, such as to deprive the charterers of substantially the whole benefit which it was the intention of the parties they should obtain from further use of the vessel under the charterparty.

The principles governing intermediate terms set out by Lord Diplock in the *Hong Kong Fir Shipping* case have met with approval in Caribbean courts.[74]

Principles applying to classification of terms

Sale of Goods legislation defines certain implied terms as either conditions or warranties.[75]

The parties may also designate a term as a condition (or condition precedent[76]), warranty or intermediate term. Where they do so, this designation will generally be respected by the court. For example, in the case of a breach of a condition, that breach, however small, will give rise to a right to repudiate, unless such a construction produces a result so unreasonable that the parties could not have intended it, and if there is some other possible and reasonable construction.[77]

Use of terminology in commercial contracts

In contractual drafting, particularly in commercial contexts, parties may describe terms as 'conditions' or 'warranties' without intending them to bear their technical meaning at law. It is common for the words 'representations' and 'warranties' to be used interchangeably to connote statements the accuracy of which is promised by a party. These are often contained in a dedicated section of the agreement entitled 'representations and warranties'. It does not necessarily follow that the parties intend these designations to govern the consequences of a breach. For example, a typical representation may be that the seller in a transaction has a good,

---

74 See also *Locke (JR) v Bellingdon Ltd* 2002 CA 42.

75 See, for example, s 11 Sale of Goods Act, Cap 318 (Barbados); s 11; Sale of Goods Act (Jamaica); s 12 Sale of Goods Act, Ch 337 (The Bahamas) and ss 12–17 Sale of Goods Act, Cap 261 (Belize).

76 *Byron v Caines* (1995) Court of Appeal, Bermuda, No 12 of 1994, unreported [Carilaw BM 1995 CA 1].

77 *L Schuler A G v Wickman Machine Tool Sales Ltd* [1973] 2 All ER 39.

unencumbered title to the property being sold. It is arguable that a breach of such a term is a fundamental breach, and that the parties intended it to be a condition, in the technical sense, and not merely a warranty entitling the buyer to sue for damages. On the other hand, a party may, for example, warrant that its accounts are prepared in compliance with international accounting standards, and it might be similarly arguable that breach of this term would be unlikely to give rise to a right in the non-defaulting party to rescind the agreement.[78]

Similarly, 'undertakings' will generally refer to obligations which one or both of the parties will undertake to perform. Undertakings are common, for example, in financing contracts, where a typical undertaking given by a corporate borrower might be to provide the lender bank with regular updates on the borrower's financial condition. Undertakings and representations/warranties are often agreed to be repeated by the performing party at certain points during the parties' contractual relationship, for example, on drawdown of a loan or at the beginning of an interest period.

Further, in commercial contexts, the designation 'condition' will often be interpreted as being a condition precedent rather than a condition in the technical sense. Here, the transaction or agreement may not be fully effected until the relevant condition has been satisfied. Sometimes the drafting of the written agreement may provide that even if a condition precedent fails to be met, certain provisions of the agreement may become and remain binding on execution. An example of such a term would be a provision to the effect that confidentiality obligations of the party will survive, notwithstanding the failure of the transaction contemplated by the agreement by reason of a condition precedent not being satisfied.

INTERPRETATION OF WRITTEN TERMS

Where the terms of a written contract are unclear, the court must interpret them so as to give effect to the meaning which the parties intended to convey by using the words in the document. In doing so, the courts will examine the parties' intention objectively. Therefore, the courts will be concerned with the parties' intention as manifested by them, and shown by evidence adduced, rather than the actual state of mind of each party. It must be determined how a reasonable person would interpret the contract, given the relevant background. The periods of negotiation before[79] and conduct after[80] finalisation of the contract are generally not relevant for these purposes. This is because the bargain reached by the parties will frequently be the result of a compromise between them, rather than reflecting the terms which each party had hoped to achieve during and after negotiations.

78 For example, see *Hamiltonian Hotel & Island Club Ltd v Daulphin* (1990) Court of Appeal, Bermuda, No 10 of 1989, unreported [Carilaw BM 1990 CA 2], where the Bermudian Court of Appeal held that breach of a clause requiring the plaintiff to audit the company books annually was not a fundamental breach, as the defendant had 'attached precious little importance to the obligation during the currency of the agreement'.

79 *Prenn v Simmonds* [1971] 3 All ER 237.

80 *Schuler AG v Wickman Machine Tool Sales* [1974] AC 235.

The court's attitude towards the interpretation of express contractual terms was famously described by Lord Hoffmann in *Investors Compensation Scheme Ltd v West Bromwich Building Society*,[81] as follows:

> But I think I should preface my explanation of my reasons with some general remarks about the principles by which contractual documents are nowadays construed. I do not think that the fundamental change which has overtaken this branch of the law, particularly as a result of the speeches of Lord Wilberforce in *Prenn v Simmonds*[82] and *Reardon Smith Line Ltd v Yngvar Hansen-Tangen*[83] is always sufficiently appreciated. The result has been, subject to one important exception, to assimilate the way in which such documents are interpreted by judges to the common sense principles by which any serious utterance would be interpreted in ordinary life. Almost all the old intellectual baggage of 'legal' interpretation has been discarded. The principles may be summarised as follows:
>
> (1) Interpretation is the ascertainment of the meaning which the document would convey to a reasonable person having all the background knowledge which would reasonably have been available to the parties in the situation in which they were at the time of the contract.
>
> (2) The background was famously referred to by Lord Wilberforce as the 'matrix of fact,' but this phrase is, if anything, an understated description of what the background may include. Subject to the requirement that it should have been reasonably available to the parties and to the exception to be mentioned next, it includes absolutely anything which would have affected the way in which the language of the document would have been understood by a reasonable man.
>
> (3) The law excludes from the admissible background the previous negotiations of the parties and their declarations of subjective intent. They are admissible only in an action for rectification. The law makes this distinction for reasons of practical policy and, in this respect only, legal interpretation differs from the way we would interpret utterances in ordinary life. The boundaries of this exception are in some respects unclear. But this is not the occasion on which to explore them.
>
> (4) The meaning which a document (or any other utterance) would convey to a reasonable man is not the same thing as the meaning of its words. The meaning of words is a matter of dictionaries and grammars; the meaning of the document is what the parties using those words against the relevant background would reasonably have been understood to mean. The background may not merely enable the reasonable man to choose between the possible meanings of words which are ambiguous but even (as occasionally happens in ordinary life) to conclude that the parties must, for whatever reason, have used the wrong words or syntax (see *Mannai Investments Co Ltd v Eagle Star Life Assurance Co Ltd*).[84]
>
> (5) The 'rule' that words should be given their 'natural and ordinary meaning' reflects the common sense proposition that we do not easily accept that people have made linguistic mistakes, particularly in formal documents. On the other hand, if one would nevertheless conclude from the background that something must have gone wrong with the language, the law does not require judges to attribute to the parties an inten-

81 [1998] 1 All ER 98. See also: *Charter Reinsurance Co Ltd v Fagan* [1997] AC 313, *Mannai Investment Co Ltd v Eagle Star Life Assurance Co Ltd* [1997] AC 749, *Chartbrook Ltd v Persimmon Homes Ltd* [2009] UKHL 38 and the Antigua and Barbuda case, *Dries v Barbuda Express Ltd* (2008) High Court, Antigua and Barbuda, No 0429 of 2006, unreported [Carilaw AG 2008 HC 21].

82 [1971] 1 WLR 1381, 1384–1386.

83 [1976] 1 WLR 989.

84 [1997] 2 WLR 945.

tion which they plainly could not have had. Lord Diplock made this point more vigorously when he said in *The Antaios Compania Neviera SA v Salen Rederierna AB*:[85]

> ... if detailed semantic and syntactical analysis of words in a commercial contract is going to lead to a conclusion that flouts business commonsense, it must be made to yield to business commonsense.

In the conjoined appeals, *Re Sigma Finance Corporation (in administrative receivership)* and *In Re The Insolvency Act 1986*,[86] the UK Supreme Court took the approach of contextual interpretation one step further, holding that an express term of a contract was invalid.

Sigma Finance was a company which functioned as an investment vehicle. It held certain assets in its investment portfolio which produced a return, which was then passed on to investors. The financial crisis of 2008 affected the validity of those assets such that it held approximately $500 million but had liabilities of approximately $6 billion.

The appeal turned on the construction of an express term of one of the transaction documents, at clause 7.6, that purported to provide for the discharge of certain short term liabilities in circumstances where the company was insolvent.

The document also provided for a 'waterfall' system on insolvency of the company, which stipulated that creditors of the company were to be paid in accordance with a system of priorities. This meant that if the assets of the company were insufficient to cover all of its debts, those assets would have to be applied to discharge the debts at the 'top' of the waterfall first, meeting lower prioritised debts in turn according to the waterfall. In such a system, the creditors at the bottom of the waterfall would be unlikely to have their debts satisfied, on account of an insufficiency of assets.

The difficulty with the contractual drafting arose out of the provision for discharge of short term liabilities. This provision appeared to allow the beneficiary under this provision to take a 'short cut', so that it would have the discharge of certain of its debts prioritised over and above the waterfall mechanism.

The Court held the provision allowing the one party to receive payments outside of the waterfall repayment process to be invalid, on the basis that it was in conflict with the tenor of the agreement. Lord Mance SCJ said:

> In my opinion, the conclusion reached below attaches too much weight to what the courts perceived as the natural meaning of the words of the third sentence of clause 7.6, and too little weight to the context in which that sentence appears and to the scheme of the Security Trust Deed as a whole. Lord Neuberger was right to observe that the resolution of an issue of interpretation in a case like the present is an iterative process, involving 'checking each of the rival meanings against other provisions of the document and investigating its commercial consequences' (para. 98, and also 115 and 131). Like him, I also think that caution is appropriate about the weight capable of being placed on the consideration that this was a long and carefully drafted document, containing sentences or phrases which it can, with hindsight, be seen could have been made clearer, had the meaning now sought to be attached to them been specifically in mind (paras. 100–1). Even the most skilled drafters sometimes fail to see the wood for the trees, and the present

85 [1985] 1 AC 191, 201.

86 [2009] UKSC 2; [2008] EWCA Civ 1303.

> document on any view contains certain infelicities, as those in the majority below acknowledged (Sales J, paras. 37–40, Lloyd LJ, paras. 44, 49–52 and 53, and Rimer LJ para. 90). Of much greater importance in my view, in the ascertainment of the meaning that the Deed would convey to a reasonable person with the relevant background knowledge, is an understanding of its overall scheme and a reading of its individual sentences and phrases which places them in the context of that overall scheme. Ultimately, that is where I differ from the conclusion reached by the courts below. In my opinion, their conclusion elevates a subsidiary provision for the interim discharge of debts 'so far as possible' to a level of pre-dominance which it was not designed to have in a context where, if given that pre-dominance, it conflicts with the basic scheme of the Deed.

The commercial position in this type of transaction and in these types of documents would generally support the court's view. Therefore, this decision can be applauded on the basis that it shows a willingness on the part of the judges to take a commercial and not overly textual approach.

At first glance, this decision appears to be in line with previous case law demonstrating a movement towards a less formalistic approach towards contractual interpretation.

On the other hand, the decision in *Sigma Finance* can be criticised for a number of reasons. In considering these reasons, it is useful to recall the effect of the decision. There, an express term was held to be ineffective on the basis that it was inconsistent with the tenor of the document, in circumstances where, on a strict reading, that express term was not necessarily inconsistent with the other provisions of the document.

First, it actually departs from previous analysis (in particular, in relation to the binding effect of signature and the parol evidence rule) and extends the principle that ambiguous contracts are to be interpreted so as to determine the intention of the parties. It is established that, generally, parties who sign a contract are bound even where they do not read the terms and that they cannot admit extrinsic evidence as to terms without rebutting a presumption of completeness.[87] Parties should therefore be bound even where their lawyers failed to correct poor drafting.

Secondly, the decision undermines the importance of certainty. The Hoffman principles of interpretation in *Investors Compensation Scheme Ltd v West Bromwich Building Society*[88] relate to instances of ambiguity, that is, where there are multiple interpretations of the express words used in the contract. In *Sigma Finance,* the Supreme Court held an express term to be completely invalid.

Thirdly, the rationale of facilitating the commercial purpose of the contract ignores the fact that the parties to the contract were sophisticated and experienced in commercial matters and were being advised by legal experts. Those experts were also drafting the agreements, and were under contractual and tortious duties to do so with sufficient skill and care. The fact that the draftsmen were highly skilled lawyers provides further justification for holding the parties to their explicit terms; the documents were drafted and negotiated by experts who are at fault if the drafting fails by reason of incompetence potentially amounting to negligence.

Fourthly, it is necessary to examine the remedy in this case. The remedy was one of rectification of the contract to include or exclude the term in question. While the

87 See *L'Estrange v Graucob* [1934] 2 KB 394 and *Jacobs v Batavia and General Plantations Trust Ltd* [1924] 1 Ch 287.

88 [1998] 1 All ER 98.

court's pragmatism might be helpful in cases of ambiguity, it is questionable whether a party should be allowed to retrospectively amend an express term of an agreement after execution. Allowing rectification in these circumstances could afford an aggrieved party a better bargain than it was able to negotiate for in the first place. This result would undermine the principle of freedom to contract.

Finally, it is worth noting that, in *Sigma Finance*, rectification was allowed in circumstances where it is hard to see how the parties could have contemplated that there would have been a shortfall of $6 billion to meet the company's liabilities. Lord Walker SCJ stated in his dissenting judgment that the Court should have upheld the strict meaning of the agreement, on the basis that 'the parties cannot have contemplated that Sigma would have insufficient assets to meet its liabilities even to secured creditors – especially not on the scale of the extraordinary loss that has actually occurred'. He did not consider it tenable that the parties had intended that the drafting should cater for this unlikely result, when the express drafting of the agreement indicated that they had not.

The effect of the *Sigma Finance* case is to inject an element of uncertainty into the principles of contractual interpretation. It highlights the importance of precise, consistent drafting that reflects as closely as possible the parties' agreed terms.

EXEMPTION AND LIMITATION CLAUSES

An exemption or exclusion clause is an express contractual term which seeks to exclude or limit the contractual or tortious liability of one of the parties under the contract. The exclusion of or limitation on liability can relate either to exclusion of terms implied by the *court, by statute, or by custom* or to statements made during negotiations before entry into the agreement.

The common law rules governing exemption clauses are examined below. The statutory rules which supplement the common law rules are discussed in Chapter 7.

Standard form agreements

Exemption clauses are often found in standard form contracts, such as contracts made subject to the printed terms drawn up by one of the parties.[89] Examples include the 'conditions of carriage' in airline tickets, or 'terms and conditions' in mobile phone contracts. Standard form contracts are increasingly common, and the average person may enter into these contracts without ever having negotiated their terms.

From a consumer's perspective in particular, a person is rarely in a position to negotiate or question the terms presented to him in a typical standard form contract. Even if he is in a position to read and understand the terms, it is unlikely that he will be able to vary those terms.

From a commercial perspective, the use and imposition of exclusion clauses as part of a standard form document are also common. This is often the case in financing transactions, where banks are generally in a position of dominant bargaining power

89 See Lawson, *Exclusion Clauses and Unfair Contract Terms*, 7th edn (2003); Yates, *Exclusion Clauses in Contracts*, 2nd edn; MacDonald, *Exemption Clauses and Unfair Terms*, 2nd edn.

relative to the borrower (whether corporate or individual). Banks will often insist on the inclusion of their 'standard' terms in transaction documents, together with other requirements which are pre-set and must be met by the borrower.[90]

Typical examples of exclusion clauses in contracts for the sale of goods are clauses excluding all conditions and warranties, whether express or implied,[91] and clauses excluding liability for misrepresentation.

Limitation clauses are clauses which cap the liability of a party with reference to a set monetary limit or a formula for determining a set monetary limit (for example, 'Party A's liability shall not exceed $1000', or 'Party A's liability shall not exceed the purchase price').

Exemption clauses must be part of the contract

Sufficiency of notice

In the case of signed contracts, parties will generally be bound on the basis that they are deemed to have understood and agreed to those terms on signature. Where a party signs a contractual document containing an exemption clause, the clause is binding on the signatory whether or not he read it or understood it.[92]

In the case of exemption clauses which are not part of a signed document, the essential ingredient for that clause to be binding is notice. Only if the party had notice of a term can it be said that he agreed to it. There are principles governing what constitutes valid notice for this purpose.

The question of timing of the notice of an exemption clause is important in determining whether it can be said to be incorporated into the contract between the parties. An exemption clause is not binding unless it was brought to the attention of the other party before the contract was made.

Thus, an exemption clause printed on a receipt for money paid will not be valid, as a receipt is not a contractual document.[93]

Similarly, in *Olley v Marlborough Court*,[94] P arrived at a hotel and filled out the usual forms at the reception desk, paying for one week's stay. On reaching the bedroom, P saw a notice on the wall stating that the hotel would not be liable for articles lost or stolen unless handed in to the manager for safekeeping.

---

90 This may include, for example the delivery of certain documents by the borrower, such as financial statements and certified copies of constitutional documents (in the case of corporate borrowers).

91 *L'Estrange v Graucob* [1934] 2 KB 394.

92 *Parker v South Eastern Railway* (1877) 2 CPD 416; *L'Estrange v Graucob* [1934] 2 KB 394; *Levison v Patent Steam Carpet Cleaning Co Ltd* [1978] QB 69. Cf *Interfoto Picture Library Limited v Stiletto Visual Programme Ltd* [1989] QB 433.

93 *Chapelton v Barry UDC* [1940] 1 All ER 356. As to timing and incorporation of terms generally, see also *Robinson v Somers Isles Shipping Ltd* (2008) Supreme Court, Bermuda, No 275 of 2007, unreported [Carilaw BM 2008 SC 9] (standard terms, including an exclusive jurisdiction clause, brought to the plaintiff's attention after conclusion of a contract for shipping of cargo did not form part of the contract).

94 [1949] 1 KB 532. See also *Chapelton v Barry UDC* [1940] 1 All ER 356 and *Thornton v Shoe Lane Parking Ltd* [1971] 2 QB 163 (Denning LJ held that a customer paying to use parking facilities who received the ticket at the entrance to the car park was not bound by an exclusion clause brought to his attention after receipt of the ticket).

P's fur coat was stolen, and P sued the hotel, which sought to rely on the clause to be exempted from liability. The question to be decided was whether the defendant, the hotel, was protected by the notice in the plaintiff's bedroom. It was held that the hotel could not rely on the clause, as it was not brought to P's notice until after the contract had been made at the reception desk. Denning LJ, after stating that the hotel owed P a duty of care to ensure that P's room key was not taken by an unauthorised person, continued:

> The only other point is whether the defendants are protected by the notice which they put in the plaintiff's bedroom providing:
>
>> The proprietors will not hold themselves responsible for articles lost or stolen unless handed to the manageress for safe custody.
>
> The first question is whether that notice formed part of the contract. People who rely on a contract to exempt themselves from their common law liability must prove that contract strictly. Not only must the terms of the contract be clearly proved, but also the intention to create legal relations – the intention to be legally bound – must also be clearly proved. The best way of proving it is by a written document signed by the party to be bound. Another way is by handing him, before or at the time of the contract, a written notice specifying certain terms and making it clear to him that the contract is in those terms. A prominent public notice which is plain for him to see when he makes the contract would, no doubt, have the same effect, but nothing short of one of these three ways will suffice. It has been held that mere notices put on receipts for money do not make a contract: see *Chapelton* v *Barry UDC*.[95] So, also, in my opinion, notices put up in bedrooms do not of themselves make a contract. As a rule, the guest does not see them until after he has been accepted as a guest. The hotel company, no doubt, hope that the guest will be held bound by them, but the hope is vain unless they clearly show that he agreed to be bound by them, which is rarely the case.
>
> Assuming, however, that the plaintiff did agree to be bound by the terms of this notice, there remains the question whether on its true interpretation it exempted the defendants from liability for their own negligence. It is said, and, indeed, with some support from the authorities, that this depends on whether the hotel was a common inn with the liability at common law of an insurer, or a private hotel with liability only for negligence. I confess that I do not think it should depend on that question. It should depend on the words of the contract. To exempt a person from liability for negligence, the exemption should be clear on the face of the contract. It should not depend on what view the courts may ultimately take on the question of common inn or private hotel. In cases where the establishment is clearly a common inn or, indeed, where it is uncertain whether it is a common inn or a private hotel, I am of opinion that a notice in these terms would not exempt the defendants from liability for negligence but only from any liability as insurers. Indeed, even if it were clearly not a common inn, but only a private hotel, I should be of the same opinion. Ample content can be given to the notice by construing it as a warning that the hotel proprietor is not liable in the absence of negligence. As such it serves a useful purpose. It is a warning to the guest that he must do his part to take care of his things himself, and, if need be, insure them. It is unnecessary to go further and to construe the notice as a contractual exemption of the defendants from their common law liability for negligence. I agree that the appeal should be dismissed.

Thus, in addition to meeting the conditions for contemporaneity, the parties must also, at the time at which the exemption clause is brought to their attention, intend to be bound by those terms.

---

95 [1940] 1 All ER 356.

In the case of *Williams v Cornwall Betting Services Ltd*,[96] the Jamaican Court of Appeal held that a partially obliterated notice of an exemption clause put on the back of a race programme by a bookmaker was sufficient notice to the plaintiff, notwithstanding that he was illiterate.

There, the plaintiff, who was illiterate, had for a number of years been in the habit of placing bets with the defendant, and taking the race programme home to be read to him by his daughter. On a particular day, the plaintiff had placed and won a bet that would have entitled him to nearly $10,000. On arrival at the bookmaker to collect his winnings, he was told that the defendant had capped its liability to pay out money for that type of win so that, in accordance with the exemption clause, the plaintiff would be entitled only to approximately $100. The exemption clause had been printed in full on every race programme, except for the programme which had been taken up by the plaintiff, on which was printed only a portion of the relevant provision. The Court of Appeal held that the portion of the exemption clause which had been printed on the notice was sufficient to bring the exemption clause to the plaintiff's notice, so that it formed part of the contract and was valid to cap the defendant's liability.

It is also settled that where a similar exemption clause has been included in *previous* dealings between the parties, the clause will be binding, since the party against whom the clause was inserted will be deemed to have had notice of it.[97] This course of dealing must be consistent.[98]

Liability for negligence

An exemption clause purporting to exempt liability for negligence must be adequate. This proposition was stated by Scrutton LJ in *Rutter v Palmer*:[99]

> In construing an exemption clause, certain general rules may be applied: First, the defendant is not exempted from liability for the negligence of his servants unless adequate words are used; secondly, the liability of the defendant apart from the exempting words must be ascertained; then the particular clause in question must be considered; and if the only liability of the party pleading the exemption is a liability for negligence, the clause will more readily operate to exempt him.

The decision in *Olley v Marlborough Court*[100] reaffirms this principle and demonstrates that even where a clause purporting to exempt the defendant from liability for negligence has been brought to the parties' attention, the exemption must be sufficiently clear on the face of the contract.

96 (1984) Court of Appeal, Jamaica, No 57 of 1981, unreported [Carilaw JM 1984 CA 4].
97 *Spurling v Bradshaw* [1956] 1 WLR 461. See also *Hollier v Rambler Motors (AMC) Ltd* [1972] 2 QB 71.
98 *McCutcheon v David MacBrayne Ltd* [1964] 1 WLR 165.
99 [1922] 2 KB 87.
100 [1949] 1 KB 532.

Liability for misrepresentation

Where the party seeking to rely on an exemption clause has misrepresented the meaning or extent of the clause then it will not be binding on the representee.[101]

Unreasonable clauses

As already discussed, standard form contracts containing terms which are non-negotiable are increasingly common. As a general rule (not restricted to exemption clauses), where a contract contains terms that are unusually unreasonable or burdensome to perform, special steps must be taken to bring those terms to the notice of the party who did not draft those terms.

This principle was laid down by Dillon LJ in *Interfoto Picture Library Ltd v Stiletto Visual Programmes Ltd*:[102]

> At the time of the ticket cases in the last century it was notorious that people hardly ever troubled to read printed conditions on a ticket or delivery note or similar document. That remains the case now. In the intervening years the printed conditions have tended to become more and more complicated and more and more one-sided in favour of the party who is imposing them, but the other parties, if they notice that there are printed conditions at all, generally still tend to assume that such conditions are only concerned with ancillary matters of form and are not of importance. In the ticket cases the courts held that the common law required that reasonable steps be taken to draw the other parties' attention to the printed conditions or they would not be part of the contract. It is in my judgment a logical development of the common law into modern conditions that it should be held, as it was in *Thornton v Shoe Lane Parking*,[103] that, if one condition in a set of printed conditions is particularly onerous or unusual, the party seeking to enforce it must show that that particular condition was fairly brought to the attention of the other party.

Interpretation of exemption clauses

In cases of unequal bargaining power, where one party can dictate the terms to another, courts have tended to curtail the exclusion of liability wherever possible, except where to do so would clearly violate accepted principles of contractual interpretation.

This approach was confirmed in *Boyack & McKenzie Ltd v Lock Joint American (Trinidad) Ltd*.[104] Here, the defendant had subcontracted to the plaintiff the road reinstalment obligations under its contract with the Government of Trinidad and Tobago for the construction of sewers and sewage disposal plants. The defendant later performed the road reinstalment work itself, depriving the plaintiff of the

101 *Curtis v Chemical Cleaning Co* [1951] KB 805. See also *Harbour Cold Stores Ltd v Chas E Ramson Ltd et al* (1982) Court of Appeal, Jamaica, No 57 of 1978, unreported [Carilaw JM 1982 CA 4].

102 [1989] QB 43, para 19.

103 [1971] 2 QB 163.

104 *Boyack & Mckenzie Ltd v Lock Joint American (Trinidad) Ltd* (1966) High Court, Trinidad and Tobago, No 1557 of 1963, unreported [Carilaw TT 1966 HC 12]. See *also Pearson & Sons Ltd v Dublin Corp* [1907] AC 351.

opportunity to do so and therefore of the profits under the contract. The plaintiff then sued for breach of contract. The defendant sought to rely on an exemption clause in the contract dealing with stoppage and suspension. However, that clause sought to exonerate the plaintiff from liability in cases where stoppage, suspension or delay of the work related to acts or orders of the Government; it was not clear that the clause would permit the defendant to stop the work and do it itself. The court held that the defendant's interpretation of the contract was incorrect; if the defendant wanted the clause to have the purported effect, it should have used clear and precise language; in the absence of such language, the defendant was liable for breach of contract. The court disapproved of the defendant's attempt to rely on the exemption clause, particularly because the balance of bargaining power lay distinctly in its favour, relative to the plaintiff. Rees J said:

> The contention of the defendants, as I understand it, is that Art. (XII) is an exemption clause. From the circumstances, it is clear that the defendants, who had the option of sub-contracting the work of reinstatement to the plaintiffs or to any other person with the necessary experience, materials and equipment, were in a far superior position than the plaintiffs at the time of signing the sub-contract, and could, therefore, dictate their own terms to the plaintiffs. In situations such as these 'the courts have tended to set their faces against the exclusion of liability, and so far as rules of construction allow, to confine the operation of exemption clauses within the narrowest limits'. It is enough to say that I find that the defendants were in breach of the sub-contract by preventing the plaintiffs from doing the reinstatement work and wrongfully doing it themselves.

The 'fundamental breach' doctrine and exemption clauses

In order to protect consumers from unscrupulous dealers, the courts have developed the doctrine of fundamental breach. The doctrine has been developed and refined over time. Whereas it had previously been suggested that it was a rule of law that *any* fundamental breach would disentitle the breaching party from relying on an exemption clause,[105] the principle governing the interaction between exemption clauses and fundamental breach was restated in *Photo Production Ltd v Securicor.*[106] The current position is that a party may be deprived of the benefit of an exemption clause only where that was the intention of the parties.

The essence of the current principle is that where a defaulting party has committed a breach which is arguably within the scope of an exemption clause, the question of the liability or otherwise of that party for the breach will be a question of the interpretation of the contract. This is so, even where the breach is fundamental in nature. The parties are free to agree that liability for a breach (whether fundamental or otherwise) may be absolved under an exemption clause. By the same token, the court in interpreting a contract may find that the parties could not have intended that a defaulting party should be absolved from liability by virtue of an exemption clause.

105 *Karsales (Harrow) Ltd v Wallis* [1956] 1 WLR 936, *Boshali v Allied Commercial Exporters Ltd* [1961] 1 All NLR 917; *Harbutt's Plasticine v Wayne Tank Co* [1970] 1 QB 44; *Suisse Atlantique v Rotterdamsche Kolen Centrale* [1967] AC 361.

106 [1980] AC 827.

In the *Photo Production* case, Lord Diplock drew a distinction between (1) primary obligations (such as terms of the contract) and (2) secondary obligations (such as liability to pay damages for a breach). He held that the parties to a contract are free to determine their primary obligations in order to fix their secondary obligations, and that therefore they can choose to govern their liability after termination. On this basis, it is for the parties to determine whether an exemption clause operates to relieve a party of liability for fundamental or non-fundamental breaches.

The approach taken in *Photo Production* was affirmed by the Jamaican Court of Appeal in *Harbour Cold Stores Ltd v Chas E Ramson Ltd*.[107] Here, ewe carcasses delivered to the defendant for cold storage were spoilt as a result of the defendant's negligence. The plaintiff bailor sued the defendant as bailee of the goods, and the defendant sought to rely on an exemption clause which capped its liability where notice of claim in cases of spoilage was not given within a certain time period. The plaintiff argued that the limitation clause was ineffective on the basis that the defendant had committed a fundamental breach which brought the contract to an end.

It was held that, notwithstanding the defendant's negligence, the defendant could rely on an exclusion clause exempting it from liability for negligence. This was because it could not have been within the contemplation of the parties that the defendant's breach should bring the agreement to an end. This was demonstrated in part by the fact that the plaintiff had continued to make orders pursuant to the terms of the agreement, even after the alleged breach by the defendant.

Carey JA stated that:

> if the freedom to contract exists, it is not that a rule of law exists to nullify such clauses, but that it is difficult to conceive any other result in construing the effect of such a fundamental breach on an exception clause. In other words, [where] it would be absurd to construe the particular clause as applicable to a situation that was clearly never in contemplation. . .Clause 3 is unambiguous: it prescribed a time limit for notice of claim in the event of spoilage or deterioration of the carcasses . . . Plainly, therefore, the clause contemplated that claims would be made from time to time as and when there was spoilage.

Applying these principles, three questions are helpful in determining whether a defaulting party can rely on an exemption clause to exonerate him from liability for breach (whether fundamental or otherwise):

(1) Did the parties intend to be bound by the exemption clause?

(2) Is the clause effective? In particular, was it properly incorporated into the contract and are the terms sufficiently reasonable, clear and precise?

(3) Do the terms of the exemption clause as drafted cover the breach or fundamental breach in question? Or is the breach so serious and so fundamental that the parties could not have intended for the clause to exempt the parties for breach?

---

107 (1982) Court of Appeal, Jamaica, No 57 of 1978, unreported [Carilaw JM 1982 CA 4]; cf *Oncology Association Ltd v The Attorney-General* (2005) Court of Appeal, The Bahamas, No 64 of 2005, unreported [Carilaw BS 2005 CA 311], where the Bahamian Court of Appeal appeared to suggest that the line of cases supported *by Suisse Atlantique Societe d'armament Maritime SA v NV Rotterdamscher Kolen Centrale* [1967] AC 361 remains good law.

In *Bevad Limited v Oman Limited*,[108] the Jamaican Court of Appeal held that the vendor in a contract for the sale of land could not rely on an exemption clause purporting to exclude all conditions, warranties and representations, whether implied or express, on account of the fact that he had fraudulently misrepresented that planning permission for the development of the land had been obtained, when it had not. Harris LJ summarised the court's position on this point as follows:

> A party seeking to rely on an exemption clause may be denied the right so to do, if he is found to be in fraudulent breach of a contract. In the instant case, the appellant has been found to have made fraudulent representations knowing fully well that 11 Hopedale Avenue was not suitable for the construction of 23 habitable rooms. The approved building plans were defective. No planning approval was in existence. This was not disclosed to the respondent. Mr. Harris was misled into believing approval for parking was granted. This clearly taints the entire contract. This being so, it would be barred from relying on the warranty clause.

The breach in this case was so fundamental that, on an interpretation of the contract, the vendor could not rely on the exemption clause to exempt it from liability.

Similarly, where X bought a second-hand truck from Y under a hire-purchase agreement which contained a clause excluding all warranties and conditions as to fitness or roadworthinesss, and the truck turned out to be completely unroadworthy, Y could not rely on the exemption clause as he had committed a fundamental breach in supplying a useless vehicle.[109] Similarly, a dealer who sold an unroadworthy 4-year-old truck, having contracted to sell a 1-year-old one, was not protected by a clause exempting him from liability for breach of warranty since he was not carrying out the contract in its essential respects.[110]

The doctrine has also been applied where a railway authority employee allowed a stranger to have access to a left luggage office with the result that the plaintiff's luggage deposited at the office was stolen[111] and where an insurance company had delayed repairs on a vehicle after it had been involved in an accident, so that the owner lost profits, the company could not rely on an exemption clause excluding liability for consequential loss.[112]

The contra proferentem *rule*

One key rule of interpretation is the *contra proferentem* rule. Exemption clauses are construed strictly against the party who inserted them. Thus, in *Ammar & Azar Ltd v Brinks Jamaica Ltd*,[113] the Jamaican Supreme Court held that 'such limitation as a party seeks to rely on must be clearly and unambiguously stated in the contract relied on'.

---

108 (2008) Court of Appeal, Jamaica, No 133 of 2005, unreported [Carilaw JM 2008 CA 54], 28. See also *JB Astwood & Son Ltd v Marra* (1980) Court of Appeal, Bermuda, No 28 of 1979, unreported [Carilaw BM 1980 CA 27].

109 *Shotayo v Nigerian Technical Co Ltd* [1970] NCLR 159.

110 *Ogwu v Leventis Motors Ltd* [1969] NRNLR 115.

111 *Alexander v Railway Executive* [1951] 2 KB 882.

112 *Niger Insurance Ltd v Abed* (1976) 6 UILR 61.

113 (1984) Supreme Court, Jamaica, No A051 of 1981, unreported [Carilaw JM 1984 SC 35].

Implied terms

In addition to terms which are expressed by parties orally or in writing, the law will, in some instances, imply into a contract terms which were not expressly included as a part of the agreement. These terms will derive from (1) statute, (2) custom or (3) implication by the court. In deciding what terms are to be implied into a contract, as when interpreting express terms, the court will look to establish what the parties must have meant to agree, taking into consideration both the commercial purpose of the contract and the circumstances of the agreement.[114] Terms will generally not be implied where they have been excluded by the express terms of the agreement. This is captured by the phrase *expressum facit cessare tacitum* (what is expressed makes the implied silent).

Terms implied by statute

In some cases, statutory provisions will deem terms to be implied into certain types of contracts to protect parties who ostensibly lack equal bargaining power, for example, purchasers and employees. Examples of these are contracts relating to the sale of goods, hire purchase and employment. Importantly, these terms will not be implied where to do so would violate or contradict the express terms of the agreement.[115] For this reason, commercial contracts commonly expressly exclude any such implied terms. Thus, in *Johnstone v Bloomsbury Health Authority*[116] it was held that a provision requiring a doctor to work 88 hours a week was an exclusion clause, as it prevented the operation of an implied term that an employer would not overwork an employee to the detriment of his health.

Terms implied by sale of goods legislation are discussed in detail in Chapter 7.

Terms implied by custom

Terms may be implied where there is a defined and general custom of a locality or by the usage of a particular trade. Such custom or usage must be notorious, certain and reasonable and must not be inconsistent with any statute. For example, in *Hutton v Warren*[117] an outgoing tenant was entitled to rely on a local custom that he should be paid a reasonable allowance for labour and materials expended on the land even though the lease contained no express term to that effect.

Similarly, in *Produce Brokers Co Ltd v Olympia Oil and Cake Co Ltd*,[118] the House of Lords held that, where an agreement referred 'all disputes arising out of [the]

---

114 *Codelfa Construction Pty Ltd v State Railway Authority of New South Wales* (1982) 149 CLR 337, 345; *South Australia Asset Management Corp v York Montague* [1997] AC 191, 212.

115 Cf *Johnstone v Bloomsbury HA* [1992] QB 333; *Yarm Road Ltd v Hewdon Tower Cranes Ltd* [2002] EWHC 2265, (2002) 85 Const LR 142.

116 [1992] QB 333.

117 (1836) 1 M & W 466.

118 [1915] 1 KB 233.

contract' to arbitration, the arbitral panel was correct in considering custom when making its award.

The rationale for this is that 'the courts are spelling out what both parties know and would, if asked, unhesitatingly agree to be part of the bargain'.[119]

Thus, in *Pierre v Port Authority of Trinidad and Tobago*, it was held that in a contract for the carriage of goods there is invariably an implied term that the goods will be carried safely and properly.[120]

A custom or usage may be excluded by the parties either expressly or impliedly; thus, terms will not be implied by reason of custom or usage where to do so would contradict one or more of the express terms of the contract.[121] Subsequent case law has clarified this principle, such that the test has two parts. First, a term will not be implied in contravention of express contractual terms, and, secondly, a term will not be implied unless it is consistent with the tenor of the document as a whole.[122]

Terms implied by the courts

Terms necessary to achieve business efficacy: the Moorcock principle

Where the parties, by inadvertence or by incompetent drafting, fail to incorporate into a contract terms which they would certainly have included had they addressed their minds properly to the drafting of the contract, the court may imply such terms in order to give 'business efficacy' to the transaction.[123] This principle was famously laid down by Bowen LJ in *The Moorcock*[124] as follows:

> Now, an implied warranty, or, as it is called, a covenant in law, as distinguished from an express contract or express warranty, really is in all cases founded on the presumed intention of the parties, and upon reason. The implication which the law draws from what must obviously have been the intention of the parties, the law draws with the object of giving efficacy to the transaction and preventing such a failure of consideration as cannot have been within the contemplation of either side; and I believe if one were to take all the cases, and they are many, of implied warranties or covenants in law, it will be found that in all of them the law is raising an implication from the presumed intention of the parties with the object of giving to the transaction such efficacy as both parties must have intended that at all events it should have. In business transactions such as this, what the law desires to effect by the implication is to give such business efficacy to the transaction as must have been intended at all

---

119 *Liverpool City Council v Irwin* [1977] AC 239, 253; *Baker v Black Sea & Baltic General Insurance Co Ltd* [1998] 1 WLR 974, 979.

120 (1969) High Court, Trinidad and Tobago, No 20 of 1966, unreported [Carilaw TT 1969 HC 23].

121 *Les Affréteurs Réunis v Walford* [1919] AC 801. See also *Budget Hardware Supplies Ltd v First Citizens Bank Limited* (2007) Court of Appeal, Trinidad and Tobago, No 59 of 2005, unreported [Carilaw TT 2007 CA 5] (no implied term that overdrawn cheques must be honoured by a bank where express terms gave the bank the right to postpone payment of cheques drawn against uncleared effects).

122 *London Export Corporation Ltd v Jubilee Coffee Roasting Co* [1958] 2 All ER 411.

123 *The Moorcock* (1889) LR 14 PD 64.

124 (1889) LR 14 PD 64. See also *Basanta-Henry v National Commercial Bank Jamaica Ltd* (2004) Supreme Court, Jamaica, No E-132 of 2002, unreported [Carilaw JM 2004 SC 108].

events by both parties who are business men; not to impose on one side all the perils of the transaction, or to emancipate one side from all the chances of failure, but to make each party promise in law as much, at all events, as it must have been in the contemplation of both parties that he should be responsible for in respect of those perils or chances.

For example, where D employed P to carry out 'bush clearing' in the course of extending electricity lines, a term was implied that trees along the route should be cut down by P, as these would obstruct the line.[125] And a term was implied in a hire-purchase agreement for a truck that instalments should be withheld so long as the truck was incapable of carrying goods due to frequent breakdowns.[126]

It should be noted that courts will not imply a term pursuant to the *Moorcock* principle where the parties have clearly expressed their intentions to the contrary in a written agreement.[127] This is consistent with the maxim *expressum facit cessare tacitum*, which is to the effect that express terms will override incompatible implied terms.

The decision in *The Moorcock* was restated in *Equitable Life Assurance Society v Hyman*,[128] where Lord Steyn said as follows:

It is necessary to distinguish between the processes of interpretation and implication. The purpose of interpretation is to assign to the language of the text the most appropriate meaning which the words can legitimately bear . . . If a term is to be implied, it could only be a term implied from the language of [the provision] read in its particular commercial setting. Such implied terms operate as ad hoc gap fillers.

The decision of the Privy Council in *Attorney General of Belize v Belize Telecom Ltd*[129] is demonstrative of the court's willingness to favour an interpretation of contractual terms which fulfils the legacy of the 'business efficacy' principle laid down in *The Moorcock*.

There, the court had to consider provisions in the articles of association of B, a company formed for the specific purpose of taking over a telecommunications business which was a public authority with an effective monopoly of telecommunications services in Belize. A key consideration in forming the company was that the government would be able to sell part of its interest in the business, while maintaining control. This control was facilitated, in part, by provisions in the company's articles giving the government special rights to appoint and remove directors.

Counsel for the respondents suggested an interpretation of the articles of association that would clearly contradict the purpose for which the company had been established. The court found in favour of the appellants on the basis that it implied a term into the articles of association which was 'required to avoid defeating what appears to have been the overriding purpose of the machinery of appointment and removal of directors, namely to ensure that the board reflects the appropriate

125 *Oketete v Electricity Corp of Nigeria* [1970] NCLR 53.
126 *WAAEC Ltd v Balogun* (1979) FCA/C/82/77 (unreported).
127 *Hugh v Yap* (2003) Court of Appeal, Jamaica, No 11 of 2000, unreported [Carilaw JM 2003 CA 7], 16.
128 [2002] 1 AC 408.
129 [2009] UKPC 10.

shareholder interests in accordance with the scheme laid out in the articles'. Lord Hoffman, after discussing previous case law in support of the *Moorcock* principle, said as follows:

> The Board considers that this list is best regarded, not as series of independent tests which must each be surmounted, but rather as a collection of different ways in which judges have tried to express the central idea that the proposed implied term must spell out what the contract actually means, or in which they have explained why they did not think that it did so. The Board has already discussed the significance of 'necessary to give business efficacy' and 'goes without saying'. As for the other formulations, the fact that the proposed implied term would be inequitable or unreasonable, or contradict what the parties have expressly said, or is incapable of clear expression, are all good reasons for saying that a reasonable man would not have understood that to be what the instrument meant.

In the St Lucian case of *Marcus v Lawaetz*,[130] the Privy Council held that, in the circumstances of that case, it would not be appropriate to imply a contractual term on the basis of the 'business efficacy' principle. There, the Privy Council held that there was no implied term obliging the defendant to hypothecate its property in order to assist its business partner, the plaintiff, with its preliminary negotiations for the financing for development of the property. The only term that could have been implied was an obligation to mortgage the property as security in order to secure the financing once negotiations were complete. The plaintiff was held to have wrongfully repudiated the agreement because it did so prematurely, at a time when the defendant was not yet obliged to hypothecate the property. The Court gave its decision on this point in the following terms:

> In this appeal the appellants challenge all three findings of the Court of Appeal. On the question of breach they submit that on the true construction of the addendum dated 25th January 1973, Mr. Lawaetz was in breach of the agreement by refusing, when called upon to do so by the appellants, to cause the company to pass a resolution agreeing to hypothecate its property in order to secure loan finance for the development. There is no express term to this effect in the addendum agreement but it is submitted that it is a necessary implication to be read into the actual wording, which provides:
>
>> For the above consideration LAWAETZ agrees to subordinate the Grande Anse Beach Property, St. Lucia consisting of between 1,900 and 2,000 acres for the purpose of SLICL obtaining interim and mortgage monies.
>
> Their Lordships are satisfied that no such term is to be implied. It was argued that such a term must necessarily be implied in order to enable the appellants to hold preliminary discussions with prospective lenders. But such a resolution, a proposed draft of which was placed before their Lordships during the course of argument, would add virtually nothing by way of assurance to a prospective lender to that which is contained in the clause in the addendum set out above.
>
> The term to be implied to give business efficacy to the clause is that the company would mortgage its property as security in order to assist the appellants to obtain a loan provided upon reasonable and prudent terms. Until the time that such a proposal could be placed before Mr. Lawaetz and considered by him and the company the obligation to subordinate did not arise. Their Lordships agree with the trial judge and the Court of

130 (1986) Privy Council, St. Lucia, No 3 of 1983, unreported [Carilaw LC 1986 PC 2].

> Appeal that the time for Mr. Lawaetz to cause the company to mortgage its property had not arrived at the date when the appellants repudiated the agreements. It follows that the appellants were rightly held to have wrongfully repudiated the agreements.

An implied duty of good faith or fair dealing

In a recent Belizean case, *Bella Vista Development Co Ltd v AG*,[131] it was suggested by Legall J that, in some circumstances, the courts would be willing to imply a duty of good faith or fair dealing. This case concerned a 'termination for convenience' clause in favour of the government. Such clauses purport to allow the beneficiary of the clause to terminate the agreement without cause. The clause in question read as follows:

> 59.4 Notwithstanding the above, the Contracting Agency may terminate the contract for convenience at anytime.

General elections in Belize were held in February 2008, and the government changed hands. The new government then served notice on the claimant that it was terminating the contract. The claimant sued the government for breach of contract. The claimant relied on precedents from United States courts and an Australian case, *GEC Marconi Systems Pty Limited v BHP Information Technology Pty Ltd*,[132] to argue that there were legal limits on the defendants' ability to terminate. The claimant argued that, in exercising its right under the termination for convenience clause, the government was obliged to act in good faith. Legall J confirmed that such a duty was implied in termination for convenience clauses, but he noted that the burden of proof lies on the party asserting bad faith, and that the claimant had failed to discharge this burden. Further, there is a presumption of good faith. He said:

> On the authorities, it is safe to come to the conclusion that bad faith, unfair dealings, an abuse of contracting discretion, and an attempt to acquire a better bargain from another source, are limitations legally placed on the use of the convenience clause. These cases clearly show that although there is a right to terminate a contract with or without cause, under a convenience clause, that right is subject to the rule not to act in bad faith or in abuse of discretion, or in an attempt to get a better bargain from another source.
>
> In my judgment, where a termination for convenience clause appears in a contract, whether it is a contract involving private individuals or government, if there is nothing to the contrary in the contract, the termination for convenience clause may be acted upon with or without cause. The right to terminate such a contract with or without cause would, however, amount to breach of contract by the terminating party, if the termination was done in bad faith or without fair dealing or in an abuse of discretion or in an attempt to get a better bargain from another source. Even though the words of the convenience clause may be clear and unambiguous, any such termination would amount to a breach of contract, unless the contrary appears in the contract.
>
> But the parties alleging bad faith have a very weighty burden to discharge and they rarely succeed . . .
>
> The Convenience Clause is subject to the limitations of acting in good faith, fair dealing or without an abuse of discretion. These terms are implied in the contract. There is a heavy burden on the part of the claimants to prove bad faith, and on the facts, they have failed to satisfy this burden. The claimants have also failed to satisfy the burden of

131 (2009) Supreme Court, Belize, No 199 of 2008, unreported [Carilaw BZ 2009 SC 14].
132 2003 FCA 50.

> proving abuse of discretion and unfair dealing and an intention to contract with others. Moreover, there is a presumption of good faith. There is no evidence that the defendants acted unconscionably as that term is legally defined.

It remains to be seen whether other Caribbean courts will follow the approach in *Bella Vista Development* and find in favour of a general implied duty of good faith, even where the express contractual terms provide for termination without cause. It seems unlikely that they will do so, given that in this case the doctrine was asserted on the basis of United States and Australian precedents. Except in certain circumstances, such as in the case of insurance contracts, the doctrine of good faith does not have general application in English law, and this is likely to carry significant weight with judges in the Commonwealth Caribbean.[133]

The 'officious bystander' test

The court will also imply terms into a contract where it is obvious that both of the parties must have had an intention for that term to form part of the agreement. The test was described in *Shirlaw v Southern Foundries Ltd* in the following terms:

> *Prima facie* that which in any contract is left to be implied and need not be expressed is something so obvious that it goes without saying; so that if, while the parties were making their bargain, an officious bystander were to suggest some express provision for it in the agreement, they would testily suppress him with a common, 'oh, of course'.[134]

In *Costa v Murray and Murray*,[135] the High Court of Trinidad and Tobago applied both the *Moorcock* principle and the 'officious bystander' test in finding that the defendant, who had agreed to grand to the plaintiff a licence to occupy the defendant's land, was in breach of an implied term in the licence agreement that he would give the plaintiff possession of the lands in question.

---

133 For reference, see Brownsword, *Contract Law: Themes for the Twenty-First Century*, 2nd edn (OUP, 2006) 53, 59–511, 514–21; Brownsword, 'Good Faith in Contracts Revisited' (1996) 49 *Current Legal Problems* 111; Brownsword, Hird and Howells (eds) *Good Faith in Contract: Concept and Context* (1999). Cf Bridge, 'Does Anglo-Canadian Contract Law Need a Doctrine of Good Faith?' (1984) 9 Canadian JBL 385.

134 [1939] 2 KB 206, *per* MacKinnon J. See also *Basanta-Henry v National Commercial Bank Jamaica Ltd* (2004) Supreme Court, Jamaica, No E-132 of 2002, unreported [Carilaw JM 2004 SC 108].

135 (1977) High Court, Trinidad and Tobago, No 1249 of 1975, unreported [Carilaw TT 1977 HC 82]. See also *Sengupta v Woods Development Limited* (2003) High Court, Antigua and Barbuda, No 0366 of 1998, unreported [Carilaw AG 2003 HC 15] where it was held that this was an implied term in a building contract that the building would conform to the soil requirements.

CHAPTER 7

SALE OF GOODS

RIGHTS AND OBLIGATIONS

Introduction – the sale of goods legislation

In the Commonwealth Caribbean, the law relating to contracts for the sale of goods is derived from both common law and statutory sources. The body of case law governing contracts for the sale of goods grew up out of a willingness of courts to mitigate the harshness of the early common law '*caveat emptor*' rule, according to which a buyer in a transaction is responsible for examining the goods to be purchased, so that, in the absence of an express warranty (on which he could insist to protect himself), he could not bring an action against the seller if the item failed to meet his expectations.

Over time, this rule was modified and supplemented by case law in which the courts recognised that, in certain circumstances, the parties must implicitly have intended certain terms to apply: for instance, terms in a bulk order that the goods would correspond with a sample provided by the seller,[1] and that the seller would transfer good title in the property.

As discussed in Chapter 6, contractual terms can be implied into contracts by legislation, notwithstanding they were not contemplated or expressly incorporated into the contract by the parties. Under the sale of goods legislation, terms are implied into contracts for the sale of goods, unless they are expressly excluded.[2]

Many Commonwealth Caribbean territories have passed legislation regulating contracts for the sale of goods in relation to various matters including formation, capacity to contract, terms, and remedies available to the parties in such contracts.[3]

Sale of goods legislation has only partially codified, and has not replaced, the common law principles governing these types of contracts.

By way of example, the Sale of Goods Act of Trinidad and Tobago states as follows:

> 59. (1) The rules in bankruptcy relating to contracts of sale shall continue to apply thereto notwithstanding anything contained in this Act.
>
> (2) The rules of the Common Law, including the law merchant, save in so far as they are inconsistent with the express provisions of this Act, and in particular the rules relating to the law of principal and agent, and the effect of fraud, misrepresentation, duress or coercion, mistake or other invalidating cause, shall continue to apply to contracts for the sale of goods.
>
> (3) Nothing in this Act shall affect the written laws relating to bills of sale or any other written law relating to the sale of goods.

---

1 *Parker v Palmer* (1821) 4 B & Ald 387; *Lorymer v Smith* (1822) 1 B & C 1. See s 16 and s 13, Sale of Goods Act, Cap 318 (Barbados).

2 Section 54 and s 15(d), Sale of Goods Act, Cap 318 (Barbados); s 55, Sale of Goods Act; Cap 393 (Antigua and Barbuda); and s 64, Sale of Goods Act 1978 (Bermuda).

3 See, for example, Sale of Goods Act, Cap 318 (Barbados); Sale of Goods Act, Cap 393 (Antigua and Barbuda); Sale of Goods Act 1978 (Bermuda); Sale of Goods Act, Cap 261 (Belize); Sale of Goods Act, Ch 337 (The Bahamas); Sale of Goods Act (Jamaica); and Sale of Goods Act, Ch 82:30 (Trinidad and Tobago).

(4) The provisions of this Act relating to contracts of sale do not apply to any transaction in the form of a contract of sale which is intended to operate by way of mortgage, pledge, charge or other security.[4]

Similar savings clauses are contained in the legislation of other Commonwealth Caribbean countries.[5]

The sale of goods legislation enacted in the various jurisdictions of the Commonwealth Caribbean is based closely on the UK Sale of Goods Acts of 1893 and 1979. To the extent that the Caribbean legislation is ambiguous or silent, judicial decisions relating to the UK legislation are useful supplements to local case law in interpreting the Caribbean statutes. This process of interpretation must, however, be informed by an examination of the intention of the parties, so that the legislation is not interpreted so strictly as to produce a result that the parties could not reasonably have intended.

Types of goods covered

Sale of goods legislation applies to contracts for the sale of goods, whether absolute or conditional.[6] Contracts for the sale of goods are defined as contracts whereby the seller transfers or agrees to transfer the property in goods for consideration (that is, for a price). This definition includes contracts of sale between one part owner and another.[7] Goods are defined as all chattels personal other than *choses in action* and money, and can include ships,[8] building materials,[9] cars,[10] cattle[11] and alcoholic beverages.[12]

Contracts for the sale of goods are classified as 'agreements to sell' where transfer of the property is to take place at a future time. Agreements to sell become 'sales' when the relevant time elapses or the conditions in the contract for the transfer of property are fulfilled.

A contract for the sale of goods is called 'a sale' where the transfer takes place at the time when the contract is made.

---

4 See s 59, Sale of Goods Act, Ch 82:30 (Trinidad and Tobago); s 62, Sale of Goods Act 1978 (Bermuda); and s 59, Sale of Goods Act (Jamaica).

5 For example, see s 59, Sale of Goods Act, Cap 318 (Barbados); s 59, Sale of Goods Act, Cap 393 (Antigua and Barbuda); s 70, Sale of Goods Act 1978 (Bermuda); s 61, Sale of Goods Act, Cap 261 (Belize); s 59, Sale of Goods Act, Ch 337 (The Bahamas); and s 59, Sale of Goods Act (Jamaica).

6 See s 2, Sale of Goods Act, Cap 318 (Barbados); s 3, Sale of Goods Act, Cap 393 (Antigua and Barbuda); and s 3, Sale of Goods Act, Ch 82:30 (Trinidad and Tobago).

7 See s 3, Sale of Goods Act, Cap 318 (Barbados); s 3 Sale of Goods Act, Cap 393 (Antigua and Barbuda); and s 2, Sale of Goods Act 1978 (Bermuda).

8 See the Bahamian case of *Canadian Imperial Bank of Commerce v Owners of and all parties interested in the motor vessel 'New Light'* (1997) Supreme Court, The Bahamas, No 1217 of 1994, unreported [Carilaw BS 1997 SC 87]. See also *Behnke v Bede Shipping Company Limited* [1927] 1 KB 649; *Re Blythe Shipbuilding and Dry Docks Co* [1926] Ch 494.

9 *Baksh Trading as Rassul Baksh Sawmill and Hardware v Emile Ellias and Company Ltd* (1994) High Court, Trinidad and Tobago, No 950 of 1990, unreported [Carilaw TT 1994 HC 115].

10 *Mitchell v Petroleum Products Ltd* (1988) Supreme Court, The Bahamas, No 321, unreported [Carilaw BS 1988 SC 48].

11 *Sanchez v Quesnel* (1990) Court of Appeal, Trinidad and Tobago, No 49 of 1986, unreported [Carilaw TT 1991 CA 24].

12 *Panday v Baksh* (1981) High Court, Guyana, No 2139 of 1976, unreported [Carilaw GY 1981 HC 42].

The terms of the Sale of Goods Acts apply by analogy to contracts for work and materials. Thus, in *Samuels v Davis*,[13] the plaintiff, a dentist, contracted with the defendant to make a set of dentures for the defendant's wife. He made and delivered the dentures, but the defendant refused to pay for them on the ground that they were unusable. It was held that a term could be implied into the contract that the dentures were to be fit for their purpose, arising either (1) under the sale of goods legislation itself, or (2) by analogy with the legislation.

Subject matter of the contract

The Acts apply to contracts for the sale of goods, which may be *existing* goods already owned by the seller, or *future* goods, which are goods to be acquired or manufactured by the seller after the contract has been made.[14]

If, in the case of a contract for specific goods (that is, goods which are identified when the contract is made), those goods have been destroyed at the time the contract is made without the knowledge of the seller, then the contract is void.[15]

Further, if the goods perish *before the risk passes to the buyer* under the contract without any fault of either party, then the contract will be void.

The risk *prima facie* passes with the property. So, generally, the risk will pass to the buyer when the property is delivered to the buyer. This means that before the sale but after the agreement to sell, the risk remains with the seller.[16]

It should be noted that the parties are free to determine the time at which the property passes or the risk passes to the buyer and, in the case of such determinations, the rule that the risk passes with the property will not apply.[17]

Capacity to contract

The ability of minors, drunken persons and the mentally ill to enter into contractual (or quasi-contractual) obligations is governed by the substantial body of common law rules concerning the capacity to contract. The general rule is that such persons cannot enter into contracts, with the exception of contracts for necessaries. Capacity to contract is discussed in detail in Chapter 5.

Sale of goods legislation expressly preserves the body of law relating to capacity. For example, section 4 of the Sale of Goods Act (Trinidad and Tobago) provides:

> 4. Capacity to buy and sell is regulated by the general law concerning capacity to contract, and to transfer and acquire property. However, where necessaries are sold

---

13 [1943] KB 526; *Young & Marten Ltd v McManus Childs Ltd* [1969] 1 AC 454 and *Gloucestershire County Council v Richardson* [1969] 1 AC 480.

14 Section 6, Sale of Goods Act, Cap 318 (Barbados); s 7, Sale of Goods Act, Ch 82:30 (Trinidad and Tobago); and s 6, Sale of Goods Act (Jamaica).

15 Section 7, Sale of Goods Act, Cap 318 (Barbados); s 8, Sale of Goods Act, Ch 82:30 (Trinidad and Tobago); and s 7, Sale of Goods Act (Jamaica).

16 Section 8, Sale of Goods Act, Cap 318 (Barbados); s 9, Sale of Goods Act, Cap 303 (Antigua and Barbuda); and s 8, Sale of Goods Act (Jamaica).

17 Section 21, Sale of Goods Act, Cap 318 (Barbados); s 19, Sale of Goods Act, Cap 393 (Antigua and Barbuda); and s 18, Sale of Goods Act (Jamaica).

> and delivered to an infant or to a person who, by reason of mental incapacity or drunkenness, is incompetent to contract, he must pay a reasonable price therefor.[18]

Notably, the legislation defines necessaries as 'goods suitable to the condition in life of such infant (that is, minor) or other person and to his actual requirements at the time of the sale and delivery'. This definition is consistent with the common law definition of necessaries (see Chapter 5, above).

Formalities

Generally, contracts for the sale of goods may be made either orally or in writing, or a combination of both. They may also be implied from the conduct of the parties.

Legislation preserves the rules governing formalities under company law. For example, a company may have certain execution requirements that must be met before it can validly enter into a contract.[19]

Obligations under the contract

Price

The parties to a contract for the sale of goods may prescribe a price for the goods, or prescribe a manner for determining the price, or may determine the price in the course of their dealings.[20]

If the parties fail to determine the price in one of the above three ways, the buyer must pay a 'reasonable' price. A 'reasonable' price is a question of fact, to be determined in each case.[21]

The contracts to which the sale of goods legislation applies must be for 'money consideration', and so the term 'price' means cash consideration.[22] The Acts do not apply to contracts the consideration for which takes a different form, for example, payment in kind.

Depending on the circumstances, where the parties have not fixed the price at the time when the contract is alleged to have been made, it may be necessary to establish that the contract was actually concluded in the first place.[23] It is, however, perfectly valid for the parties to agree the terms of a contract but to agree that the price will be

---

18 See for example s 4, Sale of Goods Act, Cap 318 (Barbados); s 4, Sale of Goods Act, Cap 393 (Antigua and Barbuda); s 3, Sale of Goods Act, 1978 (Bermuda); s 4, Sale of Goods Act, Cap 261 (Belize); s 4, Sale of Goods Act, Ch 337 (The Bahamas); s 3, Sale of Goods Act (Jamaica); and s 4, Sale of Goods Act, Ch 82:30 (Trinidad and Tobago).

19 See, for example, ss 22–25, Companies Act, Cap 308 (Barbados) and; ss 22–25, Companies Act 1995 (Antigua and Barbuda) as to the execution formalities required in order for a company to enter into contracts.

20 Section 9(1), Sale of Goods Act, Cap 318 (Barbados); s 8, Sale of Goods Act 1978 (Bermuda); and s 10, Sale of Goods Act, Cap 261 (Belize).

21 Section 9(2), Sale of Goods Act, Cap 318 (Barbados); s 10(2), Sale of Goods Act, Cap 393 (Antigua and Barbuda) and s 9(2), Sale of Goods Act (Jamaica).

22 Section 3(1), Sale of Goods Act, Cap 318 (Barbados); s 3(1), Sale of Goods Act, Cap 393 (Antigua and Barbuda); and s 3(1), Sale of Goods Act, Ch 337 (The Bahamas) .

23 *May & Butcher v The King* [1934] 2 KB 17.

fixed later on, provided that the requisite ingredients for formation of a contract are present, and that the parties have shown an intention to be bound by the contract.[24]

Third party valuation

The parties to a contract for the sale of goods may agree for a third party to determine the price at a future date.

For instance, section 11(1) of the Sale of Goods Act of Antigua and Barbuda[25] provides:

> 11. (1) Where there is an agreement to sell goods on the terms that the price is to be fixed by the valuation of a third party, and such third party cannot or does not make such valuation, the agreement is avoided:
>
> Provided that if the goods or any part thereof have been delivered to and appropriated by the buyer he must pay a reasonable price therefor.

Thus, under sub-section (1), if the third party fails to make the valuation as agreed and the agreement is executory (that is, it has not yet been performed), then the agreement is rendered void. If, however, the goods have been completely or partially delivered, the buyer must pay a reasonable price for them.

Sub-section (2) provides further that if either party prevents the third party responsible for the valuation from carrying out the valuation, the innocent party may sue that party for damages:

> 11. (2) Where such third party is prevented from making the valuation by the fault of the seller or buyer, the party not in fault may maintain an action for damages against the party in fault.

Any valuation provided honestly and in good faith by a third party in accordance with this section will be binding on the parties, who will not be able to set aside the valuation. There is an exception in cases of fraud or collusion in the determination of the valuation, and in these cases the parties will be able to set it aside. Lord Denning MR confirmed this principle in *Campbell v Edwards*:[26]

> In former times (when it was thought that the valuer was not liable for negligence) the courts used to look for some way of upsetting a valuation which was shown to be wholly erroneous. They used to say that it could be upset, not only for fraud or collusion, but also on the ground of mistake. See, for instance, what I said in *Dean v Prince*.[27] But those cases have to be reconsidered now. I did reconsider them in the *Arenson* case.[28] I stand by what I there said. It is simply the law of contract. If two persons agree that the price of property should be fixed by a valuer on whom they agree, and he gives that valuation honestly and in good faith, they are bound by it. Even if he has made a mistake they are still bound by it. The reason is because they have agreed to be bound by it. If there were fraud or collusion, of course, it would be different. Fraud or collusion unravels everything . . .
>
> In my opinion, therefore, the landlord is bound by this valuation of £10,000. I would just like to add this. The position of a valuer is very different from an arbitrator. If a valuer is

24 *Hillas & Co Ltd v Arcos Ltd* [1932] All ER Rep 494; *Foley v Classique Coaches Ltd* [1934] 2 KB 1.

25 Cap 393.

26 [1976] 1 WLR 403.

27 [1954] 1 All ER 749, at 758, 759.

28 [1976] 1 All ER 785.

> negligent in making a valuation, he may be sued by the party—vendor or purchaser—who is injured by his wrong valuation. But an arbitrator is different. In my opinion he cannot be sued by either party to the dispute, even if he is negligent. The only remedy of the party is to set aside the award; and then only if it comes within the accepted grounds for setting it aside. If an arbitrator is guilty of misconduct, his award can be set aside. If he has gone wrong on a point of law, which appears on the face of it, it can be corrected by the court. But the arbitrator himself is not liable to be sued. I say this because I should be sorry if any doubt should be felt about it.
>
> This case is just a postscript to *Arenson v Casson Beckman Rutley & Co.*[29] The valuation is binding on the parties. The master and the judge were right and we dismiss the appeal.

This decision also confirms that where the basis for the valuation is wholly unfounded, the parties may sue the valuer for negligence.[30]

Conditions and warranties

At common law, terms are classified as conditions, warranties or intermediate terms. This is somewhat inconsistent with sale of goods legislation, which recognises only two classes of term: conditions and warranties (discussed below).

Whether time is of the essence

The condition as to time implied by the sale of goods legislation is a negative one. It specifies when time is *not* a condition, as opposed to laying down a positive term to be implied into contracts. For instance, section 11 of the Jamaican Sale of Goods Act reads as follows:

> 11. (1) Unless a different intention appears from the terms of the contract, stipulations as to time of payment are not deemed to be of the essence of a contract of sale.
>
> Whether any other stipulation as to time is of the essence of the contract or not, depends on the terms of the contract.
>
> (2) In a contract of sale, 'month' means *prima facie* calendar month.[31]

The legislation provides that, unless expressly stated in the contract, time will not be considered to be 'of the essence' of a contract for the sale of goods;[32] that is, a time stipulation will not be a condition entitling the innocent party to rescind the contract in the event of a breach. On the other hand, case law has confirmed that where time *is* made of the essence, a breach of a time stipulation will constitute a fundamental breach.[33]

Stipulations as to time of *payment* must be distinguished from stipulations as to time of *delivery*. The legislation makes it clear that the former will not be implied as

---

29 [1976] 1 All ER 785

30 See also *Arenson v Arenson and Casson Beckman Rutley & Co* [1976] 1 All ER 785 and *Wright v Frodoor* [1967] 1 WLR 506.

31 Cap 349.

32 See, for example, s 11(1), Sale of Goods Act, Cap 318 (Barbados); s 12(1), Sale of Goods Act, Cap 393 (Antigua and Barbuda); s 10(1), Sale of Goods Act 1978 (Bermuda); s 12(1), Sale of Goods Act, Cap 261 (Belize); s 12(1), Sale of Goods Act, Ch 337 (The Bahamas); s 11(1), Sale of Goods Act (Jamaica); and s 12(1) Sale of Goods Act, Ch 82:30 (Trinidad and Tobago).

33 *Steadman v Drunkle* [1916] 1 AC 275, 279; *Financings Ltd v Baldock* [1963] 2 QB 104, 120; *Bunge Corp v Tradax Export SA* [1980] 1 Lloyd's Rep 294, 305, 307, 309, 310 (affirmed [1981] 1 WLR 711); *Lombard North Central Plc v Butterworth* [1987] QB 527.

conditions in a contract for the sale of goods unless a different intention appears. For this reason, commercial contracts are often drafted so that stipulations as to time of delivery contemplate that time is of the essence. In this case, as well as under the legislation, failure to meet a specified delivery deadline will amount to breach of condition.[34]

Even where time has clearly been made of the essence under the terms of the contract, where one party gives the other party an extension of time, the parties will no longer be able to insist that time is of the essence. If the extension is granted with no fixed date for completion, time will be 'at large'.

An example of the operation of this principle is the Bahamian case of *Canadian Imperial Bank of Commerce v Owners of MV 'New Light'*.[35]

The facts were that the Admiralty Marshal entered into a contract for the sale of a ship, the 'New Light', to the plaintiff, L, on behalf of the owner. For various reasons, L was unable to complete the contract on time. L still wished to proceed with the contract, and the Admiralty Marshal agreed to an extension in time for completion in favour of L.

It later turned out that the Admiralty Marshal was unable to complete the sale after having been separately served with an injunction preventing him from selling the vessel. As the Admiralty Marshal had failed to complete the sale, L sued for return of its deposit for the sale paid under the terms of the contract. The Admiralty Marshal argued that, as the contract had made time of the essence, and L had in the first instance failed to complete on time, he was entitled to treat the contract at an end on the basis that the buyer, L, had fundamentally breached the contract. For this reason, he argued, he was entitled to forfeit the deposit.

It was held that, although time had been made of the essence at the inception of the contract, in light of the extension the Admiralty Marshal had granted and the concurrent failure to set a completion date, the Admiralty Marshal was not entitled to insist that time was of the essence, and he was ordered to return the deposit to L.

Waiver of obligations as to time

Under the sale of goods legislation, a buyer may waive any condition of a contract for the sale of goods. For instance, section 13 of the Bahamian Act provides:

> 13. (1) Where a contract of sale is subject to any condition to be fulfilled by the seller, the buyer may waive the condition, or may elect to treat the breach of such condition as a breach of warranty, and not as a ground for treating the contract as repudiated.

Thus, where time is of the essence under a contract for the sale of goods and a buyer accepts late delivery, he may be deemed to have waived the seller's breach of the condition as to time.

Time for delivery after waiver of a stipulation as to time

Where a buyer waives a stipulation as to time, but does not specify a new delivery date, it will be necessary to determine when delivery should be made. Section 30(2) of the Bahamian Sale of Goods Act[36] provides:

34 *CB Jutagir Hardware v Elegant Products Ltd* (1984) High Court, Trinidad and Tobago, No 277 of 1980, unreported [Carilaw TT 1984 HC 148].

35 (1997) Supreme Court, The Bahamas, No 1217 of 1994, unreported [Carilaw BS 1997 SC 87].

36 Ch 337. See also *Hughes v Metropolitan Railway Co* (1877), 2 App Cas 439; *Hartley v Hymans* [1920] 3 KB 475; *Charles Rickards Ltd v Oppenhaim* [1950] 1 KB 616; and *Tool Metal Manufacturing Co Ltd v Tungsten Electric Co Ltd* [1955] 1 WLR 761.

> 30. (2) Where under the contract of sale the seller is bound to send the goods to the buyer, but no time for sending them is fixed, the seller is bound to send them within a reasonable time.

Thus, where a buyer has not fixed a specific time for delivery, the seller cannot simply deliver the goods at his convenience. On the contrary, the seller will be under an obligation to deliver the goods within a reasonable time.

In such circumstances, it will be necessary to determine what is 'a reasonable time'. Where the sale of goods legislation makes references to time, the question of what is a reasonable time is a question of fact.[37]

In a Trinidadian case, *CB Jutagir Hardware v Elegant Products Ltd*,[38] the plaintiff contracted to purchase from the defendant a number of marble wash-basins and household fittings. The parties agreed that time was to be of the essence of the contract, and the delivery date was set for 12 October 1979. The first consignment was delivered late, on 16 October 1979, but the plaintiff nevertheless accepted the goods. However, a second consignment was rejected by him. It was held that the plaintiff had waived its right to insist that time was of the essence. Blackman J said:

> I come to the other point at issue which arises and it is whether the time for delivery, that is, 12th October, was of the essence of the contract and if so, whether there was a waiver as to time. In this regard, the plaintiff has not quarreled with the defendant in respect of the late delivery of the first batch; but he has been aggrieved by the second delivery . . .
>
> Now, Section 12(1) of the Sale of Goods Act, Ch 82:30 (the Act) provides that:
>
>> Unless a different intention appears from the terms of the contract, stipulations as to time of payment are not deemed to be of the essence of a contract of sale. Whether any other stipulation as to time is of the essence of the contract or not depends on the terms of the contract.
>
> The stipulation as to time . . . reads as follows:
>
>> Complete delivery to be effected no later than 12th October, 1979.
>
> Did the plaintiff waive its right to insist that the defendant comply with the date of delivery?
>
> In *WJ Alan Ltd v El Nasr Co*,[39] Lord Denning MR said:
>
>> The principle of waiver is simply this: if one party, by his conduct, leads another to believe that the strict rights arising under the contract will not be insisted on, intending that the other should act on that belief, and he does act on it, then the first party will not afterwards be allowed to insist on the strict legal rights when it would be inequitable for him to do so: see *Plasticmoda Societa per Azioni v Davidsons (Manchester) Ltd*.[40] There may be no consideration moving from him who benefits by the waiver. There may be no detriment to him by acting on it. There may be nothing in writing. Nevertheless, the one who waives his strict rights cannot afterwards insist on them. His strict rights are at any rate suspended so long as the waiver lasts. He may on occasion be able to revert to his strict legal rights for the future by giving reasonable notice in that behalf, or

37 Section 55, Sale of Goods Act, Cap 318 (Barbados); s 65, Sale of Goods Act 1978 (Bermuda); and s 57, Sale of Goods Act, Cap 261 (Belize).

38 (1984) High Court, Trinidad and Tobago, No 277 of 1980, unreported [Carilaw TT 1984 HC 148].

39 [1972] 2 All ER 127, at 140.

40 [1952] 1 Lloyd's Rep 527.

> otherwise making it plain by his conduct that he will thereafter insist on them: see *Tool Metal Manufacturing Co Ltd v Tungsten Electrical Co Ltd.*

Now Jutagir, having accepted the first batch of goods and having communicated with the defendant to the effect that future deliveries would be accepted provided of course that in the case of wash basins these would be round, in my view either waived his right to insist that the delivery date of 12th October was still of the essence or at least was estopped by his conduct in complaining that the goods were not delivered on time. Indeed, the only reason why the goods were rejected by Jutagir was that the goods did not conform to a sample submitted by the defendant, not because they were delivered out of time. He cannot reject goods on one ground and rely on another ground later for their non-acceptance. *Panchaud Freres SA v Etablissements General Grain Co,*[41] where Lord Denning MR said:

> If a man, who is entitled to reject goods on a certain ground, so conducts himself as to lead the other to believe that he is not relying on that ground, then he cannot afterwards set it up as a ground of rejection, when it should be unfair or unjust to allow him so to do.

Since he had waived his right to reject the goods or is estopped by his conduct in insisting on delivery at the stipulated time, the plaintiff ought to have given the defendant a reasonable time within which to deliver them thus making time of the essence before resorting to repudiating the contract. He did not do so. I think it was wrong in not giving the defendant reasonable notice to deliver the items of goods other than the wash basins if he intended to insist on making time of the essence in respect of those articles: *Hartley v Haynes.*[42] In that case, McCardie J based his decision on the variation of the original agreement with respect to the contract time; but I think the principle is applicable as well to this case. See also *Panoutsos v Raymond Hadley Corporation of New York*[43] and *Charles Rickards Ltd v Oppenheim.*[44] In the latter case, Denning LJ said:

> But in my view it is unnecessary to determine whether it was a contract for the sale of goods or a contract for work and labour. Because, whatever it was, the defendant was entitled to give notice bringing the matter to a head. It would be most unreasonable if the defendant, having been lenient and waived the initial expressed time, should, by so doing, have prevented himself from ever thereafter insisting on reasonably quick delivery. In my judgment he was entitled to give a reasonable notice making time of the essence of the matter. Adequate protection to the suppliers is given by the requirement that the notice should be reasonable.

In other words, the plaintiff acted unjustly and wrongly in not giving notice to the defendant before terminating the contract, since he had previously behaved in a manner which led the defendant to believe that he was not insisting on deliveries being made at the stipulated date.

Implied terms as to title

The sale of goods legislation implies certain terms relating to title. For example, section 13 of the Jamaican Act provides:

> 13. In a contract of sale, unless the circumstances of the contract are such as to show a different intention, there is –

41 [1970] 1 Lloyd's Rep 53, at 57.
42 [1920] 3 QB 475, at 495.
43 [1917] 2 KB 473, at 478.
44 [1950] 1KB 616, at 624.

(a) an implied condition on the part of the seller that in the case of a sale he has a right to sell the goods, and that in the case of an agreement to sell he will have a right to sell the goods at the time when the property is to pass;

(b) an implied warranty that the buyer shall have and enjoy quiet possession of the goods;

(c) an implied warranty that the goods shall be free from any charge or incumbrance in favour of any third party, not declared or known to the buyer before or at the time when the contract is made.

Thus, the sale of goods legislation implies a condition into contracts for the sale of goods that the seller has (or, at the time when the property is to pass, will have) the right to sell the goods. It also implies warranties that the buyer will enjoy quiet possession, and that the goods are unencumbered (that is, that they are free from liens, security or other third party interests) with respect to interests not known or declared to the buyer before or at the time when the contract was made.

In a Jamaican case, *Noble's Executive Auto Brokers Ltd v Brantner*,[45] N sold a car to B, who subsequently spent money putting it in order. While B's wife was driving the car, it was seized by the police, who took the keys. Neither the purchase price nor the car were returned to B. B sued N for breach of contract. It was held by the Jamaican Court of Appeal that N had breached the implied condition that it had the right to sell the goods and the implied warranty that B should enjoy quiet possession of the goods.

Where the parties have excluded the terms implied under the legislation, the purchaser in a contract for the sale of goods may wish to protect his interests by insisting on an express warranty from the seller that he has the right to sell the goods, and that the goods are unencumbered by third party interests (such as security interests over the property in respect of a loan made by a third party to the seller).

Implied conditions as to fitness for purpose and merchantable quality

Section 16 of the Bahamian Sale of Goods Act[46] reads:

16. Subject to the provisions of this Act and of any Act in that behalf, there is no implied warranty or condition as the quality or fitness for any particular purpose of goods supplied under a contract of sale, except as follows –

(a) where the buyer, expressly or by implication, makes known to the seller the particular purpose for which the goods are required, so as to show that the buyer relies on the seller's skill or judgment, and the goods are of a description which it is in the course of the seller's business to supply (whether he be the manufacturer or not), there is an implied condition that the goods shall be reasonably fit for such purpose:

Provided that in the case of a contract for the sale of a specified article under the patent or other trade name, there is no implied condition as to its fitness for any particular purpose; . . .

(b) where goods are bought by description from a seller who deals in goods of that description (whether he be the manufacturer or not), there is an implied condition that the goods shall be of merchantable quality:

45 (1996) Court of Appeal, Jamaica, No 89 of 1995, unreported [Carilaw JM 1996 CA 13].

46 Ch 337.

Provided that if the buyer has examined the goods, there shall be no implied condition as regards defects which such examination ought to have revealed;

(c) an implied warranty or condition as to quality or fitness for a particular purpose may be annexed by the usage of trade;

(d) an express warranty or condition does not negative a warranty or condition implied by this Act unless inconsistent therewith.

Implied condition as to fitness for purpose

The legislation implies a condition that goods are fit for the purpose that they were intended to fulfil, subject to the following requirements. First, the buyer must have expressly or by implication made the purpose of the goods known to the buyer. Second, it must have been shown that the buyer was relying on the seller's skill or judgment in relation to those goods. Finally, the goods must have been purchased from a seller in the course of his business, involving the sale of goods of that description.[47]

THE BUYER MUST MAKE THE PURPOSE KNOWN

A buyer cannot rely on the implied condition as to fitness for purpose unless he has made the purpose known to the seller.

In a Trinidadian case, *Baksh v Emile Elias & Co Ltd*,[48] B purchased sheets of plywood from E, stating that he required plywood for concrete decking, but without specifying the grade of plywood required. E supplied the plaintiff with 'sturdi-floor' plywood, which was of poor quality and became damaged on its first use. B sued E for damages for breach of the implied condition, under section 16 of the Trinidad and Tobago Sale of Goods Act, that the plywood was to be fit for its intended purpose. Evidence submitted by E, which was accepted by the court, showed that sturdi-floor plywood could, in some circumstances and with varying success, be used for concrete decking if handled in a certain manner. It was held that if B had required a specific grade of plywood which would be capable of multiple uses, he ought to have made this clear to the seller, and he had failed to do so. Consequently, B's action failed.

THE BUYER MUST HAVE RELIED ON THE SELLER'S SKILL AND JUDGMENT

The first two conditions required for the implication of the condition as to fitness for purpose (that is, the 'purpose' and 'reliance' conditions) are independent, but, by choosing a seller who trades in the goods in question, the buyer will generally be taken to have indicated his reliance. In *Grant v Australian Knitting Mills Ltd*,[49] Lord Wright described the court's approach:

47 Section 15(a), Sale of Goods Act, Cap 318 (Barbados); s 16(a), Sale of Goods Act, Ch 337 (The Bahamas); s 16(3), Sale of Goods Act, Ch 82:30 (Trinidad and Tobago); and s 15(a), Sale of Goods Act (Jamaica). See also *Kraakman (dba The Woodshop) v Sterling* (2011) High Court, BVI, HCVAP 2010/012, unreported.

48 (1994) High Court, Trinidad and Tobago, No 950 of 1990, unreported [Carilaw TT 1994 HC 115]. See also *Pries v Last* [1903] 2 KB 148; *Grant v Australian Knitting Mills Ltd* [1936] AC 85; *Steele v Gemini Concrete Supplies Ltd* (1997) High Court, Trinidad and Tobago, No 1536 of 1987, unreported [Carilaw TT 1997 HC 143]; *Nabbie v HE Robinson and Co Ltd* (1986) High Court, Trinidad and Tobago, No 426 of 1972, unreported [Carilaw TT 1986 HC 118]; and *International Meters Ltd v Thomas* (2004) Court of Appeal, BVI, No 7 of 2002, unreported [Carilaw VG 2004 CA 6].

49 [1936] AC 85.

> The reliance will seldom be express: it will usually arise by implication from the circumstances; thus to take a case like that in question, of a purchase from a retailer, the reliance will be in general inferred from the fact that a buyer goes to the shop in the confidence that the tradesman has selected his stock with skill and judgment.

The conjoined appeals in *Ashington Piggeries Ltd v Christopher Hill Ltd* and *Christopher Hill Ltd v Norsildmel*[50] are instructive on the question of what constitutes reliance. That case raised several issues, including fitness for purpose and reliance, merchantable quality, and sale by description.

The facts were that the plaintiff purchased mink feed from the defendants which turned out to contain an ingredient which was poisonous to mink. The mink that ate the feed died as a result of the poison. The defendants were principally in the business of making feed for poultry, pheasants, calves and pigs, and did not have prior experience or knowledge of making food for mink.

It was held that the defendants were liable for breach of the implied conditions as to fitness for purpose and merchantable quality. The court held that the buyer had relied on the skill and judgment of the sellers, even though that reliance was only partial. It was not necessary for the buyer's reliance to be total and exclusive. The fact that the buyer had placed the order with the sellers was evidence of reliance. The plaintiff buyer had relied on the defendant to ensure that the ingredients used in the mink feed were of a suitable quality for the purpose for which it was intended, namely, compounding animal foodstuffs.

Notably, if the sellers had been able to prove that the offending ingredient was fatal to mink by reason of an idiosyncrasy of mink unknown within their sphere of expertise and that the feed could have been safely fed to animals generally, then it would not have been possible to say that the buyer had relied on the sellers' skill and judgment as to the ingredients in the food.

The judgment in *Ashington Piggeries* was affirmed by the Jamaican Court of Appeal in *Appleton Hall Ltd v T Geddes Grant Distributors Ltd*.[51] Here, it was held that the defendant seller was liable to the plaintiff buyer for breach of an implied condition that a fungicide purchased by the buyer would be fit for its intended purchase, which was to treat papaya plants being cultivated for export.

In this case, the seller's representative, who held a Bachelor of Science degree in Zoology and Biology and had training and experience in the application of fungicides, had visited the buyer's farm and advised on the choice of pesticide to be used. The pesticide had a destructive effect on the papaya crops and the buyer brought an action against the seller, who argued that the fungicide was appropriate as it had been successfully used in parts of Jamaica, and whether the fungicide would have negative effects on the plants depended on the way in which it was applied.

It was held that the seller was liable for breach of the contract of sale because, although not explicitly stated, it would be reasonable to conclude that the buyer was seeking a product that would have little or no deleterious effect on the papaya plants. Further, reaffirming the principle as to reliance laid down in the *Ashington Piggeries* case, the court held that in deciding to place an order with the seller, the buyer was placing reliance on the seller to provide a fungicide fit for the use for which it was intended.

50 [1971] 1 All ER 847.
51 [2011] JMCA Civ 30.

Sale in the course of business

This requirement was considered in a Bermudian case, *Sousa v Warner*,[52] where it was held that a marine services engineer, who also undertook motor vehicle spray painting, was not selling goods in the course of his business when he sold a defective boat to a purchaser, a medical doctor. There was no evidence that the seller under the contract was in the habit of selling boats; rather, it was a 'one-off' transaction relating to a boat which he had bought and used for fishing. The buyer's contention that there was an implied term as to fitness for purpose deriving from the Bermudian Sale of Goods Act[53] was rejected. Instead, the buyer was able to successfully plead breach of express warranties as to the model of the boat, and to the effect that the boat was in excellent condition.

Similarly, in *Kempadoo v Chin*,[54] it was held that the plaintiff, K, had failed to establish that C, the seller of a racehorse, was selling the horse in the course of a business. There, C had suggested to K that the horse would be capable of performing as a stud horse, although the horse had never been used before for that purpose. It was later discovered by K that the horse was impotent and therefore unable to impregnate any mares. K sued C for breach of the implied condition of fitness for purpose under the Sale of Goods Ordinance[55] of Guyana. It was held that C, being 'an experienced owner and trainer of racehorses . . . and . . . not a professional breeder of racehorses' could not have been taken to warrant the fitness of the horse for stud purposes, and K's action was dismissed.

Goods 'of that description'

As for the provision in the legislation that goods 'of that description' must be sold by the seller in the course of business, this requirement will not be construed restrictively. 'Goods of that description' will be taken to mean 'goods of that kind'. Thus, in the *Ashington Piggeries* case, the sale by the defendants of mink feed was held to be in the course of their business notwithstanding that they primarily sold feed for other types of animals. Furthermore, a person could be in the course of selling goods of a particular description even if he had not previously accepted orders for that type of goods. The 'course of business' requirement applies also to the implied condition as to merchantable quality, and so this principle applies equally in that context.

The legislation further provides that a warranty or condition as to the quality or fitness for purpose of goods may be implied by the usage of trade. Arguably, this provision adds very little, because courts are able to imply such terms in respect of a range of contracts and not just contracts for the sale of goods.[56]

Sale under trade name

There is an exception where goods are sold under a patent or other trade name, where no condition as to fitness for purpose will be implied.

---

52 (1995) Court of Appeal, Bermuda, No 4 of 1994, unreported [Carilaw BM 1995 CA 27]. See also *Davies v Sumner* [1984] 3 All ER 831.

53 Sale of Goods Act 1978.

54 (1974) High Court, Guyana, No 43 of 1971, unreported [Carilaw GY 1974 HC 2]. See also *Marcano v Quamina* (1975) High Court, Trinidad and Tobago, No 2369 of 1969, unreported [Carilaw TT 1975 HC 53].

55 Cap 333.

56 See Chapter 6, above.

However, this is only the case where it is clear from the circumstances that the buyer specified the trade name so as to indicate that he was satisfied, rightly or wrongly, that the goods would fulfil the intended purpose and that he was not relying on the judgment or skill of the seller, regardless of the extent of the seller's judgment or skill.[57]

BURDEN OF PROOF

The burden of proving that the buyer made the purpose of the goods known to the seller lies on the buyer. Once this burden has been discharged, the onus shifts to the seller to prove that the goods were, at the time of sale, fit for the purpose for which they were sold.[58]

Implied condition as to merchantable quality

Where goods are bought 'by description' from a seller who deals in goods of that description (whether as manufacturer or not), there is an implied condition that the goods will be of 'merchantable quality'.[59]

DEFINITION OF 'MERCHANTABLE QUALITY'

It is uncommon for the Commonwealth Caribbean Sale of Goods Acts to provide for a definition of the term 'merchantable quality'. This is also true in respect of the UK Sale of Goods Acts of 1873 and 1979, on which the Caribbean legislation was modelled. Consequently, there is a significant body of case law in which courts have sought to provide a definition.[60] These authorities suggest that, in essence, goods will not be of merchantable quality if they have latent defects (a) which would render the goods unfit for use and (b) in respect of which the buyer would demand either a reduction in price or special terms.

In the High Court decision in *Australian Knitting Mills v Grant*[61] (the Court of Appeal case is discussed above), it was held that, in order for goods to be of a merchantable quality, they should 'be in such a state that a buyer, fully acquainted with the facts, and therefore knowing what hidden defects exist and not being limited to their apparent condition, would buy them without abatement of the price obtainable for such goods if in reasonable sound order and condition without special terms'.

---

57 *Baldry v Marshall* [1925] 1 KB 260.

58 *Meadows v Quality Auto-Sale Ltd* (1998) Supreme Court, The Bahamas, No 206 of 1982, unreported [Carilaw BS 1988 SC 44].

59 Section 15(b), Sale of Goods Act, Cap 318 (Barbados); s 16(b), Sale of Goods Act, Ch 337 (The Bahamas); s16(2), Sale of Goods Act, Ch 82:30 (Trinidad and Tobago) and s 15(b), Sale of Goods Act (Jamaica). See also *Kraakman (dba The Woodshop) v Sterling* (2011) High Court, BVI, HCVAP 2010/012, unreported and *Steele v Gemini Concrete Supplies Ltd* (1997) High Court, Trinidad and Tobago, No 1536 of 1987, unreported [Carilaw TT 1997 HC 143].

60 See the definition of the term 'merchantable quality' at s 16(6) of the Trinidad and Tobago Act, which provides:

> 16(6) Goods of any kind are of merchantable quality within the meaning of subsection (2) if they are fit for the purpose or purposes for which goods of that kind are commonly bought (and where appropriate as durable) as it is reasonable to expect having regard to any description applied to them, the price if relevant, and all the other relevant circumstances.

61 (1930), 50 CLR 387, at 418.

When the case was later heard by the Privy Council, Lord Reid[62] elaborated on the definition, saying:

> 'Merchantable' does not mean that the thing is saleable in the market simply because it looks all right; it is not merchantable . . . if it has defects unfitting it for its only proper use but not apparent on ordinary examination.

In *Hardwick Game Farm v Suffolk Agricultural Poultry Producers Association*,[63] Lord Reid described the meaning of the phrase as 'commercially saleable'. He explained the definition in the following terms:

> I take first subsection (2) because it is of more general application. It applies to all sales by description where the seller deals in such goods. There may be a question whether the sale of a particular article is not really a sale by description but that does not arise here: these are clearly sales by description. Then it is a condition (unless excluded by the contract) that the goods must be of merchantable quality. Merchantable can only mean commercially saleable. If the description is a familiar one it may be that in practice only one quality of goods answers that description – then that quality and only that quality is merchantable quality. Or it may be that various qualities of goods are commonly sold under that description – then it is not disputed that the lowest quality commonly so sold is what is meant by merchantable quality: it is commercially saleable under that description. I need not consider here what expansion or adaptation of the statutory words is required where there is a sale of a particular article or a sale under a novel description. Here the description 'ground nut extractions' had been in common use.

In *Cehave NV v Bremer Handelsgesellschaft mbh, 'The Hansa Nord'*,[64] Lord Denning applied the definition of merchantable quality in the Supply of Goods (Implied Terms) Act 1973 (UK) by analogy to contracts for the sale of goods made before the Act's entry into force. This definition is helpful in interpreting sale of goods legislation in the Commonwealth Caribbean. It reads:

> Goods of any kind are of merchantable quality within the meaning of this Act if they are as fit for the purpose or purposes for which goods of that kind are commonly bought as it is reasonable to expect having regard to any description applied to them, the price (if relevant) and all other relevant circumstances; and any reference in this Act to unmerchantable goods shall be construed accordingly.

Having cited the above definition, Lord Denning continued:

> In applying that definition, it is as well to remember that, by the statute, we are dealing with an implied condition, strictly so called, and not a warranty. For any breach of it, therefore, the buyer is entitled to reject the goods: or, alternatively, if he chooses to accept them or has accepted them, he has a remedy in damages. In these circumstances, I should have thought a fair way of testing merchantability would be to ask a commercial man: was the breach such that the buyer should be able to reject the goods?

62 See also *Bristol Tramways Co Ltd v Fiat Motors Ltd* [1910] 2 KB 841; *Henry Kendall & Son v William Lillico & Sons Ltd* [1969] 2 AC 31; *Cammell Laird & Co Ltd v The Manganese Bronze & Brass Co Ltd* [1934] AC 402; *Bartlett v Sydney Marcus Ltd* [1965] 1 WLR 1013; *B S Brown & Son Ltd v Craiks Ltd* [1970] 1 All ER 823; *H Beecham & Co Pty Ltd v Francis Howard & Co Pty Ltd* [1921] VLR 428; and *George Wills & Co Ltd v Davids Pty Ltd* (1956–57) 98 CLR 77.

63 [1969] 2 AC 31.

64 [1976] 1 QB 44.

Goods are unmerchantable if they cannot be used for any purpose for which those goods would normally be used.[65] However, the goods need not be perfect in order to be of merchantable quality.[66]

Although the courts have grappled with the issue of the definition of 'merchantable quality', the question of whether the goods in question are merchantable depends on the tenor of the contract itself, and the circumstances of the case[67] at the time of the sale.[68] In *BS Brown & Son Ltd v Craiks Ltd*,[69] Lord Reid stated that:

> Judicial observations can never be regarded as complete definitions: they must be read in the light of the facts and issues raised in the particular case. I do not think it is possible to frame, except in the vaguest terms, a definition of 'merchantable quality' which can apply to every kind of case.

It has also been stated in a St Lucian case that 'any attempt to forge some exhaustive, positive and specific definition of the term would be an exercise in futility'.[70]

The Bahamian case of *Debarros v Quality Auto Sales Ltd*[71] is illustrative of the proposition that resolution of the issue of merchantable quality depends on the facts of each case. This case also demonstrates that the reasonable expectations of the purchaser must be taken into account when considering merchantability. Here, the plaintiff, B, purchased from the defendant, Q, a Suzuki motor car, which B later discovered to have spots of rust on its exterior and a rear window which leaked when it rained. In deciding whether or not the car was of merchantable quality within section 16(b) of the Sale of Goods Act, Ch 337, Gonsalves-Sabola CJ, in the absence of any definition of 'merchantable quality' in the Bahamian Act, adopted the statutory definition approved by Lord Denning in the *'Hansa Nord'* case (above). In the instant case, no fault had been found with the car in 'locomotive respects: the engine was good', and the vehicle 'ran flawlessly as a motor vehicle'. Referring to a previous judgment under the UK Sale of Goods Act, where a Range Rover was held not to be of merchantable quality, Gonsalves-Sabola CJ continued:

> Mustill LJ [in deciding a previous case concerning the unmerchantable quality of a Range Rover car][72] was dealing with a motor car of obviously higher class than the bottom-of-the-line Suzuki which would not induce in a purchaser the same range and level of expectations. The question to be answered is: was the Suzuki at the time of its

65 *Cammell Laird & Co Ltd v The Manganese Bronze & Brass Co Ltd* [1934] AC 402.

66 *Bartlett v Sydney Marcus Ltd* [1965] 1 WLR 1013.

67 *Ibid.*

68 *Oldham and Oldham v Maura's Marine Ltd* (1997) Supreme Court, The Bahamas, No 18 of 1995, unreported [Carilaw BS 1997 SC 54].

69 [1970] 1 WLR 752, at 754.

70 *St Lucia Motor & General Insurance Co Ltd v Northwest Ltd* (2002) High Court, St Lucia, No 473 of 1998, unreported [Carilaw LC 2002 HC 22], 15 *per* Hariprashad-Charles J].

71 (1990) Supreme Court, The Bahamas, No 1227 of 1983, unreported [Carilaw BS 1990 SC 18]. See also *Quality Auto Sales Limited v Bell* (2001) Supreme Court, The Bahamas, No 91 of 1997, unreported [Carilaw BS 2001 SC 22]; *Industria Petroquimica Dominicana C&A v Motivation Processors Ltd* (2008) Supreme Court, Jamaica, No 14 of 2000, unreported [Carilaw JM 2008 SC 50]; and *Richards v Universal Supplied Limited* (1992) High Court, Grenada, No 445 of 1987, unreported [Carilaw GD 1992 HC 9].

72 See *Rogers and Another v Parish (Scarborough) Ltd and Another* [1987] 1 QB 933, per Mustill LJ.

> purchase, with the latent defects which later manifested themselves, as fit for the purpose for which it was bought as the purchaser could reasonably expect? On the case made by the plaintiff, I cannot place his now unwanted Suzuki motor car within the 'congeries of defects' cases. Applying the authorities cited above to the facts before me, I do not conclude that, at the time of purchase of the motor car, it was not of merchantable quality, therefore the defendant has not been in breach of that implied condition under section 16(b) of the Act.
>
> The plaintiff, however, was entitled under his contract with the defendant, to feel that pride and joy which springs from the external appearance of newness of a car he bought as new and, what is more important, that sense of ordinary security from the elements and the discomfort and discomfiture of wet and malodorous carpeting which a water proof vehicle would ensure. Why else does a motor car have a roof and windows which can be closed?

Thus, while deciding that there had been no breach of condition under section 16(b), Gonsalves-Sabola CJ held that the plaintiff was 'entitled under section 53(1)(b) of the Act to a measure of damages for breach of warranty or, as Lord Denning's hypothetical commercial man would say, "a price allowance" for the latent defects' which later became apparent.

In *Baptiste v Robinson*,[73] the High Court of Trinidad and Tobago considered the definition of merchantable quality, in circumstances where the defendant had, by way of sale by description, purported to sell a new car to the plaintiff. It turned out that the car was in fact second-hand, and the plaintiff sued the defendant for breach of contract. It was held that the sale of a second-hand car as 'new' amounted to a breach of the implied condition of merchantable quality; though, since the plaintiff had accepted the car and thereby affirmed the contract, he had lost his right to rescind. Collymore J considered both the circumstances of the case, and the question of whether a reasonable person acting reasonably would have accepted the car:

> The term 'merchantable quality' is not defined in the Act, but a test frequently referred to was given by Farwell J in the case of *Bristol Tramways Carriage Co Ltd v Fiat Motors Ltd*[74] that:
>
> > The phrase in section 14(2), is, in my opinion, used as meaning that the article is of such a quality and in such a condition that a reasonable man acting reasonably would after a full examination accept it under the circumstances of the case in performance of his offer to buy that article; whether he buys it for his own use or to sell again.
>
> It is my respectful view the test enunciated above comprehensively sums up the expectations of a member of the public walking in to a showroom to buy a car . . . Being a sale by description the seller warrants the merchantability of the goods (s 16(b)).

Similarly, in *Swanson v Caribbean Cabinets Co Ltd*,[75] where a set of cabinets sold to the buyer were infested with beetles, it was held that the seller had breached the implied condition as to merchantability. It was clear from the buyer's evidence that she would not have agreed to pay the contract price for the cabinets had she known they were so infested.

---

73 (1985) High Court, Trinidad and Tobago, No 1899 of 1981, unreported [Carilaw TT 1985 HC 54].

74 [1971] 2 KB 831, at 114.

75 (2009) High Court, Barbados, No 1518 of 2002, unreported [Carilaw BB 2009 HC 21].

The price paid for the goods in question will also be relevant in determining what qualities the buyer could reasonably expect in order for the goods to be merchantable within the meaning of the legislation. For example, in *Thomas v City Motors Ltd*,[76] the High Court of Antigua and Barbuda held that the buyer of 'the cheapest bus on the market' could not reasonably have expected the bus to be durable. Accordingly, the buyer's action against the seller for breach of contract on the basis of the unfitness for purpose and unmerchantability of the bus was dismissed.

Other conditions

As is the case with implied conditions as to fitness for purpose, the condition as to merchantable quality is subject to a number of requirements. First, the goods must be bought 'by description'. Secondly, as mentioned above, the goods must be bought from a dealer in goods of that description.

As discussed above, in considering whether a seller has sold goods in the course of his business, it will be sufficient for the seller to be in the business of selling goods of that *category or kind*. It is not necessary for the seller to have been in the business of selling precisely those goods which formed the subject matter of the contract.[77]

The legislation makes clear that where the buyer has examined the goods, there will be no implied condition in relation to defects which the buyer's examination ought to have revealed. This provision reflects the *caveat emptor* (buyer beware) rule.[78]

The question of merchantability must be decided at the time when the property in the goods passes.[79]

Sale by description

Section 14 of the Jamaican Sale of Goods Act provides:

> 14. Where there is a contract for the sale of goods by description, there is an implied condition that the goods shall correspond with the description; and if the sale be by sample, as well as by description, it is not sufficient that the bulk of the goods corresponds with the sample if the goods do not also correspond with the description.

Where the sale of goods legislation applies, it is an implied condition that goods sold according to a description given by the seller will match that description. Thus, there were breaches of the condition where a car was advertised as a 1961 model, when in fact it consisted of two halves welded together, and only one of the halves dated from 1961,[80] and where the seller of a bus falsely described the engine as 'practically

---

76 (2003) High Court, Antigua and Barbuda, No 23 of 2002, unreported [Carilaw AG 2003 HC 55].

77 *Ashington Piggeries Ltd and another v Christopher Hill Ltd; Christopher Hill Ltd v Norsildmel* [1971] 1 All ER 847.

78 Section 15(b), Sale of Goods Act, Cap 318 (Barbados) s 16(6), Sale of Goods Act, Ch 337 (The Bahamas); and 16(2)(b), Sale of Goods Act, Ch 82:30 (Trinidad and Tobago).

79 *Advance Inc v National Fisheries Limited* (1989) High Court, Barbados, No 984 of 1987, unreported [Carilaw BB 1989 HC 33].

80 *Beale v Taylor* [1967] 3 All ER 253.

new', but the vehicle turned out to be 'little more than a shell'.[81] Similarly, goods sold partially by way of sample and partially by way of description must match the description. It is not sufficient for them to simply match the sample.

Sale by sample

As to sale by sample, section 17 of the Trinidad and Tobago Sale of Goods Act provides:

> 17. (1) A contract of sale is a contract for sale by sample where there is a term in the contract, express or implied, to that effect.
>
> (2) In the case of a contract for sale by sample, there is –
>
> (a) an implied condition that the bulk shall correspond with the sample in quality;
>
> (b) an implied condition that the buyer shall have a reasonable opportunity of comparing the bulk with the sample;
>
> (c) an implied condition that the goods shall be free from any defect rendering them unmerchantable which would not be apparent on reasonable examination of the sample.
>
> (3) In subsection (2)(c) 'unmerchantable' is to be construed in accordance with section 16(6).

This section provides that in a sale by sample, three conditions will be implied: (1) that the bulk corresponds to the sample in quality; (2) that the buyer will have a reasonable chance to compare the goods with the sample; and (3) that the goods will be free from defects rendering them unmerchantable (except in the case of defects which would be apparent on reasonable inspection of the sample).

Where condition to be treated as warranty

The legislation allows the buyer (but not the seller) to waive any condition in a contract for the sale of goods, or to treat the breach as a breach of warranty instead of a breach of condition.[82]

The legislation appears to affirm the common law test for classifying terms by providing that whether a stipulation in a contract for sale is a condition or a warranty depends on the construction of the contract.[83] Thus, in *Debarros v Quality Auto Sales Ltd*,[84] as we have seen, Gonsalves-Sabola CJ, found that the fact that the car sold had rust spots and a leaky window was not sufficient to constitute a breach of an implied condition as to merchantable quality. Accordingly, the buyer was not entitled to rescind the contract of sale; but the court went on to hold that he was 'entitled under section 53(1)(b) of the [Bahamian] Act to a measure of damages for breach of warranty

---

81 *Procope v Stanley* (1994) High Court, St Kitts and Nevis, No 165 of 1993, unreported [Carilaw KN 1994 HC 9].

82 Section 12(1)(a), Sale of Goods Act, Cap 318 (Barbados); s 13(1), Sale of Goods Act, Cap 393 (Antigua and Barbuda); and s 12(1)(a), Sale of Goods Act (Jamaica) and; *Kraakman (dba The Woodshop) v Sterling* (2011) High Court, BVI, HCVAP 2010/012, unreported.

83 *L Schuler A G v Wickman Machine Tool Sales Ltd* [1973] 2 All ER 39. See also Chapter 6.

84 (1990) Supreme Court, The Bahamas, No 1227 of 1983, unreported [Carilaw BS 1990 SC 18].

or, as Lord Denning's hypothetical commercial man would say, "a price allowance" for the latent defects which became patent after purchase and use'.

An important provision in the Sale of Goods Acts is that, subject to contrary terms in the contract, where the buyer has accepted goods under the contract, any conditions which are breached by the seller must be treated only as warranties and not as a basis for terminating the contract.[85] Under the Acts, 'the buyer is deemed to have accepted the goods when he intimates to the seller that he has accepted them, or when the goods have been delivered to him, and he does any act in relation to them which is inconsistent with the ownership of the seller, or when, after the lapse of a reasonable time, he retains the goods without intimating to the seller that he has rejected them.'[86]

Thus, for instance, in *Procope v Stanley*,[87] where, in a contract for the sale of a bus, there was a breach of the implied condition that goods shall correspond with their description, the High Court of St Kitts/Nevis held that since the buyer had taken delivery of the vehicle and driven it for a distance of more than 23,000 miles, the breach of condition was to be treated as a breach of warranty giving rise only to a claim for damages.

The time at which property transfers

The question of when property passes is important as it determines, among other things, when the goods are at the seller's risk and when this risk passes to the buyer. This is so because there is a presumption that risk passes with the property in the goods.[88]

On the one hand, for the purpose of determining whether goods are the subject matter of a contract, goods may be classified according to when they are acquired by the seller or when they come into existence. The legislation distinguishes, in that instance, between existing goods, that is, goods which are owned or possessed by the seller at the time of the contract, and future goods, which are goods to be made or acquired by the seller after the contract is made.

On the other hand, for the purpose of determining the time at which property in the goods passes, the legislation draws a distinction based on whether or not the goods have been identified and agreed. Thus, the legislation categorises goods passing to the buyer as either specific goods or ascertained goods.

For example, sections 17 and 18 of the Jamaican Sale of Goods Act provide as follows:

---

85 Section 12(1)(c), Sale of Goods Act, Cap 318 (Barbados); s 13(2), Sale of Goods Act, Cap 393 (Antigua and Barbuda); and s 12(1)(b), Sale of Goods Act (Jamaica).

86 Section 36, Sale of Goods Act, Ch 337 (The Bahamas); s 36, Sale of Goods Act (Jamaica); and s 13(3), Sale of Goods Act, Cap 393 (Antigua and Barbuda).

87 (1994) High Court, St Kitts and Nevis, No 165 of 1993, unreported [Carilaw KN 1994 HC 9]. See also *Abbott (WJ) & Sons Ltd v Duncan* (1971) Court of Appeal, St Vincent and the Grenadines, Civ App No 3 of 1970, unreported [Carilaw VC 1971 CA 6]; and *Lambourne (LW) & Co Ltd v Seecharan* (2008) High Court, Trinidad and Tobago, No 836 of 2002, unreported [Carilaw TT 2008 HC 86].

88 Section 21(1), Consumer Protection Act, Cap 326D (Barbados).

17. Where there is a contract for the sale of unascertained goods, no property in the goods is transferred to the buyer unless and until the goods are ascertained.

18. (1) Where there is a contract for the sale of specific or ascertained goods, the property in them is transferred to the buyer at such time as the parties to the contract intend it to be transferred.

(2) For the purpose of ascertaining the intention of the parties, regard shall be had to the terms of the contract, the conduct of the parties, and the circumstances of the case.

Specific goods are goods identified and agreed upon when the contract is made.[89] Goods which need to be identified after the contract are either 'ascertained' or 'unascertained', and will only be capable of passing to the buyer once they are 'ascertained'.[90]

The property which is the subject matter of the contract of sale cannot change hands unless it is ascertained. The property will pass at the time when the parties intend for it to pass, as discerned from the contractual terms, the conduct of the parties and the surrounding circumstances.

While there is no definition provided for 'ascertained' or 'unascertained' goods in the legislation, case law suggests that the term 'ascertained' is meant to apply to goods which are identified *after* formation of the contract. This contrasts with the definition of specific goods which, as already seen, are goods which were identified at the time when the contract was made.[91]

Rules to determine the intention of the parties regarding time of transfer

As stated above, the property will pass at the time when the parties intend it to. The question of what the parties intended must be informed by the terms of the agreement and the conduct of the parties, and must be considered in light of the prevailing circumstances. In the absence of the appearance of a different intention, the legislation sets out certain rules for determining the intention of the parties.

First rule: unconditional contracts for specific goods

In the case of unconditional contracts for the sale of specific goods, the property passes when the contract is made, regardless of whether the time of payment or delivery is postponed.[92]

In a Jamaican case, *Francis v Taylor*,[93] where the seller (the defendant) sold a truck cylinder head to the buyer (the plaintiff), who was acting through an agent, it was

---

89 See s 60, Sale of Goods Act (Jamaica); s 2(1), Sale of Goods Act, Cap 393 (Antigua and Barbuda); and s 2(1), Sale of Goods Act, Ch 337 (The Bahamas).

90 See s 7, Sale of Goods Act, Ch 337 (The Bahamas); s 18, Sale of Goods Act, Cap 393 (Antigua and Barbuda); and s 18, Sale of Goods Act, Ch 337 (The Bahamas).

91 *Re Stapylton Fletcher Ltd (in administrative receivership), Re Ellis Son & Vidler Ltd (in administrative receivership)* [1995] 1 All ER 192, [1994] 1 WLR 1181.

92 See s 19, Sale of Goods Act, Cap 318 (Barbados); s 20, Sale of Goods Act, Cap 393 (Antigua and Barbuda); s 18, Sale of Goods Act 1978 (Bermuda); s 20, Sale of Goods Act, Cap 261 (Belize); s 20, Sale of Goods Act, Ch 337 (The Bahamas); s 20, Sale of Goods Act (Jamaica); and s 20, Sale of Goods Act, Ch 82:30 (Trinidad and Tobago).

93 (1982) Supreme Court, Jamaica, No 31 of 1979, unreported [Carilaw JM 1982 SC 37]. See also *Coggins v Garage and Rolling Door Company Ltd* (2007) High Court, Trinidad and Tobago, No 2550 of 2004, unreported [Carilaw TT 2007 HC 262].

held that the property in the goods had passed to the buyer even though the price was in dispute. The fact that the buyer and the seller could not agree on the price of the cylinder head, after the buyer had already modified and installed the part in his truck, was not relevant.The cylinder head constituted ascertained goods within the meaning of section 18(1) of the Jamaican Sale of Goods Act, and the property had therefore passed to the buyer at the time when the parties intended it to pass. To determine this intention, the court looked at the first rule regarding ascertainment of intention. Although the first rule makes mention only of 'specific goods in a deliverable state', the court, without adverting to the discrepancy, applied the provision by analogy to ascertained goods, namely, the cylinder head, and held that the property passed when the contract was made between the buyer's agent and the seller, even though no price had been agreed or determined.

Thus, the Jamaican Supreme Court held that the property in the cylinder head had passed to the buyer even though the price was in dispute.

Second rule: conditional contracts where the seller is obliged to put goods in a deliverable state

In contracts for the sale of specific goods which are made conditional on the seller putting the goods into a deliverable state, the property passes when (a) the seller has done so, and (b) the buyer has had notice that he has done so.

In a Bahamian case, *Mitchell v Petroleum Products Ltd*,[94] it was held that a new car with 'lack lustre paint, missing hubcaps, a windshield wiper which is only partially working, a non-functioning odometer and a dent with rust at the back' was not in a deliverable state. The property in the car did not, therefore, pass on the making of the contract, and the plaintiff's right to reject the car for breach of warranty had not for that reason been lost.

Third rule: contracts for specific goods where the price must be determined

The third rule is that, in the case of contracts for specific goods, where the seller has to measure or test the goods in order to determine their price, the property passes when (a) the seller has done so, and (b) the buyer has had notice that he has done so.

Fourth rule: contracts for 'sale or return'

The fourth rule applies to contracts for the sale of goods on concession, or for 'sale or return'. An example of such a contract is where a person organising a social event purchases soft drinks from a beverage company on the basis that he need only pay for what he uses. The unused portion of the delivery of soft drinks will be returned to the seller. In the case of this type of contract, the legislation provides that the property passes to the buyer when the buyer signifies his approval or otherwise adopts the transaction. If the buyer does not do so, but keeps the goods without giving the seller notice of rejection, and if a deadline for return has been set, the property passes on the expiration of this time. If no deadline for return has been set, the property will pass after the passage of a reasonable period of time.

94 (1988) Supreme Court, The Bahamas, No 321, unreported [Carilaw BS 1988 SC 48].

FIFTH RULE: CONTRACTS FOR UNASCERTAINED OR FUTURE GOODS BY DESCRIPTION

Finally, in the case of sale of unascertained goods or future goods by description, the property passes when the goods are appropriated to the contract. The goods may be appropriated either by the seller with the buyer's agreement or by the buyer with the seller's agreement. This agreement may be either express or implied and may be before or after the appropriation is made.

However, in such circumstances, where the seller delivers the goods to the buyer or to a carrier or other bailee for the purpose of transmission to the buyer and does not reserve the right of disposal, he is deemed to have unconditionally appropriated the goods to the contract.

The passing of risk with the property

Section 22 of the Bahamian Sale of Goods Act provides:

> 22. Unless otherwise agreed, the goods remain at the seller's risk until the property therein is transferred to the buyer, but when the property therein is transferred to the buyer, the goods are at the buyer's risk whether delivery has been made or not:
>
> Provided that where delivery has been delayed through the fault of either buyer or seller, the goods are at the risk of the party in fault as regards any loss which might not have occurred but for such fault:
>
> Provided also that nothing in this section shall affect the duties or liabilities of either seller or buyer as a bailee of the goods of the other party.

Thus, there is a presumption that the goods remain at the risk of the seller until the property has passed to the buyer. This is so even if the goods have not been delivered; except that where one of the parties has caused a delay in delivery, that party will be at risk and be liable for any loss which could have been avoided if the delay had not occurred.

The legislation preserves, by explicitly stating that it does not overrule, the principles governing bailment relationships.[95]

Sale of goods by a person not the owner

Generally, a person who does not have a good title to property cannot pass good title on to someone else. Put in another way, a person cannot transfer a better title in property than he himself owns. This is captured by the maxim *nemo dat quod non habet* (one cannot give what he does not have). This basic common law principle is reflected in the legislation. Section 23(1) of the Sale of Goods Act of Antigua and Barbuda[96] provides:

95 Bailment arrangements involve one party, the bailor, delivering goods to another party, the bailee, to be held by the bailee. The goods will be held by the bailee and returned at a later date or will be dealt with according to the bailor's instructions.

96 Cap 165. See also the Bahamian case of *De Gregory v National Workers Co-operative Credit Union* (2010) Supreme Court, The Bahamas, No 1791 of 2008, unreported [Carilaw BS 2010 SC 143].

23. (1) Subject to the provisions of this Act, where goods are sold by a person who is not the owner thereof, and who does not sell them under the authority or with the consent of the owner, the buyer acquires no better title to the goods than the seller had, unless the owner of the goods is by his conduct precluded from denying the seller's authority to sell:

(2) Provided also that nothing in this Act shall affect –

(a) the provisions of the Factors Act, or any enactment enabling the apparent owner of goods to dispose of them as if he were the true owner thereof;

(b) the validity of any contract of sale under any special common law or statutory power of sale or under the order of a court of competent jurisdiction.

The legislation provides for certain exceptions to the *nemo dat* rule, whereby a person who does not have good title may pass good title to a third party. These exceptions protect innocent purchasers acting in good faith

Estoppel

The first exception to the *nemo dat* rule is indicated by the words in sub-section (1): 'unless the owner of the goods is by his conduct precluded from denying the seller's authority to sell'.

By an application of the doctrine of estoppel, the positive actions of the owner of the goods in question may preclude him from later denying the authority of the seller to sell those goods. The owner will not be permitted to deny that the seller had authority where, by his words[97] or conduct,[98] he has held out the seller as the owner of the goods.

The negligent omissions of the owner may also preclude him from denying the authority of the seller to sell the goods. If an owner negligently allows the purported seller to hold himself out as the true owner of the goods sold, that owner will be prevented by the estoppel doctrine from denying the seller's authority. In order to prove negligent omission, it must be established that the owner breached a duty of care.[99] Since it is unusual to be able to establish a duty of care owed by the owner – for example, a duty of care to ensure that goods are not stolen by thieves or lost by the person in possession of the goods – clear cases of estoppel by negligence are rare.[100]

The Factors Act and other enactments

The Sale of Goods Acts qualify the principle enshrined in the maxim *nemo dat quod non habet* by preserving rules which enable the apparent owner of goods to sell them as if he were the owner. For example, section 23(2) of the Antigua and Barbuda Act, Cap 451 states:

(2) Provided also that nothing in this Act shall affect –

(a) the provisions of the Factors Act, or any enactment enabling the apparent owner of goods to dispose of them as if he were the true owner thereof . . .

---

97 *Henderson & Co v Williams* [1895] 1 QB 521; *Rogers v Lambert* [1891] 1 QB 318.

98 *Farquarson Bros v J King & Co Ltd* [1902] AC 325.

99 *Coventry Shepherd & Co v Great Eastern Railway Co* (1883) 11 QBD 776; *Mercantile Credit Co Ltd v Hamblin* [1965] 2 QB 242; *Mercantile Co Ltd v Twitchings* [1977] AC 890.

100 *Farquarson Bros v J King & Co Ltd* [1902] AC 325; *London Joint Stock Bank v MacMillan* [1918] AC 777; *Jones v Waring & Gillow Ltd* [1926] AC 670; *Wilson & Meeson v Pickering* [1946] 1 KB 422. Cf *Lickbarrow v Mason* (1787) 2 TR 63.

This second exception to the *nemo dat* principle provided for by the sale of goods legislation is in respect of the rules governing transfer of title laid down by 'any other enactment'. The sale of goods legislation provides expressly that any such rules allowing an apparent owner of goods to dispose of goods as though he were the true owner are not affected by the sale of goods provisions.

The factors legislation may be cited as a common example of such 'other enactments'. This legislation regulates, among other things, the powers of mercantile agent with respect to the disposition of goods. For example, the Factors Acts[101] allow for a seller acting in the ordinary course of business to make a valid pledge (or other disposal other than sale) of goods to a third party, notwithstanding that the seller in question does not have title to the goods.

Several of the Caribbean Sale of Goods Acts, such as those of Antigua and Barbuda and the Bahamas,[102] make express reference to the Factors Act.[103] Others, such as the Sale of Goods Acts of Barbados, Jamaica, Bermuda and Trinidad and Tobago, do not mention any specific legislation.

Regardless of whether the relevant Factors Act is mentioned, the reference to 'any other enactment', being any other legislation, preserves other laws which set rules allowing a seller who does not own goods to pass a good title to a third party.

Performance of the contract

Delivery

Where the seller has delivered the wrong quantity of goods, the buyer's remedy varies depending on the circumstances.[104]

If the quantity of goods is less than agreed, the buyer may accept the goods and must pay for them at the agreed rate.[105]

If the quantity delivered is larger than the agreed quantity, the buyer may accept the agreed amount and reject the excess, or accept the whole delivery. In the latter case, the buyer must pay for the goods at the contract rate.[106]

If the seller delivers the agreed goods together with goods of a description not covered by the contract, the buyer may either accept the goods which were agreed under the contract and reject the rest, or the buyer may reject the whole delivery.[107]

These principles are subject to any usage of trade, special agreement or course of dealing between the parties.[108]

---

101 See, for example, Factors Act, Cap 165 (Antigua and Barbuda); Mercantile Agents Act, Ch 333 (The Bahamas); Factors Act, Cap 249 (Belize), Factors Act, Cap 78:80 (Dominica).

102 The Bahamian equivalent of the Factors Act is called the Mercantile Agents Act, Ch 333.

103 See for example s 23(2), Sale of Goods Act, Cap 393 (Antigua and Barbuda); s 23(a), Sale of Goods Act, Ch 337 (The Bahamas); s 23(2)(a), Sale of Goods Act, Cap 261 (Belize).

104 Section 30(1) of the Sale of Goods Act, Cap 318 (Barbados); s. 31, Sale of Goods Act, Cap 393 (Antigua and Barbuda); and s 30, Sale of Goods Act (Jamaica).

105 Section 30(2) of the Sale of Goods Act, Cap 318 (Barbados); s 31(1), Sale of Goods Act, Cap 393 (Antigua and Barbuda); and s 30(1), Sale of Goods Act (Jamaica).

106 Section 31(2), Sale of Goods Act, Cap 393 (Antigua and Barbuda); and s 30(2), Sale of Goods Act (Jamaica).

107 Section 30(3) of the Sale of Goods Act, Cap 318 (Barbados); s 31(3), Sale of Goods Act, Cap 393 (Antigua and Barbuda); and s 30(3), Sale of Goods Act (Jamaica).

108 Section 30(4) of the Sale of Goods Act, Cap 318 (Barbados); s 31(4), Sale of Goods Act, Cap 393 (Antigua and Barbuda); and s 30(4), Sale of Goods Act (Jamaica).

REMEDIES OF THE SELLER AND BUYER

The legislation provides for remedies of the seller and buyer under contracts for the sale of goods, which build upon the usual remedies provided for breach of contract.[109]

The sale of goods legislation states explicitly that it does not affect the parties' rights to interest, special damages or to recover consideration (money paid) arising under general legal principles.[110]

Seller's rights and remedies

Remedies against the goods

An unpaid seller has four remedies against the goods to be bought and sold. These are also referred to as real remedies. For example, section 41 of the Belize Sale of Goods Act, Cap 261, provides:

> 41. (1) Subject to this Act, notwithstanding that the property in the goods may have passed to the buyer, the unpaid seller of goods, as such, has by implication of law:
>
> (a) a lien on the goods or right to retain them for the price while he is in possession of them;
>
> (b) in case of the insolvency of the buyer, a right of stopping the goods *in transitu* after he has parted with the possession of them;
>
> (c) a right of resale as limited by this Act.
>
> (2) Where the property in goods has not passed to the buyer, the unpaid seller has, in addition to his other remedies, a right of withholding delivery similar to and co-extensive with his rights of lien and stoppage *in transitu* where the property has passed to the buyer.

Each of these remedies is discussed in turn below.

(a) **Lien.** Section 42 of the Belize Act provides that where an unpaid seller remains in possession of the goods, he may retain possession of them until they are paid for.

The seller is also able to retain possession of the goods in certain circumstances where the price has been tendered. Those circumstances are (1) where the goods have been sold without any stipulation as to terms of credit, (2) where the goods have been sold on credit, but the term of credit has expired, and (3) where the buyer has become insolvent.

(b) **Right of stoppage of goods *in transitu*.** The second remedy of the seller exercisable against the goods is the right to stop the goods that have left his possession while they are in transit, provided that the buyer had become insolvent.

The Act prescribes when the goods are to be considered 'in transit'. They will be in transit so long as they are being delivered to the buyer, and the transit will end

---

109 See ss 49–54, Sale of Goods Act, Ch 337 (The Bahamas); ss 50–55, Sale of Goods Act, Cap 318(Barbados); ss 49–54, Sale of Goods Act, Ch. 82:30 (Trinidad and Tobago); and ss 49–53, Sale of Goods Act (Jamaica).

110 See s 54, Sale of Goods Act, Ch 337 (The Bahamas); s 53, Sale of Goods Act, Cap 318 (Barbados); and s 53, Sale of Goods Act (Jamaica).

when they reach their intended destination or when they are accepted by the buyer or the buyer's agent.

The seller may exercise the right of stoppage *in transitu* by taking actual possession of the goods, or by notifying the carrier, custodian or bailee who is in possession of the goods that he is taking possession.

(c) **Right of resale.** An unpaid seller has a right of resale of the goods. The unpaid seller must give notice to the buyer of his intention to resell, unless the goods are perishable. If, after notice has been given to the buyer, the buyer fails to pay or tender the price, the unpaid seller may proceed with the resale. In that case, the buyer will be liable to compensate the seller for damages for any loss caused by the breach of contract.

In the Barbadian case of *Byer v Stuart*,[111] X sold a car to Y under the terms that Y would make payments for the car. Y failed to make these payments, and X sold the car to Z. It was held that, although the seller had a right of resale under the Sale of Goods Act, he had not notified Y of his intention to resell and therefore was not entitled to exercise the right.

(d) **Right to withhold delivery.** The fourth remedy is available only where the property has not passed to the buyer. The time at which property passes depends on the agreement of the parties and the statutory principles governing the ascertainment of the intention of the parties as to when the property is to pass.

Personal remedies

Under the sale of goods legislation, an unpaid seller will have two personal remedies against the buyer. First, the seller may bring an action against the buyer for the price of the goods. Secondly, he may bring an action for compensation in cases of wrongful rejection or non-acceptance by the buyer. In the case of non-acceptance, the buyer will generally be liable for loss and expenses arising out of a failure to accept the goods, including those incurred by the seller for storage of the refused goods.[112]

In *Francis v Taylor*,[113] the court held that under the Jamaican Sale of Goods Act, the unpaid seller's remedy was an action for the price of the goods, and not removal of the goods by a bailiff. Here, the seller of a truck cylinder head instructed a bailiff to remove the cylinder by force from the buyer's truck (thereby causing significant loss to the buyer) on the false premise that the buyer had stolen the goods. The court, remarking that the seller's behaviour was 'disgraceful and contemptuous to say the least', held that he was not entitled to recover the cylinder head. The property had passed to the buyer at the time when the contract was made and, as the buyer had taken possession of the cylinder head, and the seller had not given notice of resale, the seller could only sue for damages for the unpaid price under section 48(1) of the Jamaican Sale of Goods Act.[114]

---

111 (1980) Divisional Court, Barbados, No 24 of 1979, unreported [Carilaw BB 1980 DC 1].

112 See ss 37(1) and 49–50, Sale of Goods Act, Ch 337 (The Bahamas); s 49, Sale of Goods Act, Cap 318 (Barbados); s 50, Sale of Goods Act, Cap 393 (Antigua and Barbuda); and s 49, Sale of Goods Act (Jamaica).

113 (1982) Supreme Court, Jamaica, No 31 of 1979, unreported [Carilaw JM 1982 SC 37], discussed at n 92, above. See also *Alberga v Ross* (1980) Grand Court, Cayman Islands, No 372 of 1980, unreported [Carilaw KY 1980 GC 20].

114 Section 48(1) Sale of Goods Act (Jamaica). See also, for example, s 49(1) Sale of Goods Act, Cap 393 (Antigua and Barbuda); and s 48(1), Sale of Goods Act, Cap 318 (Barbados).

These two personal remedies are in addition to the seller's general right to sue for damages and/or rescind the contract where the buyer has breached other terms of the contract.

Buyer's rights and remedies

Defective goods

A buyer's rights in respect of defective goods will be either damages for breach of warranty or rescission and damages (for breach of a condition such as the implied condition as to merchantable quality).

Non-delivery

In cases of failure by the seller to deliver the goods, a buyer may sue for damages or for specific performance.[115]

Resale by a buyer

Generally, any resale of goods or any creation of a pledge or other disposition in respect of the goods by the buyer will be defeated by the seller's rights of lien or stoppage *in transitu*. This rule applies unless the third party to whom the buyer has transferred the goods, or in whose favour the security interest has been created or other disposition made, has paid consideration and is acting in good faith, in which case he may obtain a good title under the resale.

STATUTORY RULES GOVERNING UNFAIR TERMS AND EXCLUSION CLAUSES

The common law rules governing unfair terms and exemption clauses are discussed in Chapter 6. With the advent of increasing political and parliamentary investment in consumer protection, many jurisdictions of the Commonwealth Caribbean have supplemented the common law rules with legislation.[116] The statutory rules are largely modelled on the Unfair Contract Terms Act 1977 of the United Kingdom, and so case law decided under the provisions of that Act may be helpful in interpreting local legislation.

---

115 Sections 51–52, Sale of Goods Act, Ch 337 (The Bahamas). See also, for example, ss 51–52, Sale of Goods Act, Cap 393 (Antigua and Barbuda); and ss 50–51, Sale of Goods Act, Cap 318 (Barbados).

116 For a discussion of the need for legislative reform pre-dating the Trinidad and Tobago Unfair Contract Terms Act, Ch 82:37, see *Quammie v Trinity Motors (Robinson) Ltd* (1982) High Court, Trinidad and Tobago, No 1952 of 1979, unreported [Carilaw TT 1982 HC 31]. See also *Harbour Cold Stores Ltd v Chas E Ramson Ltd* (1982) Court of Appeal, Jamaica, No 57 of 1978, unreported [Carilaw JM 1982 CA 5].

Application

The unfair terms legislation applies only to contracts made after such legislation came into force.[117]

Exclusion of contractual liability

The legislation places specific restrictions on the ability of commercial parties to exclude contractual liability where the consumer has agreed to standard terms which he/she has not been able to influence.[118]

Standard form contracts are usually drafted in advance by the commercial party, for example, the bank or utility provider. Examples of such contracts are airline terms of carriage, mobile phone contracts and the terms and conditions applicable to credit cards. In these cases, the commercial party cannot enforce a contractual provision exempting it from liability as against the consumer, unless the provision satisfies the 'reasonableness' test.

'Unreasonable' exemption clauses

Legislation in certain jurisdictions, such as Trinidad and Tobago and Antigua and Barbuda, prohibits reliance by a commercial party on unreasonable exemption clauses.

Section 6 of the Unfair Contract Terms Act, Ch 82:37 (Trinidad and Tobago) provides:

> 6. (1) This section applies as between contracting parties where one of them deals as consumer or on the other's written standard terms of business.
>
> (2) As against that party, the other cannot by reference to any contract term–
>
> (a) when himself in breach of contract, exclude or restrict any liability of his in respect of the breach; or
>
> (b) claim to be entitled–
>
> (i) to render a contractual performance substantially different from that which was reasonably expected of him, or
>
> (ii) in respect of the whole or any part of his contractual obligation, to render no performance at all,
>
> except in so far as (in any of the cases mentioned above in this subsection) the contract term satisfies the requirements of reasonableness.[119]

Under the section, reliance on an unreasonable exemption clause by the commercial party will thus be prohibited where that party is in breach. Reliance on an

117 Section 3, Unfair Contract Terms Act, Ch 82:37 (Trinidad and Tobago); s 3, Unfair Contract Terms Act, Cap 451 (Antigua and Barbuda).

118 See ss 3(1) and 3(3), Unfair Terms in Consumer Contracts Act, Ch 337B (The Bahamas).

119 See also s 6, Unfair Contract Terms Act, Cap 451 (Antigua and Barbuda).

unreasonable clause by the commercial party is also prohibited by the legislation in circumstances where such reliance would either (i) make that party's obligation to perform the contract substantially different from what was reasonably expected of him, or (ii) allow the commercial party to be exempted from performance altogether.

Unreasonable indemnity clauses

The legislation which applies the reasonableness test also prohibits unreasonable indemnity clauses. A term purporting to make a consumer liable to indemnify the other party to the contract (or any other party) will be unenforceable against that consumer unless it satisfies the test of reasonableness.[120]

The definition of 'reasonable'

A term of a contract will be reasonable within the meaning of the legislation if it is fair and reasonable, having regard to the circumstances which were known or ought reasonably to have been known to the parties, or were in the contemplation of the parties, at the time the contract was concluded.[121]

For the purposes of determining whether the reasonableness test has been met in the case of certain specified provisions of the legislation, the matters listed in a Schedule to the legislation must be considered.[122] These matters include the relative bargaining power of the parties, and whether the consumer received any inducement for agreeing to the contractual term in question.[123]

Those specified provisions, in respect of which the scheduled matters must be considered, relate to the exclusion of liability under sale of goods and hire purchase legislation.[124]

Interaction with Sale of Goods and Hire Purchase Acts

It is common for exclusion clauses attempting to exclude warranties as to title and quiet possession under the Sale of Goods and Hire Purchase Acts to be rendered

120 Section 7(1), Unfair Contract Terms Act, Ch 82:37 (Trinidad and Tobago) and s 7, Unfair Contract Terms Act, Cap 451 (Antigua and Barbuda).

121 Section 13(1), Unfair Contract Terms Act, Ch 82:37 (Trinidad and Tobago) and s 14(1), Unfair Contract Terms Act, Cap 451 (Antigua and Barbuda).

122 Section 13(2) and Second Schedule, Unfair Contract Terms Act, Ch 82:37 (Trinidad and Tobago) and s 14(2) and Second Schedule Unfair Contract Terms Act, Cap 451 (Antigua and Barbuda). Cf Schedule, Consumer Protection Act, 2002 (Barbados).

123 Section 13(2)(a)–(b) and Second Schedule, Unfair Contract Terms Act, Ch 82:37 (Trinidad and Tobago) and s 14(2) (a)–(b) and Second Schedule, Unfair Contract Terms Act, Cap 451 (Antigua and Barbuda). Cf Schedule, Consumer Protection Act, 2002 (Barbados).

124 Sections 9–10 and Second Schedule, Unfair Contract Terms Act, Ch 82:37 (Trinidad and Tobago) and ss 9–10 and Second Schedule, Unfair Contract Terms Act, Cap 451 (Antigua and Barbuda). Cf Schedule, Consumer Protection Act, 2002 (Barbados).

unenforceable by unfair terms legislation.[125] For example, the Antigua and Barbuda Unfair Contract Terms Act[126] provides:

> 9. (1) No person may exclude or restrict ... liability for breach of obligation arising from
>
> (a) section 14 of the Sale of Goods Act (seller's implied undertakings as to title etc.);
>
> (b) section 10 of the Hire-Purchase Act (conditions and warranties to be implied in hire-purchase agreements).
>
> (2) No person may as against a person dealing as consumer exclude or restrict by reference to a contract term liability for breach of obligation arising from sections 15, 16, or 17 of the Sale of Goods Act (seller's implied undertakings as to conformity of goods with description or sample, or as to their quality or fitness for a particular purpose).[127]

Thus, in addition to providing for the protection of the consumer from unconscionable contract terms, the Unfair Contract Terms legislation serves to reinforce the protection afforded to the consumer under complementary legislation.

The operation of this provision under the equivalent Trinidad and Tobago statute was illustrated in *Steele v Gemini Concrete Supplies Ltd*.[128] There, G agreed, pursuant to a contract for sale by description, to supply concrete to S. The concrete later started to sag and crack in places, and it was then discovered to be substandard. The court implied conditions that the concrete would be fit for purpose both at the time of delivery and for a short period afterwards, and that it would be of merchantable quality. The defendant was precluded from relying on an exclusion clause in the contract on the basis of section 9(2) of the Unfair Contract Terms Act (Trinidad and Tobago).

Unfair terms

The legislation of some jurisdictions sets an 'unfairness' test rather than a reasonableness test. This is the approach followed in the legislation of Barbados and The Bahamas. Unfair terms are unenforceable against consumers.

Section 5 of the Bahamian Act provides:

> 5. (1) An unfair term in a contract concluded with a consumer by a seller or supplier shall not be binding on the consumer.
>
> (2) The contract shall continue to bind the parties if it is capable of continuing in existence without the unfair term.[129]

---

125 See, for example, s 9, Unfair Contract Terms Act, Ch 82:37 (Trinidad and Tobago) and s 9, Unfair Contract Terms Act, Cap 451 (Antigua and Barbuda). See also Sale of Goods Act, Ch 82:30 (Trinidad and Tobago); Hire Purchase Act, Ch 82:33 (Trinidad and Tobago); Sale of Goods Act, Cap 393 (Antigua and Barbuda); and Hire Purchase Act, Cap 201 (Antigua and Barbuda).

126 Cap 451.

127 Cap 451. See also, Sale of Goods Act, Cap 393 (Antigua and Barbuda); Hire Purchase Act, Cap 201 (Antigua and Barbuda); Sale of Goods Act, Ch 82:30 (Trinidad and Tobago); and Hire Purchase Act, Ch 82:33 (Trinidad and Tobago).

128 (1997) High Court, Trinidad and Tobago, No 1536 of 1987, unreported [Carilaw TT 1997 HC 143].

129 Section 5, Unfair Terms in Consumer Contracts, Ch 337B (The Bahamas). See also s 9, Consumer Protection Act, 2002 (Barbados).

A term will be classified as unfair if it causes a significant imbalance in the rights and obligations under the contract to the detriment of the consumer.[130] An assessment of unfairness must take into account the nature of the goods or services to be provided, and the prevailing circumstances at the time when the contract was concluded.[131]

Plain and intelligible language

In addition to the provision that unfair terms are not enforceable, legislation may provide that a supplier must ensure that any written contractual term is expressed in plain, intelligible language.[132] If a written term is ambiguous, the interpretation most favourable to the consumer will prevail.

Exclusion of non-contractual liability

Unfair contract terms legislation also limits the extent to which a contract can exclude liability for certain forms of non-contractual liability. For example, section 5(1) of the Unfair Contract Terms Act, Cap 82:35 of Trinidad and Tobago[133] provides that a person cannot exclude liability for death or personal injury arising out of that person's negligence. Further, pursuant to section 5(2), liability for other loss or damage attributable to a person's negligence cannot be excluded by a term of a contract unless that term is reasonable.

130 Section 4(1), Unfair Terms in Consumer Contracts, Ch 337B (The Bahamas). See also s 7, Consumer Protection Act, 2002 (Barbados).

131 Section 4(2), Unfair Terms in Consumer Contracts, Ch 337B (The Bahamas). See also s 8 and Schedule, Consumer Protection Act, 2002 (Barbados).

132 Section 6, Unfair Terms in Consumer Contracts, Ch 337B (The Bahamas). See also s 6, Consumer Protection Act, 2002 (Barbados).

133 See also s 5, Sale of Goods Act, Cap 393 (Antigua and Barbuda).

CHAPTER 8

MISTAKE

NATURE OF MISTAKE

In general, a party to a contract is bound, notwithstanding that he 'made a mistake' in entering into it. For instance, in an example suggested by Lord Atkin,[1] P agrees to purchase from V, a roadside gas station. Unknown to P, a bypass road is about to be constructed which will divert traffic away from the area. P cannot escape from the contract on the ground that he 'made a mistake', in the sense that he would not have entered into it had he known about the proposed bypass road. Similarly, if B agrees to buy goods from S for a certain price, believing that he will be able to resell them at a profit, but a sudden fall in the market value makes it inevitable that he will resell at a loss, he remains bound by his contract with S. The principle in agreements for sale is *'caveat emptor'* (let the buyer beware).

However, there are a number of types of mistake of limited scope which may render a contract void or voidable. These may be classified under the following headings.

(a) *Common mistake*, i.e. where both parties made the same fundamental mistake when entering into the contract.
(b) *Mutual mistake*, i.e. where the parties misunderstood each other and were, in effect, 'at cross purposes' when entering into the contract, so that there was no genuine offer and acceptance.
(c) *Unilateral mistake*, i.e. where only one of the parties was mistaken as to some material fact when entering into the contract, and the other knew or must be taken to have known of the mistake.

A mistake which renders a contract void or voidable is called 'operative mistake', and the extent and effects of operative mistake in equity differ in some respects from those at common law. As Denning LJ explained:[2]

> Mistake is of two kinds: first, mistake which renders the contract void, that is a nullity from the beginning, which is the kind of mistake which was dealt with by the courts of common law and, secondly, mistake which renders the contract not void, but voidable, that is, liable to be set aside on such terms as the court thinks fit, which is the kind of mistake which was dealt with by the courts of equity.

Mistake is considered to be a complex and somewhat unsettled area in the law of contract. It is an aspect of contract law which does not often appear in the modern cases, and there is a particular dearth of case law in Commonwealth Caribbean jurisdictions.[3]

---

1 *Bell v Lever Bros* [1932] AC 161, at 224.

2 *Solle v Butcher* [1949] 2 All ER 1107, at 1118.

3 In a recent Jamaican case, *Clacken v Causwell* (2010) Supreme Court, Jamaica, No 1834 of 2008, unreported [Carilaw JM 2010 SC 101], Sykes J commented that 'there are not many reported cases in which a party has been relieved from performing his contract on the ground of mistake. The reason is not hard to see. The courts lean in favour of performance. The effect of the doctrine of mistake is that the contract is nullified from the beginning.'

COMMON MISTAKE

Common mistake at common law

Common mistake arises where both contracting parties make the same mistake: where, for example, both parties to the sale of a painting mistakenly believe it to be the work of a famous artist, whereas in fact it is only a copy. It seems that common mistake will be operative at common law only in very limited circumstances, namely in cases of (i) *res extincta* and (ii) *res sua*.

Res extincta occurs where, unknown to both parties, the subject-matter of the contract has, *before* the making of the contract, already ceased to exist. A well-known example is *Coutourier v Hastie*.[4] There, P agreed to buy from V, a cargo of corn which both parties, at the time of entering into the contract, believed to be on a ship bound from Greece to England. In fact, before the contract was made, the corn had become fermented and had been sold to a buyer in Tunis. In the words of Lord Cranworth:[5]

> It appears to me clearly that what the parties contemplated . . . was that there was an existing something to be sold and bought . . . The contract plainly imports that there was something which was to be sold at the time of the contract, and something to be purchased. [Since there was] no such thing existing, there must be judgment for the defendants.

Another example of a contract being declared void on the ground of *res extincta* is *Strickland v Turner*,[6] where X bought and paid for an annuity on the life of a person who, unknown to both X and the insurance company, was already dead. It was held that the contract was void, there had been a total failure of consideration, and X could recover his money. Similarly, a deed of separation made between a man and a woman was held void because it had been made on the common assumption that the parties were legally married, whereas in fact they were not.[7]

Res sua occurs in contracts of sale where, unknown to both parties, the subject matter already belonged to the buyer. A good example is the Nigerian case of *Abraham v Oluwa*.[8] Here, in 1917 X purchased a plot of Crown land from Y, who had bought it in 1883 from the holder of a Crown grant, without any deed of conveyance being executed. In 1943, Z, mistakenly believing that the land belonged to a judgment debtor of his, attached the land under a writ of *fieri facias* and put it up for sale. X, mistakenly believing that he had a defective title or no title to the land, purchased it from Z for £68. It was later discovered that X's original title was good, and he sued to recover the £68 from Z. It was held that the contract of sale between X and Z was void since the land already belonged to X, and both X and Z were unaware of that fact. Accordingly, X was entitled to recover the £68.

Apart from cases of *res extincta* and *res sua*, it seems that a common mistake as to some fundamental underlying fact does not, *ipso facto*, render a contract void at

---

4 (1856) 5 HL Cas 673, at 681, 682.

5 *Ibid*, at 681, 682.

6 (1852) 155 ER 919.

7 *Galloway v Galloway* (1914) 30 TLR 531.

8 (1944) 17 NLR 123.

common law. In the leading case of *Bell v Lever Brothers Ltd*,[9] Bell had been the managing director of one of the respondents' subsidiary companies. Following a restructuring of the companies, Bell was made redundant and the respondents agreed to pay him a large sum as compensation for the loss of his employment. After the money had been paid, the respondents discovered that, during his directorship, Bell had committed certain breaches of duty that would have entitled them to dismiss him without compensation, a consequence of which neither Bell nor the respondents had previously been aware. The respondents sued to recover the money, arguing that the agreement to pay compensation had been based on the fundamental mistake, common to both parties, that Bell's contract of employment could not be terminated without payment of compensation. The question before the House of Lords was whether a contract which is founded on a false and fundamental assumption common to both parties is void for mistake at common law. The language of their Lordships was far from conclusive, but *Bell v Lever Brothers* has subsequently been interpreted as having answered the question in the negative, particularly since, on the facts of the case itself, the House declined to hold the compensation agreement void.

The restrictive approach to common mistake has been confirmed by subsequent cases. For instance, an agreement for the sale of a painting which both buyer and seller mistakenly believed to be the work of Constable was held not to be void at common law,[10] and a contract to buy 'horsebeans', which both parties erroneously thought to be another name for 'feveroles', was not void for common mistake, despite the fundamental nature of the mistake.[11]

Common mistake in equity

Equity follows the common law in regarding *res extincta* and *res sua* as rendering a contract void. In its equitable jurisdiction, the court may either refuse specific performance or set aside the contract, notwithstanding that it has been executed. In exercising this jurisdiction, the court may impose terms on either party in order to do substantial justice in the case. For example, where P agreed to purchase a fishery from V which, unknown to both parties, already belonged to P, the court set the agreement aside, but only on the terms that V should have a lien on the property for the money he had spent on improving it.[12]

The equitable principle was applied by the ECS Court of Appeal in *Dammer v Wallace*.[13] In this case, D had entered into a contract to sell to W her 'interest and share' in property to which both parties mistakenly believed she was entitled under her mother's will. Characterising the case as one where the parties were under a common and fundamental misapprehension as to the rights of D under the will of the testatrix, Liverpool JA held that the court could rescind the contract in its equitable jurisdiction, and he ordered D to return the purchase price to W. He explained:

9 [1932] AC 161.

10 *Leaf v International Galleries* [1950] I All ER 693.

11 *Frederick E Rose Ltd v William H Pim Jnr & Co Ltd* [1953] 2 All ER 739.

12 *Cooper v Phibbs* (1867) LR 2 HL 149.

13 (1993) Court of Appeal, Eastern Caribbean States (Anguilla), Civ App No 1 of 1991, unreported [Carilaw AI 1993 CA 3].

> Where the initial impossibility is not known to either party (and this will be so in a case where the property has never existed, even though the parties believed otherwise), the contract will, as a general rule, be void (*Galloway v Galloway*[14] and *Law v Harrigan*[15]). The parties to the contract intended to effectuate a transfer of the appellant's entitlement under the will of her mother, but such a transfer was impossible for the reasons already stated. The question which arises as a consequence is will this court assist a purchaser in a position such as this where the consideration has wholly failed? . . . The remedy of rescission may be given to set aside a contract where the parties were under a common misapprehension as to their relative or respective rights, provided that the misapprehension was fundamental and that the party seeking to set it aside was not at fault.

A similar approach was taken by the Jamaican Court of Appeal in *Stuart v National Water Commission*.[16] In this case, S entered into an agreement with the St Ann Parish Council to enable the Council to obtain a supply of water from a spring on S's land, and, pursuant to the agreement, S transferred three lots of land to the Council. Under the agreement, the water was to be used exclusively for the purpose of a public water supply in the Ocho Rios area, and the Council covenanted that it would not extract more than 750,000 gallons of water daily from the streams on the land. Later, when the demand for water increased, the Council started to extract more than the agreed amount of water, and S then sought compensation for excess water drawn. Upon proof at the trial that the stream in question was a public stream within the meaning of the Water Act, and that S had no sole and exclusive right to its use, Patterson J held that the contract between S and the Council was a nullity, and the Court of Appeal upheld that decision. Rattray P said:

> I agree with [Patterson J's] conclusions. The subject-matter of the agreement was never at any time the property of the plaintiff, but the property of the Crown. He therefore had nothing to sell to the defendant, and the foundation upon which the agreement was entered into disappears since the agreement was concluded on a wrongful assumption by both plaintiff and defendant that the defendant had property in the water which he could sell to the plaintiff and which the plaintiff could buy . . . It is clear that where the contract is entered into by the parties on the basis of an existing state of facts which turns out to be incorrect in terms of ownership of property sold, that contract cannot further be enforced against the party who, on discovery that the vendor had no title or interest in the property which he purported to sell, refuses to honour the contract. In the words of Knight Bruce LJ,[17] 'it would be contrary to all the rules of equity and common law to give effect to such an agreement'. If a final citation is needed, we may leave it in the words of Lord Westbury in *Cooper v Phibbs*:[18] 'Private right of ownership is a matter of fact; it may be the result also of matter of law; but if the parties contract under a mutual mistake and misapprehension as to their relative and respective rights, the result is that the agreement is liable to be set aside as having proceeded upon a common mistake.'

14 (1914) 30 TLR 531.
15 (1917) 33TLR 331.
16 (1996) Court of Appeal, Jamaica, Civ App No 3 of 1995, unreported [Carilaw JM 1996 CA 31].
17 *Cochrane v Willis* [1865–1866] 1 LR Ch App 58, at 64.
18 (1866) 1 LR HL 149, at 170.

The rule in Solle v Butcher

Further, it seems that, in its equitable jurisdiction, a court may set aside a contract which would not be void at common law, where the parties have made a fundamental mistake as to the subject matter of the agreement. A well-known example is *Solle v Butcher*.[19] Here, L agreed to let a flat to T, which both mistakenly believed to be outside the scope of the Rent Restriction Acts, and as a result T paid a higher rent than the maximum allowed under the Acts. It was held that the mistake did not render the lease agreement void at common law, but it could be set aside in equity, but on the terms that T could either surrender the lease entirely or remain in possession under a new lease at the full rent allowed under the Acts.

A rare example of the exercise of this jurisdiction in the Caribbean is the Bahamian case of *Johnson v Wallace*.[20] This was a case involving the application of section 4(1) of the Law of Property and Conveyancing (Condominium) Act, Ch 124, which provides, *inter alia*, that, in order to be valid, a declaration of condominium (described elsewhere as 'the foundation stone' of the condominium concept[21]) must be executed 'by the person or persons having the legal and equitable title' to the property in question. In *Johnson*, the statutory requirement had not been observed since the land had been mortgaged to a bank, which therefore had a legal title, and the bank had not joined in the execution of the declaration. Georges CJ held that the declaration was void and went on to consider the effect which this ruling had on those persons who had purchased units in the building in the belief that they were buying into a condominium scheme. He took the view that, in each contract of sale relating to a unit, both vendor and purchaser 'must have entered into the agreement on certain assumptions as to the nature of the subject matter of the contract. If in fact the property conveyed was not a condominium under the Act [because of the invalidity of the declaration of condominium], then there would have been a common mistake. In such cases equity would regard the contract as a nullity and set it aside notwithstanding that it had been executed, imposing terms if necessary to ensure justice between the parties.' Accordingly, Georges CJ set aside the conveyances to purchasers, 'based as they were on a false assumption common to both parties', and he went on to order that, on repayment of the debt owed to the bank, the vendor should execute fresh, confirmatory conveyances in favour of the purchasers.

The wider equitable approach to common mistake established in *Solle v Butcher*[22] was castigated by the English Court of Appeal in *Great Peace Shipping Ltd v Tsavrilis Salvage (International) Ltd*.[23] The Court took the view that the approach in *Solle* could not be reconciled with *Bell v Lever Brothers Ltd*,[24] and that there was no justification for allowing a broader doctrine of common mistake in equity than that which existed at common law. In particular, the Court expressed the view that the effect of the exercise of a judicial discretion to remedy a common mistake was to undermine the security of contracts, allowing a court to intervene in order to rescind a contract

---

19 [1949] 2 All ER 1107.

20 (1989) 1 Carib Comm LR 49.

21 *Goodyear v Maynard* (1983) Supreme Court, The Bahamas, No 488 of 1988, unreported, *per* Henry J.

22 [1949] 2 All ER 1107.

23 [2002] 4 All ER 689.

24 [1932] AC 161.

which had turned out to be a bad bargain for one of the parties. Whether courts in the Caribbean will embrace the *Great Peace* approach or not remains to be seen. Not being a Privy Council or a House of Lords decision, it cannot be said to have overruled *Solle v Butcher* (also a Court of Appeal decision), and Caribbean courts may continue to apply the more flexible approach advocated by Denning LJ in *Solle*, rather than 'to wind back the clock in order to restore the law on mistake as it stood before this infusion of equity'.[25] In any event, it is arguable that the facts of *Great Peace* would not have attracted the intervention of equity, as the mistake was not sufficiently fundamental to bring the case within the *Solle v Butcher* principle. In this case a ship had suffered serious structural damage while on a journey from Brazil to China and a vessel was required urgently to assist with the salvage operation. The claimants entered into a contract with the defendants, the owners of the *Great Peace*, which both parties believed, at the time the agreement was made, to be about 35 miles from the salvage site. In fact, the *Great Peace* was 410 miles away, and when the claimants realised this, they chartered another ship which was much closer, and sought to avoid the *Great Peace* contract on the ground of common mistake. It was held that the mistake concerning the proximity of the *Great Peace* was not sufficiently serious to make the contract void at common law, and it is submitted that, for the same reason, it would not have been held void in equity either. It is thus arguable that the criticisms made of *Solle v Butcher* were not necessary to the decision in the case.

Rectification

Equity may rectify a contract which, because of a common mistake of the parties, does not accurately reflect the agreement reached: for example, where, owing to a common mistake, an agreed covenant was omitted from a deed of sublease, rectification of the deed was ordered;[26] where, pursuant to an oral agreement for the sale of property, the written contract of sale embodying the agreement and the subsequent conveyance included an adjoining yard which the parties had orally agreed should not be included, the court ordered rectification of the conveyance so as to express the oral agreement;[27] and where, in a sale of land, owing to a mistake common to both vendor and purchaser, the wrong plot was conveyed to the purchaser, rectification of the deed of conveyance was ordered.[28] It has been said that,'the essence of rectification is to bring the document which was expressed and intended to be in pursuance of a prior agreement into harmony with that prior agreement.'[29] The rectification remedy affords an exception to the general rule that parol evidence cannot be admitted to contradict or to vary a written contract.

Since the basis of the remedy of rectification is the failure of the written contract to express the *common intention* of the parties, it is not available where only one of the

25 *Anson's Law of Contract*, 29th edn, p 296.

26 *Oyadiran v Baggett* [1962] LLR 96.

27 *Craddock Brothers v Hunt* [1923] 2 Ch 136.

28 *Gonsalves v Cordice* (2012) High Court, St Vincent and the Grenadines, No 339 of 2006, unreported.

29 *Lovell and Christmas Ltd v Wall* (1911) 104 LT 85, *per* Cozens-Hardy MR.

parties objects and where the other satisfies the court that he understood the agreement in the sense stated in the contract. In other words, rectification is available in cases of common mistake but generally not for unilateral mistake, except, it seems, where (i) one party was mistaken as to the construction of the agreement, (ii) the other party knew of the mistake, and (iii) that other party was likely to benefit from the mistake.[30]

In order for rectification to be available, the following requirements must be satisfied, as established in the leading case of *Craddock Brothers v Hunt*:[31]

(i) there must be a prior completed agreement;
(ii) the intention of the parties must have continued unaltered until the time of the execution of the written agreement; and
(iii) there must be clear evidence that, owing to a mistake common to both parties, the instrument as executed does not accurately represent the true agreement of the parties at the time of the execution; and
(iv) it must be shown that the instrument, if rectified, would accurately represent the true agreement of the parties.

MUTUAL MISTAKE

Mutual mistake at common law

Mutual mistake arises where, to outward appearances, a contract has been concluded, but one of the parties shows that, owing to a fundamental mistake of fact on his part, he had no intention to make that exact contract. In such a case, there will have been no genuine offer and acceptance, and the contract will be void. For example, where S, the owner of two Mercedes cars, one of 2,000 cc and the other of 3,500 cc, offers to sell 'my Mercedes car' to B for $20,000, intending to sell the one of 2,000cc, and B accepts the offer, believing that he is buying the 3,500 cc car, the parties are 'at cross-purposes' and the contract is void.

In cases of mutual mistake, the court must determine 'the sense of the promise', that is, whether an objective observer would interpret the agreement in the meaning attributed to it by S, or alternatively in the meaning attributed to it by B, or indeed whether any sense could be made out of the agreement at all. In *Wood v Scarth*,[32] L made a written offer to let a public house to T for £63 a year. T, after a meeting with L's clerk, accepted the offer in writing, believing that his only financial obligation under the lease was the payment of rent. L, on the other hand, intended that T should pay a premium of £500 in addition to the rent, and he thought that the clerk had made this clear to T. It was held that the contract was not void. T had accepted the precise written offer made to him, and L's 'mistake' could not affect the validity of that clear acceptance.

30 *Roberts v Leicestershire County Council* [1961] 2 All ER 545.
31 [1923] 2 Ch 136.
32 (1858) 175 ER 733.

On the other hand, if it is impossible to infer any agreement between the parties, the contract is void. In *Scriven v Hindley*,[33] D, at an auction sale, made a bid for some bales of tow, erroneously believing that the bales contained hemp, which was more valuable than tow, and the tow was knocked down to him. The auctioneer intended to sell tow, and D intended to buy hemp. It was held that the contract was void, as it was impossible to determine objectively whether the subject-matter of the contract was hemp or tow.

Mutual mistake in equity

The position in equity is, in principle, the same as at common law. The court determines the 'sense of the promise', and will not allow a party to obtain rectification or rescission of a contract or to resist specific performance merely because he understood it in a sense which is different from that determined objectively by the court. Thus, in one case,[34] D had been the highest bidder for a property at an auction. He resisted a suit for specific performance of the contract on the ground that he had mistakenly believed the property to include a certain field, which in fact was not the case. The court granted specific performance of the contract in the sense understood by the auctioneer, as there had been no ambiguity in the particulars of sale. Baggalay LJ said:[35]

> Where there has been no misrepresentation and where there is no ambiguity in the terms of the contract, the defendant cannot be allowed to evade the performance of it by the simple statement that he has made a mistake. Were such to be the law, the performance of a contract could seldom be enforced upon an unwilling party who was also unscrupulous.

However, as equitable remedies are discretionary, the court may refuse to decree specific performance against a mistaken party if to do so would cause exceptional hardship.[36] In such a case, the other party would be confined to an action for damages.

UNILATERAL MISTAKE

Unilateral mistake at common law

Unilateral mistake is the term used to describe the situation where X makes a fundamental mistake on entering into a contract with Y, and Y knows of X's mistake. In such a case, the contract will be void. For example, in *Hartog v Colin and Shields*,[37] S by mistake offered to sell Argentinian hareskins to B at a certain price 'per pound'. B accepted the offer, well knowing that S had intended to offer to sell at a price 'per piece' (a 'piece' being about one-third of the value of a 'pound'), which was the normal custom in the trade and which was the basis on which negotiations had

---

33 [1913] 3 KB 564. See also *Raffles v Wichelhaus* (1864) 159 ER 375.

34 *Tamplin v James* (1880) 15 Ch D 215.

35 At 217.

36 *Malins v Freeman* (1837) 48 ER 537.

37 [1939] 3 All ER 566.

been conducted. It was held that there was no contract and S was not bound to sell at the price stated.

The majority of instances of unilateral mistake concern *mistaken identity*, where A enters into a contract of sale with a person who he thinks is B, but that person turns out to be C, not B. Where A's mistake is induced by the fraud of C (as occurred in most of the cases), there are two possible solutions: either (a) the contract is void *ab initio*, or (b) the contract is voidable, i.e. valid until set aside by A. Solution (a) will prejudice a third party who may have innocently acquired the goods from C, whereas solution (b) protects the innocent third party (T), provided the original contract had not been set aside by A before T acquired the goods from C.

For a contract to be vitiated on the ground of mistaken identity, it is incumbent on the party who alleges mistake (A in the above scenario) to show:

(a) that he intended to deal with some existing person other than the person (C in the above scenario) with whom he has apparently made a contract;
(b) that C was aware of A's intention;
(c) that A regarded the identity of the other contracting party as of fundamental importance; and
(d) that A took reasonable steps to verify the identity of the other party.

With respect to (a), there must be a confusion between *two distinct existing persons*. If A contracts with C, meaning to contract with some other person who is in fact non-existent, the contract is not void for mistake, though it may be voidable if A's misapprehension was caused by C's fraud.[38]

With respect to (b), it is possible to infer that where A intends to enter into a contract of sale with B but, owing to C's fraud, he enters into a contract with C, the contract is void since A's offer was made to B alone and C, though he knew this fact, purported to accept it himself. Thus if, in the meantime, the goods have been resold by C to T, an innocent third party, T, gets no title to them.[39] Alternatively, in such a case it may be inferred that A, though deceived by the fraud of C, was content to sell the goods *to the person who accepted the offer, whoever he was*, even though, had A known that the acceptor was not B, he would not have entered into the contract. A well-known example is *Phillips v Brooks*.[40] Here, a rogue called North entered P's shop and asked to see some jewellery. He chose a pearl necklace and a ring, then took out his cheque book and wrote out a cheque for £3,000, saying: 'You see who I am, I am Sir George Bullough' (a person of distinction whose name was known to P) and gave a London address, which P checked in a directory. P then asked North whether he would like to take the articles with him, to which North replied: 'You had better get the cheque cleared first, but I should like to take the ring, as it is my wife's birthday tomorrow.' P allowed North to take away the ring, which North then pledged to D, a pawnbroker, for £350. The cheque was dishonoured and P sought to recover the ring from D. It was held that P had intended to contract with the person present in the shop, whoever he was. The mistake as to the identity of the man North did not affect the formation of the contract. North acquired a

38 *King's Norton Metal Co Ltd v Edridge, Merrett & Co Ltd* (1897) 14 TLR 98.

39 See *Ingram v Little* [1960] 3 All ER 332.

40 [1919] 2 KB 243. See also *Lewis v Averay* [1971] 3 All ER 907.

voidable title to the ring, and since the contract had not been avoided at the time of the pledge, D had acquired a good title.

Unilateral mistake in equity

Equity follows the common law in holding that if one party, to the knowledge of the other, is mistaken as to the fundamental character of the offer, and it can be shown that he did not intend to make the apparent contract, the contract is void. Equity will clinch the matter by formally rescinding the contract or by refusing a decree of specific performance. In *Webster v Cecil*,[41] for instance, C refused to sell his land to W for £2,000. C then wrote a letter to W, offering to sell for £1,250. W accepted the offer by return mail. C, realising that he had mistakenly written £1,250 when he meant £2,250, gave notice of the mistake to W. W nevertheless sued for specific performance. The court refused to grant the decree, since W obviously knew of C's mistake.

DOCUMENTS MISTAKENLY SIGNED

It is a basic rule of contract law that a person who signs a written document is bound by its terms, whether or not he has read it or has understood it,[42] for 'much confusion and uncertainty would result in the field of contract and elsewhere if a man were permitted to try to disown his signature simply by asserting that he did not understand that which he had signed'.[43] Thus where, on the dissolution of a partnership, one of the partners signed a document containing a term which he had not noticed and which had not been mentioned in a previous verbal agreement, by which he was liable to indemnify his co-partner in respect of certain liabilities, it was held that he was bound by his signature. His lack of awareness of the contents of the document was no defence.[44]

Non est factum

In restricted circumstances, the defence of *non est factum* ('it is not my deed') may be available to a signatory. The defence has been deliberately kept within a narrow compass because of the deleterious effect which a void document may have on innocent third parties. Thus, where, for instance, a rogue fraudulently induces a person to sign a written document, and a third party alters his position in reliance on that document, it is considered that the interests of the innocent third party should prevail over those of the signatory since he 'has, by signing, enabled the fraud to be carried out, and enabled the false document to go into circulation'.[45] Originally, *non est factum* was available only to illiterates or blind persons who signed deeds after the contents had been incorrectly read to them; later, the defence was extended to

41 (1861) 54 ER 812.

42 *L'Estrange v Graucob Ltd* [1934] 2 KB 394. See p 62, below.

43 *Muskham Finance Co Ltd v Howard* [1963] 1 All ER 81, at 83.

44 *Blay v Pollard and Morris* [1930] 1 KB 628.

45 *Norwich and Peterborough Building Society v Steed (No 2)* [1992] 3 WLR 669, at 676.

include persons who are senile, of very low intelligence or unable to read English; but only in very exceptional circumstances will the defence be available to literate persons of full capacity.[46] In a Trinidadian case, *Seepersad v Mackhan*,[47] for instance, the *non est factum* defence succeeded where a woman described as 'old, illiterate, of very low intelligence and unable to understand and appreciate the English language' was induced by a false representation to sign a document (a memorandum of transfer of land) which was fundamentally different from that which she contemplated (a deed of assent).

If X signs a document after being misled by Y as to its contents, the contract will in any event be voidable for misrepresentation, but where *non est factum* applies, the contract is not merely voidable but void, so that a third party who has acted on the document in good faith will be prejudiced. For example, where a rogue, Y, induces X to sign a guarantee of Y's bank overdraft by representing that it is an insurance proposal, if *non est factum* applies, the guarantee is void and the bank loses its security.

Negligence of signatory

Non est factum is not available if the signatory was negligent in signing the document, such as where he was too lazy to read it or carelessly relied on the word of another person as to its contents or effect. In a Bahamian case, *Gordon v Bowe*,[48] G signed a deed whereby, as vendor, she transferred a lot of land to a bank. The deed had been signed at the request and in the presence of S, the bank manager, for whom G had earlier worked as a maid, and there was evidence that she had been misled into signing, believing that it was a routine banking document authorising her to receive other deeds of hers which were in the bank's custody. Georges CJ held that G could not rely on *non est factum*. He explained:

> The plaintiff is a woman of intelligence. She reads quite normally. She has pursued her claim with persistence and resolve. For reasons which are obvious, she trusted Mr Somers and, because of that trust, she signed a document which he placed before her, without reading it. In *Saunders v Anglia Building Society*[49] Lord Reid stated: 'There must be a heavy burden of proof on the person who seeks to invoke this remedy. He must prove all the circumstances necessary to justify its being granted to him, and that necessarily involves his proving that he took all reasonable precautions in the circumstances. I do not say that the remedy can never be available to a man of full capacity, but that could only be in very exceptional circumstances; certainly not where his reason for not scrutinising the document before signing it was that he was too busy or too lazy. In general, I do not think that he can be heard to say that he signed in reliance on someone he trusted. But particularly when he was led to believe that the document which he signed was not one which affected his legal rights, there may be cases where the plea can properly be applied in favour of a man of full capacity.' While their Lordships in that case did not completely close the door on the availability of the plea of *non est factum* to a person of full capacity, they all make it clear that it would seldom be available. While it is the case that the plaintiff has consistently stated that she signed the document,

46 *Saunders v Anglia Building Society* [1970] 3 All ER 961.

47 (1982) High Court, Trinidad and Tobago, No 533 of 1977, unreported [Carilaw TT 1982 HC 27].

48 (1988) Supreme Court, The Bahamas, No 346 of 1975, unreported [Carilaw BS 1988 SC 75].

49 [1970] 3 All ER 961, at 963.

> believing that it was no more than a document authorising her to receive her deeds and thus not affecting her legal rights, the fact is that the document was relatively short, barely exceeding a page, and quite simple. It would not have taken a minute to look at it to grasp what it said. Failure to do so in these circumstances was, in my view, careless; and that carelessness disentitles the plaintiff from succeeding on that plea.

Fundamentally different transaction

It was established by the House of Lords in *Saunders v Anglia Building Society*[50] that, in order to rely successfully on the defence, the defendant must show that the document he signed was 'essentially', 'radically' or 'fundamentally' different from the document he *thought* he was signing. This requirement would be satisfied where, for example, he signed a guarantee, believing he was signing a bill of exchange,[51] or where he signed a mortgage, believing he was signing a power of attorney.[52] In *Saunders*, an elderly widow gave the title deeds of her leasehold house to her nephew, so that he could borrow money on the security of the property, on condition that she should remain in occupation for the remainder of her life. She knew that L, a business associate of the nephew, would assist in obtaining the loan. L asked her to sign a document, which she was unable to read because she had broken her glasses, but L told her that it was a deed of gift to the nephew. She signed the document, which was in fact an assignment of the leasehold by way of sale to L. L subsequently mortgaged the house to a building society as security for a loan but he failed to pay the mortgage installments. The widow sought a declaration that the assignment to L was void on the ground of *non est factum*.

The House of Lords held that the widow had not been careless in signing the document, as her reason for not reading it was acceptable, but the plea of *non est factum* failed since the court took the view that, in the circumstances, the document she signed was not essentially different in nature from what she thought she was signing. Looking at 'the object of the exercise', the widow's purpose was to enable L, who was apparently acting in conjunction with her nephew, to raise a loan on the security of the property for the benefit of the nephew, and that purpose would have been achieved by the signed document, if L had acted honestly throughout. There was thus, in the circumstances, no essential difference between a deed of gift to the nephew and an assignment to L.

The principles stated in *Saunders* were applied by Edoo J in a Trinidadian case, *Seepersad v Mackhan*.[53] Here, M, who was described as being 'old, illiterate, of very low intelligence and unable to understand and appreciate the English language', was induced by a false representation to sign a document the effect of which was fundamentally different from that which she contemplated. She believed she was signing or putting her thumbprint to a deed of assent vesting certain property in herself and her children, whereas in fact the document was a transfer to R, her son, and his wife. Holding that this was a clear case of *non est factum*, Edoo J said:

---

50 *Ibid.*

51 *Foster v Mackinnon* (1869) LR 4 CP 704.

52 *Bagot v Chapman* [1907] 2 Ch 222.

53 (1982) High Court, Trinidad and Tobago, No 533 of 1977, unreported [Carilaw TT 1982 HC 27].

> In *Saunders v Anglia Building Society*, which can be considered as the leading case on the doctrine of '*non est factum*', the House of Lords extended the doctrine as enunciated in previous cases to apply not only to the blind and illiterate but also to persons who are senile, of very low intelligence or unable to read English, and to persons who are tricked into signing a document. According to Lord Reid, the doctrine applies to 'those who are permanently or temporarily unable, through no fault of their own, to have without explanation any real understanding of the purport of a particular document, whether through defective education, illness or innate incapacity'. *Saunders* rejected the distinction between the 'character' and 'contents' of a document and put in its place the requirement that the difference between the document as it was and as it was believed to be, must be radical or substantial or fundamental, and to be judged by 'difference in practical result' rather than by 'difference in legal character'. I consider that this principle applies most aptly to the instant case.

In *Jamaica Citizens Bank Ltd v Reid*,[54] the defendant, who described himself as a 'responsible businessman', stated that he had signed certain mortgage documents in blank, leaving the details to be filled in by other persons at a later date, and relying on the advice of the mortgagee's agent whom he trusted. Beckford J (Ag) held that the defendant could not rely on *non est factum*; in the first place, the defendant had not been induced to sign a document which was radically different from what he believed it to be, as he knew what he was signing was meant to deal with his land and, secondly, it was 'not open to him to say that he did not consent to whatever the completed documents contained'. The learned judge cited the following passage from the judgment of Lord Reid in *Saunders v Anglia Building Society*:[55]

> The plea [of *non est factum*] cannot be available to anyone who was content to sign without taking the trouble to try to find out at least the general effect of the document. Many people do frequently sign documents put before them for signature by their solicitors or other trusted advisers without making any enquiry as to their purpose or effect. But the essence of the plea *non est factum* is that the person signing believed that the document he signed had one character or one effect, whereas in fact its character or effect was quite different . . . Further, the plea cannot be available to a person whose mistake was really a mistake as to the legal effect of the document, whether that was his own mistake or that of his adviser.

54 (1995) 32 JLR 1.

55 [1970] 3 All ER 961, at 963.

CHAPTER 9

MISREPRESENTATION, UNDUE INFLUENCE AND DURESS

MISREPRESENTATION

Material statements made by the parties during negotiations leading up to a contract may constitute either *contractual terms* or *mere representations*. A contractual term is a statement by which the parties *intend to be bound* and which therefore forms part of the agreement. A mere representation is a statement by which the parties *did not intend to be bound* but which nonetheless *induced* the contract.[1]

Definition of 'representation'

A mere representation is a statement:

(a) of fact,

(b) made by one party to the other,

(c) during negotiations leading to a contract,

(d) which was intended to operate, and did operate, as an inducement to enter into a contract, but

(e) which was not intended to be a binding contractual term.

If such a statement turns out to be *false*, there is *misrepresentation*

False statement of fact

A representation may be by words, which is the usual case, or by conduct. An example of mirepresentation by words would be where D induces C to buy a boat which he describes as a '2010 model', when in fact it is a 2001 model (the statement as to the date not being a term of the contract), or to purchase a 'genuine Renaissance Italian vase', when in fact the vase is an imitation, manufactured two years ago in Taiwan (the origin and date of the vase not being made a term of the contract). An example of a misrepresentation by conduct would be where D, a rogue, enters C's shop dressed in a barrister's wig and gown, in order to induce C to sell him goods on credit. Another example of misrepresentation by conduct is to be found in *Spice Girls Ltd v Aprilia World Service BV*.[2] Here, the 'Spice Girls', a five-member pop group, had entered into a contract with the defendants under which the defendants agreed to sponsor the group's tour in return for promotional work. Three weeks after signing the contract, one of the Spice Girls, Gerry Halliwell, left the group. When the defendants became aware that the other members of the group had known *prior to* the signing of the contract, of Halliwell's intention to leave they claimed that they had been induced to enter into the contract by misrepresentation, and the

---

1 See pp 58–61, above.

2 [2002] EWCA 15.

English Court of Appeal upheld that contention. By participating in a costly commercial photo shoot, and supplying logos, images and designs of the entire five-member group, at a time when they knew that one member of the group was about to leave, the Spice Girls had made a misrepresentation by conduct which entitled the defendants to rescission of the contract.

Silence is not misrepresentation

Generally, silence cannot amount to a representation, and the mere non-disclosure of the truth is not misrepresentation. In contracts of sale, the maxim is *caveat emptor* ('let the buyer beware'), so that the seller, subject to any statutory duties under consumer legislation,[3] is not bound to disclose defects in the *quality* in the land or goods he is selling.[4] As Lord Campbell explained:[5]

> There being no fiduciary relation between vendor and purchaser in the negotiation, the purchaser is not bound to disclose any fact exclusively within his knowledge which might reasonably be expected to influence the price of the subject to be sold. Simple reticence does not amount to legal fraud, however it may be viewed by moralists.

However, silence may constitute misrepresentation in the following cases:

(i) Where silence distorts a positive representation, for example where a vendor of a building described the premises as 'fully let', but omitted to disclose to the purchaser that the tenants had given notice to quit ('a half truth may be as good as a lie');[6] and where a defendant, on accepting a dress for cleaning, stated that a document required to be signed by the customer exempted the defendant from liability for damage to beads and sequins, whereas in fact it exempted the defendant from 'any damage howsoever arising'.[7]

(ii) Where a statement, though true when made, later becomes false, to the representor's knowledge, and the representor fails to inform the representee of the change of circumstances.[8]

(iii) Where there is active concealment of a fact, for example where the seller covers up defects in an article in order to mislead the buyer into believing that the article is in a good condition[9]

(iv) Where the contract is *uberrimae fidei* (see pp 157–163, below).

Statements of opinion

A statement expressing the speaker's opinion on a matter is not a statement of fact and will generally not be treated as a representation. Thus, for example, in *Bissett v*

---

3 See pp 106–116, above.

4 *Keates v Lord Cadogan* (1851) 138 ER 234.

5 *Walters v Morgan* (1861) 45 ER 1056.

6 *Dimmock v Hallett* (1866) LR 2 Ch App 21.

7 *Curtis v Chemical Cleaning and Dyeing Co* [1951] 1 All ER 631.

8 *With v O'Flanagan* [1939] Ch 575. See also *Davies v London and Provincial Marine Insurance Co* (1878) 8 Ch D 469.

9 *Horsfall v Thomas* (1862) 158 ER 813.

Wilkinson,[10] W entered into a contract to purchase land in New Zealand from B in reliance upon B's statement that he estimated the land 'would carry two thousand sheep'. The land had not previously been used for sheep farming by B or anyone else. When B sued W for the balance of the purchase price, W counterclaimed for rescission of the contract on the ground of misrepresentation. The Privy Council held that B's statement was merely one of opinion, honestly held, and that the claim of misrepresentation failed. On the other hand, an opinion may be treated as a fraudulent misrepresentation if it is proved that the representor had no such opinion, since an expression of opinion will usually be based on facts and may imply that the representor has knowledge of facts which would justify his opinion. In other words, an expression of opinion may be treated as a statement of fact, especially where the representor is in a better position than the representee to know the relevant facts. A well-known example is *Smith v Land and House Property Corporation*,[11] where the vendor of a hotel being sold at an auction stated in the auction particulars that the hotel was 'let to a most desirable tenant', whereas in fact the tenant was much in arrears with the rent. It was held that the 'opinion' stated about the tenant would be treated as a statement of fact, since it constituted an assertion that nothing had transpired in the course of the landlord/tenant relationship to justify regarding the tenant as 'undesirable'.

Statements of intention

A statement as to what the speaker intends to do in the future is not treated as a representation and will not generally be actionable; but it may be actionable if the representee can show that the representor had no such intention. Thus, for example, where a company in its prospectus stated that money lent to the company would be used to expand the business, whereas, as the directors well knew, it was to be used to pay existing debts, the apparent statement of intention was regarded by the court as a statement of fact and an actionable misrepresentation since, in the words of Bowen LJ, 'the state of a man's mind is as much a fact as the state of his digestion'. He went on to say:[12]

> It is true that it is very difficult to prove what the state of a man's mind at a particular time is, but if it can be ascertained, it is as much a fact as anything else. A misrepresentation as to the state of a man's mind is, therefore, a statement of fact.

Mere 'puffs'

Advertisements containing commendatory and exaggerated descriptions of products being offered for sale (such as the laundry detergent manufacturer that

10 [1927] AC 177. See also *Economides v Commercial Union Assurance Co plc* [1998] QB 587 (statement by 21-year-old student estimating cost of replacing contents of flat at £16,000 held mere expression of opinion and not actionable).

11 (1884) 28 Ch D 7.

12 *Edgington v Fitzmaurice* (1885) 29 Ch D 459, at 483.

advertises its product as 'washing whitest', or the manufacturer of a beverage that proclaims its product 'fortifies the over-forties') are not treated as representations of fact, but are regarded as mere puffs and without legal effect.

False statement must have been addressed to the party misled

A party who is misled by a misrepresentation must be able to show that the false statement was addressed to him, either directly or through another person intended by the representor to convey the statement. In *Peek v Gurney*,[13] P purchased shares in a company in reliance on certain false statements contained in the company's prospectus. He brought an action against the promoters of the company for rescission on the basis of misrepresentation. It was held that the statements in the prospectus had been addressed only to the original allottees of shares on the formation of the company, and since P was not one of those original purchasers, but one to whom the shares had been resold, he could not rely on the misrepresentation.

Representation must induce the contract

A misleading statement will not be an actionable representation unless (i) it was intended to be an inducement to the other party to enter into the contract, and (ii) it did in fact operate as an inducement. In the first place, the misleading statement must have been addressed to the party misled. Secondly, it is not necessary that the representor's statement should have been the *sole* inducement to entering into the contract; it is sufficient if the false statement was 'actively present in the representee's mind' when he entered.[14] If, on the other hand, the representee does not rely on the representor's false statement but on his own independent investigations about the subject-matter of the contract, the representor will not be liable. Thus, for instance, where the vendor of a mine made certain misleading statements about its earning capacity and the purchaser's agent reported that the statements were correct, the misrepresentations were not actionable since the purchaser did not rely on them but on the investigations and advice of his own agent.[15] Again, there may be situations where there was a misrepresentation but the representee was not aware of it and so could not have been induced by it. One such case was *Horsfall v Thomas*,[16] where the seller of a gun, in order to conceal a serious defect in its barrel, inserted a metal plug into the weak spot. The buyer bought the gun without inspecting it, and when he attempted to use the gun, it disintegrated. It was held that concealment of the defect in the gun constituted misrepresentation by conduct but, as the buyer never inspected the gun, it could not be said that the misrepresentation had induced him to purchase it.

There is no actionable misrepresentation where the representee knows that the representation is false, but mere *constructive* notice of the falsity does not prevent

13 (1873) LR 6 HL 377.

14 *Edgington v Fitzmaurice* (1885) 29 Ch D 459, at 483.

15 *Attwood v Small* (1838) 7 ER 684.

16 (1862) 158 ER 813.

the misrepresentation from being actionable. In other words, if D makes a representation to C which induces C to enter into a contract with D, D cannot argue that C could have discovered the truth if he had made proper enquiries.[17]

TYPES OF MISREPRESENTATION

A misrepresentation may be (i) fraudulent, (ii) negligent, or (iii) innocent.

Fraudulent misrepresentation

A misrepresentation is fraudulent when it is made:

(i) knowingly;
(ii) without belief in its truth; or
(iii) recklessly careless whether it be true or false.

This definition of fraudulent misrepresentation (otherwise known as the tort of deceit) was established by Lord Herschell in *Derry v Peek*;[18] in essence, it is a false statement which the representor did not honestly believe to be true, and which was made not merely carelessly but dishonestly. In this case, a company had acquired the right under a special Act of Parliament to operate horse-drawn trams, but wished to run steam or mechanically powered trams, for which the consent of the Board of Trade was required. The directors believed that this consent would be given as a matter of course, as plans previously submitted by them had been approved without objection, and they issued a prospectus in which it was stated that the company had the right to operate trams by steam or mechanical power in place of horses. The claimant took up shares on the faith of the representation. The Board of Trade ultimately refused consent, and the company was wound up. The claimant's action for deceit against the directors failed in the House of Lords. In Lord Herschell's words:[19]

> The prospectus was . . . inaccurate. But that is not the question. If [the directors] believed that the consent of the Board was practically concluded by the passing of the Act, has the plaintiff made out, which was for him to do, that they have been guilty of a fraudulent misrepresentation? I think not. I cannot hold it proved as to any one of them that he knowingly made a false statement, or one which he did not believe to be true, or was careless whether what he stated was true or false. In short, I think they honestly believed that what they asserted was true.

In a Jamaican case, *Bevad Ltd v Oman Ltd*,[20] a real estate agent, acting on behalf of the appellant vendor, approached the respondent offering for sale a lot of land at Hopedale Avenue, St Andrew, owned by the appellant, together with approved building plans for 14 apartments of varying dimensions. Shortly afterwards, H, the respondent's representative, was taken to the site where A, the appellant's principal director, pointed out a lot, approximately half an acre in dimension,

17 *Sule v Aromire* (1950) 20 NLR 20.
18 (1889) 14 App Cas 337.
19 At 379.
20 (2008) Court of Appeal, Jamaica, Civ App No 133 of 2005, unreported [Carilaw JM 2008 CA 54].

outlined the boundaries and frontage of the land, and gave an explanation as to the design and proposed location of the buildings. The parties subsequently entered into an agreement for the sale of lot 2 (No 11 Hopedale Avenue), together with approved building plans for the construction of apartments on the property. Before the sale was completed, the respondent obtained a surveyor's identification report in respect of the land, and, following the receipt of the report, the sale was completed and the land transferred to the respondent. Six years later, the respondent was informed by another surveyor that the boundaries on earth did not correspond with those on the plan annexed to the certificate of title, and it then became apparent that the lot which A had pointed out to H was not the lot referred to in the agreement for sale and in the appellant's certificate of title. The respondent brought an action against the appellant, seeking damages and rescission of the contract of sale. The trial judge found for the claimant on the ground that A's pointing out of the wrong lot constituted fraudulent misrepresentation. In the Court of Appeal, Harris JA stated that the critical issue was whether A had induced the respondent to enter into the contract by making false representations about the land, 'without belief in their truth, or reckless in not caring whether they were true or false', so that liability in the tort of deceit could be ascribed to the appellant. The trial judge had found as a fact that A had pointed out the wrong lot to H, but it was argued on appeal that this did not constitute fraudulent misrepresentation as there was no proof of fraud or recklessness on the part of A; further, that A's misrepresentation did not induce the respondent to enter into the contract of sale, in that the respondent did not place reliance on A's statement but rather on the acumen and expertise of H, who was an experienced purchaser of lands, and the confirmation in their own surveyor's report, which they had received after the signing of the contract but before completion of the sale. Rejecting these contentions, Harris JA said:

> In *Derry v Peek*, the *locus classicus* on the tort of deceit, Lord Herschell, speaking over a hundred years ago, stated that for an action to lie in the tort, it must be shown that the statement was not only false but was 'made knowingly, or without belief in its truth, or recklessly, careless whether it be true or false'. In that case it was held, *inter alia*, that a false statement made carelessly, without reasonable belief in its truth, did not amount to fraud but may furnish evidence of it. The principal elements of the tort which must be established [are]:
>
> (i) There must be a false representation of fact. This may be by word or conduct.
>
> (ii) The representation must be made with the knowledge that it is false, that is, it must be willfully false or made in the absence of belief in its truth.
>
> (iii) The false statement must be made with the intention that the claimant should act upon it . . . sustaining damage in so doing.
>
> If fraud is proved, there is no necessity to establish that there was an intention to injure or defraud the claimant. The true test is whether the claimant was induced by the false statement to act as he did. The issue as to whether a misrepresentation is fraudulent is one of fact. When, therefore, is a statement willfully false within the context of the principles laid down in *Derry v Peek*? The answer lies in the intention of the defendant as to whether he had a genuine belief in the truth of his statement. Liability may be imposed on a defendant if it can be shown that he did not honestly believe the truth of the statement. If a man makes a statement, intending it to be acted upon by others, knowing it to be untrue, or has reasonable grounds to believe it to be untrue, he commits a fraud. To establish liability, it is not necessary to show that he should have known the statement was false. Once it is made and it is shown that he has no belief in it, this is affirmation

> which renders him liable. In *Smith v Chadwick*[21] Lord Bramwell said: 'An untrue statement, as to the truth or falsity of which the man who makes it has no belief, is fraudulent; for, in making it, he affirms he believes it, which is false.' It is sometimes sufficient to assign liability to a defendant by showing that he acted recklessly in making the representation . . . It must be shown that there was a conscious indifference on the part of a defendant as to whether the statement was true or false.

Having upheld the trial judge's finding that the representations made by A, the appellant's managing director, were fraudulent, Harris JA proceeded to consider whether it was those representations that had induced the respondent to enter into the contract, or whether the respondent had relied on the expertise of its own representative, H, and the original surveyor's report which it had obtained. In this connection, a dictum of the Earl of Devon in *Attwood v Small*[22] was apposite:

> If a party engaged in negotiating for a purchase of property, having employed competent agents to inspect that property, either did not call for or obtain any report from those agents, or, having got such a report, did not act upon it, he could not afterwards turn round and say that he had been deceived by placing reliance upon the statements of the vendor instead of availing himself of the means of information which were open to him.

On the other hand, in *Aaron's Reefs Ltd v Twiss*,[23] Lord Halsbury LC had had this to say:

> If a man is induced to enter into a contract by a false representation, it is not a sufficient answer to him to say, 'if you had used due diligence you would have found out that the statement was untrue. You had the means afforded you of discovering its falsity, and did not choose to avail yourself of them'. I take it to be a settled doctrine of equity . . . that this is not an answer unless there is such delay as constitutes a defence under the statute of limitations.

Harris JA took the view that the second of these two *dicta* applied in this case. It was no answer to the respondent's claim that the appellant's fraudulent misrepresentation had induced the contract, to argue that the respondent, through its representative, H, had the means of discovering the true position regarding the lot being purchased. Further, the first surveyor's report obtained by the respondent was irrelevant to the case because it was secured *after* the contract of sale had been concluded, and therefore could not be said to have been a factor influencing the respondent's entry into the contractual relationship with the appellant.

Negligent misrepresentation

At the time *Derry v Peek* was decided, there was no separate category of negligent misrepresentation (apart from the equitable liability of fiduciaries for careless statements, for example those made by a solicitor to his client);[24] at common law, a misrepresentation was either fraudulent or innocent. It was only 75 years later, in 1964, that the House of Lords held in *Hedley Byrne & Co v Heller & Partners*

21 (1884) 9 App Cas 187, at 203.
22 [1835–1842] All ER Rep 258, at 261.
23 [1896] AC 273, at 279.
24 *Nocton v Ashburton* [1914] AC 932.

Ltd[25] that there could be liability in damages for a misrepresentation that was not fraudulent but merely careless. In that case, which was an action in tort, it was established for the first time that a negligent misstatement which causes financial loss may give rise to an action in damages for the tort of negligence. There was no contractual relationship between claimant and defendant in *Hedley Byrne*, but the principle established in that case can apply whether or not the misstatement leads to a contract between representor and representee. The facts were that the claimants, who were advertising agents, asked their bankers to inquire into the financial stability of E Co, with whom the claimants were contemplating entering into certain advertising contracts. In answer to inquiries by the claimants' bankers, the defendants, who were E Co's bankers, carelessly gave favourable references about E Co. Relying on these references, the claimants went ahead with the advertising contracts, but shortly afterwards E Co went into liquidation and the claimants lost a large sum of money. The claimants' action against the defendants for negligence failed because the defendants had expressly disclaimed responsibility for the references, but it was held that, if it were not for the express disclaimer, the defendants would have owed a duty of care to the claimants not to cause financial loss by their statements. There was little uniformity of approach among the five Law Lords as to the basis of liability for negligent misstatements; however, it was stated that a duty of care to avoid negligent misstatements will arise if there is, between the claimant and the defendant, a 'special relationship' – a term that has not been definitively explained, but seems to require 'reasonable reliance' by one party on the representation made by the other. Presumably, in the majority of cases there would be no difficulty finding a 'special relationship' between two contracting parties, so that where one party carelessly makes a pre-contractual misstatement to the other, the latter should have a cause of action for negligent misrepresentation. An example where such an action succeeded is *Esso Petroleum Co Ltd v Mardon*.[26] In this case, Esso granted to M a three-year lease of a filling station located on a newly developed site. During the negotiations for the lease, a dealer sales representative employed by Esso, who had over 40 years' experience in the field, had advised M that, by his estimate, the 'throughput' of the filling station in its third year of operation would be approximately 200,000 gallons. In the event, the throughput for the third year was only 86,000 gallons, which made operation of the business uneconomic, and M decided not to renew the lease. Esso sued M for arrears of rent, and M counterclaimed for damages for negligent misrepresentation. It was held that M's counterclaim succeeded. Since Esso had a financial interest in the advice given to M and they knew that M was relying on the expertise of their representative, there was a special relationship between the parties and Esso owed M a duty of care. In the circumstances, the overestimate of the throughput constituted a breach of Esso's duty of care for which they were liable.

25 [1963] 2 All ER 575.
26 [1976] 2 All ER 5.

Negligent misrepresentation under the Misrepresentation Acts

In two Caribbean jurisdictions, Trinidad and Tobago and Bermuda, legislation modelled closely on the UK's Misrepresentation Act 1967 has been enacted. Unlike tortious liability in deceit or under the rule in *Hedley Byrne*, which are not limited to pre-contractual misrepresentations, the Misrepresentation Acts were designed specifically to cover such misrepresentations.

Section 3(1) of the Misrepresentation Act, Ch 82:35 (Trinidad and Tobago) provides:

> Where a person has entered into a contract after a misrepresentation has been made to him by another party thereto and as a result thereof he has suffered loss, then, if the person making the representation would be liable to damages in respect thereof had the representation been made fraudulently, that person shall be so liable notwithstanding that the misrepresentation was not made fraudulently, unless he proves that he had reasonable ground to believe and did believe up to the time the contract was made that the facts represented were true.

Apart from the *Hedley Byrne* rule in tort, the common law position in the law of contract before the enactment of the Misrepresentation Acts was that there were only two categories of misrepresentation – fraudulent and innocent – and no damages could be awarded for an innocent representation; only the equitable remedy of rescission was available. This is still the position in those Caribbean jurisdictions (the vast majority) in which there is no Misrepresentation Act, but in Trinidad and Tobago and Bermuda the Acts have had the effect of (i) imposing liability in damages for *negligent misrepresentation*, and (ii) placing the onus on the representor to disprove negligence on his part. A claimant in either of these two jurisdictions who alleges that he was induced to enter into a contract because of the other party's negligent misrepresentation will thus have alternative causes of action: (i) under the *Hedley Byrne* rule; and (ii) under the Act. As to which of the two causes of action would be the more beneficial to the claimant, it would seem, in most cases, to be more advantageous to sue under the Act, since the burden of disproving negligence would be on the defendant, whereas, under *Hedley Byrne*, the onus would always be on the claimant to show both the existence of a special relationship between the parties and a breach of duty by the defendant. On the other hand, there may be a prospect of a higher award of damages in a tort claim, in which case a claim under *Hedley Byrne* would be preferable.

A case in which there were claims both under *Hedley Byrne* and under the UK Misrepresentation Act 1967 is *Howard Marine and Dredging Co Ltd v A Ogden & Sons (Excavations) Ltd*.[27] Here, the respondents chartered two barges from the appellants, whose manager, during negotiations leading up to the contract, represented to the respondents that the barges had a carrying capacity of 1,600 tons. This figure was based on the manager's recollection of a deadweight figure of 1,800 tons stated in Lloyd's Register, which was in fact erroneous; the true deadweight figure was 1,195 tons, as stated in the German shipping documents which the manager had seen, giving a carrying capacity of only 1,055 tons. The charterparty made no mention of these figures. When the respondents ultimately refused to continue paying the

27 [1978] 2 All ER 1134.

hire charges, the appellants withdrew the barges and sued for the outstanding payments. The respondents counterclaimed for damages both under section 2(1) of the Misrepresentation Act 1967 and under *Hedley Byrne*. All the requirements for a claim under section 2(1) were present, and it was for the appellants to disprove negligence with respect to their manager's erroneous statement by showing that they 'had reasonable ground to believe . . . that the facts represented were true'.

A majority of the English Court of Appeal held that the appellants had not discharged their burden of proof, as it was not reasonable for their manager not to have referred to the German shipping documents before giving information about so important a matter as the barges' carrying capacity. It was emphasised that the Act imposed a strict obligation on the representor not to state facts without being able to prove that he had reasonable grounds to believe them to be true, and this may be a heavy burden to discharge. Accordingly, the appellants were liable under section 2(1). On the other hand, the Court was divided as to whether the appellants were liable under *Hedley Byrne*, and so no decision was reached on that cause of action. The *Howard Marine* case thus shows how a claimant may have an easier path to success under the Acts than under the *Hedley Byrne* principle.

A similar result, based on the Misrepresentation Act, Ch 82:35 of Trinidad and Tobago, was reached in *Montrichard v Franklin*.[28] Here, S Ltd sold a pick-up vehicle to M Ltd, receiving a Mazda car in part-payment of the price. Later, after S Ltd had sold the car to X, it was discovered that the car was subject to a hire purchase agreement and that a finance company, A Ltd, had a lien on the vehicle. S Ltd paid to A Ltd the sum outstanding under the hire purchase to avoid repossession, then purported to rescind the sale agreement with M Ltd by repossessing the pick-up, which by that time had been sold and transferred to the claimants. The latter sought damages and recovery of the pick-up from S Ltd. S Ltd argued that the contract of sale with M Ltd and the agreement to accept the car in part exchange had been induced by the misrepresentation of B, a director of M Ltd, that the car was the property of M Ltd, contending that B had warranted that the car was not subject to any hire purchase at the time of the sale. Blackman J considered that this was not a case of fraudulent misrepresentation, but rather one within the Misrepresentation Act, Ch 82:35, so that under section 3 the person responsible for the misrepresentation had, in order to escape liability, to demonstrate that he had reasonable grounds to believe and did believe up to the time the contract was made that the facts he represented were true. In the circumstances of the present case, where there was evidence that personnel of M Ltd knew that the car was subject to a hire purchase agreement with A Ltd, Blackman J thought it inconceivable that B had not been told about A Ltd's connection with the car, and since B made no effort to contact A Ltd to ascertain the true position, it was difficult to see how he could be said to have discharged the onus of proof placed upon him by the Act to show reasonable grounds for his belief that his representation to S Ltd concerning the ownership of the car was true. The learned

28 (1996) High Court, Trinidad and Tobago, No 4416 of 1987, unreported [Carilaw TT 1996 HC 215]. See also *Caribbean Atlantic Life Assurance Co Ltd v Nassief* (1970) Court of Appeal of ECS (Dominica), Civ App No 1 of 1970, unreported [Carilaw DM 1970 CA 6], where N took out a life assurance policy with the appellant company, having been assured by the company's agent that premiums payable under the policy were deductible for income tax purposes. This was held to be an innocent misrepresentation which rendered the contract voidable, and N was entitled to recover the premiums he had paid.

judge considered the situation in the instant case to be similar to that in *Howard Marine* where, as we have seen, there was an unexplained failure on the part of the representor to examine the German shipping documents which would have revealed the true carrying capacity of the barges. On the issue of the seizure of the pick up by S Ltd from the claimants, Blackman J held that the contract between M Ltd and S Ltd was voidable on account of misrepresentation, but that since the claimants had purchased the vehicle in good faith, S Ltd no longer had a right to rescind as against them; they were 'not involved in the misrepresentation, being in the position of an innocent third party in relation to B's misrepresentation'.

Innocent misrepresentation

A misrepresentation which is neither fraudulent nor negligent, that is, made without fault, will be classed as 'innocent'. A party who has been induced to enter into a contract through the other party's innocent misrepresentation has no cause of action for common law damages against the representor, but he has a right in equity to rescission of the contract. The Misrepresentation Acts give the court power to refuse rescission and to award damages in lieu.

An instance of innocent misrepresentation is to be found in the Bahamian case of *American British Canadian Motors Ltd v Caribbean Bottling Co Ltd*.[29] Here, the claimants had supplied the defendants with two 150-kw generators, after advising the defendants that the energy demand would be less than 150 kw, and that two 150-kw generators would be more suitable for the defendants' needs than one 300-kw generator. In particular, the claimants' manager had suggested to the defendants that their plant could be run from one 150-kw generator, thus leaving the other one available as a stand-by in case the first one broke down or required servicing; and, if the demand increased in the future to more than 150 kw, the two generators could be put in dual paralleling at a cost of only $1,500, and would function together so as to provide the additional energy required. It transpired that a single 150-kw generator was not adequate for the defendants' needs, and that the linking of the two generators cost $19,000.

In an action by the claimants to recover the price of the generators, Bryce CJ found that the claimants' manager's representations were not fraudulent, but he set aside the contract on the ground of innocent misrepresentation, as it was clear that the defendants had been induced to purchase the generators by the claimants' manager's innocent misrepresentations. Bryce CJ ordered the return of the generators to the claimants and a refund to the defendants of the deposit they had paid.

RESCISSION FOR MISREPRESENTATION

A contract which has been induced by misrepresentation is *voidable*, not void; thus it will remain in force unless and until it is set aside by the representee. The act of setting aside the contract is known as 'rescission', the effect of which is that 'the

29 (1973) Supreme Court, The Bahamas, No 46 of 1971, unreported [Carilaw BS 1973 SC 5].

contract is terminated *ab initio* as if it had never existed'.[30] Rescission is available whether the misrepresentation is fraudulent, negligent, or innocent.

As in the case of a breach of contract by one party, where the innocent party has a choice whether to affirm or to rescind the contract, a misrepresentee similarly must decide whether to proceed with the contract (affirmation) or to refuse to be bound by it (rescission). Both affirmation and rescission can be by express words or may be inferred from conduct.

If the misrepresentee chooses to rescind, he must make his decision clear to the representor within a reasonable time. However, if it is impossible or impracticable to communicate this intention to the representor, then some other overt act showing an intention to terminate the contract may suffice. An example of such a case is *Car and Universal Finance Co Ltd v Caldwell*.[31] Here, the defendant sold and delivered a car to R, who handed over a cheque in payment. The cheque was dishonoured, and both R and the car disappeared without trace. The defendant immediately reported the matter to the police and to the Automobile Association, requesting them to find the car. Meanwhile, R had sold the car to M who in turn sold to the claimant, who had no notice of the fraud. One of the issues in the case was whether the defendant had sufficiently communicated his intention to rescind the contract between himself and R. It was held that, in the circumstances, he had done so by contacting the police and the Automobile Association, which had the effect of immediately revesting title to the car in him, so that the claimant had acquired no title.

Although rescission thus occurs by act of the representee, he may further reinforce his position by bringing an action in court for the equitable remedy of rescission. This may have at least two advantages: first, it may protect him against the possibility that the representor, having received notice of the representee's intention to rescind, nevertheless proceeds to sell the goods to an innocent third party; second, he may be able to obtain consequential orders from the court, designed to achieve *restitutio in integrum* for both representor and representee. As Lord Blackburn said in one case:[32]

> The court can take account of profits and make allowance for deterioration. And I think the practice has always been for a court of equity to give this relief whenever, by the exercise of its powers, it can do what is practically just, though it cannot restore the parties precisely to the state they were in before the contract.

Loss of the right to rescind

The right to rescind a contract for misrepresentation will be lost in any of the following circumstances.

(i) *Affirmation*. If, with full knowledge of the facts and of the misrepresentation, the misrepresentee affirms the contract by words or conduct, he will no longer have the right to rescind. For example, a person who purchases shares in a company on the faith of certain misleading information contained in a prospectus, will lose

30 Cheshire, Fifoot and Furmston, *Law of Contract*, 15th edn, p 352.

31 [1964] 1 All ER 290.

32 *Erlanger v New Sombrero Phosphate Co* (1878) 3 App Cas 1218, at 1278, 1279.

his right to rescind if, after becoming aware of the misrepresentation, he attempts to sell the shares or accepts dividends paid to him, as such acts show an intention to affirm the purchase.[33] Another example is afforded by the case of *Long v Lloyd*.[34] Here, the claimant was induced to buy a truck from the defendant following the latter's representation that it was 'in first class condition'. On the first journey after the claimant had taken delivery, the dynamo ceased working and other serious defects became apparent. The defendant offered to pay half the cost of the necessary repairs, but on the next long journey the truck broke down completely, and the claimant then sought to rescind the contract. It was held that the first journey did not constitute affirmation of the contract, since it could be regarded as having been undertaken to test the truth of the defendant's representation, but the second journey amounted to affirmation, since by that time the claimant had become aware of the falsity of the defendant's representation. The right to rescind had thus been lost.

(ii) *Lapse of time*. Where, after becoming aware of a misrepresentation, the representee fails for a considerable time to show an intention to rescind, he may be regarded as having affirmed the contract; but, in the absence of knowledge of the falsity of the representation, mere lapse of time will not bar the representee from rescinding.[35] Further, it is established that where the misrepresentation is fraudulent, time does not begin to run against the representee until he has become aware, or ought to have become aware, of the fraud.[36]

However, it seems that where the misrepresentation is *innocent*, lapse of time may bar rescission by the representee, despite his lack of awareness of the falsity of the representation, if the court takes the view that the representee has failed to rescind within a 'reasonable' time of the making of the contract. The authority for this proposition is *Leaf v International Galleries*,[37] where the claimant purchased from the defendants a painting of Salisbury Cathedral which the defendants innocently represented to have been by Constable, whereas in fact, as the claimant discovered five years later when he tried to sell it, it was the work of a lesser artist. On discovering this, the claimant immediately sought rescission of the contract of sale and recovery of the price. It was held that the right of rescission had been lost because of the lapse of time. In the words of Jenkins LJ:[38]

> Contracts such as this cannot be kept open and subject to the possibility of rescission indefinitely . . . It behoves the purchaser either to verify or, as the case may be, to disprove the representation within a reasonable time, or else stand or fall by it. If he is allowed to wait five, ten, or twenty years and then reopen the bargain, there can be no finality at all.

(iii) *Third party rights*. Since a contract induced by misrepresentation is voidable and not void, the right to rescind is lost if, in the meantime, a third party has *bona fide* and without notice acquired rights in the subject-matter of the contract. This equitable rule is based on the notion that the interests of innocent third parties

---

33 *Scholey v Central Railway Co of Venezuela* (1868) LR 9 Eq 266.

34 [1958] 1 WLR 753, 761.

35 *Armstrong v Jackson* [1917] 2 KB 822, at 830.

36 *Redgrave v Hurd* (1881) 20 Ch D 1, 13.

37 [1950] 1 All ER 693.

38 *Ibid*, at 696.

should prevail over those of the party misled. Thus, for example, where a rogue obtains goods from C by means of a fraudulent misrepresentation, then sells them to D, an innocent purchaser, C, will not afterwards be able to rescind so as to displace D's title.[39] Similarly, a contract to take up shares in a company which has been procured by a misrepresentation cannot be rescinded by the representee once winding-up proceedings have commenced, as that would prejudice the rights of the company's creditors, who are regarded as being in the same position as *bona fide* purchasers for value.[40]

(iv) *Impossibility of restitutio in integrum*. The main objective of rescission for misrepresentation is to restore the parties as far as possible to the position in which they were before the contract was entered into. It is also important that the party rescinding should not be unjustly enriched at the expense of the guilty party. Thus, for instance, in a contract of sale induced by the seller's misrepresentation, the seller will be required to return the purchase price to the buyer, but the buyer will be under a reciprocal obligation to return to the seller any goods delivered to him under the contract.[41] In Lord Wright's words,[42] 'though the defendant has been fraudulent, he must not be robbed, nor must the plaintiff be unjustly enriched, as he would be if he both got back what he had parted with and kept what he had received in return. The purpose of relief is not punishment, but compensation'.

If, therefore, events or activities occurring since the date of the contract have made restitution impossible, as, for example, where the subject-matter of a sale is a mine which has, since the date of the contract, been virtually exhausted,[43] or goods which have been consumed or drastically altered by the buyer,[44] the right to rescind will have been lost.

On the other hand, mere deterioration of the property before the misrepresentation comes to light will not prevent rescission,[45] as the court in its equitable jurisdiction can make such orders as are 'practically just',[46] such as making an allowance for the deterioration or the improvement of the subject-matter of the contract,[47] or ordering compensation for losses incurred by the representor,[48] or payment for benefits conferred on the representee.[49]

---

39 *Phillips v Brooks Ltd* [1919] 2 KB 243. See p 137, above. See also *Montrichard v Franklin* (1996) High Court, Trinidad and Tobago, No 4416 of 1987, unreported [Carilaw TT 1996 HC 215], p 151, above.

40 *Oakes v Turquand* (1867) LR 2 HL 325.

41 See, e.g., *American British Canadian Motors Ltd v Caribbean Bottling Co Ltd* (1973) Supreme Court, The Bahamas, No 46 of 1971, unreported [Carilaw BS 1973 SC 5].

42 *Spence v Crawford* [1939] 3 All ER 271, at 288, 289.

43 *Vigers v Pike* (1842) 8 ER 220.

44 *Clarke v Dickson* (1858) 120 ER 463.

45 *Hoines v Laverick* (1991) 26 Barb LR 52, at 55, 59, *per* Williams CJ, following *Armstrong v Jackson* [1916–17] All ER Rep 1117, at 1122, *per* McCardie J, who said: 'The phrase *restitutio in integrum* is somewhat vague. It must be considered with respect to the facts of each case. Deterioration of the subject-matter does not, I think, destroy the right to rescind nor prevent *restitutio in integrum* . . . If mere deterioration of the subject-matter negatived the right to rescind, the doctrine of rescission would become a vain thing.'

46 *Erlanger v New Sombrero Phosphate Co* (1878) 3 App Cas 1218, at 1278, *per* Lord Blackburn.

47 *Ibid*.

48 *Spence v Crawford* [1939] 3 All ER 271.

49 *Atlantic Lines and Navigation Co Inc v Hallam Ltd* [1983] 1 Lloyd's Rep 188, at 202.

(v) *Executed contracts*. Under the rule in *Seddon v North Eastern Salt Co Ltd*,[50] a contract induced by an *innocent* misrepresentation cannot be rescinded once it has been executed by a transfer of property under it. The rule applies to transfers of both land and chattels. It has been criticised as unjust, since its effect might be that a person who has been induced, for example, to take a lease on the faith of a misrepresentation, will be unable to rescind once the lease has been executed and he has gone into possession of the premises.[51] The Misrepresentation Acts[52] have abolished the rule, but it is arguably still applicable in other jurisdictions where the common law applies.

On the other hand, in *Hoines v Laverick*,[53] Williams CJ expressed the view, *obiter*, that the Barbadian courts were not bound by the rule in *Seddon's* case. Here, H had purchased and taken delivery of an aircraft from L, following L's representation that it was a 1972 model, whereas in fact it was a 1960 model. Though ultimately coming to the conclusion that L's misrepresentation was fraudulent, Williams CJ stated that even if it had been innocent, the court could rescind the contract, notwithstanding that it had been executed. He said:

> The head note to *Seddon v North Eastern Salt Co Ltd* states that the court will not grant rescission of an executed contract for sale of a chattel or chose in action on the ground of an innocent misrepresentation and that, in order for the plaintiff to succeed in such a case, fraud must be proved. In that case, Joyce J referred to the judgment of Lord Campbell in *Wilde v Gibson*[54] ... as stating the rule in equity. Lord Campbell said: 'If there be, in any way whatever, misrepresentation or concealment, which is material to the purchaser, a court of equity will not compel him to complete the purchase; but where the conveyance has been executed ... a court of equity will set aside the conveyance only on the ground of actual fraud'. Joyce J said that he did not entertain the slightest doubt about that being a correct statement of the law ... The matter received legislative attention in England with the enactment of the Misrepresentation Act, 1967, but not before some doubt was thrown on whether *Seddon's* case was authoritative ... *MacKenzie v Royal Bank of Canada*[55] ... appears to be authority for the view that the High Court in this jurisdiction can grant rescission of an executed contract on the ground of innocent misrepresentation, and irrespective of whether fraud has been proved.

DAMAGES FOR MISREPRESENTATION

At common law, damages are available only for fraudulent and negligent misrepresentation, and not for innocent misrepresentation. Under the Misrepresentation Acts, however, the court has power to award damages to the victim of an innocent misrepresentation *instead of, but not in addition to* rescission, if the court considers it equitable to do so.

---

50 [1905] 1 Ch 326.

51 See *Anson's Law of Contract*, 29th edn, p 319.

52 Misrepresentation Act, Ch 82:35 (Trinidad and Tobago), s 3(2); Law Reform (Misrepresentation and Frustrated Contracts) Act 1977 (Bermuda), s 3(2).

53 (1991) 26 Barb LR 52, at 55, 56.

54 (1848) 1 HL Cas 605, at 632–633.

55 [1934] AC 468.

In cases of fraudulent or negligent misrepresentation, the claimant may claim both rescission of the contract and damages for loss suffered.

In all claims for damages for misrepresentation, whether fraudulent, negligent or under the Acts, the tort and not the contract measure is applied;[56] that is, the aim of an award is to restore the injured party to the position in which he was before the tort was committed, not to put him into the position in which he would have been if the contract had been performed (the contract measure). The effect of applying the tort measure is that generally the victim cannot recover damages for loss of profits, but this may not always be so, as *East v Maurer*[57] shows. In this case, M, the owner of two hairdressing salons, sold one of them (salon 1) to E, after fraudulently misrepresenting to E that he (M) did not intend to work at the other salon (salon 2) retained by him, except in emergencies. In fact, M continued to work at salon 2, thus causing E to lose customers. If it had been a term of the contract of sale that M should not continue to work in salon 2, E would have been able to recover the profits they would have made if they had not had competition from M; but since there had merely been a misrepresentation by M, the tort measure of damages applied, which *prima facie* would not include E's loss of profits. However, by an adroit judicial sleight of hand, the court held that, applying the tort measure of damages (that is to restore E to the position in which they would have been, but for the misrepresentation by M), if E had not bought salon 1, they could have invested their money in another business which would have generated profits. Accordingly, E was entitled to damages based on the profits they might have been expected to have made in another business.

It has been held that recovery of damages for consequential loss caused by fraudulent misrepresentation is not restricted to loss which was foreseeable, but extends to 'all the actual damages directly flowing from the fraudulent inducement', since 'it does not lie in the mouth of the fraudulent person to say that the damage could not reasonably have been foreseen'.[58] In the case of negligent misrepresentation, on the other hand, in accordance with normal tort principles, damages are recoverable only for foreseeable loss.[59]

NON-DISCLOSURE

We have seen[60] that, as a general rule, silence does not amount to misrepresentation, and there is no general duty on the part of a contracting party, such as a seller of goods, to disclose material facts or information about the subject-matter of the contract. However, an important exception to this principle is the duty in contracts *uberrimae fidei* ('of the utmost good faith') to disclose material facts which are likely to influence the decision of the other party whether or not to enter into the contract.

56 *McGregor on Damages* (15th edn), paras 1718–1722.

57 [1991] 2 All ER 733.

58 *Doyle v Olby (Ironmongers)* [1969] 2 All ER 119, at 122.

59 *Howard Marine and Dredging Co Ltd v A Ogden & Sons (Excavations) Ltd* [1978] 2 All ER 1134.

60 P 143, above.

The most important classes of contract *uberrimae fidei* in the Caribbean context are contracts of insurance.[61]

Disclosure of material facts

In contracts of insurance, whether marine,[62] motor,[63] fire[64] or burglary[65] insurance, the proposed assured is under a duty to disclose to the insurer all material facts which might influence the insurer in deciding whether or not to accept the risk, and a fact is 'material' if it 'would affect the mind of a prudent insurer, even though its materiality is not appreciated by the assured'.[66] As Bayley J explained:[67]

> I think that in all cases of insurance, whether on ships, houses, or lives, the underwriter should be informed of every material circumstance within the knowledge of the assured; and that the proper question is, whether any particular circumstance was in fact material, and not whether the party believed it to be so. The contrary doctrine would lead to frequent suppression of information, and it would often be extremely difficult to show that the party neglecting to give the information thought it material.

The rationale for the duty of disclosure was further explained by Scrutton LJ:[68]

> As the underwriter knows nothing and the man who comes to him to ask him to insure knows everything, it is the duty of the assured, the man who desires to have the policy, to make full disclosure to the underwriters without being asked of all the material circumstances, because the underwriters know nothing and the assured knows everything. This is expressed by saying that it is a contract of the utmost good faith.

---

61 In *Pereira v British American Insurance Company (Trinidad) Ltd* (2004) High Court, Trinidad and Tobago, No S–781 of 1999, unreported [Carilaw TT 2004 HC 87], Tiwary-Reddy J stated that, in order to conclude a binding contract of insurance, there must be agreement between the insurance company and the assured as to every material term of the contract. In non-marine insurance, it is usual for an offer to be made by the proposer who completes a proposal form and sends it to the insurance company for its consideration for acceptance. The material terms of an insurance contract are: the definition of the risk to be covered and the duration of the insurance cover; the amount and mode of payment of the premium; the amount payable by the insurance company in the event of a loss. There must either be express agreement on these terms, or it must be possible reasonably to infer that there was tacit agreement between the parties.

62 See *Lighthouse Reef Resort Ltd v Regent Insurance Co* (2005) Supreme Court, Belize, No 173 of 2003 [Carilaw BZ 2005 SC 25].

63 See *Insurance Co of the West Indies v Elkhalili* (2008) Court of Appeal, Jamaica, Civ App No 90 of 2006 [Carilaw JM 2008 CA 107]; *Alleyne v Colonial Fire and General Insurance Co Ltd* (2005) Court of Appeal, Trinidad and Tobago, Civ App No 58 of 2004, unreported [Carilaw TT 2005 CA 45]; *Harris v Guyana and Trinidad Mutual Fire Insurance Co* (1971) High Court, Guyana, No 510 of 1968, unreported [Carilaw GY 1971 HC 25]; *Motor and General Insurance Co Ltd v Narine* (2003) High Court, Trinidad and Tobago, No 388 of 1999, unreported [Carilaw TT 2003 HC 149] (decided under s 10(3) of the Motor Vehicles Insurance (Third Party Risks) Act, Ch 48: 51, as well as under common law principles).

64 See *East Bay Shopping and Marina Resort Ltd v Security and General Insurance Co Ltd* (2002) Supreme Court, The Bahamas, No 987 of 1994, unreported [Carilaw BS 2002 WSC 57]; *CLICO International General Insurance Ltd v Matheson* (2004) Court of Appeal, Eastem Caribbean States, Civ App No 2 of 2003, unreported [Carilaw GD 2004 CA 15]; *Feanny v Globe Insurance Co of the West Indies Ltd* (1997) Supreme Court, Jamaica, No E245A of 1983, unreported [Carilaw JM 1997 SC 61].

65 See *Elivique v NEM (West Indies) Insurance Ltd* (2004) High Court, St Lucia, No 0456 of 2002, unreported [Carilaw LC 2004 HC 35].

66 Cheshire, Fifoot and Furmston, *Law of Contract*, 15th edn, p 373; *Hosein (S) & Co v Goodwill Life and General Insurance Co Ltd* (1990) High Court, Trinidad and Tobago, No 6603 of 1988, unreported [Carilaw TT 1990 HC 165], *per* Hamel-Smith J.

67 *Lindenau v Desborough* (1828) 108 ER 1160.

68 *Rozanes v Brown* (1928) 32 Lloyds LR 98, at 102.

Thus, for example, where, in a proposal form for fire insurance, an applicant failed to disclose that he had suffered loss in a previous fire, as well as a burglary and a flood,[69] or that there had been a threat to burn down the premises,70 the insurer was discharged from liability under the policy; similarly, a motor insurance policy was vitiated by the assured's omission to state that another insurance company had declined to insure his motor vehicle;[71] and where a motor insurance proposal form requested 'particulars of accidents or losses', the assured's failure to disclose that one of his vehicles had been involved in an accident was sufficient to vitiate the policy.[72]

Proof of inducement

It has also been held, however, that, 'for an insurer to avoid a policy for non-disclosure, not only does the non-disclosure have to be material but, in addition, it must have induced the making of the policy upon the relevant terms. Accordingly, an insurer who was not induced by the non-disclosure of a material fact, cannot rely on the non-disclosure to avoid the contract'.[73] In *Assicuriazioni Generali SpA v Arab Insurance Group*[74] it was stated that:

> In order to prove inducement, the insurer or reinsurer must show that the non-disclosure or misrepresentation was an effective cause of his entering into the contract on the terms on which he did. He must therefore show at least that, but for the relevant non-disclosure or misrepresentation, he would not have entered into the contract on those terms. On the other hand, he does not have to show that it was the sole effective cause of his doing so.

Although inducement must normally be proved, and cannot generally be inferred from proof of material non-disclosure, it is accepted that there may be cases where the materiality of the non-disclosure or misrepresentation is so obvious as to justify an inference of fact that the insurer was actually induced. Thus, for example, in *Wire*

---

69 *Feanny v Globe Insurance Co of the West Indies Ltd* (1997) Supreme Court, Jamaica, No E245A of 1983, unreported [Carilaw JM 1997 SC 61]; see also *Gordon v Bankers Insurance Company of Trinidad and Tobago Ltd* (2009) High Court, Trinidad and Tobago, No S 410 of 2002, unreported [Carilaw TT 2009 HC 34]. See also *S&S Building Supplies Ltd v Caribbean Home Insurance Co Ltd* (2008) Court of Appeal, Trinidad and Tobago, Civ App No 103 of 2005, unreported [Carilaw TT 2008 CA 37], where Hamel-Smith JA emphasised that although the proposal form required the assured to answer certain questions, that did not relieve him of his general common law duty to disclose any further material facts which might affect the insurer's mind in accepting the risk; and, as Goddard LJ had stated in *Zurich General Accident & Liability Insurance Co Ltd v Morrison* [1942] 2 KB 53, at 64–65, it is not of itself a good answer for the claimant to say, 'If it was material, why did you not ask?'

70 *Ghany (Solomon) Oil & Engineering Ltd v NEM (West Indies) Insurance Ltd* (2000) High Court, Trinidad and Tobago No S 3114 of 1986, unreported [Carilaw TT 2000 HC 93].

71 *London Assurance Co v Mansel* (1879) 11 Ch D 363.

72 *Alleyne v Colonial Fire and General Insurance Co Ltd* (2005) Court of Appeal, Trinidad and Tobago, Civ App No 58 of 2004, unreported [Carilaw TT 2005 CA 45], following *Pan Atlantic Insurance Co Ltd v Pine Top Insurance Co Ltd* [1994] 3 All ER 581.

73 *Insurance Company of the West Indies v Elkhalili* (2008) Court of Appeal, Jamaica, Civ App No 90 of 2006, unreported [Carilaw JM 2008 CA 107]. See also *Alleyne v Colonial Fire and General Insurance Co Ltd* (2005) Court of Appeal, Trinidad and Tobago, Civ App No 58 of 2004, unreported [Carilaw TT 2005 CA 45] (motor insurance policy avoided where assured failed to disclose loss of sight in one eye).

74 [2002] EWCA Civ 1642, cited by Warner JA in *Hosein v Gulf Insurance Ltd* (2005) Court of Appeal, Trinidad and Tobago, Civ App No 105 of 2004, unreported [Carilaw TT 2005 CA 47].

Converters Ltd v Trinidad and Tobago Insurance Ltd,[75] machines were described in a policy of marine insurance as 'new', but the assured had failed to disclose that they had been manufactured several years previously. Mendonca J had no doubt that 'the materiality of the non-disclosure [was] clear and obvious', and gave 'rise to the presumption that, had the insurers been informed of the material facts, they would not have accepted the risk or would have done so on different terms', and there was no evidence to displace that presumption. Accordingly, the insurer was entitled to avoid the policy.

Although the vast majority of cases are concerned with non-disclosure by an assured, it was pointed out by Lord Lloyd in *Pan Atlantic Insurance Co Ltd*[76] *v Pine Top Insurance Co Ltd* that 'the obligation of utmost good faith is reciprocal and ... operates both ways'. He continued:

> Although, in the usual case, it is the assured who knows everything, and the insurer who knows nothing, there may be special facts within the knowledge of the insurer which it is his duty to disclose, as where (to take an example given by Lord Mansfield in *Carter v Boehm*[77]) the insurer knows at the time of entering into the contract that the vessel has already arrived ... Nor is the obligation of good faith limited to one of disclosure. As Lord Mansfield warned in *Carter*, there may be circumstances in which an insurer, by asserting a right to avoid for non-disclosure, would himself be guilty of want of good faith.

In practice, it is common for insurance companies to give themselves even greater protection against non-disclosure by inserting a 'basis of the contract' clause in the proposal form, the effect of which is that the assured warrants the accuracy of the information supplied to the insurance company, so that the accuracy of the information becomes a condition of the validity of the policy. The legal effect of a 'basis of the contract' clause is that 'if his answer to a direct question is inaccurate, or if he fails to disclose some material fact long forgotten, or even some fact that was never within his knowledge, the contract may be avoided despite his integrity and honesty of purpose'.[78] Further, the presence of such a clause makes it 'unnecessary to consider whether the fact inaccurately stated is material or not, or whether the applicant knew or did not know the truth'.[79]

The practice of inserting 'basis of the contract' clauses has been much criticised on the ground that they give too wide a scope for insurance companies to repudiate policies on what are essentially technical grounds. The Law Commission in England has twice recommended that such clauses should be considered void,[80] but the recommendation has yet to be implemented. It remains to be seen whether legislatures in Commonwealth Caribbean jurisdictions will outlaw the use of these clauses, in the face of likely opposition from the region's powerful insurance industry.

---

75 (2003) High Court, Trinidad and Tobago, No 441 of 1995, unreported [Carilaw TT 2003 HC 132]. See also *S&S Building Supplies Ltd v Caribbean Home Insurance Co Ltd* (2008) Court of Appeal, Trinidad and Tobago, Civ App No 103 of 2005, unreported [Carilaw TT 2008 CA 37].

76 [1995] AC 501, at 555.

77 (1766) 97 ER 1162.

78 Cheshire, Fifoot and Furmston, *Law of Contract*, 15th edn, p 376; *Singh v Ruby General Insurance Co Ltd* (1968) High Court, Trinidad and Tobago, No 1823 of 1964, unreported [Carilaw TT 1968 HC 15], *per* Rees J.

79 *Insurance Co of the West Indies v Elkhalili*, n 71 above, *per* Harrison JA; *Elivique v NEM (West Indies) Insurance Ltd* (2004) High Court, St Lucia, No 0456 of 2002, unreported [Carilaw LC 2004 HC 35].

80 Law Com No 104 (1980); Law Com No 319 (2009).

Completion of proposal form by agent

An issue which has arisen in a number of Caribbean cases concerns the effect of non-disclosure or misrepresentation in a proposal form, where the insurer's agent assists with filling in the form. In *Beacon Insurance Co Ltd v Jackson*,[81] the claimant company sought to avoid a motor insurance policy on the ground of misrepresentation as to a material fact, namely that LP, the 'other driver' of the defendant's vehicle, was born on 10 November 1979, and not on 10 November 1971, as stated on the proposal form. According to the evidence, it was not the assured but the claimant's agent who, in the exercise of her authority to complete proposal forms, had written '1971' on the form, after asking the assured's representative 'how old LP looked'. Thom J held that the defendant assured was not responsible for the misrepresentation, and the claimant was not entitled to avoid the policy. He explained:

> Mrs Samuel, an experienced insurance personnel of nine years, was fully aware that Mrs Richards [the defendant's representative] did not know the age of the driver. Mrs Samuel knew that the claimant would not issue coverage for an 'other driver' under the age of 25 years but, armed with this knowledge, she induced Mrs Richards to speculate as to the age of the driver by asking how old Leon Payne looked. When she was given an age range of twenties or thirties, she determined the year of birth as 1971 and inserted it on the form. Like in *Stone v Reliance Mutual Insurance Society Ltd*,[82] the erroneous answer was brought about by the fault of Mrs Samuel ... who did not discharge her duties properly ... I am of the opinion that Mrs Samuel was the agent of the claimant. She was authorised to fill out proposal forms ... She inserted information which she knew was inaccurate. When she required Mrs Richards to sign the form after she had filled in the information, she led Mrs Richards to believe that it was not necessary to have the accurate information but an estimate would suffice ... The claimant cannot rely upon the erroneous answer to avoid the policy.

Similar issues were present in *Clico International General Insurance Ltd v Matheson*,[83] where the company refused to pay to the claimants compensation under a fire insurance policy, on the ground of misrepresentation and/or material non-disclosure, in that it was stated in the proposal form that the walls of the insured building were made of concrete and timber, whereas in fact the building consisted entirely of timber. The trial judge found on the evidence that the proposal form had in fact been completed by the insurance company's agent, J, who was knowledgeable about the claimants' affairs, having previously dealt with them in previous insurance transactions, and that J had led the claimants to understand that it was sufficient for them to sign the proposal in blank and to submit it to him. In these circumstances, Saunders CJ upheld the decision of the trial judge and ruled that the company was not entitled to avoid the policy on the ground of material non-disclosure. He explained:

> The proposal form in question had the usual provision that it was to be the basis of the contract. There are therefore two questions that must be answered. Was the proposal form completed by the agent of the Mathesons or by CLICO's agent? If it was completed

81 (2007) High Court, St Vincent & The Grenadines, No 340 of 2006, unreported [Carilaw VC 2007 HC 23].

82 [1972] 1 Lloyd's L Rep 469.

83 (2004) Court of Appeal, Eastern Caribbean States, Civ App No 2 of 2003, unreported [Carilaw GD 2004 CA 15].

> by the former, was the misdescription material? ... In *Western Australian Insurance Co Ltd v Daytona*,[84] a proposal form contained untrue answers filled in by an agent of the company after the agent had obtained the signature of the assured. By a majority, the court held that the proposal was binding on the company, as the agent had acted within the scope of his authority and the company was êstopped from relying on the untruth of the answers ... In the instant case, the judge relied on section 73 of the Insurance Act, 1973 to find that Mr John was acting as the agent of the company for all material purposes. Section 73 states: 'An agent, broker or salesman shall, for the purposes of receiving an initial premium for a contract of insurance, be deemed to be the agent of the insurer notwithstanding any conditions or stipulations to the contrary'. I don't think it is necessary for me to determine the scope of this section because, either way, there was evidence to support the learned judge's finding that ... it was within Mr John's actual or ostensible authority to assist in the completion of proposal forms ... The trial judge found as a fact that the residents of Carriacou looked up to Mr John with trust in transacting their insurance business. There was evidence that, in Grenada, Mr John was and still is regarded as 'Mr CLICO'. I fail to see why Mr John's knowledge of the Mathesons' wooden building ought not to be imputed to CLICO ... In all the above circumstances, it is my view that the learned trial judge was right to hold that in completing the proposal form Mr John was the agent of CLICO and that, for this reason, CLICO was not entitled to avoid the policy on the ground of material non-disclosure.

It was clear in the *Matheson* case that the representative who completed the proposal form had the authority of the insurance company to do so and that he was therefore acting as the company's agent at the material time. It is otherwise, however, if the form is filled out by a representative who has no such authority. In such a case, the person completing the form will be deemed to have done so as the agent of the assured and not that of the insurer, so that any wrong answers or information will constitute misrepresentation or non-disclosure on the part of the assured, which may enable the insurance company to avoid the policy. Such was the position in a Jamaican case, *Feanny v Globe Insurance Company of the West Indies*,[85] where, in a fire insurance proposal form completed by an insurance agency employee, who had no authority to fill out such forms as agent of the insurance company, there was a failure to disclose certain previous insurance claims. Courtenay Orr J held that the insurance company was entitled to avoid the policy on account of the non-disclosure. Following the reasoning of Scrutton LJ in *Newsholme Bros v Road Transport and General Insurance Co*,[86] the learned judge said:

> In writing down the answers, the agent could only have been acting as the agent or amanuensis of the insured. He could not be the agent of the [insurance] company, because a man cannot contract with himself, and therefore when someone fills up a proposal form he cannot be at the same time the agent of the person to whom the proposal is made. Therefore, any error in writing down the answers was not perpetrated by the agent in performance of any duty to the insurance company.

84 (1924) 35 CLR 355.

85 (1997) Supreme Court, Jamaica, No E245A of 1983, unreported [Carilaw JM 1997 SC 61].

86 [1929] All ER Rep 442, at 444, 448.

Non-disclosure in other contracts

Apart from contracts of insurance, there are a number of other contracts in which there may be a duty of disclosure, namely:

(i) *Company prospectuses.* Under the companies legislation, certain matters must be included in prospectuses inviting the public to subscribe for shares. A contract to purchase company shares will be voidable if there is material non-disclosure in the prospectus.

(ii) *Partnership contracts.* Not only are partners required to show good faith towards each other in carrying out the business of the partnership, but it has also been held that mutual duties of good faith and disclosure apply to those who are negotiating for entry into a partnership. Accordingly, each party must disclose to the other negotiating parties all material facts of which he has knowledge and of which the other parties might be unaware, and which might influence a party's decision whether or not to enter into the partnership.[87]

(iii) *Family arrangements.* Agreements or arrangements between family members concerning the protection or distribution of family property are *uberrimae fidei*, and if any family member withholds material information from other members, the agreement may be set aside. Thus, for example, where a family arrangement was entered into without a secret marriage being disclosed by one party to the other, the arrangement was set aside.[88]

(iv) *Guarantee and suretyship.* Contracts of guarantee or suretyship are generally not considered to be *uberrimae fidei*. Thus, for instance, where a surety guarantees the account of a customer of a bank, the latter is under no duty to disclose to the surety details of the customer's indebtedness;[89] similarly, a creditor is not bound to reveal, to the prospective guarantor of a debt, details of sums already owed by the debtor at the time of the making of the contract of guarantee.[90]

    On the other hand, an employer who takes a fidelity bond, by which the honesty of one of his employees is guaranteed, must disclose to the surety any acts of dishonesty by the employee of which he has knowledge. For example, where an employer told a prospective surety that the employee was 'a good produce-buyer', without disclosing that the employee had defaulted to the extent of £600 on previous dealings, the surety was entitled to avoid his obligations under the bond into which he later entered.[91]

UNDUE INFLUENCE

The equitable doctrine of undue influence was described by Lord Millett in the Privy Council in *National Commercial Bank (Jamaica) Ltd v Hew*,[92] thus:

---

87 *Conlon v Simms* [2006] 2 All ER 1024.

88 *Gordon v Gordon* (1821) 36 ER 910.

89 *Cooper v National Provincial Bank* [1946] KB 1.

90 *United Africa Co Ltd v Jazzar* (1940) 6 WACA 208.

91 *John Holt & Co Ltd v Oladunjoye* (1936) 13 NLR 1.

92 [2003] UKPC 51; (2003) 63 WIR 183, at 192.

> Undue influence is one of the grounds on which equity intervenes to give redress where there has been some unconscionable conduct on the part of the defendant. It arises whenever one party has acted unconscionably by exploiting the influence to direct the conduct of another which he has obtained from the relationship between them. As Lord Nicholls observed, it arises out of a relationship between two persons where one has acquired over another a measure of influence, or ascendancy, of which the ascendant person then takes unfair advantage.

Accordingly, when one party (A) enters into a contract in circumstances where equity finds (i) that the other party (B) exercised a dominating influence over him, (ii) that B abused that influence, and (iii) that A suffered a detriment in so doing, the contract will be voidable by A.

Traditionally, the courts have treated cases of undue influence as falling into two categories, (a) those in which there was a special relationship between the parties, such as solicitor/client and doctor/patient, and (b) other cases where there was no special relationship. The issue was thoroughly examined in 1993 by the House of Lords in *Barclays Bank plc v O'Brien*,[93] which established the modern classification,[94] as follows:

Class 1: Actual undue influence

Here, the burden of proof rests on A (the party claiming that the contract should be set aside) to show that B (the other party) exerted undue influence on him to enter into the contract. In order to succeed in having the contract set aside, A must adduce affirmative evidence of 'some unfair and improper conduct, some coercion from outside, some overreaching, some form of cheating and generally, though not always, some personal advantage obtained' by B. Thus, for example, actual undue influence was proved where a father was induced to agree to make an equitable mortgage in favour of a bank, after being made to believe that if he did not do so, his son would be prosecuted for forging the father's signature – a felony punishable by 'transportation for life'.[95]

Class 2: Presumed undue influence

Here, A needs to show, in the first place, only that there was a *relationship of trust and confidence* between him and B of such a nature that it can be presumed that B abused that relationship in procuring A to enter into the contract. A does not need to show any actual undue influence; once a confidential relationship has been shown to have existed, the burden of proof then shifts to B to show that no undue influence was in fact exerted by him, and that A exercised his own free will in entering into the contract, for example after obtaining independent legal advice.

Class 2 has two sub-classes.

93 [1993] 3 WLR 786, at 791, 792.

94 Approved in *Murray v Deubery* (1996) 52 WIR 147 (Court of Appeal, Eastern Caribbean States), at 151, *per* Floissac CJ.

95 *Williams v Bailey* (1866) LR 1 HL 200.

Class 2A

Certain relationships give rise to a legal presumption that undue influence was exercised; those relationships are:

(i) parent and child;
(ii) guardian and ward;
(iii) trustee and beneficiary;
(iv) legal adviser and client;[96]
(v) doctor and patient; and
(vi) spiritual or religious adviser and pupil.

However, the relationships of husband and wife[97] and banker and customer[98] do not give rise to such a presumption. An example of the legal presumption of undue influence arising from the relationship in (vi) is the leading case of *Allcard v Skinner*,[99] where Lindley LJ opined that 'the influence of one mind over another is very subtle, and of all influences religious influence is the most dangerous and the most powerful, and to counteract it courts of equity have gone very far'. Although *Allcard* was a case of gift rather than contract, the same principles apply equally to gifts and contracts. There, A entered an order of nuns, having been introduced to the defendant, the Lady Superior, by N, the 'spiritual director and confessor' of the sisterhood, and after taking vows of poverty, chastity and obedience. During an eight-year period, while A was a member of the order, she gave to the defendant property to the value of over £7,000, most of which was spent on the purposes of the sisterhood. Six years after leaving the order, A sued the defendant to recover the remainder of the property which had not already been disposed of, on the ground that it had been given under undue influence. It was held that A's action was barred on account of her acquiescence and the delay in bringing the claim, but that if it were not for the acquiescence and delay, the property would have been recoverable as it had been given under pressure which, in the circumstances, A could not resist; an important factor was the lack of opportunity for A to obtain independent advice, in the light of a rule of the order that no sister should seek external advice without the consent of the Lady Superior.

Regarding the significance of obtaining independent advice before entering into a transaction, it has been emphasised in the Privy Council[100] that independent legal

---

96 *Brown v Dillon* (1983) 20 JLR 37 (Supreme Court, Jamaica), at 39, 40, *per* Downer J; *Lalor v Campbell* (1987) 24 JLR 67 (Supreme Court, Jamaica); *Smith v Salmon* (2006) Court of Appeal, Jamaica, Civ App No 67 of 2004, unreported [Carilaw JM 2006 CA 69] ('An attorney-at-law who purchases from a vendor who is his client at the time of the sale will be presumed to have exerted undue influence over such vendor. The sale will be treated as void unless it is shown that the vendor was afforded the opportunity to obtain and did receive independent advice at the time of such sale' – *per* Harrison P).

97 *Barclays Bank plc v O'Brien* [1993] 3 WLR 786, at 792, *per* Lord Browne-Wilkinson. See also *Barbados National Bank v Lehtinen* (1992) High Court, Barbados, No 1410 of 1988, unreported [Carilaw BB 1992 HC 38], *per* Chase J; *Dailey v Dailey* (2003) 63 WIR 63, (Privy Council appeal from the Court of Appeal, Eastern Caribbean States), at 70 *per* Lord Hope.

98 *National Commercial Bank (Jamaica) Ltd v Hew* (2003) 63 WIR 183, at 192, *per* Lord Millett.

99 (1887) 36 Ch D 145.

100 *Inche Noriah v Shaik Allie Bin Omar* [1929] AC 127.

advice is not the only way in which the presumption of undue influence can be rebutted; nor, on the other hand, may such advice be sufficient to rebut the presumption unless it is shown that the advice was followed. Above all, it is necessary to prove that A made the gift or entered into the transaction as the result of 'the free exercise of independent will', and the most obvious way to establish that would be to prove that the nature and effect of the transaction had been fully explained to A by some independent and qualified person.

On the other hand, the proposition that there is no legal presumption of undue influence as between husband and wife was emphasised most recently in *Royal Bank of Scotland plc v Etridge (No 2)*[101] by Lord Nicholls, who said:

> It is now well established that husband and wife is not one of the relationships to which this latter principle applies. In *Yerkey v Jones*,[102] Dixon J explained the reason. The Court of Chancery was not blind to the opportunities of obtaining and unfairly using influence over a wife which the husband often possesses. But there is nothing unusual or strange in a wife, from motives of affection or for some other reasons, conferring substantial financial benefits on her husband. Although there is no presumption, the court will nevertheless note, as a matter of fact, the opportunities for abuse which flow from a wife's confidence in her husband. The court will take this into account with all the other evidence in the case.

Further, in *Dailey v Dailey*,[103] a Privy Council Appeal from the Eastern Caribbean States Court of Appeal, Lord Hope pointed out that care needs to be taken to distinguish between cases (a) where a wife has entered into a *gratuitous* transaction with her husband, and (b) those in which there is an *agreement under which the wife is to receive full value* for the property or interest which she is transferring to the husband. In the former case, the onus is on the doneê to support the gift if it is so large as not to be reasonably accounted for on the ground of the relationship, but a transaction which is entered into for full value needs no such explanation; there is no presumption to rebut. Accordingly, in the instant case it was held that since the husband had paid to his wife the agreed sum for the property transferred by her, there was no need for her to have been separately advised before she signed the instrument of transfer. The transfer was 'at arm's length', and the wife failed to establish that her agreement to it had been obtained by undue influence.

Class 2B

Here, A proves that there was in fact a relationship of confidence between him/her and B, such as to give rise to a presumption that B exercised undue influence over A.[104] In such cases, the burden of proof is on B to show that he did not exert undue

---

101 [2001] 4 All ER 449.

102 (1939) 63 CLR 649, at 675.

103 (2003) 63 WIR 63.

104 An isolated demonstration by a complainant of trust and confidence in a dominant party is insufficient to engender a Class 2(B) relationship between the complainant and the dominant party. There must be evidence that the complainant 'generally reposed trust and confidence' in the dominant party. The evidence required is evidence that before or at the time of the execution of the transaction, the complainant had habitually, frequently or repeatedly expressed or indicated his trust and confidence in the dominant party: *Murray v Deubery* (1996) 52 WIR 147, at 153, *per* Floissac CJ.

influence over A, so that once A has established that he/she reposed confidence in B, the burden shifts to B to disprove undue influence. If he fails to do so, the contract will be set aside, without A having to prove that B actually exerted influence over him/her or otherwise abused trust or confidence in relation to the particular transaction. Cases falling within Class 2B very often concern undue influence as between husband and wife.

Two key modern cases on undue influence, which have delineated the boundaries of the concept, particularly in the context of the husband/wife relationship, are the decisions of the House of Lords in *Barclays Bank plc v O'Brien*[105] and *Royal Bank of Scotland plc v Etridge (No 2)*.[106]

In *O'Brien*, a husband, who was a shareholder in a company, wished to obtain an increase of the company's overdraft with the claimant bank, to be secured by a charge on the matrimonial home which he owned jointly with his wife. Both spouses were required to sign the relevant documents, and the husband falsely told the wife that the security was limited to £60,000, whereas in fact it was for £130,000. The bank employee who presented the documents for the wife's signature omitted to follow the bank manager's instructions to explain the documents to both spouses, and to advise the wife that if she had any doubts she ought to get independent legal advice. Both husband and wife signed the documents without reading them. When the bank later sought to enforce the security, the wife claimed that she had been pressurised by her husband to sign the documents, and that he had misled her into believing that the limit of her liability was £60,000. The issue was therefore whether the undue influence or misrepresentation by the husband could affect the liability of the wife to a third party (the bank). In the House of Lords, Lord Browne-Wilkinson opined that such issues should be decided on the basis of notice, so that 'where a wife has agreed to stand surety for her husband's debts as a result of undue influence or misrepresentation, the creditor will take subject to the wife's equity to set aside the transaction, if the circumstances are such as to put the creditor on enquiry as to the circumstances in which she agreed to stand surety'. Accordingly, a lender, contemplating making a loan to a husband for his business purposes on the security of a matrimonial home or under his wife's guarantee, must take reasonable steps to ensure that the wife's consent to the arrangement was properly obtained and not procured by the undue influence or misrepresentation of the husband. In the *O'Brien* case, it was held that the bank should have been aware of the risk of undue influence and misrepresentation by the husband, and had failed to ensure that she had obtained independent legal advice. The wife was thus entitled to rescind her agreement with the bank.

The other modern case, *Royal Bank of Scotland plc v Etridge (No 2)*, involved a number of conjoined appeals, each of which concerned a wife who had charged her interest in the matrimonial home in favour of a bank as security for her husband's business loans, and in each of which there was an allegation of undue influence by the husband. The case is particularly noteworthy for Lord Nicholls' checklist of matters on which a wife should be advised by an attorney or solicitor (not necessarily, according to his Lordship, an *independent* solicitor, which would mean that the lender's solicitor would be eligible), as follows:[107]

---

105 [1993] 3 WLR 786.

106 [2001] 4 All ER 449.

107 *Ibid*, at 434, 435.

> Typically, the advice a solicitor can be expected to give should cover the following matters as the core minimum. (1) He will need to explain the nature of the documents and the practical consequences these will have for the wife if she signs them. She could lose her home if her husband's business does not prosper. Her home may be her only substantial asset, as well as the family's home. She could be made bankrupt. (2) He will need to point out the seriousness of the risk involved. The wife should be told the purpose of the proposed new facility, the amount and principal terms of the new facility, and that the bank might increase the amount of the facility, or change its terms, or grant a new facility without reference to her. She should be told the amount of her liability under her guarantee. The solicitor should discuss the wife's financial means, including her understanding of the value of the property being charged. The solicitor should discuss whether the wife or her husband has any other assets out of which repayment could be made if the husband's business should fail. These matters are relevant to the seriousness of the risks involved. (3) The solicitor will need to state clearly that the wife has a choice. The decision is hers and hers alone. Explanation of the choice facing the wife will call for some discussion of the present financial position, including the amount of the husband's present indebtedness, and the amount of his current overdraft facility. (4) The solicitor should check whether the wife wishes to proceed. She should be asked whether she is content that the solicitor should write to the bank confirming he has explained to her the nature of the documents and the practical implications they may have for her, or whether, for instance, she would prefer him to negotiate with the bank on the terms of the transaction. Matters for negotiation could include the sequence in which the various securities will be called upon or a specific or lower limit to her liabilities. The solicitor should not give any information to the bank without the wife's authority.

Caribbean cases on undue influence

Undue influence has been frequently invoked in Commonwealth Caribbean jurisdictions, in the contexts both of gifts and of contracts. With regard to the latter, one of the earliest Caribbean cases is *Turnbull & Co v Duval*,[108] a Privy Council appeal from the Jamaican Supreme Court. In this case, the respondent's husband was in business in Jamaica and was in financial difficulties and indebted to the appellants, T & Co, who also carried on business in Jamaica, as well as in London and New York. C was the appellants' agent as well as one of the executors and trustees of the will of the respondent's father. The respondent was the beneficiary as to one-fifth of her father's residuary estate. At the instigation of the husband and C, the respondent signed a deed of indenture, charging her share in her father's residuary estate in favour of the appellants as security for the repayment of the husband's debts owed to the appellants. The evidence accepted by the Court was that the respondent knew nothing about any document she was to sign until it was brought to her by her husband; she had no advice about it; and she signed it because her husband told her he was being pressed by C, and because she believed that if she signed it for £1,000, that would enable her husband to settle a particular debt he owed in connection with the supply of beer to the military forces in Jamaica. The Privy Council held that the appellants were not entitled to enforce the charge on the respondent's share in her father's estate. In the words of Lord Lindley:[109]

108 [1902] AC 429.
109 At 434.

> It is quite impossible to uphold the security given by Mrs Duval. It is open to the double objection of having been obtained by a trustee from his *cestui que trust* by pressure through her husband and without independent advice, and of having been obtained by a husband from his wife by pressure and concealment of material facts. Whether the security could be upheld if the only ground for impeaching it was that Mrs Duval had no independent advice has not really to be determined. Their Lordships are not prepared to say it could not. But there is an additional and even stronger ground for impeaching it. It is, in their Lordships' opinion, quite clear that Mrs Duval was pressed by her husband to sign, and did sign, the document, which was very different from what she supposed it to be, and a document of the true nature of which she had no conception. It is impossible to hold that Campbell or Turnbull & Co are unaffected by such pressure and ignorance. They left everything to Duval, and must abide the consequences.

Another example of a fiduciary relationship giving rise to a relationship of confidence is the Dominican case of *Dib v Karam*.[110] D was a widow, whose husband had been a substantial merchant in Roseau and the owner of several commercial properties. K, a valued friend to whom D had invariably turned for advice and assistance in times of difficulty, was given a general power of attorney, and he had full powers and control over D's business and financial affairs. K expressly undertook to arrange the sale of the properties and stock-in-trade to which D had become entitled, but he omitted to canvas prospective purchasers, and purchased the properties for himself at prices well below market value, procuring formal transfers from D. Ultimately, it fell to the Court of Appeal of the West Indies Associated States to decide whether the transfers should be set aside as having been procured by undue influence exerted by K on D. It was held that, in view of the fiduciary relationship between K and D, it had been incumbent on K to ensure that D had received independent advice before she sold and transferred the properties to K. Since D had placed special reliance and confidence in K as her agent, the onus was on K to satisfy the court that he took no undue advantage of his position; that he made full disclosure of all facts which he knew or ought to have known might be likely to influence D's judgment; and that the transactions were fair as to price and in every other respect. K clearly had not satisfied that onus, and the transactions would be set aside. AM Lewis CJ explained:[111]

> The low purchase price placed on the properties, ie, values considerably below the current market value, particularly at a time when, as the evidence disclosed, other persons had evinced interest in purchasing the properties, would seem to suggest that these interested persons should have been canvassed by the respondent; . . . and, had he in fact canvassed these prospective purchasers, it was equally his duty to apprise the appellant of the result of these discussions before personally concluding a purchase of the properties at bargain prices in his personal favour. In order that any taint of suspicion should be removed from the action of the respondent in the circumstances, he would have to show that 'he acted in keeping with perfect good faith, and made full disclosure of the material circumstances and everything known to him respecting the subject matter of the transaction, which would be likely to influence the conduct of the principal'.[112] Nothing in the record discloses that the respondent did make these particular disclosures to the appellant . . . The failure of the respondent to make full disclosures and to discharge the onus placed on him, by virtue of the fiduciary relationship

110 (1968) 11 WIR 499.

111 At 514.

112 *Bowstead on Agency*, 12th edn, p 93.

> which existed between him and the appellant, of proving that the appellant had independent legal advice before she entered into the agreement the terms of which were so highly disadvantageous to the respondent, is such that in my opinion the court should interfere on the ground of public policy, as stated by Cotton LJ in *Allcard v Skinner*,[113] 'to prevent the relations which existed between the parties and the influence arising therefrom being abused'.

In considering allegations of undue influence, Caribbean courts have in numerous cases applied the principle espoused by Lord Scarman in *National Westminster Bank v Morgan*,[114] to the effect that a transaction will not be set aside on the ground of undue influence without proof of 'manifest disadvantage' to the claimant. Lord Scarman said in that case:[115]

> I know of no reported authority where the transaction set aside was more manifestly disadvantageous to the person influenced. It would not always be a gift; it can be a 'hard and inequitable' agreement,[116] or a transaction 'immoderate and irrational',[117] or 'unconscionable' in that it was at an undervalue.[118] Whatever the legal character of the transaction, the authorities show that it must constitute a disadvantage sufficiently serious to require evidence to rebut the presumption that, in the circumstances of the relationship between the parties, it was procured by the exercise of undue influence.

The principle in *Morgan* was applied by the Guyana Court of Appeal in *De Freitas v Alphonso Modern Record Store Ltd*.[119] In this case, C entered into an agreement with her brother, D, to transfer to D her shareholding in a private company for the sum of $61,700, and D gave C a cheque for that amount, which she cashed. Five and a half years later, C instituted legal proceedings for a declaration that the transfer of the shares was void, and that she remained the owner of the shares, on the ground of undue influence. It was held that even if the combined circumstances of C's advanced age, her close relationship with her brother, and the fact that she 'relied on what he told her' amounted to evidence of a confidential relationship giving rise to a presumption of undue influence (which, in the view of George C, was doubtful), such evidence could avail C nothing, 'unless conjoined with the additional evidence that the transfer of the shares at par value was manifestly disadvantageous to her'.[120] In the absence of evidence of such disadvantage, C's plea of undue influence failed.

The 'manifest disadvantage' requirement was also applied by the Court of Appeal of the Eastern Caribbean States in *Murray v Deubery*,[121] where Floissac CJ pointed out that, in *CIBC Mortgages plc v Pitt*,[122] Lord Browne-Wilkinson had stated that 'manifest disadvantage' was irrelevant in cases of actual undue influence (Class 1), and was relevant and required only in cases of presumed undue influence (Class 2). Lord Browne-Wilkinson said:[123]

---

113 (1887) 36 Ch D 145, at 171.

114 [1985] 1 All ER 821.

115 At 827.

116 *Ormes v Beadel* (1860) 66 ER 70, at 74.

117 *Bank of Montreal v Stuart* [1911] AC 120, at 137.

118 *Poosathurai v Kannappa Chettai* (1919) LR 47 Ind App 1, at 3, 4.

119 (1991) 45 WIR 245.

120 *Ibid*, at 249, *per* George C.

121 (1996) 52 WIR 147.

122 [1993] 3 WLR 802.

123 *Ibid*, at 808.

> I have no doubt that the decision in *Morgan* does not extend to cases of actual undue influence. Despite two references in Lord Scarman's speech to cases of actual undue influence, as I read his speech he was primarily concerned to establish that disadvantage had to be shown, not as a constituent element of the cause of action for undue influence, but in order to raise a presumption of undue influence within Class 2. That was the only subject matter before the House of Lords in *Morgan* . . . I therefore hold that a claimant who proves actual undue influence is not under the further burden of proving that the transaction induced by undue influence was manifestly disadvantageous: he is entitled as of right to have it set aside.

The meaning of 'disadvantage' in this context was again considered by the Privy Council in *National Commercial Bank (Jamaica) Ltd v Hew*.[124] In this case, the appellant bank sought to recover from the respondent property developer over J$32 million owed on an overdraft facility at the bank. One of the grounds on which the respondent resisted the claim was that the loan agreement had been procured by undue influence on the part of the bank. The Jamaican Court of Appeal had identified three features of the loan agreement which were disadvantageous to the respondent: (i) the agreement stipulated that the loan money was to be spent on a development at Barrett Town; (ii) the funding was inadequate to finance more than the initial infrastructure and (iii) the security taken by the bank was excessive. The Court of Appeal went on to hold that, on the facts, a relationship of trust and confidence existed between the bank and the respondent, and that the bank had taken unfair advantage of that relationship, the loan being commercially disadvantageous to the respondent. The Court therefore set aside the agreement.

The Privy Council, on the other hand, advised that the Court of Appeal's decision be overturned. Lord Millett[125] was prepared to accept the lower court's finding that there was a relationship of trust and confidence between the respondent and C, the bank manager with whom the loan was negotiated, but he went on to emphasise that, 'however great the influence which one person may be able to wield over another, equity does not intervene unless that influence has been abused. Equity does not save people from the consequences of their own folly; it acts to save them from being victimised by other people.' He went on to state that there must be evidence of exploitation of the vulnerable party by the ascendant one. It was always highly relevant that the transaction was 'manifestly disadvantageous' to the person seeking to set it aside, but this was not always necessary.[126] Further, 'disadvantageous' in this context meant disadvantageous *as between the parties*, and 'unless the ascendant party has exploited his influence to obtain some unfair advantage from the vulnerable party, there is no ground for equity to intervene'. However commercially disadvantageous the transaction may be to the vulnerable party, equity will not set it aside if it is a fair transaction *as between the parties to it*. Lord Millett concluded by expressing the view that the Court of Appeal had 'confused the question whether the transaction was commercially disadvantageous to [the respondent] with the very different question whether it was unfair as between him and the bank'.

124 (2003) 63 WIR 183.

125 At 193.

126 *CIBC Mortgages plc v Pitt* [1993] 4 All ER 433.

In one respect, Lord Millett's approach is difficult to reconcile with that of Lord Browne-Wilkinson in *Barclays Bank plc v O'Brien*.[127] That concerns Lord Millett's statements that, 'however great the influence which one person may be able to wield over another, equity does not intervene unless that influence has been abused', and that, 'it must be shown that the ascendant party has unfairly exploited the influence he is shown or presumed to possess'. The statement that it was incumbent on the vulnerable party to prove positively that he was exploited seems to directly contradict the principle expressed in *O'Brien* that, 'in a Class 2B case, in the absence of evidence disproving undue influence, the complainant will succeed in setting aside the impugned transaction merely by proof that the complainant reposed trust and confidence in the wrongdoer, *without having to prove that the wrongdoer exerted actual undue influence or otherwise abused such trust and confidence* in relation to the particular transaction impugned'. In this connection, Lord Millett's requirement of positive proof of exploitation seems to blur the distinction so carefully made in *O'Brien* between 'Class 1' cases (actual undue influence) and 'Class 2B' (presumed undue influence). It thus remains to be seen whether courts in the Commonwealth Caribbean will follow Lord Millett's approach or that of Lord Browne-Wilkinson. Since *Hew* is a Jamaican case, the Jamaican courts will no doubt consider themselves bound by that decision, so long as the Privy Council remains the final court of appeal for Jamaica, and it is conceivable that courts in other Caribbean jurisdictions where the Privy Council is the final court of appeal will also consider themselves bound by *Hew*. On the other hand, the courts of Barbados, Belize, and Guyana, where final appeals no longer lie to the Privy Council, *O'Brien* and *Hew* will both be persuasive authorities only, and the courts will be free to adopt either approach.

The principles laid down in *Royal Bank of Scotland plc v Etridge (No 2)*[128] were applied in a recent Trinidadian case, *Republic Bank Ltd v Plus Enterprises (1990) Ltd*,[129] where a wife had executed in favour of the bank a continuing guarantee in respect of the indebtedness of a company controlled by her husband, Delzin J held the guarantee void for undue influence in the following circumstances:

> The evidence discloses a consistent attitude by the [wife] of reposing both trust and confidence in her husband in relation to the affairs of the [company], coupled with an obedient attitude to his decision-making on behalf of the [company] ... Further, the evidence discloses a marked reluctance by the husband to explain relevant documents to his wife and a consistent attitude of pressuring the wife into executing previously unexplained documents in circumstances where her attentions were actively focused elsewhere, coupled with a desire to maintain matrimonial peace. Given her reluctance to challenge her husband in these circumstances, and his obvious intention to suppress any independent judgment being exercised by his wife, I have no hesitation in finding that the husband took unfair advantage of his influence over his wife or her confidence in him. I therefore find the existence of circumstances that establish the factual inference of undue influence which, in my view, has not been rebutted by the [bank]. It is precisely these types of situations that have influenced the development of the policy of the courts disclosed in the case law, which effectively places the onus on the beneficiary of the guarantee to ensure the exercise of free will in the grant of the benefit. Accordingly, I also hold, in accordance with the evidence, that there was a duty on the [bank] to satisfy

127 [1993] 3 WLR 786.

128 [2001] 4 All ER 449.

129 (2009) High Court, Trinidad and Tobago, No 2839 of 1995, unreported [Carilaw TT 2009 HC 21].

> itself that the wife had freely entered into the transaction and that she understood the nature of the transaction. The [bank], in the circumstances disclosed by the evidence in this case, was under the duty to follow the guidelines laid down in *Royal Bank of Scotland plc v Etridge (No 2)*. There is no evidence in this case that there was any compliance with those guidelines. Indeed, the evidence establishes that the banking official did not witness the signature of the [wife], nor did [the bank] have any direct dealings with her.

DURESS

Duress at common law meant actual violence or threats of violence to the person, calculated to produce fear of loss of life or bodily harm, as, for example, where there were threats to kill a party or a close relative.[130] More recently, the concept has been extended to 'duress of goods', where a contract is induced by the illegal seizure or threat to seize a party's goods. Any contract procured by duress of either type can be set aside by the court.[131]

Economic duress

More significant in the modern law is the concept of 'economic duress', which occurs when D makes threats of such serious economic consequences to C that C is constrained to enter into an agreement. It is now established that a contract entered into as a result of such pressure is voidable at the option of the victim, as, for example, where D, a party to an existing contract with C, threatened to encourage its employees to go on strike unless C agreed to make a payment additional to the contract price; this constituted economic duress because a strike would have been so economically detrimental to C that C had no practical option other than to agree to pay.[132] Similarly, X, a carrier, entered into a contract with Y to deliver consignments of basketware to Z, a chain of retail shops with whom Y had an agreement to supply the goods. When X realised that the contract with Y might not be economically viable, X refused to continue the delivery unless Y agreed to pay a higher price for the transportation. Y agreed to the higher charges because it could not find an alternative carrier and its commercial survival depended on its fulfilling the agreement with Z. It was held that Y was not bound to pay the additional amount as Y's promise had been procured by economic duress.[133] As Lord Scarman stated in the Privy Council case of *Pao On v Lau Yiu Long*:[134]

---

130 *Anson's Law of Contract*, 29th edn, p 352; *Barton v Armstrong* [1976] AC 104, at 118.

131 On the relationship between duress, inequality of bargaining power and undue influence, see *Stechers Ltd v Cheesman* (1977) High Court, Trinidad and Tobago, No 2614 of 1972, unreported [Carilaw TT 1977 HC 66]; and *Barbados National Bank v Lehtinen* (1992) High Court, Barbados, No 1410 of 1988, unreported [Carilaw BB 1992 HC 38].

132 *B&S Contracts and Design Ltd v Victor Green Publications Ltd* [1984] ICR 419.

133 *Atlas Express Ltd v Kafco (Importers and Distributors) Ltd* [1989] 1 All ER 641.

134 [1979] 3 All ER 65, at 79.

> There is nothing contrary to principle in recognising economic duress as a factor which may render a contract voidable, provided always that the basis of such recognition is that it must always amount to a coercion of will which vitiates consent.

A well-known example of economic duress is the case of *D&C Builders Ltd v Rees*[135] where, as we have seen,[136] the claimants were a small firm who were owed £482 by the defendant for building work done. The defendant's wife, knowing that the claimants were in financial difficulties, offered them £300 in full settlement, saying that if they did not accept the offer they would get nothing. Lord Denning MR held that the claimants were not bound by their promise to accept the lesser amount in full settlement; this, he said, was 'no true accord: the debtor's wife held the creditor to ransom. The creditor was in need of money to meet its own commitments and she knew it.'[137]

Economic duress was also an element of the decision in *Lloyds Bank Ltd v Bundy*.[138] In this case, B was an elderly farmer who owned a farmhouse which was his only substantial asset. Both B, his son, and his son's company were customers of the appellant bank. When the company experienced financial difficulties, B guaranteed its overdraft at the bank up to £1,500, charging the house as security. Later, B guaranteed the overdraft for a further £5,000 and charged the house for a further £6,000. The company's difficulties continued, and the bank manager advised B that the bank would continue to extend overdraft facilities to the company only on condition that B executed a further guarantee of £11,000 and a charge of £3,500. B complied but, six months later, the company went into receivership and the bank sought to enforce the guarantee and the charge. The English Court of Appeal held that both the guarantee and the charge should be set aside. Significantly, Lord Denning, with or from whom the other Justices of Appeal neither concurred nor dissented, propounded a wide principle of 'inequality of bargaining power' which, in the circumstances of this case, required the bank to ensure that B received independent legal advice on the affairs of the company and on the effect of the guarantee and charge in question. Since the bank had failed to do so, the transactions were voidable. Lord Denning said:[139]

> English law gives relief to one who, without independent advice, enters into a contract upon terms which are very unfair or transfers property for a consideration which is grossly inadequate, when his bargaining power is grievously impaired by reason of his own needs or desires, or by his own ignorance or infirmity, coupled with undue influences or pressures brought to bear on him by or for the benefit of the other. When I use the word 'undue', I do not mean to suggest that the principle depends on proof of any wrongdoing. The one who stipulates for an unfair advantage may be moved solely by his own self-interest, unconscious of the distress he is bringing on the other. I have also avoided any reference to the will of the one being 'dominated' or 'overcome' by the other. One who is in extreme need may knowingly consent to a most improvident bargain, solely to relieve the straits in which he finds himself.

Lloyds Bank Ltd v Bundy can thus be regarded as an application of three principles: economic duress, undue influence, and inequality of bargaining power, though economic duress is perhaps the most justifiable basis of the decision, given that it

135 [1965] 3 All ER 837.
136 See p 42, above.
137 *Ibid*, at 841.
138 [1974] 3 All ER 757.
139 *Ibid*, at 765.

was Lord Denning alone who promoted the concept of 'inequality of bargaining power', and that this was not a case where it had been proved that the bank stood in a position of undue influence over the party seeking to avoid the transaction.

A Caribbean example of economic duress is *Ting v Borelli*.[140] Here, the liquidators of a Bermudian company, in order to raise funds, proposed a scheme of arrangement under section 99 of the Bermuda Companies Act. The scheme was opposed by T and two companies under his control which were owners of a portion of the share capital of the Bermudian company. The liquidators was under pressure to meet a deadline, as the scheme was destined to fail if the deadline were not met. Accordingly, the liquidators entered into a settlement agreement with T and his two companies whereby the latter undertook to withdraw their opposition to the scheme in return for the liquidators' 'irrevocable covenant' not to pursue any claims whatsoever against T and the companies. The Privy Council held that the settlement was voidable on the ground of economic duress, since the liquidators 'entered into the settlement agreement as the result of the illegitimate means employed by [T], namely opposing the scheme for no good reason and in using forgery and false evidence in support of that opposition, all in order to prevent the liquidators from investigating his conduct of the affairs of [the Bermudian company] or making claims against him arising out of that conduct'. As Lord Saville explained:[141]

> An agreement entered into as the result of duress is not valid as a matter of law. Duress is the obtaining of agreement or consent by illegitimate means.[142] Such means include what is known as 'economic duress', where one party exerts illegitimate economic or similar pressure on another. An agreement obtained through duress is invalid in the sense that the party subject to the duress has the right to withdraw from the agreement, though that right may be lost if that party later affirms the agreement or waives the right to withdraw from it.

On the other hand, in *Martin Brower Co v Burbank Development Ltd*,[143] the Barbados High Court found no evidence of economic duress. In this case, E and F signed an unconditional written guarantee in which they agreed to be responsible for all debts owed by D to the claimant company for goods supplied to D. Belgrave J examined the correspondence between the parties and could find no evidence therein or elsewhere that the claimant had exerted any undue pressure or coercion against the guarantors; it was also significant that the guarantors who were claiming to have been subjected to duress had made no protest, and had taken no steps to avoid the guarantee. In coming to the conclusion that there had been no duress, Belgrave J cited[144] the following extract from the judgment of Lord Scarman in *Pao On v Lau Yiu*:[145]

> Duress, whatever form it takes, is a coercion of the will so as to vitiate consent. Their Lordships agree with the observation of Kerr J in *The Siboen and The Sibotre*[146] that in a

140 (2010) 79 WIR 204.

141 *Ibid*, at 213, 214.

142 *DPP for Northern Ireland v Lynch* [1975] 1 All ER 913; *Universe Tankships Inc of Monrovia v International Transport Workers' Federation* [1982] 2 All ER 67.

143 (1992) 28 Barb LR 9.

144 *Ibid*, at 16.

145 [1979] 3 All ER 65, at 78.

146 [1976] 1 Lloyds Rep 293, at 336.

> contractual situation commercial pressure is not enough. There must be present some factor which could in law be regarded as coercion of his will so as to vitiate his consent. This conception is in line with what was said in this Board's decision in *Barton v Armstrong*[147] by Lord Wilberforce and Lord Simon of Glaisdale: 'In determining whether there was a coercion of the will such that there was no true consent, it is material to enquire whether the person alleged to have been coerced did or did not protest, whether, at the time he was allegedly coerced into making the contract, he did or did not have an alternative course open to him, such as an adequate legal remedy; whether he was independently advised; and whether, after entering into the contract, he took steps to avoid it. All these matters are . . . relevant in determining whether he acted voluntarily or not.'

Unconscionable bargains

Whereas the English courts have generally been willing to set aside contracts only where either undue influence or economic duress was established according to well defined principles, some Caribbean judges, like courts in Canada[148] and Australia,[149] have been prepared to apply a broader principle of unconscionability of bargains having much in common with Lord Denning's concept of 'inequality of bargaining power', thus enabling the court to set aside transactions in which neither undue influence nor economic duress can be proved according to substantive law principles. Haynes C, in a Guyanese case, *Singh v Singh*,[150] explained the concept as follows:

> This rule of equity which places the onus of proof that an impeached transaction is just, on him who seeks to uphold it, may come into play whenever the transaction (be it a sale, gift or a settlement or any other property arrangement) has been entered into between parties whose bargaining positions are so unequal for any of the reasons explained in the cases that, in equity, the one needs protection against the other, and it is, on the face of it, an improvident one . . . [Improvidence] most frequently involves the adequacy of the price, in the case of a sale, or the disadvantages of the financial provisions in transactions other than sales. In some cases, depending on the circumstances, it may be sufficient to discharge this onus to prove that the party affected fully understood and appreciated the nature and effect of what he was doing, and that his consent to it was free and voluntary. In some cases, proof that the sale price was either the full market price or, if not, was still a just one, might be adequate. In some, perhaps in most cases, the absence of independent legal or other competent advice would be fatal or might make it more difficult to discharge the onus. And in other cases, it might call for proof of more than one of these factors. It is neither practicable nor desirable to essay to pronounce an exhaustive statement of the evidential positions which may exist. But, at the end of the day, for the impeached transaction to stand or to be legally enforceable, the court must be satisfied that no undue advantage has been taken of the party who was in the weaker bargaining position and so needed to be protected.

In a Canadian case, *Morrison v Coast Finance Ltd*,[151] Davey JA pointed out that although the equitable concepts of unconscionable bargains and undue influence are

147 [1975] 2 All ER 465.

148 *Morrison v Coast Finance Ltd* (1966) 55 DLR (2d) 710.

149 *Commercial Bank of Australia Ltd v Amadio* (1983) 151 CLR 447.

150 (1978) 25 WIR 410, at 419, discussed by Crane J in *Gayadharsingh v Jones* (1982) High Court, Trinidad and Tobago, No 1969 of 1976, unreported [Carilaw TT 1982 HC 34].

151 (1966) 55 DLR (2d) 710.

closely related, they are nevertheless separate and distinct. Thus, where a court finds against undue influence, that is not the end of the matter, for it may yet give relief if it considers the transaction to be unconscionable. In his view, 'a plea of undue influence attacks the sufficiency of consent, [whereas] a plea that a bargain is unconscionable invokes relief against an unfair advantage gained by an unconscientious use of power by a stronger party against a weaker'. Davey JA continued:[152]

> On such a claim, the material ingredients are proof of inequality in the position of the parties arising out of the ignorance, need or distress of the weaker, which left him in the power of the stronger, and proof of substantial unfairness of the bargain obtained by the stronger. On proof of these circumstances, it creates a presumption of fraud which the stronger must repel by proving that the bargain was fair, just and reasonable.

It is debatable whether the narrow English approach or the broader view favoured in Canada and Australia is more suitable in the Caribbean context. On the one hand, the large gap between the wealthier and the poorer classes in most Caribbean jurisdictions would suggest that the concept of unconscionable bargains and inequality of bargaining power has a useful role to play; on the other, application of the concept has the potential to cause uncertainty and lead to instability in contractual relations, particularly as different courts and judges are likely to have divergent views as to the meaning and scope of unconscionability and improvidence in the contractual context. It may be preferable to address issues of unconscionability through legislation such as that relating to consumer protection and unfair contract terms.

152 *Ibid.*

CHAPTER 10

ILLEGALITY

Introduction

A contract which, on its face, has all the necessary characteristics of a valid, enforceable agreement, may be struck down on the ground that some statutory provision renders it illegal, or that it is tainted with a degree of moral turpitude that, on public policy grounds, renders it void and unenforceable at common law. Apart from the element of deterrence, perhaps the main reason for the courts' refusal to entertain claims founded on illegal or immoral behaviour is that the dignity of the court would be undermined if it were seen to be encouraging or condoning reprehensible acts. The twin pillars of the law relating to illegal contracts are the Latin maxims, *'ex turpi causa non oritur actio'* ('no action can be founded on an illegal act') and *'in pari delicto, potior est conditio defendentis'* ('where the parties are equally at fault, the defendant's position is the stronger'). The combined effect of these maxims, subject to certain exceptions, is that (i) an illegal contract cannot be enforced in a court of law, and (ii) where the parties are equally at fault, any property which has been handed over to a party to an illegal contract cannot be recovered by order of a court of law.

The law relating to illegal contracts is complex, for several reasons: first, there are two recognisable species of illegality – 'statutory illegality' and 'common law illegality' – which require differing approaches; secondly, some contracts are held to be expressly prohibited by a statute (contracts 'illegal as formed'), while others are held not to be expressly prohibited by the statute, but may have been performed in a way which is illegal (contracts 'illegal as performed'), a distinction that is often difficult to draw, and which may give rise to tricky points of statutory interpretation; thirdly, there are often difficulties concerning the effects of illegality, the determination of which may depend on the application of a large number of technical rules and principles; and fourthly, the 'unruly horse' of public policy rides chaotically over the whole area of illegal contracts, which may make the outcome of a given case difficult to predict. The inherent difficulty of this area of the law has been expressed by the authors of *Chitty on Contracts*[1] thus:

> The diversity of the fields with which policy is concerned, and of the circumstances in which a contractual claim may be affected by it, combine to make this branch of the law of contract inevitably complex – a complexity which has been aggravated by lack of systematisation and by the confusing terminology which has often been adopted.

STATUTORY ILLEGALITY

Contracts expressly prohibited by statute

Where a contract is expressly forbidden by a statute, there is no doubt that the intention of the legislature is that it shall not be enforced, for 'what is done

---

1 25th edn, Vol 1, para 1031, p 546, cited with approval by Meerabux J in *Acuzena v de Molina* (1991) 50 WIR 85, at 88. See pp 192, 193, below.

in contravention of the provisions of an Act of Parliament cannot be made the subject-matter of an action'.[2] Such a contract is often described as a contract 'illegal as formed'. A well-known example is *Re Mahmoud and Ispahani*.[3] Here, a wartime statutory order prohibited the sale of certain goods, including linseed oil, without a licence from the Food Controller. The claimant contracted to sell a quantity of linseed oil to the defendant. The claimant had a licence, while the defendant did not, but the latter deceived the claimant into believing that he was licensed. Ultimately, the defendant refused to take delivery of the oil, and the claimant sued him for damages for non-acceptance. It was held that, once it had been shown that the parties were prohibited by statute from entering into the contract, the court could not entertain an action on the agreement by either party, and the fact that the defendant was alone at fault, and was relying on his own illegal conduct, was immaterial. In the words of Bankes LJ, 'the statutory order is a clear and unequivocal declaration by the legislature, in the public interest, that this particular kind of contract shall not be entered into.'[4]

A clear example of statutory illegality in the Caribbean is to be found in *Off Course Betting (1955) Ltd v Chen*,[5] which concerned the application of the Betting, Gaming and Lotteries Act, 1965 (Laws of Jamaica). Section 4(1)(b) provided that, 'no person shall use, or cause or knowingly permit any other person to use, any premises for the purpose of the effecting of any . . . betting transactions by that person . . . and every person who contravenes any of the provisions of this subsection shall be guilty of an offence'. Section 9(1) provided that, 'where in the case of any premises there is for the time being in force a licence authorising the holder of the licence to use those premises as a betting office . . . section 4(1)(b) shall not apply to the use of those premises for the effecting of betting transactions with or through the holder of the licence or any servant of his.'

In this case, C sued the defendants to recover the sum of £4,225, which he claimed he had won on bets placed with the defendants on English horse races. C had been in the habit of placing bets with the defendants through his wife, the manager of the betting office, not in the office itself but in an adjacent shop where he carried on his grocery business, and this is what happened on the day in question, the bets being evidenced by a voucher written up by the wife. The trial judge, Hercules J, found in favour of C, on the basis that, even if there had been breaches of the Act, they did not render the betting contract unenforceable.

The Jamaican Court of Appeal, by a majority, found for the defendants. In the view of Graham-Perkins JA, there was no ambiguity in the language of sections 4(1)(b) and 9(1). Their combined effect was to prohibit the making of betting transactions in unlicensed premises, and any such contract was illegal and void. He explained:

> It is to be noted that Hercules J does not appear to have made any findings on the two critical questions involved in the submissions before him, namely (1) whether the

2 Langton v Hughes (1813) 1 M & S 593, at 596, *per* Lord Ellenborough CJ.

3 [1921] 2 KB 716. See also *Chai Sau Yin v Liew Kwee Sam* [1962] AC 304 (contract to purchase rubber, where one of the parties did not have a licence as required by statute, held illegal and unenforceable); *Esi v Moroku* (1940) 15 NLR 116 (sublease of Crown land without the Governor's consent, as required by statute, held illegal: sub-lessor unable to sue for rent).

4 [1921] 2 KB 716, at 724.

5 (1972) Court of Appeal, Jamaica, Civ App No 27 of 1969, unreported [Carilaw JM 1972 CA 27].

> questioned transaction was or was not in breach of any of the prohibitory provisions of the Act or of the relevant regulations, and (2) assuming any such breach, and depending on the nature thereof, what consequences flowed therefrom as a matter of law. Let me say at once that in my view the answers to the questions posed above depend essentially on the meaning of the very plain language of sections 4(1)(b) and 9(1) of the Act. They do not involve any searching analysis of the structure, scope or purpose of the Act, nor an examination of its moral implications. Neither do they require this Court to embark on a dissertation on that popular hobby-horse – public policy . . . The language of these subsections is unmistakably clear. Section 9(1) removes from the operation of section 4(1)(b) any premises in respect of which there is in force a betting office licence. It is only on such licensed premises that betting transactions may lawfully be effected. In the absence of such a licence, section 4(1)(b) prohibits the user by any person of any premises for the purpose of effecting betting transactions. It is the user for a particular purpose without a licence that offends against the subsection. Put in another way, betting transactions may be effected on premises licensed for that purpose, and on no other . . . There is, in my view, not the least ambiguity in the language of section 4(1)(b). What is therein prohibited in very positive and clear language is the effecting of betting transactions on unlicensed premises. It must follow, therefore, that such transactions are unlawful. In this circumstance, there cannot be the least doubt as to the principle to be applied. A contract which is expressly forbidden can give rise to no cause of action to a party who seeks to enforce it. It has been suggested that to hold that the transaction with which I am here concerned is illegal is to put a premium on deceit. This may very well be, but this cannot be the concern of this Court in the particular circumstances of this case. It is no doubt true that the objection that a contract is illegal as between a plaintiff and a defendant sounds very ill in the mouth of the defendant. Nearly two hundred years ago, Lord Mansfield observed: 'It is not for his [a defendant's] sake that the objection is ever allowed, but it is founded on general principles of policy, which the defendant has the advantage of, contrary to the real justice, as between him and the plaintiff, by accident, if I may so say. The principle of public policy is this: *ex dolo malo non oritur actio*. No court will lend its aid to a man who founds his cause of action upon an immoral or illegal act . . . It is upon that ground that the Court goes; not for the sake of the defendant, but because it will not lend its aid to such a plaintiff. So if the plaintiff and the defendant were to change sides, and the defendant were to bring his action against the plaintiff, the latter would then have the advantage of it' . . . These words are as relevant today as they were when Lord Mansfield spoke.

Another example of an express statutory prohibition rendering a contract illegal is the Bahamian case of *Albury v Webster*.[6] Section 4 of the Real Estate (Brokers and Salesmen) Act 1995, provides that 'a person shall not engage in the practice of real estate business . . . in the capacity of a real estate broker unless he is the holder of a valid licence . . . authorising him so to do', and section 40 goes further by providing that a person who engages in such practice without a licence 'shall not be entitled to bring any suit or action for the recovery of any fee or reward for . . . anything done by him on behalf of any other person in the course of engaging in such practice'. Accordingly, actions by an unlicensed company and its agent to recover a sum allegedly due from the defendant as sales commission, in respect of the sale of certain property, failed. In the words of Osadebay Sr J:

> The court will not enforce an agreement which is expressly or impliedly prohibited by statute. If a contract is of the nature that the court will not enforce, it does not matter what the intent of the parties is, nor does it matter what the practice of the parties is. Once it is determined that an agreement is of this class, then it is unenforceable, whether

6 (2000) Supreme Court, The Bahamas, No 517 of 1999, unreported [Carilaw BS 2000 SC 51].

> the parties meant to break the law or not . . . The agreement is illegal and sales commission cannot be recovered.

In another Bahamian case, *Bowe v Mitchell*,[7] the claimant taxi-driver, believing that he could no longer drive because of an eye condition, agreed to rent his licence plate, taximeter and radio call instrument to the defendant for the sum of $100 a week. The agreement was in breach of section 68 of the Road Traffic Act (Laws of the Bahamas, Cap 204), which provided that, 'the controller may, in his discretion, transfer a taxi-cab . . . licence . . . from the holder to another person, but such transfer shall not be claimed as of right . . . A taxicab . . . licence shall become void and of no effect and shall forthwith be surrendered to the controller . . . unless the licence is transferred under this section.' An action by the claimant for arrears of rental failed. Without stating whether he regarded this as a case of express or of implied statutory prohibition, Georges CJ said:

> The Act plainly has as one of its objectives that of ensuring that taxicab licences are not transferred from one holder to another without the consent of the controller. On any such attempted transfer, the licence becomes void and must be surrendered. The contract for the hiring of the 'plate' was thus unenforceable by statute and the claimant's claim for the rental allegedly in arrears must fail.

Contracts impliedly prohibited by statute

A contract which is impliedly prohibited by a statutory provision will, as in the case of an express prohibition, be illegal and unenforceable. It may be a difficult task for the court to decide whether a particular contract is impliedly prohibited, and it is essentially a matter of statutory interpretation and ascertainment of the intention of the legislature. An important test is whether the purpose of the statute is to protect the public from damage or fraud, or whether it is merely for revenue preservation. If it is the former, then a contract made in contravention of the statute is more likely to be held to be illegal; if the latter, the court is more likely to regard it as valid and enforceable.[8] It is clear also that the courts take into account the fact that, in today's world, there is a proliferation of statutory rules and regulations affecting many aspects of commercial activity, many of which impose penalties for even minor infringements, and the courts are reluctant to strike down contracts on the ground of statutory illegality, in the absence of a clear intention to that effect on the part of the legislature.[9]

A case in which an implied statutory prohibition was found by the court is *Cope v Rowlands*.[10] Here, the claimant, who was acting as a broker in the City of London without having a licence as required by statute, sought to recover from the defendant payment for work done in buying and selling stock. The statute did not expressly

---

7 (1985) Supreme Court, The Bahamas, No 457 of 1984, unreported [Carilaw BS 1985 SC 11].

8 *Victorian Daylesford Syndicate Ltd v Dott* (1905) 74 LJCR 673, at 676, *per* Buckley J; *Gonzales v Hassanali* (1965) 8 WIR 146, *per* Wooding CJ; *Grant v Williams* (1987) Court of Appeal, Jamaica, Civ App No 20 of 1985 (unreported) [Carilaw JM 1987 CA 103], *per* Carberry JA.

9 *St John Shipping Corp v Joseph Rank Ltd* [1956] 3 All ER 683, at 690,691; *Shaw v Groom* [1970] 2 QB 504, at 522; *Vita Food Products v Unus Shipping Co Ltd* [1939] 1 All ER 513, at 523.

10 (1836) 150 ER 711; cf *Jose's Ltd v Esso Standard Oil Co* (2000) Court of Appeal, Cayman Islands, unreported [Carilaw KY 2000 CA 11].

prohibit contracts concerning payment to unlicensed brokers, but it did provide that any person who acted as a broker in the City without first obtaining a licence should forfeit and pay to the City £25 for each such offence. It was held that, since one of the objectives of the legislature was the benefit and security of the public in transactions negotiated by brokers, 'the clause which imposes a penalty must be taken to imply a prohibition of all unadmitted persons to act as brokers, and consequently to prohibit, by necessary inference, all contracts which such persons make for compensation to themselves for so acting.' The claimant's action accordingly failed.

On the other hand, *Archbolds (Freightage) Ltd v S Spanglett Ltd*[11] is an example of a case where the court declined to hold that the contract had been impliedly rendered illegal by the statute. Under the provisions of the Road Traffic Act 1933, no person should use a vehicle for the carriage of goods by road unless he held an 'A' or a 'C' licence. The former entitled him to carry the goods of others for reward, while the latter was restricted to carriage of the person's own goods. The defendants agreed with the claimants to transport a consignment of whisky belonging to third parties from Leeds to London. Unknown to the claimants, the vehicle to be used for the journey did not have an 'A' licence. Owing to the driver's negligence, the whisky was stolen en route, and the claimants sued the defendants for damages for the loss. The defendants contended that they were not liable on the contract, their argument being that contracts of carriage made with unlicensed carriers were *implicitly* prohibited by the statute, so that the contract in this case was illegal and unenforceable. The court rejected that contention. Pearce LJ emphasised that the question of whether a contract was impliedly prohibited was to be answered by construing the statute and identifying its fundamental purpose. In this instance, 'The object of the [Act] was not to interfere with the owner of goods or his facilities for transport, but to control those who provided the transport, with a view to promoting its efficiency. Transport of goods was not made illegal, but the various licence holders were prohibited from encroaching on one another's territory, the intention of the Act being to provide an orderly and comprehensive service.' Accordingly, the claimants were entitled to damages for breach.

In deciding whether a statute impliedly prohibits or nullifies a contract, an important consideration is whether the purpose of the statute was (a) to protect the public, or (b) merely to protect the revenue; for only in the case of the former is it likely to be construed as nullifying or prohibiting the contract.[12]

An example of the application of this distinction is *Weekes v Gibbons*,[13] the central issue in which was whether the Registration of Building and Civil Engineering Contracting Undertakings Ordinance 1968 (Montserrat) nullified building contracts which had not been registered as required by the Ordinance, so that a contractor who was in breach of the Ordinance would be unable to recover from the building owner the contract price for building works carried out by him. Floissac CJ opined[14]

---

11 [1961] 1 All ER 417.

12 The same distinction is made in cases of illegal *performance* of contracts which are *ex facie* valid: *Anderson Ltd v Daniel* [1924] 1 KB 138, at 147, *per* Scrutton LJ; *Ambrose v Boston* (1993) 55 WIR 184, at 193, 194, *per* Bernard JA.

13 (1993) 45 WIR 142 (Court of Appeal, Eastern Caribbean States).

14 *Ibid*, at 143.

that, in order to resolve the issue, and in the absence of any express nullification or prohibition in the statute, the issue was whether such nullification or prohibition ought to be implied, which was a matter of ascertaining the intention of the legislature. The learned Chief Justice took the view that there were a number of surrounding circumstances that militated against the implication of a legislative intent to nullify unregistered building contracts, among which were (i) that the statute did not prescribe contractual terms for the protection of the building owner or the public, and (ii) that there was no discernible ground of public policy which could justify the illegality and nullity of unregistered building contracts and the severe consequences of such illegality and nullity.

Similarly, Satrohan Singh JA stated[15] that the issue was 'whether the Act absolutely prohibited, as being against morality or public policy, building or civil engineering undertakings of $10,000 or more, unless such undertakings were performed pursuant to a registered agreement, or whether the Act was created mainly for revenue purposes'. He did not find that it was the intention of the legislature that the requirement for registration in the Ordinance was for any purpose other than the protection of the revenue. In his view, the only remedy contemplated by the statute for the infringement of its provisions was a penalty in the form of a $500 fine; the requirement for registration of a building contract was not created either expressly or by implication for the protection of the public, and it could not therefore be construed as absolutely prohibiting the performance of a contract which had not been registered. He therefore held that the non-registration of the contract in the instant case did not affect its enforceability, and the contractor was entitled to sue on it.

Illegal performance of a contract

A contract which is not *ex facie* illegal and which is perfectly valid in its inception may be *performed* in a way that contravenes a statute. Indeed, *Archbolds (Freightage) Ltd v S Spanglett Ltd* (above) may be categorised as such a case. Where a contract is legal in its formation but is performed in an unlawful way, the party who is guilty of illegal performance cannot enforce the contract. Thus, where sellers of artificial fertilisers were required by statute to give to the buyer an invoice stating the percentages of certain chemicals contained in the goods, the sellers of a consignment of artificial manure who had failed to comply with the statute were held to be unable to recover the purchase price from the buyer.[16] And even the party who is not guilty of a breach of the statute will be unable to enforce the contract if he acquiesced in the other's wrongdoing. Thus, where C entered into a contract with D, a road haulage contractor, to transport heavy machinery, and D, with the acquiescence of C's manager, overloaded the vehicle, contrary to statutory regulations prescribing maximum loads, so that it toppled over and the load was damaged, C could not sue D for damages under the contract (nor could D have sued C).[17]

15 *Ibid*, at 144, 147, 148.

16 *Anderson Ltd v Daniel* [1924] 1 KB 138.

17 *Ashmore, Benson, Pease and Co Ltd v AV Dawson Ltd* [1973] 2 All ER 856.

On the other hand, where the illegal performance is by one party only, without the assent of the other, the latter has his usual remedies under the contract. The rationale for this rule is that, since the contract is legal and therefore valid from its inception, and becomes illegal only because of the other party's unlawful performance, there is no reason why the innocent party should be prevented from suing.[18]

Statutes imposing only a penalty

Where a statute provides a penalty for the commission of an offence during the performance of a contract, the contract will not necessarily be rendered illegal. Again, it is a question of statutory interpretation as to whether the intention of the legislature was that the contract should be unenforceable by the party guilty of illegal performance, or whether it intended merely to impose a penalty. If the imposition of a penalty only was intended, then even the guilty party may enforce the contract. Thus, for instance, a landlord who failed to provide a tenant with a 'rent book' containing all the information required by statute, was not debarred from suing for rent, as the purpose of the legislation was not to interfere with the contractual rights and obligations of the parties, but rather to impose a criminal penalty for non-compliance.[19]

A leading example is *St John Shipping Corp v Joseph Rank Ltd*.[20] Here, the claimants, who were shipowners, contracted to carry grain from the United States to England. During the course of the voyage, the master of the ship allowed the ship to become overloaded, contrary to the Merchant Shipping Act 1932. The master was prosecuted and fined for the offence. The defendants, the consignees of part of the cargo, withheld part of the freight due, arguing that the claimants were not entitled to enforce a contract which had been performed in an illegal manner. The court rejected the defendants' contention. The Act did not render illegal the contract of carriage; it merely imposed a penalty for infringement, and the overloading was merely an incident in the course of performance

Void contracts

Where a statute declares a contract, or a particular kind of contractual term, to be void, the provisions of the statute may declare what are to be the consequences of such voidness. Although neither party to such a contract can enforce it, money or property transferred under it may be recoverable, provided recovery is consistent with the terms of the statute.[21]

18 *Anderson Ltd v Daniel*, above, n 14, pp 145,147,149; *Marles v Philip Trant and Sons Ltd (No 2)* [1953] 1 All ER 651. See also *Maragh v Williams* (1970) Court of Appeal, Jamaica, Civ App No 89 of 1969 [Carilaw JM 1970 CA 60].

19 *Shaw v Groom* [1970] 1 All ER 72.

20 [1956] 3 All ER 683.

21 *North Central Wagon Finance Co Ltd v Brailsford* [1962] 1 WLR 1288.

Contract unenforceable by one party only

A statute may impose a duty on one party to comply with a particular regulation, and go on to provide expressly or impliedly that, in the event of a breach by that party, the contract will be unenforceable by him, but may be enforced by the other party. Again, it is always a question of construction as to whether the statute has this effect.[22] In *Anderson Ltd v Daniel*,[23] a statutory provision required sellers of fertilisers to give to each buyer an invoice stating the percentage of certain chemical substances contained in the fertilisers sold. In this case, the seller had failed to provide an invoice to the buyer, and in an action to recover the price of the goods, the buyer pleaded that the contract was unenforceable on account of the seller's illegal performance. It was held that the seller's action failed. Since he was the party responsible for the breach of the statutory requirement, the contract was unenforceable by him. On the other hand, the innocent buyer would have been entitled to enforce the agreement against the seller if, for instance, the seller had failed to deliver the goods.

Moneylending contracts and contracts subject to exchange control

Moneylending contracts

In most jurisdictions, statutory provisions seek to regulate moneylending transactions, and the issue in a number of Caribbean cases has been whether a moneylending contract which is shown to have been formed or performed in breach of such provisions is thereby rendered illegal and unenforceable. The courts in Trinidad and Tobago have dealt with this issue on a number of occasions. In *Gonsalves v Hassanali*,[24] for instance, the claimant sought to recover from the defendant the sum of $240 lent on a promissory note. The claimant was shown to have been carrying on the business of a moneylender without being licensed to do so under section 4(b) of the Moneylenders Ordinance. Wooding CJ, delivering the judgment of the Court of Appeal, held that the effect of the breach was that the loan contract on which the claimant was suing was illegal and void, so that she could not recover the amount of the loan. The learned Chief Justice cited the following passage from the judgment of Buckley J in *Victorian Daylesford Syndicate Ltd v Dott*:[25]

> There is no question that a contract which is prohibited, whether expressly or by implication, by a statute is illegal and cannot be enforced. I have to see whether the contract is in this case prohibited expressly or by implication. For this purpose, statutes may be grouped under two heads – those in which a penalty is imposed upon an act not merely for revenue purposes, but also for the protection of the public . . . If I arrive at the conclusion that one of the objects is the protection of the public, then the act is impliedly prohibited by the statute, and is illegal . . . The present case is one that is upon this point

22 *Victorian Daylesford Syndicate Ltd v Dott* (1905) 74 LJ CR 673.

23 [1924] 1 KB 138.

24 (1965) 8 WIR 146, applied in *Ramai v Sooknanan* (2006) High Court, Trinidad and Tobago, No 1534 of 1999, unreported [Carilaw TT 2006 HC 132], *per* Ibrahim J and *Noel v Samuel* (1991) High Court, Trinidad and Tobago, No 6011 of 1988, unreported [Carilaw TT 1991 HC 72], *per* Ramlogan J.

25 (1905) 74 LJCR 673, at 676.

> abundantly plain. There is no question of protection of the revenue here at all. The whole purpose is the protection of the public.

A similar approach was taken in another Trinidadian case, *South Western Atlantic Investment and Trust Co Ltd v Millette*,[26] where a borrower was in default in payment of $222,106, allegedly due to the lender on a promissory note. The borrower contended that the loan contract was illegal and unenforceable on the grounds, *inter alia*, (i) that the loan was at a higher rate of interest than that permitted by section 12 of the Moneylenders' Act, Ch 84:04; and (ii) that the loan was for a period of less than one year, contrary to section 15(1)(b) of the Financial Institutions (Non-Banking) Act, No 2 of 1979. Davis J accepted both of these arguments and held that the contract was illegal and unenforceable. With respect to (ii), he explained:

> In order to determine whether the promissory note in this case is illegal or not, I am of opinion that the test laid down in *Chitty on Contracts*, 25th edn, para 1146, must be applied to the Act. That test has been stated thus: 'Where the Act does not expressly deprive the plaintiff of his civil remedies under the contract, the appropriate question to ask is whether, having regard to the Act and the evils against which it was intended to guard and the circumstances in which the contract was made and to be performed, it would in fact be against public policy to enforce it.' The evils which the Financial Institutions (Non-Banking) Act intended to guard against clearly are that financial institutions must not carry on the business of banking. For this purpose that Act by Part IV under the heading 'Prohibitions' prohibits certain activities, one of which is the granting of loans for less than one year. It is to be noted that while by section 38 of that Act the Minister is empowered to exempt a financial institution which makes application for that purpose from certain of the prohibitions in Part IV, the prohibition against granting loans for less than a year is not one for which an exemption may be granted. The prohibition is therefore absolute in terms . . . The penalty for contravention of section 15(1)(b) is revocation of the institution's licence. In other words, a breach of section 15(1)(b) of the Act can lead to the demise of a financial institution. The financial institution can cease to exist. I feel justified, therefore, in concluding that Parliament intended to treat the granting of loans for less than a year as an act forbidden by statute as illegal and an act against which there could be no relief.

By contrast, in a more recent case, *Fort Vue Ltd v Young*,[27] the Trinidad and Tobago Court of Appeal came to a different conclusion regarding the effect of a breach of section 12 of the Moneylenders' Act. The main issue in the case was whether a contract for the loan of money by a person other than a licensed moneylender, at a rate of interest higher than that stipulated by the section, was illegal and unenforceable. The trial judge had held, following *Gonzales v Hassanali* and *Victorian Daylesford Syndicate Ltd v Dott*, that, 'the authorities make it clear that where the act is prohibited and a penalty is prescribed every time the act is performed, it is an illegal act, so both money and security are irrecoverable.' In his view, the purpose of the Moneylenders' Act was not merely the protection of the revenue 'but rather the protection of the public, in which case the entire transaction must be struck down as being illegal and void'. Warner JA, however, delivering the judgment of the Court of Appeal, stated that the proper interpretation of section 24 of the Act pointed to a different conclusion, as it provided a remedy for the infringement of section 12, in

26 (1985) High Court, Trinidad and Tobago, No 5555 of 1983, unreported [Carilaw TT 1985 HC 81].

27 (1988) Court of Appeal, Trinidad and Tobago, Civ App No 133 of 1986, unreported [Carilaw TT 1988 CA 11].

addition to the criminal sanction, that was not premised upon the loan contract being treated as void. In particular, section 24 provided that, where there has been a breach of section 12, the court 'may re-open the transaction and take an account between the lender and the person sued': provisions which were inconsistent with the contract being void or unenforceable. In Warner, JA's words, it was 'abundantly clear that the intention of the legislature [was] to protect the borrower by way of section 24 without taking the extreme step of rendering the contract unenforceable'. Warner JA further observed that in *South Western Atlantic Investment and Trust Co Ltd v Millette*,[28] the provisions of section 24 were not considered, and he expressed the view that, 'so far as the judgment [in that case] declares that a contract for a loan at a rate of interest in excess of the maximum permitted under section 12 is void and unenforceable, it is erroneous.'

Contracts subject to exchange control

Although the majority of Commonwealth Caribbean countries have abolished exchange control regulations, such controls continue to apply in Barbados, Belize and, to a limited extent, The Bahamas. An issue which has often been litigated is whether a contract subject to exchange control, but concluded without compliance with the regulations, is illegal and void. A number of cases dealing with this question were decided at a time when exchange control legislation was the norm throughout the Caribbean, in jurisdictions which have since abolished exchange control; but these cases remain useful illustrations of the nature and scope of statutory illegality.

In general, where contracts have been entered into in breach of exchange control regulations, the courts in the Caribbean have tended not to regard such contracts as illegal and void. As has been pointed out in a number of cases,[29] exchange control legislation was designed to stabilise and protect the national economies by making it necessary for the permission of the exchange control authority to be obtained for certain transactions involving foreign currency but, as Blackman J pointed out in a recent case in the Barbados High Court,[30] the modern tendency in the interpretation of exchange control legislation is to adopt a purposive, rather than a narrow, literal approach, and 'to avoid harsh, punitive measures'.

One of the earlier cases, *Watkis v Roblin*,[31] concerned the Jamaican Exchange Control Act (since repealed),[32] section 7 of which provided that, 'Except with the permission of the Authority, no person shall ... make any payment to or for the

---

28 Above, n 24.

29 E.g. *Bank of London & Montreal Ltd v Sale* (1967) 12 WIR 149, at 166, *per* Waddington JA; *Chase Manhattan Bank v Sanitary Laundry Co Ltd* (1988) Court of Appeal, Barbados, Civ App No 9 of 1985 (unreported) [Carilaw BB 1988 CA 21], *per* Husbands CJ (Ag); and *Kings Beach Hotel Ltd v Marks* (2006) High Court, Barbados, No 995 of 2006 (unreported) [Carilaw BB 2006 HC 20], and *per* Blackman J.

30 *Kings Beach Hotel Ltd v Marks* (2006) High Court, Barbados, No 995 of 2006 (unreported) [Carilaw BB 2006 HC 20].

31 (1964) 6 WIR 533. See also *Grant v Williams* (1987) Court of Appeal, Jamaica, Civ App No 20 of 1985 (unreported) [Carilaw JM 1987 CA 103], approving the reasoning in *Watkis v Roblin* and in *Bank of London & Montreal v Sale* (1967) 12 WIR 149, and (*per* Carberry JA) regarding it as significant that, under s 20, breaches of the Act could be cured by *ex post facto* approval from the Exchange Control Authority.

32 By the Exchange Control (Repeal) Act, 1992; see *Friend v Tulloch* (1994) 44 WIR 345.

credit of a person resident outside the scheduled territories.' Douglas J held that, in view of section 35(1) of the Act, which provides, in effect, that the parties can opt out of the provisions of section 7, the Act must be interpreted as 'going to the performance of the contract and not its formation', so a breach of section 7 did not render illegal a contract for the sale of land made in breach of its provisions. Accordingly, the contract was not void on the ground of breach of the Exchange Control Act. On the other hand, the contract was declared illegal and void because of the vendor's failure to deposit a map of the land with the Parish Council before subdivision of the land for the purpose of selling in lots, as required by the Local Improvements Act, Cap 227. Douglas J, following *Re Mahmoud and Ispahani*,[33] considered that, unlike the Exchange Control Act, the latter Act went 'to the formation of the contract and not only to its performance'. He continued:

> It ill becomes a defendant to put forward the illegality of his own act as a means of escaping liability, but when the legislature declares in the public interest that a particular kind of contract shall not be entered into, then, however shabby it may appear to be, it is open to a party sued to say that the legislature has prohibited the contract sought to be enforced, and that the case is one in which the court will not lend its aid to a man who founds his cause of action on such a contract.

In *Chase Manhattan Bank v Sanitary Laundry Co Ltd*,[34] however, the Barbados Court of Appeal took a stricter view of the effect of section 34(3)(a) of the Exchange Control Act, Cap 71, which provided that, 'Except with the permission of the Authority, no person resident in the Island shall lend any money or securities to any body corporate resident in Barbados which is by any means controlled (whether directly or indirectly) by persons resident outside Barbados.' In this case, exchange control permission had been granted for a loan of up to $385,000 by the appellant to the respondent. A loan was eventually made of an amount in excess of that permitted, secured by an assignment and mortgage which recited the loan transaction. The question before the court was whether the contract of loan had been rendered illegal and unenforceable, so that the whole amount lent was irrecoverable and the assignment and mortgage void, or whether the correct view was that the contract was valid and the appellant was merely precluded from recovering the excess amount lent. The Court of Appeal preferred the former view, as expressed by Douglas CJ in the lower court:

> It is beyond doubt that [the Exchange Control Act] is a penal statute. Its purpose is to protect the economy of Barbados. It prohibits any resident lending money to any company resident in Barbados which is controlled by persons resident outside Barbados, unless the lender has permission of the Central Bank. It provides that breaches of the statute constitute offences punishable by fine and imprisonment. It therefore makes transactions which are prohibited by the statute illegal and invalid for any purpose. Adopting the language of Lord Devlin in *St John Shipping Corp v Joseph Rank Ltd*,[35] the way in which the contract for the provision of banking services was performed ... turned it into the sort of contract that was prohibited by the statute. In the result, the assignment and mortgage is void.

33 [1921] 2 KB 716.

34 (1988) Court of Appeal, Barbados, Civ App No 9 of 1985 (unreported) [Carilaw BB 1988 CA 21].

35 [1956] 3 All ER 683.

In *Kings Beach Hotel Ltd v Marks*,[36] it was contended that a debenture/mortgage executed by the defendant in favour of the claimant to secure a loan of $1,403,391 was ineffective and void as it had been executed without the permission of the exchange control authority. The decision turned on an interpretation of section 33(1)(a) of the Act which provides that, 'Except with the permission of the Authority, no person resident in Barbados shall transfer or do any act forming part of a series of acts calculated to result in the transfer by way of sale, lease, exchange or mortgage of any land buildings or other hereditaments situate in Barbados or any instrument or certificate of title thereto, to a person resident outside Barbados.' Blackman J commented that, given that the exchange control legislation was designed for the protection of the national economy, the modern approach of the courts to the interpretation of such legislation was 'to avoid harsh, punitive measures'. He also noted that, since the mid-1990s, the Central Bank of Barbados had moved to gradually liberalise the exchange control regime. He distinguished the present case from *Chase Manhattan* on the ground that whereas section 34 addresses cases of loans of money to companies controlled by non-residents of Barbados, section 33 deals with the qualitatively different situation of monies being remitted to Barbados for investment in Barbados, and he continued:

> On a consideration of issues relating to the economy, one is dealing with a dynamic and not a static situation. Accordingly, factors or considerations that were relevant a generation ago may no longer be appropriate or valid in the current financial crisis . . . In that context, it seems to me that to declare a transaction null and void for want of the permission of the Authority, would be harmful to the economy rather than an action to protect it, and that a declaration for a transaction to be declared null and void is more appropriate in matters that are manifestly offensive to public policy, tainted with criminality or expressly stipulated by statute.

A somewhat different approach to the question of illegality in the context of breach of exchange control regulations was taken by the Guyana Court of Appeal in *Ambrose v Boston*.[37] Here, the parties had entered into a contract for the sale of land situated in Guyana. When the purchaser sought specific performance of the agreement, the vendor claimed that the contract was illegal and unenforceable on account of the fact that the purchaser, who was resident outside of the scheduled territories, had paid the deposit in a foreign currency, without the consent of the Minister of Finance, contrary to sections 3 and 4 of the Exchange Control Act. Kennard JA pointed out that the contract of sale was not, on its face, expressly prohibited by the statute, and, following *Thackwell v Barclays Bank*[38] and *Tinsley v Milligan*,[39] which, he stated, 'amply demonstrate that the law is not static and that there will be different approaches to any legal problem with the passing of time', he held that it would be 'an affront to the public conscience' to deny the purchaser the relief he sought. Bernard JA took a similar approach. She emphasised that the contract of sale entered into by the parties was, on the face of it, not one prohibited by the Exchange Control Act. The question to be decided, therefore, was: 'ought the [purchaser] to be deprived of his legal

---

36 (2006) High Court, Barbados, No 995 of 2006 (unreported) [Carilaw BB 2006 HC 20].
37 (1993) 55 WIR 184.
38 [1986] 1 All ER 676.
39 [1992] 2 All ER 391.

remedy against the [vendor] for breach of contract merely because the deposit was paid in a foreign currency in breach of the statute?' She continued:

> From a perusal of the cases involving illegality and the infringement of a statute, the courts take into account the effect of breach of the statute on public policy and public morality; in fact, Lord Wright in *Vita Food Products Inc v Unus Shipping Co Ltd*[40] was of the view that disobedience to a statute which may nullify a contract not expressly forbidden by the statute is a rule of public policy only, and public policy in a wider sense may at times be better served by refusing to nullify a bargain save on serious and sufficient grounds. There can be no hard-and-fast rule in determining the degree of moral turpitude in infringing the provisions of a statute, and the facts of each case must be scrutinised before a court turns a blind eye to a contract tainted with illegality. A court must not be seen to be indirectly encouraging breaches of laws enacted by Parliament for the protection of the public at large, in order to protect the narrow personal interests of individuals. One has to guard against sending the wrong signals. However, a court cannot be unmindful of the realities of the society in which it functions, and ought not to be seen as stultifying business transactions of individuals by adhering rigidly to statutes. This was commented upon by Bingham LJ in *Saunders v Edwards*:[41] 'Where issues of illegality are raised, the courts have (as it seems to me) to steer a middle course between two unacceptable positions. On the one hand, it is unacceptable that any court of law should aid or lend its authority to a party seeking to pursue or enforce an object or agreement which the law prohibits. On the other hand, it is unacceptable that the court should, on the first indication of unlawfulness affecting any aspect of a transaction, draw up its skirts and refuse all assistance to the plaintiff, no matter how serious his loss nor how disproportionate his loss to the unlawfulness of his conduct.' Beldam LJ in *Pitts v Hunt*[42] also commented on the new pragmatic approach of the courts in adjusting the application of the maxim '*ex turpi causa non oritur actio*' to changing social conditions, and expressed the belief that the determinative factor in the application of the maxim should be the conduct of the person seeking to base his claim upon an unlawful act. This is in keeping with 'the public conscience test' enunciated by Hutchison J in *Thackwell v Barclays Bank plc*,[43] [which] required 'involving the court looking at the quality of the illegality relied on by the defendant and all the surrounding circumstances, without fine distinctions, and seeking to answer two questions: first, whether there had been illegality of which the court should take notice and, second, whether in all the circumstances it would be an affront to the public conscience if, by affording him the relief sought, the court was seen to be indirectly assisting or encouraging the plaintiff in his criminal act'.

Bernard JA went on to point out that there had, during the previous five or so years, been 'a noticeable relaxation of the fiscal laws and dealings in foreign currencies' in Guyana, 'no doubt in an effort to stimulate economic growth and encourage foreign investment'. There had also been a decrease in the number of prosecutions for offences involving breach of the Exchange Control Act. Consonant with this development, the public interest in the stimulation of the economy would be better served by refraining from nullifying transactions in foreign currencies, except on serious and sufficient grounds. Accordingly, it would not be an affront to the public conscience to afford the purchaser the remedy, especially in view of the evidence

40 [1939] 1 All ER 513, PC.
41 [1987] 2 All ER 651, at 665.
42 [1990] 3 WLR 542, at 553.
43 [1986] 1 All ER 676.

that the vendor's motive for avoiding the contract was to secure another purchaser at a higher price.

ILLEGALITY AT COMMON LAW

Certain types of contract which are not illegal by statute are deemed to be contrary to public policy and therefore illegal at common law. These species of contract may be divided into two groups: the first group includes those which involve or contemplate conduct which is clearly reprehensible; the second, those in which the conduct is regarded as less pernicious, but which is nonetheless contrary to public policy. Contracts falling within the first group are referred to as 'illegal', whilst those in the second group are normally called 'void'.[44]

Contracts illegal at common law

Contract to commit a crime, a tort or a fraud on a third party

It is not surprising that the common law regards as illegal any contract which contemplates the commission of a crime such as, for instance, murder, assault,[45] or obtaining goods by false pretences.[46] However, the fact that a criminal offence is committed in the course of carrying out an otherwise legal agreement will not necessarily cause the contract to be treated as illegal.[47]

Similarly, a contract that involves the commission of a civil wrong, such as a libel[48] or deceit,[49] a fraudulent preference in favour of one creditor over others,[50] or the defrauding of prospective shareholders,[51] will be illegal at common law.

Contract to defraud the revenue

Any contract in which the purpose of either or both parties is the defrauding of the revenue, whether national or local, is illegal and void. For instance, in *Miller v Karlinsky*,[52] a contract of employment provided that the employee should receive a salary of £10 per week, plus 'expenses', which were to include the income tax due on the salary. When the employee sought to recover ten weeks' arrears of salary and expenses, it was revealed that part of the amount claimed as expenses represented his income tax liability. It was held that the action failed as to both expenses

44 Cheshire, Fifoot and Furmston, *Law of Contract*, 15th edn (2007), p 470.
45 *Allen v Rescous* (1677) 83 ER 505.
46 *Berg v Sadler and Moore* [1937] 1 All ER 637.
47 *Shaw v Groom* [1970] 1 All ER 702.
48 *Clay v Yates* (1856) 156 ER 1123.
49 *Brown Jenkinson & Co Ltd v Percy Dalton (London) Ltd* [1957] 2 All ER 844.
50 *Mallalieu v Hodgson* (1851) 16 QB 689.
51 *Begbie v Phosphate Sewage Co* (1875) LR 10 QB 491.
52 (1945) 62 TLR 85.

and salary. The contract was illegal, being a fraud on the revenue, and it was not possible to sever the lawful term concerning salary from the tainted one regarding expenses.

Another example is *Alexander v Rayson*.[53] In this case, L agreed to let an apartment to T at an annual rent of £1,200. The agreement was expressed in two documents: (i) a lease of the apartment at an annual rent of £450, which contemplated the provision of certain services by L and (ii) a contract for the provision by L of certain services (which were substantially the same as those contemplated by the lease) for £750 annually. A dispute arose, and T refused to pay an instalment due under the contract. When sued by L for the amount, T pleaded that the purpose for executing two documents was to enable L to present only the lease to the local authority, in order to deceive it as to the true rateable value of the property, and that, at the time of the agreement, T had been ignorant as to L's fraudulent purpose. It was held that, on proof that the documents were to be used for that purpose, L would not be able to enforce either the lease or the contract.

A Jamaican example of the application of this principle is *Halsall v Marshallek*.[54] Here, H sought specific performance of an agreement whereby M agreed to sell and H to purchase 158 acres of land in St Mary. The agreed purchase price was $200,000, but the transaction was expressed in two documents: (i) an agreement for the sale of the property for $100,000, and (ii) an agreement which stated that, in consideration of being given the option to purchase the property, H would pay to M $100,000 on execution of the option agreement. It was admitted in evidence that the purpose for splitting the consideration between the two documents was to avoid payment of stamp duty on the second $100,000. Edwards J refused to order specific performance. He said: 'the option payment would have been paid to the seller without stamp duty, transfer tax and any other fees being paid ... the agreement is tainted with illegality in that there is a common intention to defraud the revenue, and the splitting of the consideration was designed to achieve that end ... The authorities show that a contract to defraud the revenue is properly to be called illegal at common law on the ground of public policy.'

A similar situation arose in a Belizean case, *Azucena v de Molena*,[55] where, following an agreement to sell certain land for $200,000, false prices of $100,000 and $55,000 were inserted in the contract of sale and the deed of transfer respectively, in order to reduce the amount of stamp duty payable on the transaction. It was held that the contract and the transfer were tainted with illegality by reason of the fraud on the revenue, and in such circumstances public policy precluded the court from giving effect to the agreement; additionally, the transaction was rendered void by section 36 of the Stamp Duty Ordinance, Ch 51, which provided that, 'if, with intent to evade the payment of duty under this Ordinance, a consideration or sum of money expressed to be paid on any instrument is less than the amount actually paid, every such instrument shall be void'. Meerabux J said:[56]

53 [1936] 1 KB 169.

54 (1994) Supreme Court, Jamaica, No 1987/H005, unreported [Carilaw JM 1994 SC 49].

55 (1995) 50 WIR 8.

56 *Ibid*, at 90, 91, 92.

> If the illegality of a transaction is brought to the notice of the court, or if an illegality appears or surfaces during the course of the proceedings and the person invoking the aid of the court is himself implicated in the illegality, the court will not assist him, even if the defendant has not pleaded the illegality.[57] I find that illegality was not pleaded by the defendant, but that the matter of illegality was revealed in the evidence when both parties admitted that the consideration quoted in the contract was false ... I find that both parties ... knew that the consideration on the deed of transfer was $55,000 and were parties to the false figure ... I therefore find that the whole transaction, i.e. the contract and the transfer, is tainted with illegality and the only plausible or reasonable inference to draw from the transparently false consideration stated on the transfer of land was to defraud the revenue by inserting a lower amount rather than the actual consideration ... Further, it is apparent that the plaintiff in invoking the aid of the court is himself implicated in the illegality.

Contract to indemnify an assured against his own deliberate criminal or tortious conduct

A person may enter into a contract with an insurance company to indemnify him against the consequences of his *negligence*, such as with a motor insurance policy giving 'third party' cover. Such an agreement is perfectly legal and enforceable, even where the insured's negligence is so gross as to give rise to criminal liability. But a person may not contract for an indemnity against his deliberate criminal or tortious conduct. In *Geismar v Sun Alliance and London Insurance Ltd*,[58] for instance, the claimant had taken out an insurance policy covering the theft or loss of his jewellery. He brought jewellery into the United Kingdom without declaring it to customs, and without paying customs duty, which was a criminal offence. The jewellery was later stolen from his home, and he claimed to recover his loss through the insurance policy. It was held that it would be contrary to public policy to allow him to enforce the insurance contract, and so he had no claim.

Another example is *Gray v Barr*.[59] Here, D, in the course of a violent assault with a loaded firearm, involuntarily killed E – an act which amounted to manslaughter. In a subsequent civil action, judgment was given against D and in favour of E's widow in the sum of £6,668. D then sought to claim an indemnity from his insurers under a policy whereby they undertook to indemnify him in respect of any damages he might become liable to pay in respect of personal injuries caused by an accident. It was held that D's claim failed. Although the killing itself was involuntary, the fact that it had happened in the course of a violent attack meant that it would be contrary to public policy to permit him to claim an indemnity from the insurers.

The decision in *Gray v Barr*, though seemingly justifiable on the facts, has been criticised[60] on the ground that, where the insured is denied an indemnity, the person who is most adversely affected is the victim of the accident, who, in the vast majority of cases, looks not to the impecunious defendant but to the 'deep pockets' of the insurance company as the source of his compensation. Fortunately, as we have seen,

---

57 Applying *Scott v Brown, Doering, McNab & Co* [1892] 2 QB 724.

58 [1977] 3 All ER 570.

59 [1970] 2 All ER 702; affd [1971] 2 All ER 949.

60 Fleming, (1971) 34 MLR 176.

a motorist is not denied an indemnity under his 'third party' insurance policy, even where his gross negligence or recklessness amounts to manslaughter.

Contracts with a sexually immoral element

Because of the profound changes in public attitudes towards sexual morality that have occurred during the past century, many of the earlier cases on this topic may no longer be reliable authorities or even relevant at all. Conduct such as extramarital cohabitation and same-sex relationships no longer carry the stigma that they once did. In the words of Stable J, 'the social judgments of today upon matters of "immorality" are as different from those of the last century as the bikini from a bustle.'[61] Thus, for instance, in some Commonwealth Caribbean jurisdictions the 'common law' spouse who has cohabited with his/her partner for at least five years is given the same statutory rights to property as a lawfully married spouse,[62] and it has been held in England that an agreement to advertise a telephone sex dating service was not unenforceable on the ground of immorality.[63]

Contracts involving prostitution may be one type of case that has been less affected by the more liberal attitudes towards sexual morality developed during the past 150 or so years. The best-known case is *Pearce v Brooks*,[64] dating from 1866. There, the claimants agreed to hire an ornamental carriage to the defendant. The claimants knew that the defendant was a prostitute, and that she intended to use the carriage as a means of soliciting clients. An action by the claimants to recover the hire charges for the carriage failed; the court held the hiring contract unenforceable on the ground that it promoted sexual immorality. In another case, it was held that a landlord could not bring an action to recover arrears of rent from a tenant, since he knew the premises would be used for the purposes of prostitution;[65] nor, more recently, could an action be brought on a contract of employment which required the employee to acquire prostitutes for the employer's customers.[66]

Contracts which injure the state in its relations with other states

This would include, for instance, a contract to be performed in breach of the laws of another friendly state, or a contract with an enemy alien.

Contracts prejudicial to the administration of justice

This would include, for instance, an agreement to stifle a prosecution for an offence which is of public concern, such as theft or forgery.

---

61 *Andrews v Parker* [1973] Qd R 93, p 104.

62 For example, under the Family Law Act, Cap 214 (Barbados), and the Property (Rights of Spouses) Act, 2004 (Jamaica).

63 *Armhouse Lee Ltd v Chappell*, The Times, 7 August 1996.

64 (1866) LR 1 Ex 213.

65 *Girardy v Richardson* (1793) 1 Esp 13.

66 *Coral Leisure Group Ltd v Barnett* [1981] ICR 503.

Contracts involving corruption in public life

Any contract which involves or tends to corruption in public life is contrary to public policy and illegal at common law. Contracts illegal under this head would include those involving the sale of public offices, and those in which one person corruptly agrees to secure for another person some benefit from the government, such as a title or a contract; for example, where X gave to Y, the secretary of a charitable organisation, £3,000 in return for Y's promise to procure a knighthood for him;[67] where a Member of Parliament, in consideration of receiving emoluments from a political association, agreed to vote in Parliament according to the association's directions;[68] and where P, a contractor, handed over £7,500 and a car to Q, a government official, in return for Q's promise to secure a government contract for him.[69]

A striking example of this type of illegality occurred in Trinidad in the case of *Abu Bakr v Attorney General*,[70] which concerned an agreement between the Prime Minister and Abu Bakr, the leader and Imam of the 'Jamaat al Muslimeen', whereby certain advantages were to be given to the Jamaat out of state property in return for securing voting support for the Prime Minister's political party. Both the Court of Appeal of Trinidad and Tobago and the Privy Council were of the view that, in addition to being illegal under section 3 of the Prevention from Corruption Act, 1987, the agreement was illegal at common law. In the words of Lord Carson:

> It is not strictly necessary to decide this point, in view of the Board's conclusion on statutory illegality, and it is desirable to be cautious about the extent of the concept of public policy. There is, however, a well recognised head of illegality of contracts which tend to corruption in the administration of the affairs of the nation. The proposition that the agreement in question in the present appeal falls into that category appears to be well founded . . . The agreement was illegal from its inception, with the consequence that no person can claim any right or remedy under it, irrespective of his knowledge of its illegality.

THE CONSEQUENCES OF ILLEGALITY

Relevance of the state of mind of the parties

Where a contract is illegal in its inception, such as where the parties have agreed to do something which is illegal at common law on grounds of public policy, or which is expressly or impliedly forbidden by statute,[71] the agreement is intrinsically illegal; the state of mind of the parties is irrelevant, and neither can escape the consequences of illegality by pleading innocence, in the sense that he did not realise the agreement was illegal: *ignorantia iuris haud excusat* ('ignorance of the law is no excuse').

67 *Parkinson v College of Ambulance Ltd* [1925] 2 KB 1.
68 *Osborne v Amalgamated Society of Railway Servants* [1910] AC 87.
69 *Okoronkwo v Nwoga* (1973) 2 ECSLR 615.
70 (2009) Privy Council Appeal No 30 of 2008.
71 *Re Mahmoud and Ispahani* [1921] 2 KB 716.

Where a contract is apparently lawful, but both parties intend to exploit it for an illegal purpose (for example, an agreement to let a house which both parties know is to be used for the purpose of prostitution), it is treated in the same way as a contract illegal in its inception.[72]

Where a contract is apparently lawful, but only one of the parties intends to exploit it for an illegal purpose (for example, an agreement to let a house which the tenant intends to use for prostitution and the landlord is unaware of that intention), the innocent party is not affected by the guilt of the other and has his usual remedies under the contract.[73] On the other hand, the party who intends to exploit the contract for an illegal purpose or to perform it in an illegal manner will be unable to enforce the contract or bring any action on it;[74] though it has recently been held that this principle cannot be regarded as applying to all intended illegality of performance, however partial or peripheral, so that a 'minor' illegality in performance will not deprive that party of his remedies under the contract.[75]

Consequences where the contract is illegal in its inception

The contract cannot be enforced or sued upon

According to the maxims *'ex turpi causa non oritur actio'* or *'ex dolo malo non oritur actio'*, a contract which is illegal in its inception, whether by statute or at common law, cannot be enforced in any court of law. The classic statement is that of Lord Mansfield in *Holman v Johnson*:[76]

> The principle of public policy is this: *ex dolo malo non oritur actio*. No court will lend its aid to a man who founds his cause upon an immoral or an illegal act. If, from the plaintiff's own stating or otherwise, the cause of action appears to arise *ex turpi causa*, or the transgression of a positive law of this country, then the court says he has no right to be assisted. It is upon that ground the court goes; not for the sake of the defendant, but because they will not lend their aid to such a plaintiff. So if the plaintiff and defendant were to change sides, and the defendant was to bring his action against the plaintiff, the latter would then have the advantage of it; for where both are equally at fault, *'potior est conditio defendentis'*.

A Caribbean example of the application of the strict rule is *Butterworth v PC's Ltd.*[77] Here, the claimant, a computer expert and a foreign national, came to Anguilla on contract with a local company. When that contract came to an end, he wished to remain in Anguilla in gainful employment, which required him to obtain a work permit. Instead of applying for a self-employment work permit, which would have been more costly for him, he came to an arrangement with H, one of the directors of the defendant company, whereby the defendant company would apply for the

72 *Pearce v Brooks* (1866) LR 1 Exch 213.

73 *Ibid.*

74 *Alexander v Rayson* [1936] 1 KB 169.

75 *Parkingeye Ltd v Somerfield Stores Ltd* [2012] EWCA Civ 1338.

76 (1778) 98 ER 1364, at 1366.

77 (2000) High Court, Anguilla, No 70 of 2000, unreported [Carilaw AI 2000 HC 10].

permit, stating in the application, falsely, that the claimant was to be employed at a stated monthly salary. After obtaining the permit, the claimant proceeded on his own in soliciting clients, invoicing them, and keeping the income for himself. Later, the parties came to an agreement that the company should retain 10 per cent of any income earned by the claimant. The agreed procedure was that the claimant would invoice his clients in the name of PC's Ltd and hand over to the company the cheques received in payment; in turn the company would pay over to the claimant 90 per cent of the monies received and retain the rest. Subsequently, the claimant was successful in obtaining a lucrative government project, and although it was clear that the claimant, as a computer expert with no equal in Anguilla, was the person being chosen by the government to execute the project, in keeping with the pretence that the claimant was an employee of PC's Ltd, the contractual documents were signed by one of the directors of the company, and the claimant was named as PC's 'representative'. Eventually, after a dispute between the parties, the company ceased handing over to the claimant the agreed 90 per cent, whereupon the claimant purported to 'resign', and subsequently sued the company for 90 per cent of the money earned by him but not handed over by the company.

Saunders J had no hesitation in dismissing the claim, saying:

> Mr Butterworth is asking the court to compel the defendants to perform his arrangement with them during the time when it lasted. This court will do no such thing. The arrangement was a farce contrived to enable Mr Butterworth to obtain a work permit. The Labour Authorities were deceived and the public revenue defrauded. What was happening here is that, in local parlance, PC's Ltd was 'fronting' for the claimant. Whatever contract or arrangement there was in existence between these parties was contrary to public policy and illegal, and the court will grant no relief thereon ... Mr Butterworth's claim cannot be prosecuted without reference to and reliance upon the continuing illegal arrangement in which he and the defendants participated. Indeed, his claim is rooted in that arrangement.

A similar outcome was reached in *Holt v Endless Summer Charters Ltd*.[78] Here the claimant, H, who was 18 years old at the time, entered into an agreement with the defendants whereby he was to proceed from England to the BVI in order to work on the defendants' boat. A fixed salary was agreed, and it was also agreed that H would be covered by the defendants' medical insurance policy. Both parties knew that, as a 'non-belonger', H was required by the Labour Code, Cap 293, to obtain a work permit before taking up gainful employment in the BVI. H stated on the immigration form at the airport that he was entering as a tourist, and he was given permission to remain for four weeks for that purpose only. H started working on the defendants' boat almost immediately, without having applied for or obtained a work permit. As fate would have it, on the day following that of his arrival in the BVI, H suffered catastrophic injuries while swimming, and he was rendered a paraplegic. Subsequently, H sued the defendants for unpaid wages and for their alleged breach of his contract of employment in failing to provide the agreed medical insurance cover. Moore J dismissed the claim. He said:

> It was within the contemplation of the contracting parties that the plaintiff would have worked for four weeks or a little less time in violation of the plain prohibition against

78 (1999) High Court, British Virgin Islands, No 174 of 1989, unreported [Carilaw VG 1999 HC 8].

> unauthorised employment contained in section F4 of the Code ... In all the circumstances of the case, I am fully satisfied that, without a valid work permit, the contract itself, so far as it was performed, was performed in violation of the provisions of the Labour Code Ordinance, Cap 293 ... The plaintiff's engagement in employment without a work permit is prohibited by that law. Furthermore, the contract, even though made abroad in England, is illegal since its purpose was the infringement of the laws of the British Virgin Islands. In essence, therefore, the plaintiff, in relying upon the contract in support of his claim for damages, is in effect seeking to invoke the assistance of the Court to enforce rights under an illegal contract. This he cannot do.

A court will refuse to enforce an illegal contract notwithstanding that the defendant does not plead or rely on the illegality. Once the illegality has been revealed to the court, the contract will not be enforced. As Willmer LJ put it:[79]

> The principle to which we must give effect ... is the principle that the court will not lend its assistance for the purpose of enforcing an illegal contract, once the illegality has come to light and the court is satisfied of the illegality.

In *First National Credit Union Co-operative Society Ltd v Trinidad and Tobago Housing Development Corporation*,[80] the claimant credit union (FNCU) lent a sum of money to DC Ltd. In accordance with the loan agreement, DC Ltd assigned to FNCU all monies due to it from the Housing Development Corporation (HDC) under a previous construction contract. In an action brought by FNCU against HDC for the amount of the loan, it emerged in evidence that the loan to DC Ltd was illegal since DC Ltd was not a member of the credit union and the consent required for loans to non-members under section 43 of the Co-operative Societies Act, Cap 81:03, had not been obtained from the Commissioner of Co-operatives; and there was a further illegality in that no instrument of charge as required by regulation 40 of the Co-operative Societies Regulations had been executed by the borrower.

Jones J held that the illegality of the loan agreement meant that FNCU's action could not be entertained by the court, notwithstanding that the defendant (HDC) had not pleaded the illegality. She explained:

> In the instant case, while the question of the illegality of the contract was not raised in the claim, according to the cases there can be no doubt that once the question of the illegality of the contract has come to my attention, I am bound to consider this fact and its effect on the merits of the claim. On the evidence before me as presented, the contract between the FNCU and [D C Ltd] is that a loan was made to [D C Ltd] by the FNCU. The evidence is that [D C Ltd] is not a member of the credit union. In accordance with the Act, the only defence that could possibly be raised by the FNCU is that the loan was granted to a non-member with the consent of the Commissioner ... Since the loan agreement ... is illegal, the FNCU cannot rely on it as the basis for the enforcement of the assignment on which it sues. The FNCU is not entitled to rely on the illegal transaction to establish its cause of action and the court will not lend its aid to such an action. To do so would, in my opinion, offend against the intention of the Act and public policy.

79 *Snell v Unity Finance Ltd* [1963] 3 All ER 50, at 58.
80 (2010) High Court, Trinidad and Tobago, No 2682 of 2006, unreported [Carilaw TT 2010 HC 312].

Money paid or property transferred under the contract is irrecoverable

The applicable maxim here is *'in pari delicto, potior est conditio defendentis'* (where the parties are equally at fault, the defendant's position is stronger). Accordingly, where a contract is found to be illegal in its inception, no action will lie on the part of either party to recover money or property transferred to the other under the agreement. A well-known example is *Parkinson v College of Ambulance Ltd.*[81] Here, P gave the secretary of a charitable organisation a sum of money in return for the secretary's promise to procure a knighthood for P. When the knighthood failed to materialise, P sued to recover the money. It was held that the agreement was illegal at common law, as it tended to corruption in public life, and although there had been a total failure of consideration which ordinarily would have entitled the claimant to recover the money, because of the illegality the court would not entertain P's action and the sum was irrecoverable.

EXCEPTIONS TO THE '*IN PARI DELICTO*' RULE

The following exceptions to the rule of non-recovery in the case of an illegal contract are well established.

(i) *Where the parties are not* 'in pari delicto'. There are two types of circumstance where the court may regard the parties as not being equally at fault, and so give relief to the less guilty party. The first is where one party (the claimant) has been induced to enter into a contract by fraud, duress or oppression at the hands of the other (the defendant), or where the defendant stood in a fiduciary position towards the claimant and abused that position. Thus, for example, a woman who was fraudulently induced by the agent of an insurance company to take out five insurance policies which were in fact illegal, was able to recover the premiums she had paid.[82]

The second is where a contract is made illegal by a statute which has as its objective the protection of a class of persons to which the claimant belongs. As Lord Mansfield explained:[83]

> Where contracts or transactions are prohibited by positive statutes, for the sake of protecting one set of men from another set of men, the one, from their situation and condition being liable to be oppressed and imposed upon by the other, there, the parties are not *in pari delicto* and, in furtherance of these statutes, the person injured, after the transaction is finished and completed, may bring his action and defeat the contract.

For example, it was held in *Kiriri Cotton Co Ltd v Dewani*[84] that where a statute prohibits a landlord from taking a premium from a prospective tenant, the purpose of the statute is to protect tenants and the duty to observe the legislation rests on the landlord; accordingly, the tenant can recover from the landlord any

---

81 [1925] 2 KB 1. See also *Taylor v Chester* (1869) LR 4 QB 309.

82 *Hughes v Liverpool Victoria Legal Friendly Society* [1916] 2 KB 452.

83 *Browning v Morris* (1778) 98 ER 1364, at 1366.

84 [1960] 1 All ER 177.

illegal premium he has paid, even though the statute itself does not provide this remedy. As Lord Denning stated:[85]

> If there is something in the defendant's conduct which shows that, of the two of them, he is the one primarily responsible for the mistake – then it may be recovered back. Thus if, as between the two of them, the duty of observing the law is placed on the shoulders of the one rather than the other – it being imposed on him specially for the protection of the other – then they are not *in pari delicto* and the money can be recovered back.

This principle was applied by the Jamaican Court of Appeal in *Richards v Alexander*.[86] In this case, the respondent was in the process of building a house when she was approached by the appellant, who told her that he wanted the contract to do the electrical work on the house. The respondent pointed out to the appellant that he was not an electrician but 'a man that plant coal'. The appellant allayed the respondent's fears by telling her, 'I do two jobs', whereupon the respondent agreed to pay him $3,000 for the job. The respondent paid the full amount by instalments, but the appellant did very little work, and, when asked by the respondent for the return of her money, he refused to do so. In an action brought by the respondent to recover the money, the appellant contended that the action should fail since the contract was illegal under section 35 of the Electric Lighting Act, which required any person making any installation of electric light or power to be duly licensed by the proper authority, and the appellant was not so licensed. Forte JA rejected that argument and held that the money was recoverable since the parties were not *in pari delicto*. Following the principle in the *Kiriri Cotton* case, where a contract is in breach of a statute, and that statute is designed for the protection of a class of persons to which the claimant belongs, the latter can recover money or property transferred under the contract. He explained:[87]

> There can be no doubt that the purpose of requiring that ... 'no person other than a licensee ... shall make or cause to be made any installation of wires or fittings of any kind or extent for electric light or power ... unless such person has been duly licensed' ... must be for the protection of the users of the object of such installation, for example, a householder or worker in a commercial building or factory. Indicative of this is the power given to the Minister under the same section 35 to make regulations with respect to, *inter alia*, the licensing of persons, and generally for securing the safety of the public from personal injury or from fire or otherwise in respect of installations of the nature specified in the section. The statute, the breach of which the appellant contends creates the illegality of the contract, is therefore one designed for the protection of the public or the beneficiaries of the installation of wires, etc, and consequently the appellant, when entering into the agreement, well knowing he was in breach of the statute, could never be deemed to be *in pari delicto* with the respondent, whose interest the very statute sets out to protect.

(ii) *Where a party to an executory contract repents before performance (the* 'locus poenitentiae' *exception)*. A party who withdraws from the transaction while the illegality is still executory (i.e. where the illegal agreement has not yet been performed) is

85 At 180.
86 (1991) 28 JLR 342.
87 At 345.

entitled to a '*locus poenitentiae*', i.e. an opportunity to 'repent' from the illegal purpose, and he may recover money or property handed over in pursuance of the agreement, provided the withdrawal was 'genuine' and that it was not a case of the purpose being simply frustrated by the other party's failure to perform the contract.[88] In *Bigos v Bousted*,[89] C, whose wife and daughter were about to travel to Italy, in breach of exchange control regulations entered into a contract with D whereby D agreed to provide a sum of money in Italian currency. C deposited a share certificate with D as security. When D failed to provide the currency, C sued him to recover the certificate, arguing that he was entitled to a *locus poenitentiae*, as the contract had not been performed. The court rejected this contention, holding that C's 'withdrawal' was not genuine and that his action failed.

Although the concept of *locus poenitentiae* is traditionally understood as requiring some genuine 'repentance' on the part of the claimant, in the more recent case of *Tribe v Tribe*,[90] Millett LJ said that, 'genuine repentance is not required ... Voluntary withdrawal from an illegal transaction when it has ceased to be needed is sufficient.' In this case, a father who had transferred some shares to his son in order to put them out of reach of his creditors, which was an illegal purpose, was held to be entitled to recover them from the son, after the creditors' claims had been settled and the father's property was thus no longer in jeopardy. The court took the view that the father was entitled to rely on the *locus poenitentiae* principle. Clearly, there had been no 'repentance' on the part of the father, but since no creditors had actually been defrauded it was not too late for him to change his mind and recover the shares.

(iii) *Where the claimant does not rely on the illegal contract.* A party may recover property which he has transferred in pursuance of an illegal agreement if he can frame his claim in such a way that he does not have to rely on or disclose that agreement. For example, if L grants to T a two-year lease of an apartment which, to the knowledge of both parties, is to be used for the purpose of prostitution, the lease will be tainted with illegality and L will not be permitted to sue for non-payment of rent or for breach of any other covenant in the lease, nor will he be able to recover possession of the property by bringing an action for forfeiture during the continuance the lease, as such claims would entail disclosure of the illegal contract; but once the two-year period has expired and the lease has come to an end by effluxion of time, L will be able to recover possession by virtue of his independent legal title to the property. In *Amar Singh v Kulubya*,[91] a statutory provision in Uganda prohibited the sale or lease of land by an African to a non-African without the Governor's consent. Without having obtained such consent, L, an African, granted a yearly tenancy of land of which he was the registered owner to T, an Indian. The tenancy was thus void for illegality. After T had been in possession for several years, L gave him notice to quit and ultimately brought an action for recovery of the property. It was held by the Privy Council that L's claim succeeded, as it was not based on the illegal agreement but on his own

88 *Taylor v Bowers* (1876) 1 QBD 291.

89 [1951] 1 All ER 92.

90 [1996] Ch 107, at 135.

91 [1963] 3 All ER 499.

registered title. As du Parcq LJ had said in an earlier case,[92] 'prima facie a man is entitled to his own property, and it is not a general principle of our law that when one man's goods have got into another's possession in consequence of some unlawful dealings between them, the true owner can never be allowed to recover those goods by an action.'

The exception has now been held to apply equally to recovery by those entitled to equitable interests in property, as was established by the House of Lords in *Tinsley v Milligan*.[93] Here the parties, T and M, who were lesbian lovers, contributed equally to the purchase of a house with the intention of sharing the beneficial interest equally, but had the legal title conveyed into the sole name of T, so that M could fraudulently obtain certain social security benefits, which were treated as part of their shared income. Later, after a quarrel, T moved out of the house and subsequently sued for possession of the property, asserting her sole legal title. M counterclaimed for, *inter alia*, a declaration that T held the property on trust for M and T in equal shares. It was clear that through their contributions to the purchase price, T and M had equitable interests in the house, and that T was holding the legal title on a resulting trust for both parties equally. T, however, argued that, because of her fraudulent social security claim, M should be debarred from claiming any interest in the property, invoking the maxims, 'He who comes to Equity must come with clean hands' and '*Ex turpi causa non oritur actio*'. The House of Lords held, by a majority, that M's counterclaim succeeded since her claim was founded not on the illegal arrangement vesting the legal title in the sole name of T, but rather on the equitable interest she had acquired by virtue of her contribution to the purchase price. It was further held that, since it had been established in *Bowmakers Ltd v Barnet Instruments Ltd*[94] that the legal title to property, whether land or chattels, can pass under an illegal contract if the parties so intend, an equitable title should be capable of passing in the same way. In this case, M's equitable title depended solely on the presumption of resulting trust which had arisen in her favour, and she was not impelled to disclose her illegal purpose.

The approach of the majority of the House in *Tinsley* was followed by Graham J in a Cayman case, *Bonotto v Boccaletti*.[95] This case involved two Italian businessmen who entered into an agreement whereby the defendant was to assist the claimant in transferring large amounts of capital from Italy, in breach of Italian exchange control laws, for conversion into US dollars and investment in the Cayman Islands. Part of the money handed over was used by the defendant to purchase a villa which was conveyed into the name of E Ltd, a company controlled by the defendant; the remainder was then allegedly misappropriated by the defendant. The claimant brought an action in the Cayman court for a declaration, *inter alia*, that the entire shareholding of E Ltd was held on trust for the claimant and his wife; also that E Ltd held its property on trust for the claimant. In finding for the claimant, Graham J rejected the argument that

92 *Bowmakers Ltd v Barnet Instruments Ltd* [1945] KB 65, at 70.

93 [1993] 3 All ER 65.

94 [1945] 3 All ER 499.

95 (2000) Grand Court, Cayman Islands, unreported [Carilaw KY 2000 G 16].

the claimant was precluded from asserting his beneficial interest in the property on account of the illegal agreement relating to the export of currency out of Italy. He said:

> It is submitted to me that [the claimant] must rely on the illegal contract in order to establish his beneficial interest in Elbo Ltd and the subsequent wrongful assets, to the detriment of [the claimant]. [The claimant's] reply to this is that he, his wife and daughter were the beneficial owners of all the shares in that company. When Elbo Ltd was formed ... by [the defendant] and his legal advisers, the nominee companies which subscribed to Elbo Ltd and appointed themselves directors and shareholders expressly declared that they held the shares on behalf of [the claimant], his wife and daughter. All the trustees ever had, therefore, was the legal estate . . . The express declaration of trust fulfills the requirements of the three certainties in terms of intent, subject-matter and objects of the trust . . . [The claimants] remained the beneficial owners of the shares. It is that interest which they seek to enforce in these courts. They do not have to set up the illegal transaction which took place in Italy as proof of that fact. They seek to enforce their proprietary rights as beneficial owners of Elbo Ltd, a company governed by the laws of the Cayman Islands ... There is the clearest possible distinction between trying to enforce the Italian agreement and seeking to enforce the terms of a Cayman trust in a Cayman company. The law on this topic has been laid down in the most authoritative manner by the decision of the majority of the House of Lords in *Tinsley v Milligan*[96] . . . The leading judgment in *Tinsley* is that of Lord Browne-Wilkinson. He referred to a series of cases beginning with *Bowmakers Ltd v Barnet Instruments Ltd*,[97] where it was held that although goods had been sold on hire-purchase in breach of defence regulations, nevertheless property in the goods had passed. His Lordship then said: 'The following propositions emerge: (1) property in chattels and land can pass under a contract which is illegal and therefore would have been unenforceable as a contract; (2) a [claimant] can at law enforce property rights so acquired, provided that he does not need to rely on the illegal contract for any purpose other than providing the basis of a claim to a property right . . .' Applying the test laid down by Lord Browne-Wilkinson, I conclude that the factual basis concerning the hand-over of cash in Italy by [the claimant] to [the defendant] for illegal export and conversion into dollars merely provided the 'basis of his claim to a proprietary right', namely, the beneficial ownership of the shares in Elbo Ltd. For that reason, I reject the argument that unenforceability arising out of the Bretton Woods Agreement and/or illegality in Italy is a bar to the [claimant's] claim.

Contracts in restraint of trade

An agreement in restraint of trade has been defined as 'one in which a party (the covenantor) agrees with any other party (the covenantee) to restrict his liberty in the future to carry on trade with other persons not parties to the contract in such a manner as he chooses'.[98] However, although the definition of a contract in restraint of trade is easy enough to state, it is not always easy to decide whether or not a particular restriction is within the restraint of trade doctrine. Certainly, there are two classes of agreement which have long been recognised as being in restraint of trade,

96 [1993] 3 All ER 65.

97 Above, n 90.

98 *Petrofina (Great Britain) Ltd v Martin* [1966] Ch 146, at 180, *per* Diplock LJ.

namely (i) an agreement whereby an employee undertakes that, after leaving his present employment, he will not set up a competing business on his own account or take up employment with a rival firm, and (ii) an agreement between the vendor and purchaser of a business together with its goodwill, whereby the vendor agrees not to carry on a business that will compete with that of the purchaser. But apart from these two well established categories, there is no definitive way of determining whether a particular contract is or is not subject to the doctrine, since such a question may be answered only by reference to the demands of public policy; indeed, it has been said that, 'it would be mistaken, even if it were possible, to try to crystallise the rules of this, or any aspect of public policy into neat propositions. The doctrine of restraint of trade is one to be applied to factual situations with a broad and flexible rule of reason . . . The classification must remain fluid and the categories can never be closed'.[99]

The leading case on the restraint of trade doctrine is *Nordenfelt v Maxim Nordenfelt Guns and Ammunition Co Ltd*.[100] Here, the appellant, a manufacturer of guns and ammunition, sold his business to the respondent for £287,500 and covenanted that he would not, for 25 years, 'engage . . . either directly or indirectly in the trade or business of a manufacturer of guns, gun mountings or carriages, gunpowder explosives or ammunition, or in any business competing or liable to compete in any way with that for the time being carried on by the [respondent] company'. It was held by the House of Lords that an agreement in restraint of trade made between a vendor and a purchaser of a business was *prima facie* void, but would be valid if found to be reasonable (a) in the interests of the parties and (b) in the interests of the public. In this case, whereas it was reasonable in the interests of the parties that the appellant should be restrained from trading in guns, ammunition and explosives, as the business sold was devoted to the manufacture of those items and the purchaser had paid a substantial price for it, it was not reasonable to restrain him from engaging in *any competing business*, as such a restriction was wider than necessary to protect the proprietary interest purchased by the respondent. It was also held that the narrower restriction was reasonable in the interests of the public, as it protected the interests of an English company and therefore supported British trading interests.

Some 20 years after the *Nordenfelt* case, the House of Lords in *Mason v Provident Clothing and Supply Co Ltd*[101] and *Herbert Morris Ltd v Saxelby*[102] confirmed the general approach taken in that case, and further established that a distinction is to be made between restrictions imposed on vendors of businesses and those imposed on employees. In the former type of case, 'the law upholds such a bargain, and declines to permit a vendor to derogate from his own grant',[103] whereas, in the latter, 'the only reason for upholding such a restraint on the part of an employee is that the employer has some proprietary right, whether in the nature of trade connection or in the nature of trade secrets, for the protection of which such a restraint is – having regard to the duties of the employee – reasonably necessary. Such a restraint has . . . never been upheld, if directed only to the prevention of competition or against the use of the

99 *Esso Petroleum Co Ltd v Harper's Garage (Stourport) Ltd* [1968] AC 269, at 331,337, *per* Lord Wilberforce.

100 [1894] AC 535.

101 [1913] AC 724.

102 [1916] 1 AC 688.

103 [1913] AC 724, at 713, *per* Lord Shaw.

personal skill and knowledge acquired by the employee in his employer's business'.[104]

Other types of restriction may be said to have 'passed into the accepted and normal currency of commercial or contractual or conveyancing relations'[105] and are therefore outside the restraint of trade doctrine. Instances are: (i) 'sole agencies', i.e. where a manufacturer agrees to make the claimant the sole and exclusive agent for the sale of his products; (ii) 'tied houses', i.e. where the lessee of a public house agrees to sell no beer other than that manufactured by the lessor; and (iii) the normal restrictive covenants found in conveyances of land. On the other hand, there are many other types of restriction which may or may not be void, depending upon the balancing exercise carried out by the court in addressing the two countervailing freedoms based on public policy, viz (a) freedom to contract and (b) freedom to trade.

An important case in which many of these difficulties were discussed is *Esso Petroleum Co Ltd v Harper's Garage (Stourport) Ltd*.[106] Here, the respondents owned two garages. They entered into 'solus' agreements with Esso relating to each garage. In the first, they undertook to buy exclusively from Esso all their supplies of petrol for a period of four years and five months, and to keep the garage open at all reasonable times for the sale of petrol. In return, the respondents received a rebate on the wholesale price of each gallon of petrol. In relation to the second garage, the respondents mortgaged the premises to Esso as security for a loan of £7,000, covenanting to repay the loan and interest within 21 years, and not to redeem the mortgage before that time. Also, as in the first agreement, the respondents bound themselves to purchase all their petrol supplies from Esso during the continuance of the mortgage. After some time, the respondents began to sell other brands of petrol. Esso brought an action for breach of contract and the respondents pleaded that both agreements were in restraint of trade and unenforceable. It was held that both agreements were within the restraint of trade doctrine and needed to satisfy the test of reasonableness in order to be enforceable. The court found that there was nothing intrinsically unreasonable in a solus agreement of this nature, since both parties benefited from it, but whereas the first agreement was to last for a reasonable period (four years and five months), the second was unreasonably long (21 years). Accordingly, the first contract was valid and the second void.

Some cases do not fall neatly into the commonly encountered types of situation to which the restraint of trade doctrine applies, namely restraints on employees, restraints on vendors of businesses, and solus agreements. An example is the Bahamian case of *Dell Quay Overseas Ltd v Stevens*.[107] Here, the claimant, the owner of

---

104 *Herbert Morris Ltd v Saxelby* [1916] 1 AC 688, at 701, *per* Lord Parker.

105 *Esso Petroleum Co Ltd v Harper's Garage (Stourport) Ltd* [1968] AC, at 333, *per* Lou Wieberforce.

106 *Ibid*. Some of the elements in this case were discussed in *Gonzalez v Trinidad and Tobago Petroleum Marketing Co Ltd* (1985) High Court, Trinidad and Tobago, No 1656 of 1985, unreported [Carilaw TT 1985 HC 75], *per* Hosein J, where the issue was whether an interlocutory injunction should be granted to restrain the defendants (who complained of breach of a solus agreement) from withholding supplies of petroleum products from the claimant.

107 (1998) Supreme Court, The Bahamas, No 956 of 1997, unreported [Carilaw BS 1998 SC 24].

'Green Turtle Cay Club' (GTC) and marine facilities, contracted to lease part of its premises on the Cay to the defendant for the purpose of operating a diving business. One of the terms of the agreement was that the defendant would not, for a period of three years after the termination of the contract, establish a similar business within 50 miles of the Cay. Strachan J held that, in the circumstances, the restriction failed the reasonableness test; it was too wide both as to area and as to time to be enforceable. He said:

> I remind myself that the correct target is the respective obligations and, for reasons which follow, I take the view that the contract is unenforceable for lack of reasonableness. First, as to the nature of the relationship, I am, I think, well justified in following Lord Fraser's approach in *Deacons (a Firm) v Bridges*.[108] 'A decision on whether the restrictions in this agreement are enforceable or not cannot be reached by attempting to place the agreement in any particular category, or by seeking for the category to which it is most closely analogous.' The proper approach is that adopted by Lord Reid in *Esso Petroleum Co Ltd v Harper's Garage (Stourport) Ltd* where he said[109], 'I think it better to ascertain what were the legitimate interests of the appellants which they were entitled to protect, and then to see whether these restraints were more than adequate for that purpose'... It is difficult to see how, in the circumstances of this case, the test of reasonableness, of what amounts to a fair bargain, is not infringed. No legitimate interest of GTC, which has the backing of public policy, supports a restraint clause which is so widely drawn both as to area and time. GTC has, I would emphasise, contributed to the creation of such a business, but never operated the type of business that it seeks to restrain; it bore no part of the risk; operating it would be ancillary to its main business, whereas for the defendant, it's his sole business or livelihood and one for which he is trained, experienced and committed. *Prima facie* the law favours his doing so. There is nothing in the legal relationship, that is, respective obligations between the parties, which is strong enough to displace it, as to render the restraint clause enforceable.

Covenants between employer and employee

A restraint imposed on an employee under a contract of employment which is to operate *during the continuance of the contract*, for example a provision that he is not to do work for any other person whose business is in competition with that of the employer, cannot be impugned on the ground that it is an unreasonable restraint of trade, as an employer is entitled to the exclusive services of his employee.[110] But a covenant which seeks to restrict an employee's freedom to work *after the termination of his contract* of employment will be *prima facie* void and will be unenforceable unless it is shown to be reasonable in the interests of the parties and of the public.[111]

It is generally accepted that an employer is entitled to protect (a) its trade secrets and other confidential information, and (b) its trade connection (that is to prevent the employer's customers from being enticed away from it by its former employee),[112]

---

108 [1984] 2 WLR 837, at 841.

109 *Esso Petroleum Co Ltd v Harper's Garage (Stourport) Ltd* [1968] AC 269, at 301.

110 *Esso Petroleum Co Ltd v Harper's Garage (Stourport) Ltd* [1968] AC 269.

111 *Mason v Provident Clothing and Supply Co* [1913] AC 724.

112 *Forster and Sons Ltd v Suggett* (1918) 35 TLR 87; *Faccenda Chicken Ltd v Fowler* [1987] Ch 117; *Lansing Linde Ltd v Kerr* [1991] 1 WLR 251.

but that it is not entitled to restrain an employee from using his own skill and experience, even where acquired during the period of employment.[113]

Reasonableness

A contract in restraint of trade as between employer and employee which protects a legitimate interest of the employer will be upheld if the restraint is shown to be reasonable. Reasonableness is normally adjudged according to the scope, the area and the duration of the restraint, taking into account also the status of the employee and the public interest. Thus:

(a) An employer is not entitled to restrain the employee from carrying on a business which is different in character from that in which the employer's trade secrets or business connection were developed, and in which the employee was employed.[114]
(b) The area of the restraint must not be wider than necessary for the protection of the employer's interests.[115]
(c) The duration of the restraint must not be longer than necessary to protect the employer's interests.[116]
(d) The status of the employee in the employer's organisation is a relevant factor in determining the reasonableness of the restraint; in general, the more senior the employee in the employer's organisation, the more reasonable it will be to impose restrictions on his future activities.[117]
(e) Where the employee is particularly outstanding or distinguished in his field, it may be contrary to the public interest to restrict his future activities; but, apart from such cases, a restriction which is found to be reasonable as between the parties is unlikely to be held to be unreasonable in the interests of the public.[118]

Severance

In certain restricted circumstances, the court may be willing to 'sever', i.e. delete, the objectionable part of a void contract, thus leaving the rest of the agreement valid and enforceable. Severance is not permitted in the case of contracts which are rendered illegal by statute[119] or which are void on the ground that they are contrary to public policy (such as an agreement which contemplates the commission of a criminal offence or which is tainted with immorality),[120] and so the doctrine of severance is

---

113 *Herbert Morris Ltd v Saxelby* [1916] 1 AC 688, at 710, *per* Lord Parker.
114 *Bromley v Smith* [1909] 2 KB 235.
115 *Mason v Provident Clothing and Supply Co* [1913] AC 724; cf *Foster and Sons Ltd v Suggett* [1918] 35 TLR 87.
116 *Wyatt v Kreglinger and Fernau* [1933] 1 KB 793.
117 *Nordenfelt v Maxim Nordenfelt Guns and Ammunition Co Ltd* [1894] AC 535.
118 *Wyatt v Kreglinger and Fernau*, above n 112.
119 *Ritchie v Smith* (1848) 6 CB 462.
120 *Bennett v Bennett* [1952] 1 KB 249, at 253, 254; *Napier v National Business Agency Ltd* [1951] 2 All ER 264.

most applicable to contracts in restraint of trade. An example is the *Nordenfelt* case,[121] where, as we have seen, the court severed the part of the contract containing the unreasonable restraint and upheld the other, reasonable part. Again, where the vendor of a perfumery business in London covenanted that he would not carry on a similar business 'within the cities of London or Westminster or within 600 miles from the same', it was held that the covenant would be reasonable and valid if its area were confined to London and Westminster; accordingly, the reference to the 600-mile range could be severed and the agreement enforced.[122]

It is established that severance is possible only where the agreement can, for this purpose, be construed as falling into two distinct parts, so that the objectionable part can be deleted without destroying the whole, or substituting an agreement which is fundamentally different from that reached by the parties. In this connection, the court may apply the 'blue pencil' rule, whereby 'the part severed can be removed by running a blue pencil through it',[123] without affecting the rest of the agreement. Thus, where the seller of an imitation jewellery business in London agreed not to sell jewellery, both real or imitation, in the UK, USA, France, Spain, Russia, Germany and Austria, it was held that the restraint relating to the sale of imitation jewellery in the UK was valid, but the part relating to real jewellery and to the other countries named was void but could be severed by running a 'blue pencil' through it, without affecting the valid part of the agreement.[124]

121 [1894] AC 535, p 204 above.

122 *Price v Green* (1847) 16 M&W 346.

123 *Attwood v Lamont* [1920] 3 KB 571, at 578, *per* Lord Sterndale MR.

124 *Goldsoll v Goldman* [1915] 1 Ch 292.

CHAPTER 11

PRIVITY OF CONTRACT

THE PRIVITY DOCTRINE

According to the doctrine of privity, a contract creates enforceable rights and obligations only between the parties to it; thus, only the original parties can sue and be sued on it.[1] The difficulty with the doctrine has always been that it excludes third parties for whose benefit a contract was intended to be made. The exceptions to the doctrine seek to address this difficulty.

The doctrine of consideration rationale

One of the earliest enunciations of the doctrine was in *Price v Easton*,[2] where it was held that an action for breach of contract must be brought by the person from whom the consideration moved, thus linking the privity rule with the rule that consideration must move from the promisee. The facts were that D owed £13 to C. D promised to do certain work for T, and T in return agreed to discharge D's debt by paying £13 to C. D completed the work but T failed to pay the money to C. C sued T to recover the amount. It was held that C had no right of action against T, but the three judges in the English Court of Appeal used differing reasoning. According to Lord Denman CJ, C's action failed because he did not 'show any consideration for the promise moving from him' to T; Littledale J, on the other hand, said: 'No privity is shown between the plaintiff (C) and the defendant (T)'; while Patteson J remarked that there was 'no promise to the plaintiff alleged'.

The decisive case laying down the doctrine in the late nineteenth century was *Tweddle v Atkinson*,[3] in which the plaintiff's father, in consideration of the plaintiff's intended marriage, made an agreement with the future bride's father that each father would pay the plaintiff a sum of money in connection with the intended marriage. The bride's father failed to pay the plaintiff the promised amount and later died. The plaintiff sued the father's executors.

The court rejected the plaintiff's argument that an agency relationship had arisen between the plaintiff's father and the bride's father, entitling the plaintiff to sue the deceased father's executors. Wightman J stated the position as follows:

> Some of the old decisions appear to support the proposition that a stranger to the consideration of a contract may maintain an action upon it, if he stands in such a near relationship to the party from whom the consideration proceeds, that he may be considered a party to the consideration . . . But there is no modern case in which the proposition has been supported. On the contrary, it is now established that no stranger to the consideration can take advantage of a contract, although made for his benefit.

---

1 *Dunlop Pneumatic Tyre Co Ltd v Selfridge & Co Ltd* [1915] AC 847, *per* Lord Haldane.
2 (1833) 4 D & Ad 433.
3 [1861] EWHC QB J57.

Thus, it is clear that these earlier cases focused on the doctrine of consideration as the basis for the privity rule.

The rationale that contractual rights are rights *in personam*

The privity rule was revisited and reformulated in a unanimous decision of the House of Lords in *Dunlop Pneumatic Tyre Co Ltd v Selfridge & Co Ltd*.[4] There, the facts were as follows:

> Dew & Co had entered into a contract with the appellants to purchase a number of tyres and other goods from them at the prices in their list, in consideration of receiving certain discounts. As part of their contract Dew & Co. undertook, *inter alia*, not to sell to certain classes of customer at prices below the current list prices of the appellants. They were, however, at liberty to sell tyres to a class of customer that included the respondents at a discount which was substantially less than the discount they were themselves to receive from the appellants. In the case of any such sale, they undertook, as the appellants' agents in this behalf, to obtain from the customer a written undertaking to observe the terms which Dew & Co. had undertaken to observe. The respondents, Dunlop, agreed with Dew & Co. to pay to the appellants a penalty for every article sold in breach of this stipulation. Dunlop subsequently sold goods below the stipulated price and the appellants sued Dunlop for payments pursuant to this agreement.

Holding that the appellants could not sue to enforce the contract between Dunlop and Dew & Co, Viscount Haldane LC set out the reasoning behind the decision, thus:

> On January 2 the respondents contracted with Messrs Dew, in terms of a letter of that date addressed to them, that, in consideration of the latter allowing them discounts on goods of the appellants' manufacture which the respondents might purchase from Messrs Dew, less, in point of fact, than the discount received by the latter from the appellants, the respondents, among other things, would not sell the appellants' goods to private customers at prices below those in the appellants' current list, and that they would pay to the appellants a penalty for every article sold in breach of this stipulation.
>
> The learned judge who tried the case has held that the respondents sold goods of the appellants' manufacture supplied through Messrs Dew at less than the stipulated prices, and the question is whether, assuming his finding to be correct, the appellants, who were not in terms parties to the contract contained in the letter of January 2, can sue them.
>
> My Lords, in the law of England certain principles are fundamental. One is that only a person who is a party to a contract can sue on it. Our law knows nothing of a *jus quaesitum tertio* [a third party right] arising by way of contract. Such a right may be conferred by way of property, as, for example, under a trust, but it cannot be conferred on a stranger to a contract as a right to enforce the contract *in personam*.

Notably, the modern rule, as captured by Lord Haldane in the *Dunlop* case shows a shift from a focus on the doctrine of consideration towards a rationale based on the nature of contractual obligations, that is, obligations which are *in personam* and attach to the contracting parties only.

Subsequent case law has buttressed this formulation of the privity concept. In *Beswick v Beswick*,[5] B entered into an agreement with his nephew whereby he would

---

4 [1915] AC 847, 853.

5 [1967] 3 WLR 932.

transfer his business to the nephew in return for the nephew's employing B as a consultant for the rest of B's life and, after B's death, paying an annuity of £5 per week to B's widow. After B's death, the nephew failed to pay the annuity to the widow and she brought an action against him, both as intended beneficiary of the agreement and in her capacity as administratrix of B's estate. It was held by the House of Lords that she could not succeed in her personal capacity as beneficiary, not being a party to the contract, but that she did have a good cause of action as administratrix of B's estate since, in that capacity, she was B's personal representative and therefore deemed to be a party to the agreement.

Thus, according to the privity rule, if A promises B (for consideration provided by B) to do work for or pay money to T, and A fails to carry out his promise, T cannot sue A as T is not a party to the contract, nor has any consideration moved from him.[6] And where C entered into an enforceable agreement with E that C would manage E's business and that all proceeds would be paid towards settling E's overdraft at the Bank, it was held that the Bank could not sue C as 'guarantor' of E's overdraft since it was not a party to the contract between C and E.[7]

It has been commented, persuasively, that the consideration rationale for the privity rule (as set out in *Price v Easton* and *Tweddle v Atkinson*) overlaps with, and is indistinguishable from, the rationale based on the nature of contractual obligations as *in personam* obligations.[8] The key principle is therefore that a contract will be primarily a matter between the contracting parties.[9]

Remedies of the promisee

It was thus established in *Beswick v Beswick*[10] that a third party beneficiary cannot enforce an agreement against a party to a contract. There, as already seen, the plaintiff's widow was able to bring an action against her nephew only in her capacity as administratrix of her late husband's will. In that way, she was able to enforce the agreement on behalf of her husband, the promisee in the agreement. Had she not been appointed administratrix, she would not have been able to enforce the agreement. This case illustrates how a promisee may be entitled to remedies under the contact which, in effect, are to the benefit of the third party.

PROMISEE BRINGING AN ACTION TO ENFORCE THIRD PARTY RIGHTS

This possibility was explored in *Snelling v John G Snelling Ltd*.[11] There, X, the former director of a company, had entered into an agreement with two other directors, Y

6 *Price v Easton* (1833) 4 B & Ad 433; *Tweddle v Atkinson* (1861) 121 ER 762.

7 *Chuba Ikpeazu v African Continental Bank Ltd* [1965] NMLR 374.

8 Beatson, Burrows, Cartwright, *Anson's Law of Contract*, 29th edn (Oxford University Press, 2010) 616.

9 Cheshire, Fifoot, Furmston, *Law of Contract*, 14th edn (Butterworths, 2010) 500.

10 [1968] AC 58.

11 [1973] QB 87.

and Z (who were X's brothers), that repayment of sums of money lent to the company by X, Y and Z would not be demanded. The company itself was not a party to the agreement. The agreement also provided that any director would lose his right to repayment on voluntary retirement from his position as director. X subsequently sued the company for repayment.

It was held that, notwithstanding that the company (the defendant in the action) was not a party to the brothers' agreement, Y and Z were entitled to a stay of proceedings and the action was dismissed. In this way, Y and Z were able to procure a result which was for the benefit of the company, even though the company was not actually a party to the agreement in question.

It is thus possible for a promisee to obtain a remedy for the benefit of a third party, even though the third party cannot enforce the agreement directly. This explains the result in *Beswick v Beswick*, where the deceased man's widow was awarded specific performance of the agreement with the nephew. Lord Pearce in that case stated: 'The estate (though not the widow personally) can enforce it.'[12] It should be noted, however, that as specific performance is an equitable remedy, it is at the discretion of the court whether to grant it in the circumstances of each case.

TYPES OF REMEDIES

In addition to specific performance, other remedies may be available to a promisee, including an injunction or a stay of proceedings, as in *Snelling*. There are two difficulties with this approach. First, the third party cannot compel a hostile or unwilling promisee to either (1) bring an action to commence proceedings which would be beneficial to that third party, or (2) to hand over to the beneficiary any damages which are won in those proceedings. If the promisee does recover damages, the third party will have little or no ground in contract to recover those damages from the promisee to which he considers himself entitled. Secondly, the most desirable remedy will generally be damages, and the promisee will only be entitled to damages for loss suffered by him, in which case the damages recoverable by him may be nominal only.

EXTENSION OF THE PRINCIPLE IN *LLOYD'S v HARPER*[13]

There are well-established exceptions to the principle that a promisee can recover only in respect of loss suffered by himself, and not for loss suffered by a third party. For example, as demonstrated by *Lloyd's v Harper*, a promisee who is regarded as a trustee of the promise for the benefit of a third party can sue to recover loss suffered by that third party; an agent can recover for loss suffered by an undisclosed principal;[14] and claimants who had taken out an insurance policy to cover goods in a warehouse were able to recover compensation both in respect of their own goods and in respect of goods held for third parties.[15] The *dicta* of Lush LJ in *Lloyd's v Harper*

12 *Ibid*, at 89.
13 (1880) 16 Ch D 290.
14 *Allen v F O'Hearn & Co* [1937] AC 213.
15 *Walter v Monarch Fire and Life Assurance Co* (1856) 5 E & B 870.

were relied on, and arguably extended, by Lord Denning in *Jackson v Horizon Holidays Ltd*,[16] where it was held that a man who had contracted with a travel agent for a package holiday in Ceylon for himself and his wife and children, could recover damages from the agent for the distress suffered not only by himself but also by the wife and children as a result of the 'sub-standard and downright disgraceful' quality of the holiday. This decision appeared to lay down a general principal that a promisee could recover on behalf of third parties even in the absence of any trust relationship. As Lord Denning explained:

> On this question a point of law arises; the Judge said that he could only consider the mental distress to Mr Jackson himself, and that he could not consider the distress to his wife and children. He said: 'The damages are the plaintiff's. I can consider the effect upon his mind of his wife's discomfort, vexation, and the like, although I cannot award a sum which represents her vexation.'
>
> Mr Davies, for Mr Jackson, disputes that proposition. He submits that damages can be given not only for the leader of the party, in this case, Mr Jackson's own distress, discomfort and vexation, but also for that of the rest of the party.
>
> We have had an interesting discussion as to the legal position when one person makes a contract for the benefit of a party. In this case it was a husband making a contract for the benefit of himself, his wife and children. Other cases readily come to mind. A [host] makes a contract with a restaurant for a dinner for himself and his friends. The vicar makes a contract for a coach trip for the choir. In all these cases there is only one person who makes the contract. It is the husband, the host or the vicar, as the case may be. Sometimes he pays the whole price himself. Occasionally he may get a contribution from the others. But in any case it is he who makes the contract. It would be a fiction to say that the contract was made by all the family, or all the guests, or all the choir, and that he was only an agent for them. Take this very case. It would be absurd to say that the twins of three years old were parties to the contract or that the father was making the contract on their behalf as if they were principals. It would equally be a mistake to say that in any of these instances there was a trust. The transaction bears no resemblance to a trust. There was no trust fund and no trust property. No, the real truth is that in each instance, the father, the host or the vicar, was making a contract himself for the benefit of the whole party. In short, a contract by one for the benefit of third persons.
>
> What is the position when such a contract is broken? At present the law says that the only one who can sue is the one who made the contract. None of the rest of the party can sue, even though the contract was made for their benefit. But when that one does sue, what damages can he recover? Is he limited to his own loss? Or can he recover for the others? Suppose the holiday firm puts the family into a hotel which is only half built and the visitors have to sleep on the floor? Or suppose the restaurant is fully booked and the guests have to go away, hungry and angry, having spent so much on fares to get there? Or suppose the coach leaves the choir stranded halfway and they have to hire cars to get home? None of them individually can sue. Only the father, the host or the vicar can sue. He can, of course recover his own damages. But can he not recover for the others? I think he can. The case comes within the principle stated by Lush LJ in *Lloyd's v Harper* (1880) 16 ChD at page 321:
>
>> I consider it to be an established rule of law that where a contract is made with A for the benefit of B, A can sue on the contract for the benefit of B, and can recover all that B could have recovered if the contract had been made with B himself.

16 [1975] 1 WLR 1468.

> It has been suggested that Lush LJ was thinking of a contract in which A was trustee for B. But I do not think so. He was a common lawyer speaking of the common law. His words were quoted with considerable approval by Lord Pearce in *Beswick v Beswick*.[17] I have myself often quoted them. I think they should be accepted as correct, at any rate so long as the law forbids the third persons themselves to sue for damages. It is the only way in which a just result can be achieved. Take the instance I have put. The guests ought to recover from the restaurant their wasted fares. The choir ought to recover the cost of hiring the taxis home. There is no one to recover for them except the one who made the contract for their benefit. He should be able to recover the expense to which they have been put, and pay it over to them. Once recovered, it will be money had and received to their use. (They might even, if desired, be joined as plaintiffs.) If he can recover for the expense, he should also be able to recover for the discomfort, vexation and upset which the whole party have suffered by reason of the breach of contract, recompensing them accordingly out of what he recovers.

The decision in *Jackson v Horizon Holidays Ltd*[18] may be rationalised (albeit tenuously) on the basis that the promisee in that case recovered for his own suffering caused by his family's distress, and it was later suggested in *Woodar Investment Development Ltd v Wimpey Construction UK Ltd*[19] that this rationale did in fact apply. Although the *Woodar* case was decided on a different point, and the comments on this issue were therefore *obiter*, the House of Lords reasoned that *Jackson v Horizon Holidays Ltd*[20] was probably decided correctly on the facts (in other words, supporting the view that the promisee had recovered for the loss he had himself sustained caused by the suffering of his family), but rejected the proposition that a promisee can recover for loss suffered by third parties. The House reaffirmed the principle in *Beswick v Beswick*, emphasising that the *dicta* of Lush LJ in *Lloyd's v Harper* to the effect that a promisee may recover damages for loss suffered by a third party can apply only where the promisee stands in a fiduciary relationship (ie a relationship of trusteeship or agency) to the third party beneficiary for whose benefit he is suing. The result, according to their Lordships, was that neither the third party nor the promisee could recover damages for failure by the promisor to provide what he had agreed to provide.

The House of Lords had the opportunity to reconsider and clarify the results of the *Jackson v Horizon Holiday Ltd*[21] and *Woodar*[22] cases in *Linden Gardens Trust v Lenesta Sludge Disposals* and *St Martin's Property v Sir Robert McAlpine*;[23] however, they did not expressly reaffirm the *Woodar* decision but instead distinguished it on the facts. In *Linden Gardens*, in grappling with the apparent unfairness of the situation where neither the promisee nor the third party can recover what the promisor has failed to deliver, Lord Browne-Wilkinson, speaking for the majority of the court, said:

> If the law were to be established that damages for breach of a supply contract were not quantifiable by reference to the beneficial ownership of goods or enjoyment of the services contracted for but by reference to the difference in value between that which was contracted for and that which is in fact supplied, it might also provide a satisfactory

17 [1968] AC 58, at 88.
18 *Ibid.*
19 [1980] 1 All ER 571.
20 See above.
21 *Ibid.*
22 See above.
23 [1994] 1 AC 85, [1993] 3 All ER 417.

> answer to the problems raised where a man contracts and pays for a supply to others, e.g., a man contracts with a restaurant for a meal for himself and his guests or with a travel company for a holiday for his family. It is apparently established that, if a defective meal or holiday is supplied, the contracting party can recover damages not only for his own bad meal or unhappy holiday but also for that of his guests or family.

For this proposition, Lord Browne-Wilkinson cited *Jackson v Horizon Holidays Ltd*[24] 'as explained' in the *Woodar*[25] case. He then continued:

> There is therefore much to be said for drawing a distinction between cases where the ownership of goods or property is relevant to prove that the plaintiff has suffered loss through the breach of a contract other than a contract to supply those goods or property and the measure of damages in a supply contract where the contractual obligation itself requires the provision of those goods or services. I am reluctant to express a concluded view on this point since it may have profound effects on commercial contracts, which effects were not fully explored in argument. In my view, the point merits exposure to academic consideration before it is decided by this House. Nor do I find it necessary to decide the point since, on any view, the facts of this case bring it within the class of exceptions to the general rule.

Later, in *Alfred McAlpine Construction Ltd v Panatown Ltd*,[26] the House of Lords held that the exceptions to the privity rule would not apply where the third party has been given an express and direct right of enforcement against the promisor in the contract.

Thus, it would appear that the principle that the promisee can recover only for his own loss and not for that of a third party remains intact, in spite of criticism from the courts of the unfairness of the result that this proposition can produce.

EXCEPTIONS TO THE PRIVITY DOCTRINE

The most important qualifications to the doctrine of privity are (a) the 'trust concept' (trust of the benefit of a contract), (b) assignment, (c) novation and (d) agency.[27]

The 'trust concept'

Equity developed the concept of the 'trust of the benefit of a contract' in order to avoid the rigours of the common law doctrine of privity, and the concept has been invoked since the eighteenth century.[28] Maitland's definition of a constructive trust appears to support the invocation of the rule:

> Where a person has rights which he is bound to exercise on behalf of another or for the accomplishment of some particular purpose, he is said to have those rights in trust for another or for that purpose, and he is called a trustee.[29]

---

24 See above.

25 See above.

26 [2001] 1 AC 518; see also the Court of Appeal decision in *Darlington Borough Council v Wiltshire* [1995] 3 All ER 895.

27 See Chapter 12, below.

28 *Tomlinson v Gill* (1756) Amb 330.

29 Maitland, *Equity* 44.

The cases of *Lloyd's v Harper*[30] and *Les Affréteurs Réunis SA v Walford*[31] are illustrative of its application.

In *Lloyd's v Harper*, Lush LJ set out the general rule:

> I consider it to be an established rule of law that where a contract is made with A for the benefit of B, A can sue on the contract for the benefit of B and recover all that B could have recovered if the contract had been made with B himself.

Thus, Lush LJ suggested that where A failed to sue on B's behalf, B himself would be able to bring an action against A and the other party to the contract as joint defendants.

The House of Lords reaffirmed the principle in the *Walford* case. By this concept, if A enters into a contract with B with the intention that A shall be the trustee of the benefit of the contract for C (the beneficiary) and the contract provides that B shall confer a benefit on C, then C can sue B directly to enforce the contract as, although he is not a party to it, he is the beneficiary under an enforceable trust. If A supports C's action, he will be joined as co-plaintiff, whilst if he refuses to support it, he will be joined as co-defendant.[32]

After *Walford*, the constructive trust exception was not widely applied, and the courts showed an unwillingness to apply it except in limited circumstances. The courts' attitude was summed up in *Re Schebsman, Official Receiver v Cargo Superintendents (London) Ltd and Schebsman*[33] by Du Parcq LJ:

> It is true that, by the use possibly of unguarded language, a person may create a trust, as Monsieur Jourdain talked prose, without knowing it, but unless an intention to create a trust is clearly to be collected from the language used and the circumstances of the case, I think that the court ought not to be astute to discover indications of such an intention. I have little doubt that in the present case both parties (and certainly the debtor) intended to keep alive their common law right to vary consensually the terms of the obligation undertaken by the company, and if circumstances had changed in the debtor's life-time injustice might have been done by holding that a trust had been created and that those terms were accordingly unalterable.

Thus, in this case the court held that an agreement between S and his employers obliging the employers to make payments to his widow and daughter did not create a trust in favour of the widow and daughter.

Similarly, in *Green v Russell*,[34] R had taken out a personal accident insurance policy on behalf of his employees, including G, the plaintiff's son. Although the case did not turn on the particular point, the court found that the policy did not give G any rights, and therefore did not give the plaintiff any rights. Romer LJ summed up the position as follows, emphasising the incompatibility of R's contractual right to terminate the insurance policy with any rights granted to G under a trust:

> An intention to provide benefits for someone else and to pay for them does not in itself give rise to a trusteeship . . . There was nothing to prevent Mr Russell at any time, had

30 (1880) 16 ChD 290.
31 [1919] AC 801.
32 *Les Affréteurs Réunis SA v Walford* [1919] AC 801.
33 [1944] Ch 83.
34 [1959] 2 QB 226.

> he chosen to do so, from surrendering the policy and receiving back a proportionate part of the premium which he had paid.

More recently, in *Swain v The Law Society*,[35] the respondents had arranged a master insurance policy for all practising solicitors in England and Wales under statutory powers. It had been agreed that a proportion of the commission earned by the insurance brokers would be paid to the Society for the benefit of the profession as a whole. Two solicitors, who were dissatisfied with the way the scheme was being operated, sought to make the Law Society accountable for the commission received, contending that the Society was a trustee of the benefit of the master policy contract for the benefit of all the solicitors. This argument was based on the fact that the contract stated that the policy had been entered into 'on behalf of' solicitors and former solicitors which, it was argued, showed an intention to create a trust of the benefit of the contract. The House of Lords rejected this contention, holding that the wording of the contract did not create a trust, either expressly or impliedly. In Lord Brightman's words:

> It would indeed be surprising if a society of lawyers, who above all might be expected to make their intention clear in a document they compose, should have failed to express the existence of a trust, if that is what they intended to create.

In the Caribbean, the trust concept was applied in a Guyanese case, *Asaram v North American Life Insurance Co*,[36] where it was held that the plaintiff, the former live-in partner of X, a deceased man, was entitled to claim under a life assurance policy taken out by X, even though she was not a party to the insurance contract. The deceased had deliberately and specifically identified the plaintiff as the named beneficiary under the policy, and the plaintiff paid the premiums. It was held that a constructive trust existed in her favour.

On the other hand, in a Barbadian case, *Rochester v Arthur*,[37] the court declined to apply the trust concept. Here, ES had, before his death, taken out two life assurance policies with the American Life Insurance Co (ALICO), in which he named his mother, GS, as beneficiary. The policy documents provided that, 'the proceeds are to be divided equally among all persons who are named as primary beneficiary and who survive the assured'. Chase J applied the principle that a trust of a life assurance policy outside the married women's property legislation was not to be inferred from a general intention to benefit a third party, but only on language clearly revealing an intention on the part of the life assured to declare himself a trustee of the benefits of the policy for the named beneficiary. Such intention was lacking in this case. He explained:

> The fundamental question [is] whether the wording of the policy of the section designated 'beneficiary' . . . is such as would lead a court of equity to the irresistible conclusion that, by naming his mother 'beneficiary', Elroy Scantlebury evinced an intention to declare himself unequivocally 'as trustee' of the benefits of the policy for his mother. In

35 [1983] 1 AC 598.

36 (1995) High Court, Guyana, No 2233 of 1993, unreported [Carilaw GY 1995 HC 4].

37 (1989) High Court, Barbados, No 1279 of 1987, unreported [Carilaw BB 1989 HC 64]. Section 139(1), Insurance Act, Ch 84:01 (Trinidad and Tobago), s 2, Insurance (Amendment) Act (Jamaica), and s 114(2), Insurance Act, Cap 310 (Barbados) have now altered the position regarding life assurance contracts in those jurisdictions. The effect of the sections is that it is no longer necessary to rely on the 'trust concept' as, on the death of the life assured, the policy monies do not fall into his estate but pass automatically and directly to the named beneficiaries.

> considering this question, it is to be borne in mind that 'men often mean to give things to their kinsfolk; they do not often mean to constitute themselves trustees'. Indeed in his work, *Life Insurance Law in the Caribbean*, Claude Denbow . . . states: 'The position of the named beneficiary at common law[38] under a life policy is governed by the well established rule . . . that a third party, not being a party to a contract made in his favour, cannot enforce it', . . . and Rees J, in the course of his judgment in *Rajkumar v First Federation Life Insurance Co Ltd*[39] observed that 'it must be borne in mind that equity leans against implying a trust for the benefit of a person not a party to the contract, unless there is a clear intention to create one' . . . Turning my attention now to the effect of the wording of the section designated 'beneficiary' in the [ALICO] policy document, can it be truly said that, by naming his mother 'beneficiary' in each of the clauses of the policies as presently worded, Elroy Scantlebury evinced an intention by that act alone to declare himself trustee of the benefits for his mother? In seeking to answer this question, it must also be borne in mind that the policies effected on the life of the deceased Elroy Scantlebury were taken out by him as a single man at the ages of 22 and 26. I find myself unable to come to the conclusion that Elroy Scantlebury at this tender age intended during his lifetime to deprive himself completely of the benefits of the policies, or to constitute himself a trustee of them for the benefit of his 62–66 year old mother.

These cases demonstrate that the 'trust concept' is of limited application as the courts will not apply it unless there is clear evidence that a contracting party entered into the agreement specifically as trustee of the benefit for the third party, and the fact that the contract purports to confer a benefit on the third party is not in itself sufficient.[40] In cases where the courts have found in favour of a trust, there was a strong indication of intention to create a trust.[41]

Assignment

A right to the performance of a contract has economic value and is treated as a right of property, called a *chose in action*. A chose in action is property which can only be claimed by action in court, and not by taking physical possession. Choses may be *legal* (e.g. debts and other contractual rights, company shares, insurance policies, bills of lading, and patents and copyrights) or *equitable* (e.g. legacies, and beneficial interests under trusts).

A chose in action, such as the right to the performance of a contract, may be assigned either by:

(a) **Statutory (or legal) assignment**, which must be (i) in writing, (ii) signed by the assignor, (iii) absolute (i.e. the whole chose must be assigned and not merely part of it), (iv) not by way of charge only, and (v) accompanied or followed by express written notice to the debtor or other person whom the assignor would have been entitled to sue. Rules relating to statutory assignment are laid down by

38 (1970) 16 WIR 447, at 451.

39 (1970) 16 WIR 447.

40 *Re Schebsman* [1944] Ch 83; *RT Briscoe (Nigeria) Ltd v Universal Insurance Co Ltd* 1966 (2) ALR Comm 263.

41 *Re Webb, Barclays Bank Ltd v Webb* [1941] Ch 225; *Re Foster Clark's Indenture Trusts, Loveland v Horsecroft* [1966] 1 All ER 43.

legislation such as section 214 of the Barbados Property Act.[42] A statutory assignee takes legal title 'subject to equities'; that is, subject to defences which arise out of the assigned contract (and not arising, for example, in tort or for fraud) and which might have been brought against the assignor.[43]

(b) **Equitable assignment**, in which no particular form is required, except where the assignment of the *chose* amounts to a disposition of an interest in land, e.g. assignment of a contract to lease property, in which case the assignment must be in writing.[44] All that needs to be shown is the intention to assign. Thus, where a father handed to his son certain assurance policies on the father's life requesting the son to erect a tombstone in his memory out of the policy monies, no notice being given to the assurance company, it was held that there was a valid equitable assignment of the policies to the son by way of charge for the cost of the tombstone.[45]

An assignment which does not comply with the statutory requirements for a legal assignment may be enforceable as a valid equitable assignment, as this outcome is not prohibited by the legislation. It must be noted, however, that an equitable assignee does not acquire a legal title to the chose in action (while a statutory assignee does acquire legal title)[46] and may not, for example, be able to bring an action in respect of the chose without joining the assignor, if the assignor still has some interest in the suit.[47]

It is not necessary for the equitable assignee to have given consideration in respect of the assignment, provided that the assignor has taken every step to complete the transaction and to perfect the assignment.[48] In the case of a chose in action, the assignment is complete or perfected when the assignor unequivocally expresses the intent to assign the chose to the assignee.[49]

In principle, the assignee cannot recover more from a debtor than the assignor could have recovered if there had been no assignment.[50]

(c) **Assignment by operation of law**. An involuntary assignment of a chose in action occurs automatically on the death or bankruptcy of the owner. On death, all contractual rights and obligations pass to the personal representative of the deceased party. Thus the personal representative can sue or be sued on contracts entered into by the deceased, except for contracts for personal services (which come to an end on the death of either party). On bankruptcy, all the property of the bankrupt vests in his trustee in bankruptcy and becomes divisible between the creditors.

---

42 Cap 236. See also s 49(f), Judicature (Supreme Court) Act (Jamaica); s 23(7), Supreme Court of Judicature Act, Ch 4:01 (Trinidad and Tobago); s 35, Real Property Act, Cap 366 (Antigua and Barbuda); s 133(1), Law of Property Act, Cap 190 (Belize).

43 *Graham v Johnson* (1869) LR 8 Eq 36; *Banco Santander SA v Bayfern Ltd* [2000] 1 All; ER (Comm) 776; cf *Stoddard v Union Trust* [1912] 1 KB 181.

44 Section 9, Statute of Frauds 1677 (United Kingdom). See also s 47, Property Act, Cap 236 (Barbados) and s 43(1), Property Act, Cap 190 (Belize).

45 *Thomas v Harris* [1947] 1 All ER 444.

46 *Warner Bros Records Inc v Rollgreen Ltd* [1976] QB 430.

47 *Ibid.*

48 *Fortescue v Barnett* (1834) 3 My & K 35.

49 *Voyle v Hughes* (1954) 2 Sm & G 18.

50 *Dawson v Great Northern & City Railway Co* [1905] 1 KB 260.

(d) **Contracts for personal services.** The right to sue on a contract of a personal or fiduciary nature (e.g. where A agrees to perform as a DJ at B's party or to write a book for B) cannot be assigned. Similarly, since the relationship between insurer and assured is a personal one, a motor insurance policy cannot be assigned to a buyer to whom the car is sold, since that would be to 'thrust a new assured upon a company against its will'.[51]

Priorities: The rule in Dearle v Hall[52]

Where an assignor makes multiple assignments of the same chose in action (whether statutory or equitable) to separate assignees, and both or several assignments cannot be satisfied by the chose, the assignments rank according to priority of notice.[53] A subsequent assignee can only be given priority over an earlier assignment if he did not know of the earlier assignment.[54] Except in assignments of equitable interests in land (in which case the notice must be in writing),[55] no specific form of notice is required. It must simply be clear and unambiguous. Thus, in *Lloyd v Banks*,[56] it was held that notice in a newspaper read by the debtor was sufficient; however, notice given to a single trustee of a trust with multiple trustees may be ineffective unless the notice is conveyed to each trustee.[57]

Rights not capable of being assigned

Contracts prohibiting assignment

A contract which precludes assignment to a third party cannot be validly assigned and in this case the contract will be unenforceable by a debtor against the purported assignee.[58] It is common for commercial contracts to either preclude assignment entirely or to stipulate that the written consent of the non-assigning party or parties be obtained before such assignment can take place.

Bare rights of action

A bare right of action (that is, a mere right of action against a particular party) cannot be assigned,[59] unless the rights being assigned are assigned together with property to which those rights attach.[60]

---

51 *Peters v General Accident and Life Assurance Corp* [1937] 4 All ER 628.

52 (1823) 3 Russ 1.

53 *Marchant v Morton, Down & Co* [1901] 2 KB 829.

54 *Re Holmes* (1885) 29 Ch D 786.

55 See, for example, s 47, Property Act, Cap 236 (Barbados) and s 43(1), Property Act, Cap 190 (Belize).

56 (1868) LR 3 Ch App 488.

57 *Re Phillips' Trusts* [1903] 1 Ch 183.

58 *Helstan Securities Ltd v Hertfordshire CC* [1978] 3 All ER 262.

59 *De Hoghton v Money* (1866) LR 2 Ch App 164.

60 *Defries v Milne* [1913] 1 Ch 98; *Ellis v Torrington* [1920] 1 KB 399.

PUBLIC POLICY

Certain types of contract have been held to be unassignable on the basis that such an assignment would be contrary to public policy. This includes, *inter alia*, maintenance payments granted to a spouse.[61]

LIABILITIES CANNOT BE ASSIGNED

At common law, only the benefit (the rights) and not the burden (the obligations) arising under the terms of a contract may be assigned.

Novation

Novation has been defined as 'the rescission of one contract and the substitution of a new one in which the same acts are to be performed by different parties'.[62] Novation, unlike assignment, requires the consent of the new party as well as that of the outgoing party and the existing party. This is because it involves entry into a whole new contract which replaces (and annuls) the contract already in place. In this way, novation allows for the transfer of both rights and liabilities.

Thus, if KFC Ltd (KFC) has a contract with Chicken 1 Ltd (Chicken 1) for the provision of chicken to its restaurant business, but Chicken 1 is selling its chicken farming business to Chicken 2 Ltd (Chicken 2), all three may agree to novate the original contract, replacing it with a contract between KFC and Chicken 2. In this way, both the burden and the benefit of the contract will be transferred to Chicken 2.

There must be consideration for the agreement,[63] but this condition would be satisfied by the promise of Chicken 2 to perform the obligations under the novated agreement formerly performed by Chicken 1.

LEGISLATIVE REFORM: THE UK CONTRACTS (RIGHTS OF THIRD PARTIES) ACT 1999[64]

In 1999, the Contracts (Rights of Third Parties) Act was passed by the UK parliament after calls for reform.[65] The Act was intended to mitigate the rigidity of the doctrine of privity of contract. For example, section 1 allows an expressly identified third party beneficiary to a contract to enforce the terms of that contract if the contract expressly provides that he may, or if (subject to the intention of the parties as discerned on a proper construction of the parties), the term purports to confer a benefit on him.

The third party can also take advantage of limitations or exclusions of liability available under the contract.[66]

61 *Re Robinson* (1884) 27 Ch D 160.

62 *Anson's Law of Contract, op cit*, p 676.

63 *Commissioners of Customs and Excise v Diners Club Ltd* [1988] 2 All ER 1016.

64 Contracts (Rights of Third Parties) Act 1999 (United Kingdom).

65 For example, see *Linden Gardens* [1994] 1 AC 85 and the UK Law Commission proposals reported in 1937.

66 Section 1(c), Contracts (Rights of Third Parties) Act 1999 (United Kingdom).

This Act would provide a remedy for cases such as *White v Jones*,[67] where a testator who intended to change his will to confer rights on his daughters, died before the amendments could be made. The failure to make the amendments was due to the negligence of the testator's solicitor. It was clear that the daughters could not sue the solicitor in contract, but they were able to maintain an action in tort for negligence. If this 1995 case had arisen after the implementation of the Contracts (Rights of Third Parties) Act, the daughters might have been able to sue in contract also.

It remains to be seen whether similar legislation will be adopted in Commonwealth Caribbean jurisdictions.

67 [1995] 2 AC 207.

CHAPTER 12

AGENCY

Formation of agency

At common law, the principal/agent relationship may arise in a variety of circumstances, for instance where an agent is appointed to negotiate a contract for the sale of goods on behalf of his principal, or to execute a conveyance of land; also, there are specialist agents who are qualified to perform specific functions, such as auctioneers, attorneys and solicitors, brokers, factors and real estate agents. In addition to these species of agent, whose relationships with their principals and the third parties with whom they have dealings are governed by the law of contract, there is also the well-known principal/agent relationship which arises in the law of tort where a 'casual agent' drives a motor vehicle for some purpose for the owner of the vehicle.[1]

As far as the law of contract is concerned, the basic function of an agent (A) is to establish a contractual relationship between his principal (P) and a third party (T) and, having done so, he normally 'drops out of the picture', leaving P and T bound by a contractual obligation.

Agency may be created in any one of four ways:

(i) by express or implied appointment giving A *actual authority* to act for P;
(ii) by *subsequent ratification* by P of a contract entered into by A without P's authority;
(iii) by *ostensible authority* conferred on A by P, although no authority was actually given; or
(iv) by authority given by implication of law in cases of *necessity*.

Actual authority

Lord Diplock has described actual authority as 'a legal relationship between principal and agent created by a consensual agreement to which they alone are parties. Its scope is to be ascertained by applying ordinary principles of construction of contracts, including any proper implications from the express words used, the usages of the trade, or the course of business between the parties.'[2]

Actual authority of an agent may be express or implied. It is *express* when P expressly selects and appoints A, and A accepts the appointment, thus creating a contract between P and A. No particular form of appointment is required; it may be written or oral, except where A is required to make contracts by deed (including conveyances of land), in which case P will need to give A a power of attorney by deed.[3]

---

1 See generally, Kodilinye, *Commonwealth Caribbean Tort Law*, 4th edn (2009), pp 331–8.

2 *Freeman and Lockyer (a Firm) v Buckhurst Park Properties (Mengel) Ltd* [1964] 1 All ER 630, at 644.

3 Cheshire, Fifoot and Furmston, *Law of Contract*, 13th edn, p 485.

Authority is implied most often where A, without any express appointment, is employed to perform certain functions within a particular trade or business; in which case, he will be deemed to have implied authority to perform those acts which are customary in the particular trade. Another instance of implied authority is that presumed to have been given by a husband to his legal or his common-law wife who is cohabiting with him, to pledge his credit for necessary goods and services.[4]

Ratification

If A, without any prior authority, purports to contract with T for and on behalf of P, and P later *ratifies and adopts* the contract, the relationship of principal and agent arises between P and A. Ratification may occur in two types of case: (i) where A, though intending to contract as P's agent, was not in fact P's agent at the time of the contract, and (ii) where A was in fact P's agent, but in making the contract he exceeded his authority. In both cases ratification has the effect of placing the parties in the same position in which they would have been if A's actions had been authorised by P from the outset. Ratification thus relates back to the moment when a concluded contract was made by A and T, and has retrospective effect.[5] This principle is illustrated by *Bolton Partners v Lambert*.[6] Here, T offered to purchase property belonging to P Co. A, who was P Co's managing director, without having authority to do so, purported to accept the offer on behalf of P Co. T then withdrew the offer, but P Co proceeded to ratify A's acceptance. It was held that, since ratification relates back to the moment the contract was concluded by acceptance of the offer, T's purported revocation of the offer came too late and he was bound.

For ratification to apply, the following two requirements must be satisfied:

(a) *The contract must have been made by A as the purported agent of a disclosed principal.* At the time he made the contract, A must have purported to act as agent of a named principal or, at least, a principal who was capable of being ascertained at that time.[7] Somewhat illogically, the doctrine of the 'undisclosed principal' is not applicable to cases of ratification, as is illustrated by *Keighley, Maxsted and Co v Durant*.[8] In this case, A was authorised by P to buy wheat at a certain price on a joint account for himself and P. A agreed to buy wheat from T at a price which was higher than that authorised; he intended to buy on the joint account but he contracted in his own name, without disclosing that he was an agent. The next day, P ratified the contract but he and A ultimately failed to take delivery of the wheat. T's action against P for breach of contract failed, since A had contracted with T without disclosing that P was his principal, and accordingly P was not contractually bound.

(b) *There must have been an existing, competent principal at the time the contract was made.* This requirement is particularly applicable to the case where, before a company

4 *Debenham v Mellon* (1880) 5 QBD 394.

5 *Bowstead and Reynolds on Agency*, 18th edn (2006), arts 14, 20, cited in *Drew v Caribbean Home Insurance Co Ltd* (1987) High Court, Trinidad and Tobago, No 2993 of 1985, unreported [Carilaw TT 1987 HC 94].

6 (1889) 41 Ch D 295.

7 *Eastern Construction Co Ltd v National Trust Co Ltd* [1914] AC 197, at 213.

8 [1901] AC 240.

has legally come into existence, its promoters enter into a contract with a third party purportedly as agents of the company; for example where promoters enter into a contract for the purchase of premises needed by the future company. In such a case, since the company was not in existence at the date of the contract, it would be incapable of ratifying the contract when it later acquired legal personalty, for 'when the company came afterwards into existence, it was a totally new creature, having rights and obligations from that time, but no rights or obligations by reason of anything which might have been done before'.[9] Whether the purported agents would themselves be liable as parties to the contract in such circumstances would depend on 'what the parties intended or must be fairly understood to have intended'.[10]

Other requirements

In addition to the above requirements, it has been held that, in order to be effective, ratification must take place within a reasonable time;[11] P must have had full knowledge of the material facts at the time of ratification;[12] and the contract must not be void[13] or *ultra vires*.[14]

Ostensible authority

Where A has not been expressly appointed agent by P, but P has, by his conduct, given the impression to T that A is his (P's) agent (i.e. where P has 'held out' A as his agent), and A has entered into a contract with T within the scope of his apparent authority, P may be estopped from denying the agency and may be bound by the contract. The nature of ostensible authority was explained by Lord Diplock in the leading case of *Freeman and Lockyer (a firm) v Buckhurst Park Properties (Mangal) Ltd*:[15]

> An 'apparent' or 'ostensible' authority . . . is a legal relationship between the principal and the contractor, created by a representation, made by the principal to the contractor, intended to be and in fact acted upon by the contractor, that the agent has authority to enter on behalf of the principal into a contract of a kind within the scope of the 'apparent' authority, so as to render the principal liable to perform any obligations imposed on him by such contract. He need not be (although he generally is) aware of the existence of the representation. The representation, when acted on by the contractor by entering into a contract with the agent, operates as an estoppel, preventing the principal

---

9 *Kelner v Baxter* (1866) LR 2 CP 174, at 183, *per* Erle CJ.

10 *Summergreene v Parker* (1950) 80 CLR 304, at 323, *per* Fullager J.

11 *Bedford Insurance Co Ltd v Instituto de Ressaguros do Brasil* [1985] QB 966, at 987.

12 *Shell Co of Australia Ltd v National Shipping Bagging Services Ltd, The Kilmun* [1988] 2 Lloyd's Rep 1, at 11.

13 *Brook v Hook* (1871) LR 6 Exch 89.

14 *Ashbury Railway Carriage and Iron Co v Riche* (1875) LR 7 HL 653.

15 [1964] 1 All ER 630, at 644, cited in *Johnstone v Ritchie* (1983) Court of Appeal, Trinidad and Tobago, Civ App No 16 of 1979, unreported [Carilaw TT 1983 CA 20]; *Clean-Away Ltd v St Tropez Marina Bahamas Ltd* (1993) Supreme Court, The Bahamas, No 1755 of 1990, unreported [Carilaw BS 1993 SC 21]; *Raymond and Pierre Ltd v HCU Communications Ltd* (2010) High Court, Trinidad and Tobago, No 1064 of 2009, unreported [Carilaw TT 2010 HC 126]; *Speedy Service Liquors Ltd v Airports Authority of Trinidad and Tobago* (2002) High Court, Trinidad and Tobago, No 586 of 1984, unreported [Carilaw TT 2002 HC 106].

> from asserting that he is not bound by the contract. It is irrelevant whether the agent had actual authority to enter into the contract . . . In ordinary business dealings, the contractor at the time of entering into the contract can in the nature of things hardly ever rely on the 'actual' authority of the agent. His information as to the authority must be derived either from the principal or from the agent or from both, for they alone know what the agent's actual authority is . . . In the ultimate analysis, he relies either on the representation of the principal, (i.e. apparent authority), or on the representation of the agent (i.e. warranty of authority). The representation which creates apparent authority may take a variety of forms of which the commonest is representation by conduct'.

Examples of ostensible or apparent authority are:

(a) Where a wife (A) has been accustomed to pledging her husband's (P's) credit for 'non-necessary' goods, such as jewellery or expensive dresses, with a store owner (T), she will have ostensible authority to do so, as P will have held her out as his agent. Accordingly, if P forbids her to continue pledging his credit, he must warn T of this change, otherwise he will be estopped from denying the agency and will remain liable for A's future purchases.[16]
(b) Where a business partner (P) retires from the partnership, he ought to give notice to the public of his retirement, otherwise he will remain liable on any contracts made by the continuing partners (A) with persons (T) who were aware of his membership of the firm.[17]
(c) Where P has been accustomed to accepting and paying for goods purchased by his employee (A) from T on behalf of P, he will remain liable to T for purchases fraudulently made by A after A has left P's employment,[18] for 'where a principal has publicly allowed the agent to assume an authority, that authority cannot be revoked privately'.[19]

Separate and apart from cases where P has held out A as his agent, and is therefore estopped from denying the agency, there are instances where P may be liable for the unauthorised acts of A, despite the absence of any representation or 'holding out' on the part of P. These are cases where the existence of P was not disclosed to T, so there was no possibility of any 'holding out' by P. In *Watteau v Fenwick*,[20] P, a brewery, purchased a public house from A but kept him on as manager. A was forbidden by P to buy cigars, although the purchase of cigars was normal and usual in this type of business. Contrary to his instructions, A bought some cigars from T who gave credit to A personally, in the mistaken belief that A was the owner of the public house. When T discovered that A was employed by P, T sued P for the price of the cigars. P argued that it could not be liable on the contract as T had been unaware of the existence of P, and there had been no 'holding out' by P. The court rejected this argument. According to Wills J, 'the principal is liable for all the acts of the agent which are within the authority usually confided to an agent of that character, notwithstanding limitations as between the principal and the agent, put upon that authority.'[21]

16 *Debenham v Mellon* (1880) 5 QBD 394.
17 *Scarf v Jardine* (1882) 7 App Cas 345, at 349.
18 *Summers v Solomon* (1857) 119 ER 1474.
19 *Anson's Law of Contract*, 29th edn (2010), p 693.
20 [1893] 1 QB 346.
21 *Ibid*, at 348.

Watteau v Fenwick is a decision which is hard to justify on principle. A clearly had no apparent or ostensible authority to contract with T for the cigars, as it is of the essence of ostensible authority that the representation ('holding out') should be made by P, and not by A himself; nor can it be justified as a case of 'usual' or 'customary' authority, since such authority is a species of implied authority, which can always be revoked or curtailed by P, as was the case here. It has been suggested, however, that the liability of P may possibly be analysed as a quasi-tortious vicarious liability for the acts of A done in the course of A's employment.[22]

Agency of necessity

It is a cardinal principle of the common law that a person who, without being requested to do so, intervenes and incurs expenditure in the 'necessary' protection of another person's property has no cause of action against that other person to recover his expenditure, for, in the oft-quoted words of Bowen LJ, 'liabilities are not to be forced upon people behind their backs'.[23] There is thus no Roman law *negotiorum gestio* in the common law. To this rule, however, there is at least one established exception, namely the rule that the master of a ship is entitled, in a case of accident and emergency, to act as an agent of the cargo owners in entering into contracts in order to salvage the cargo, which will be binding on the owners, notwithstanding that in so doing he exceeds his express authority, so long as the master acts in good faith and in the best interests of the owners.[24] In such a case, the onus is on the claimant to establish (i) that the transaction entered into was reasonably necessary in the circumstances, and (ii) that communication with the owners of the cargo was impracticable.

Relations between principal and agent *inter se*

The rights and obligations of principal and agent *inter se* are governed (a) by the express and implied terms of the agency contract and (b) by the principles of equity governing fiduciary relationships, and it has been held that the fiduciary duties owed by an agent can be varied by the terms of the contract.[25]

DUTIES OF THE AGENT

Duty to account

An agent is under a duty to keep proper accounts regarding any money or property that he receives or hands over in connection with transactions carried out by him in the course of his employment as agent, and he must be prepared at all times to produce them for inspection by the principal.[26]

---

22 *Anson, ibid*, p 694.

23 *Falcke v Scottish Imperial Insurance Co* (1886) 34 Ch D 234, at 248.

24 *The Argos* (1873) LR 5 PC 134.

25 *Kelly v Cooper* [1993] AC 205, where it was held that the agent's fiduciary duty to avoid a conflict of interest could be waived by an implied term in the contract.

26 See *Bowstead and Reynolds on Agency*, art 52; *Pearse v Green* (1819) 37 ER 327.

Duty of care and skill

In carrying out his functions, an agent must use reasonable care and exercise the degree of skill which he professes to have, and he will be liable in damages in tort or for breach of his equitable obligation if, owing to his lack of care and skill, the principal suffers loss.[27] Additionally, where A receives money which is due to P, the latter may have an action against A for an account or for money had and received.[28]

Duty not to make a secret profit

One of the two main principles arising from the fiduciary obligation of an agent towards his principal is that an agent may not, without the consent of the principal, make a profit for himself from his position as agent. If the agent does make a 'secret profit', he will hold such profit on a constructive trust for the principal and will have to disgorge it. A clear example is *Hippesley v Knee Brothers*.[29] In this case, P employed a firm of auctioneers (A) to sell certain property, agreeing to pay to A their commission on the sale and to reimburse their out-of-pocket expenses, including printing and advertising costs. A managed to obtain discounts from the printers and the advertisers, but claimed reimbursement from P of the full cost of the printing and advertising, without disclosing the discounts they had received. A acted in good faith in that they genuinely believed they were entitled to keep the amount of the discounts for themselves. It was held that A was nevertheless accountable to P for the discounts.

The modern proposition that an agent who receives a secret commission holds it on a constructive trust for the principal was established by the Privy Council in *Attorney General of Hong Kong v Reid*.[30] Here, the Attorney General brought an action for an account relating to bribes received by A, a former Acting Director of Public Prosecutions, paid to him as inducements to exploit his official position by obstructing the prosecution of certain prisoners. A used the bribe money to purchase land in New Zealand. It was held that since A was in a fiduciary position, both the bribe and the property purchased with it were held by him on a constructive trust for the government; and as the land purchased with the bribe money had decreased in value since the date of the purchase, A was liable to account for the difference between the amount of the bribe and the current value of the property. Lord Templeman, delivering the judgment of the Privy Council, emphasised that a person in a fiduciary position must not be allowed to benefit from his own breach of duty, and that such person was accountable for the bribe as soon as he received it.

The principle in *Reid* was followed in the Cayman case of *Corporacion Nacional del Cobre v Interglobal Inc*.[31] Here, the claimant company (P) had employed A as its agent and head of its futures trading department. It was an express term of his contract of employment that A was not to receive any secret commission or bribes, or make any

---

27 *Ibid*, art 42.
28 *Ibid*, art 53.
29 [1905] 1 KB 1.
30 [1994] 1 All ER 1.
31 [2002] CILR 298 (Grand Court, Cayman Islands).

secret profit in his dealings with third parties on behalf of the company. Contrary to this stipulation, A received secret payments from a third party as an inducement for A to procure the company to enter into certain contracts with commodity brokers, on terms apparently unfavourable to the company. Smellie CJ held that A was liable as constructive trustee for the amount of the secret commission. He said:

> Where a fiduciary accepts bribes and other illicit payments as an incentive for his breach of duty, he not only becomes a debtor for the amount of the bribes to the person to whom the duty was owed, but he also holds the bribes and any other property acquired therewith on constructive trust for the person. This is clear from the Privy Council decision in *Attorney General of Hong Kong v Reid*.[32] . . . [The statements of principle in the *Reid* case] are an inevitable outcome of the development of the modern law on fiduciary relationships . . . The strictness of the principle is the result of the importance which equity attaches to the fiduciary duties and the extent to which equity will operate to prevent a fiduciary from benefiting from his fraud, or even from an abuse of his fiduciary position, by which he acts in conflict with the duties owed to his principal.

Duty to avoid a conflict of interest

An agent, being in a fiduciary position towards his principal, must not place himself in a situation where his personal interests are in conflict with his duty to the principal. Perhaps the most important instance of this duty is the so-called 'rule against self-dealing', which is that an agent employed to sell P's property should not attempt to purchase the property for himself;[33] such a purchase will inevitably involve a conflict of interest as A will naturally wish to pay as low a price as possible, whereas his duty is to obtain as high a price as possible for P. Another example of a conflict of interest situation is where A, who has been appointed by P to establish contractual relations between P and T, purports to act also as agent of T. In such a case, A will be accountable to P for any benefit he has received as a result of his activities on behalf of T.[34]

Duty not to delegate his duties

An agent, having been entrusted with the task of performing services of a fiduciary nature for P, is not entitled to delegate those duties to any other person unless he obtains P's consent, or can point to a trade custom permitting delegation, or that there was an emergency which required it;[35] on the other hand, acts of a purely ministerial character not involving confidentiality or requiring any special care or skill, may always be delegated.[36]

The issue of delegation by an agent arose in a Trinidadian case, *Drew v Caribbean Home Insurance Co Ltd*.[37] Here the claimant, the owner of a yacht anchored at a marina

---

32 [1994] AC 324.

33 *McPherson v Watt* (1877) 3 App Cas 254.

34 *Armstrong v Jackson* [1917] 2 KB 822.

35 *De Bussche v Alt* (1878) 8 Ch D 286.

36 *Allam & Co Ltd v Europa Poster Services Ltd* [1968] 1 WLR 639.

37 (1987) High Court, Trinidad and Tobago, No 2993 of 1985, unreported [Carilaw TT 1987 HC 94].

in Grenada, wished to obtain a policy of marine insurance for the yacht. One DS was introduced to the claimant as 'agent' of the defendant insurance company. An insurance policy was arranged by DS, and the claimant paid a portion of the premium, receiving from the defendant a cover note which was valid for 45 days. DS then fraudulently induced the claimant to send the balance of the premium to a company which he represented as having been set up by the defendant but which in fact had no connection with the defendant. Some time later, the yacht was stolen, and when the claimant sought to recover compensation under the insurance policy, the defendant rejected the claim on the ground that the policy had lapsed on expiry of the 45-day period, owing to non-payment of the balance of the premium. Edoo J held (i) that although DS had no actual or ostensible authority to negotiate the insurance contract between the parties, the defendant had, by issuing the cover note, ratified the transaction; (ii) that the claimant was at fault in failing to ensure that DS had authority to delegate to another person the function of receiving the insurance premium; and (iii) that the claimant ought to have sent the premium directly to the defendant company. Accordingly, since the defendant company had never received the premium, the policy had lapsed and the defendant was not liable.

RIGHTS OF THE AGENT

The main right of an agent is the right to be paid the amount of the remuneration or commission agreed between himself and the principal. If no precise amount is agreed, then the agent is entitled to receive a 'reasonable remuneration', either under a term implied in the contract or on a *quantum meruit* basis.[38]

In the Commonwealth Caribbean, issues regarding rights to payment have most often arisen in the context of claims regarding commission payable to real estate agents. In considering such claims to commission, a court will invariably base its decision on a construction of the wording of the contract between P and A, and it is accepted that 'for an estate agent to be entitled to his commission, it must be shown that the parties agreed that, on the happening of an event, the commission should be paid and that event has taken place'.[39]

Real estate agents are normally employed by the prospective vendor of land to find a purchaser for such property, and the contract of agency will specify the conditions on which remuneration or commission will be payable by the vendor to the agent.[40] An instructive case from the Bahamas is *Atlantis Real Estate and Management Co Ltd v Gates*,[41] where the claimants were engaged by the defendant to sell her house, a commission of 6 per cent of the sale price being payable in the event of the claimants' introducing a person 'willing and able' to purchase the property. The claimants advertised the property in the *Nassau Guardian* newspaper, and the advertisement was answered in

38 *Way v Latilla* [1937] 3 All ER 739.

39 *Dennis Reed Ltd v Goody* [1950] 1 All ER 919, at 924.

40 A real estate agent does not become entitled to a commission merely because he makes an introduction which is the effective cause of the sale; there must be a preceding contract or at least a previous request to find a purchaser: *Mallet v Radford* (1951) 158 EG 396. See *Matthews v Ward* (1983) High Court, Barbados, No 212 of 1982, unreported [Carilaw BB 1983 HC 30].

41 (1985) Supreme Court, The Bahamas, No 703 of 1982, unreported [Carilaw BS 1985 SC 16].

February 1981 by M, who was introduced to the defendant. M viewed the property, but he was not financially in a position to purchase as he had not yet found a purchaser for his present house. One month later, the defendant took the house off the market and so informed the claimants. Early in 1982, M's financial situation changed, and in May of that year he contacted the defendant again. After negotiations, a contract of sale was signed. In August 1982, the property was conveyed to M. The claimants brought an action for 6 per cent commission. Georges CJ held that the claimants were not entitled to commission because, by the time M was financially 'able' to purchase, the agency agreement had been terminated by the defendant; he was also prepared to hold that the introduction of M to the defendant was not the effective cause of the sale. It was emphasised that where a contract of agency between a real estate agent and a prospective vendor provided that commission was to be payable to the agent upon the introduction of a person 'willing and able to purchase', the agent was obligated to introduce a person who exactly fitted that description; a person who withdrew before completion was not 'willing', and a person who did not have sufficient financial resources to proceed with the purchase was not 'able'. The legal position had been explained in a well-known dictum of Denning LJ in *Dennis Reed Ltd v Goody*[42] in the context of the particular agreement in that case:

> Whom must the agent introduce? He must produce 'a person ready, able and willing to purchase the above property for the sum of 2,825 pounds, or such other price to which I shall assent'. These words do not mean a person ready, able and willing 'to make an offer', or even 'to enter into a contract': they mean a person ready, able and willing to 'purchase', that is, to complete the purchase. He must be a person who is 'able' at the proper time to complete; that is, he must then have the necessary financial resources. He must also be 'ready', that is, he must have made all necessary preparations by having the cash or banker's draft ready to hand over. He must also be 'willing'; that is, he must be willing to hand over the money in return for the conveyance.

Similar issues of contractual interpretation were before the court in a Trinidadian case, *Bissondialsingh v Charles.*[43] Here, the claimant estate agent agreed to act as exclusive agent for the sale of the defendant's property for a commission of 5 per cent of the sale price, to be paid 'on the deposit of the property (*sic*). Should the property be sold for above the suggested price, the additional sum shall be paid to the agent'. The claimant found a prospective purchaser who entered into a written agreement for the sale of the property for $230,000 and paid a deposit of $25,750. The sale was to have been completed by a certain date. It was not, and the defendant, at the request of the purchaser, returned the deposit to the purchaser. The central question in the case was whether the claimant became entitled to payment of commission on payment of the deposit, or whether he would become entitled only on completion of the sale by conveyance of the property. Sealey J held that, on a reasonable interpretation of the agency contract, the commission was payable on completion of the sale, not on payment of the deposit. She explained:

> In *Dennis Reed Ltd v Goody*[44] the court had to consider a clause in an estate agent's contract which read in part, 'I hereby instruct you to find a person ready, willing and able to

42 [1950] 1 All ER 919.

43 (1995) High Court, Trinidad and Tobago, No 3909 of 1987, unreported [Carilaw TT 1995 HC 65].

44 [1950] 1 All ER 919.

> purchase the . . . property for the sum of 2,570 pounds or such other price to which I shall assent. Upon your introducing such a person, I will pay you a commission . . .'. It was held that the words 'upon your introducing' signified merely the services to be rendered by the agents, and not the time when the agents became entitled to commission and, under the terms of the contract, the agents became entitled to commission, not when they had introduced a person willing to make an offer, or even willing to enter into a contract, but when they had introduced a person who was ready, able and willing to complete a purchase . . . Denning LJ said: 'if estate agents desire to get full commission, not only on sales but also on offers, they must use clear and unequivocal language . . . An agent does not earn a commission as a labourer earns wages. Even though he has done his part, he does not become entitled to his commission until the purchase is completed.'

An estate agent's claim for commission succeeded in *Universal Properties and Investments Ltd v Woo*.[45] In this case, the defendant, a married man, engaged the claimant estate agent to sell his house in Freeport, Grand Bahama. The claimant found a prospective purchaser, one ET, and a contract of sale was executed by ET and the defendant. The contract stated, *inter alia*, that sale would be conditional upon the vendor conveying a title free of all encumbrances, and the defendant also entered into a commission agreement in which he agreed to pay the claimant $10,000 'as a commission for finding the above purchaser'. There was, however, a complication in that the house was subject to the defendant's wife's dower rights, which constituted an encumbrance on the property. At the time the contract of sale was executed, the wife had given her oral consent to the sale, but she later changed her mind and refused to renounce her dower rights, despite the defendant's efforts to persuade her otherwise, and so he was unable to pass a clear title free of all encumbrances.

Adams J stated that the agency agreement must always be closely examined in order to ascertain whether the agent has performed exactly what he has agreed to do, so as to be entitled to commission for finding a purchaser. The case law had established that, once matters have reached the stage of a binding contract being signed between the prospective vendor and purchaser, the vendor must pay the estate agent his commission, as it could 'be said with truth that a purchaser has been introduced by the agent',[46] and 'the event has happened upon the occurrence of which a right to the promised commission has been vested in the agent'.[47] Put in another way, 'once the signing has been done . . . the principal has accepted the benefit of the agent's work, and in these circumstances he ought not to be allowed to resile from his obligations to the agent.'[48] In order to bring about this result, and to bring business efficacy to the commission agreement, the court could imply a term that the vendor would not fail to perform his contract with the purchaser so as to deprive the estate agent of his commission. In the present case, the defendant was aware of his wife's entitlement to dower at the time he signed the contract of sale, and he had therefore to be taken to have impliedly warranted that he would obtain her renunciation of that interest. The defendant was thus liable to pay the commission.

---

45 (1986) Supreme Court, The Bahamas, No 106 of 1982, unreported [Carilaw BS 1986 SC 7].

46 *Luxor (Eastbourne) Ltd v Cooper* [1941] 1 All ER 33, 43, *per* Lord Russell.

47 *Ibid.*

48 *Ibid.*

Another example of a successful claim for commission by a real estate agent is the Jamaican case of *Lindo v Collins*.[49] Here, P entrusted A with the sale of an area of land 'for a period of two months', on the terms that, 'the property is not to be sold for less than 50,000 pounds, but you are authorised to submit offers. Should you introduce someone ready and willing to buy at the above price or at a price acceptable to me, or should the property be sold at any time during the period of two months mentioned above, or to a purchaser introduced by you, I agree to pay you a commission of 5 per centum of the sale price'. Within the two-month period, A obtained an offer from S, representing C Ltd, to purchase the property for £30,000, but the offer was unacceptable to P. About a year later, S showed a renewed interest in the property and a meeting arranged by one H between S, H and P, resulted in an agreement by C Ltd to purchase the property. A was held to be entitled to the commission. Robinson P, delivering the judgment of the Jamaican Court of Appeal, explained:

> It appears that it was the plaintiff [A], and the plaintiff alone, who had brought [S] and his company (C Ltd) into relation with the defendant [P] as an intending purchaser, and that the plaintiff had done so during the two months before the expiry of the agreement ... [H] did nothing new by way of introducing a purchaser; he merely arranged the pursuit of further negotiations between the defendant and the purchaser who had already been introduced to the defendant by the plaintiff ... But for the introduction of [C Ltd] by the plaintiff to the defendant, [C Ltd] might never have known that this property was for sale; the defendant might never have known that [C Ltd] was interested in purchasing it; and the sale to [C Ltd] might never have taken place ... A proper reading of the contract between the plaintiff and the defendant indicates that the plaintiff would be entitled to his commission on the happening of any one of three separate events. First, if during the period of two months ... he had introduced to the defendant someone ready and willing to purchase the property at a price of 50,000 pounds or at some other price acceptable to the defendant, he would have been entitled to his commission. This was not the case here. Secondly, if the property had in fact been sold at any time during the aforementioned period of two months, no matter at what price, and even if the plaintiff had played no part whatever in bringing about the sale, he would nevertheless have been entitled to his commission. This, too, was not the case here. Thirdly, if, during the aforementioned period of two months, the plaintiff had introduced a purchaser to the defendant then, should the property be sold to that purchaser, the plaintiff would be entitled to his commission. This was certainly the case here. [C Ltd] were the purchasers of the property. They had been introduced to the defendant by the plaintiff, and that introduction had taken place during the two month period of the life of the contract. In the circumstances of this case, and having regard to the terms of the contract, it seems immaterial to consider whether the introduction by the plaintiff was the effective cause of the sale, though ... it would certainly appear to be so ... Lord Atkinson, delivering the judgment of the Privy Council in *Burchell v Gowrie and Blockhouse Collieries Ltd*,[50] had this to say: 'If an agent ... brings a person into relation with his principal as an intending purchaser, the agent has done the most effective, and possibly the most laborious and expensive, part of his work, and ... if the principal takes advantage of that work, and, behind the back of the agent and unknown to him, sells to the purchaser thus brought into touch with him, ... the agent's act may still well be the effective cause of the sale.'

49 (1976) 23 WIR 156 (Court of Appeal, Jamaica).

50 [1910] AC 614, at 625.

RELATIONSHIP BETWEEN PRINCIPAL AND THIRD PARTIES

The normal rule is that when A enters into a transaction with T on behalf of P, P is bound by all acts of A performed within the scope of A's authority, whether express, implied or ostensible. P is bound by contracts made within the scope of A's authority even where A was fraudulent and acted entirely for his own purposes,[51] unless T knew or ought to have known of A's fraudulent or selfish purpose.[52]

(a) *Where the fact of the agency and the name of the principal are disclosed to the third party*, A creates a contract between P and T and A 'drops out of the picture', incurring no rights or obligations.[53] The effect is thus as if P had contracted directly with T. However, 'the parties can by their express contract provide that the agent shall be the person liable either concurrently with or to the exclusion of the principal, or that the agent shall be the party to sue either concurrently with or to the exclusion of the principal.[54]

(b) *Where the existence but not the name of the principal is disclosed to the third party*, in other words, where A clearly contracts as agent but does not disclose P's name, the effect is the same as where P is named: A drops out of the picture, unless there is an express or implied term to the effect that he undertakes liability.[55]

(c) *Where the fact of the agency and the name of the principal are not disclosed to the third party*, the doctrine of the 'undisclosed principal' will come into play.

Doctrine of the 'undisclosed principal'

The doctrine applies where A enters into a contract with T in his own name, concealing the fact that he is really an agent of P, the 'undisclosed principal'. The effect is that, on discovering that A was acting as agent for P, T can sue either A or P on the contract;[56] conversely, either A or P can enforce the contract against T.[57] The right of P to sue as undisclosed principal can be regarded as an exception to the 'privity of contract' rule, in that P is 'intervening' in a contract to which he was not a party, but the doctrine can be justified on the ground of commercial convenience. The right of the third party to sue either A or P is subject to the rule that he is not entitled to recover against both, so he must elect whether to resort to A alone or to P alone; and whether his conduct shows an unequivocal election is a question of fact to be decided in the light of the particular circumstances. Although the commencement of proceedings against either A or P is strong evidence of unequivocal election, it is not conclusive, and the circumstances may show that the right of action against the other party has not been abandoned.[58] However, where he actually obtains a

51 *Hambro v Burnand* [1904] 2 KB 10.

52 *Reckitt v Burnett, Pembroke and Slater Ltd* [1929] AC 176.

53 *Montgomerie v United Kingdom Steamship Association* [1891] 1 QB 370.

54 *Ibid*, at 372, *per* Wright J.

55 *Southwell v Bowditch* (1876) 1 CPD 374.

56 *Saxon v Blake* (1861) 29 Beav 438.

57 *Sims v Bond* (1833) 5 B & Ad 389. But P cannot sue T (i) if the terms of the contract are inconsistent with any person other than A being the principal: *Humble v Hunter* (1848) 12 QB 310, or (ii) if the personality of A is so crucial to the performance of the contract that it must be inferred that T intended to contract with no-one other than A: *Collins v Associated Greyhound Racecourses Ltd* [1930] 1 Ch 1.

58 *Clarkson Booker Ltd v Andjel* [1964] 3 All ER 260.

judgment against one, he is precluded from proceeding against the other, not on the ground that T has made a final election but because of the rule that two judgments cannot co-exist in respect of the same cause of action. In a Bahamian case, *Knowles v GAC (Eleuthera) Ltd*,[59] T entered into a contract of employment with A, by virtue of which A owed T a sum of money. Judgment was obtained against A; however, the judgment was unsatisfied and T sought to sue the defendant, P, alleging that A had contracted on behalf of P, an undisclosed principal. Georges CJ held that T could not sue P as he had already obtained a judgment against A. He explained:

> A party who concludes a contract with an agent acting for an undisclosed principal has the right to hold either of them liable. The rights against the principal and agent are in the alternative. He may elect whom he is going to pursue but he is bound by his election and, once he has elected, his rights against the other are extinguished. Where an action against the principal or the agent stops short of a judgment, it is a question of fact whether there has been an election extinguishing the right against the other ... There may be difficulties, when the first action has not yet reached the stage of judgment, in deciding whether or not the [claimant] has made an election which has extinguished his right to proceed against the other. Factually the issue can usually be resolved against concluding that there was a binding election, save in the clearest of cases. Where, however, the matter has proceeded to judgment, there would appear to be good reason for holding that since there was only one contract, recovery of judgment for breach of that contract precludes any further action upon it. It may be argued that this is unfair to a party who did not know at the time he recovered judgment against the agent that there was an undisclosed principal. The fact is that, in entering into the contract, the party was clearly relying on the creditworthiness of the agent in any event, since he was unaware that there was a principal. In these circumstances, his inability to pursue the principal after he has recovered judgment against the agent does not seem to me to result in injustice to him.

Effect of signature

If a person signs a written contractual document, he will be presumed to be a contracting party, unless it clearly appears that he signed as agent only. Thus, where an agent (A) signs a contract without indicating that he is an agent, he will be personally liable even though the other party (T) knew of the agency relationship between A and P.[60]

Warranty of authority

One who purports to act as agent is deemed to warrant that he has his principal's authority. Thus, a person who contracts as agent without having any authority to do so, or in excess of his authority, will be liable for breach of warranty of authority to any person who has suffered loss in reliance upon the purported agency. It is no defence for the 'agent' to plead that he acted in good faith or that he was unaware of his lack of authority. In *Collen v Wright*,[61] A agreed to lease to T a farm belonging to P,

59 (1986) Supreme Court, The Bahamas, No 67 of 1983, unreported.
60 *Basma v Weekes* [1950] AC 454.
61 (1857) 120 ER 241.

describing himself as the agent of P. Both T and A erroneously believed that A had authority to negotiate and sign the lease on behalf of P. When T's action for specific performance against P failed, T sued A's estate for damages for the loss incurred in the unsuccessful action against P. It was held that T's action succeeded, on the ground that the court could infer a separate and independent promise by A that he had the authority to act for P, the consideration for the promise being T's entering into the lease agreement. This principle of the 'implied warranty of authority' was defined by Bramwell LJ in another case:[62]

> If a person requests and, by asserting that he is clothed with the necessary authority, induces another to enter into a negotiation with himself and into a transaction with the person whose authority he represents that he has, in that case there is a contract by him that he has the authority of the person with whom he requests the other to enter into the transaction.

In a Bahamian case, *Stubbs v Souers*,[63] Adams J cited with approval the following definition in *Halsbury's Laws*:[64]

> Where any person purports to do any act or make any contract as agent on behalf of a principal, he is deemed to warrant that he has in fact authority from such principal to do the act or make the contract in question. If, therefore, he has no such authority, he is liable to be sued for breach of warranty of authority by any third person who was induced by his conduct in purporting to act as agent to believe that he had authority to do the act or make the contract, and who, by acting upon such belief, has suffered loss in consequence of the absence of authority.

The result is the same where A did previously have authority but, without his knowledge, it had come to an end at the material time. An example is *Yonge v Toynbee*,[65] where P instructed a solicitor, A, to defend an action on his behalf against T but, before the commencement of proceedings and unknown to A and T, P became insane and A's authority was thus automatically revoked. T, on learning of P's condition, applied to have the proceedings struck out, and later sued A to recover the costs incurred by him in pursuing his claim, on the ground that A had defended the action without authority. It was held that T's claim succeeded, since A had implicitly warranted the continued existence of his authority. There was 'no difference in principle between the case where the authority never existed at all and the case in which the authority [had] once existed and [had] ceased to exist'.[66]

Termination of agency

The agency relationship may be brought to an end in any of the following ways:

(a) *By notice of termination given by either party.* Since the agency relationship is created by mutual consent, it can equally be dissolved by consent of the parties. Such dissolution will not affect the position of third parties, unless they are given

62 *Dickson v Reuter's Telegram Co* (1877) 3 CPD 1, at 5.

63 (1986) Supreme Court, The Bahamas, No 196 of 1985, unreported [Carilaw BS 1986 SC 28].

64 4th edn, Vol 1, para E58.

65 [1910] 1 KB 215.

66 *Ibid*, at 226.

notice of the termination. If no such notice is given, P may remain liable to T, under the doctrine of ostensible authority, in respect of transactions carried out by A. P can revoke A's authority even where the authority is expressly stated to be 'irrevocable' during a certain period, but if P does revoke, he will be liable to A for damages.[67] On the other hand, the authority of an agent may be *legally* irrevocable in the following cases:

(i) Where the authority is given expressly for the purpose of protecting some interest of the agent, such as an authority to collect rents as security for a loan by him.[68]

(ii) Where an agent is given a power of attorney expressed to be irrevocable for a fixed period not exceeding one year, the power cannot be revoked during that period, either by anything done by the donor of the power, or by the death, marriage, mental incapacity or bankruptcy of the donor of the power.[69]

(b) *By completion of the transaction for which the agent is employed.*

(c) *By expiration of the stipulated period of the agency agreement.*

(d) *By operation of law.* The death,[70] insanity[71] or bankruptcy[72] of A or P will normally put an end to the agency. Similarly, where either A or P is a company, its winding up or dissolution will terminate the agency.[73] A third party who continues to deal with the agent in ignorance of the death, dissolution, bankruptcy or insanity will be able to sue the agent for breach of warranty of authority, even where the agent himself was unaware of the terminating event.[74]

(e) *By destruction of the subject-matter of the agency.* An agency will be terminated if the subject-matter of the agreement is destroyed, for example where A is employed by P to enter into an insurance policy on a building which, before the contract is concluded, is destroyed by fire.

---

67 *Temple Legal Protection Ltd v QBE Insurance (Europe) Ltd* [2009] EWCA Civ 453.

68 *Smart v Sandars* (1848) 136 ER 1132.

69 See, for example, the Powers of Attorney Act, Ch 81 (The Bahamas).

70 *Campanari v Woodburn* (1854) 139 ER 480.

71 *Yonge v Toynbee* [1910] 1 KB 215.

72 *Bailey v Thurstan & Co Ltd* [1903] 1 KB 137.

73 *Pacific and General Insurance Co Ltd v Hazell* [1997] BCC 400.

74 *Yonge v Toynbee*, n 71 above.

CHAPTER 13

DISCHARGE OF CONTRACTS

DISCHARGE BY PERFORMANCE

Performance must be complete

The general rule is that a promisor is not discharged from his contractual obligations unless he has completely and precisely performed the exact thing he has agreed to do. Where he has only partially carried out his obligations, there is no discharge. For instance, if a seller delivers to the buyer less than the agreed quantity of goods, the buyer may reject them;[1] similarly, where the seller delivers more than the quantity ordered, the buyer may reject the whole consignment, and cannot be required to select the correct quantity from the bulk delivered.[2] And where B agreed to purchase 3,000 cans of fruit from S, to be packed in cases containing 30 cans, and on delivery it was discovered that part of the consignment had been packed in cases containing 24 cans, B was held to be entitled to reject the entire consignment, notwithstanding that the correct quantity of cans had been delivered.[3] Also, failure by a party to observe a time stipulation may entitle the other party to repudiate the agreement. Thus, for example, where a contract for the sale of a flat required the purchase price to be tendered by '5pm' on a certain day, and the purchaser tendered it at 5.10 pm, it was held by the Privy Council that the vendor was entitled to repudiate the agreement and retain the deposit paid by the purchaser.[4]

Further, a party who has only partially performed his obligations cannot recover anything for the work he has done. Thus, for example, a building contractor who has agreed to construct a house for a lump sum, and who abandons the work after erecting 80 per cent of the building, is not entitled to any remuneration,[5] unless the contract provides otherwise. The leading case is *Cutter v Powell*.[6] Here, the defendant agreed to pay Cutter 30 guineas provided that he 'proceeded, continued and did his duty' as second mate on a ship sailing from Jamaica to Liverpool, England. The voyage began on 2 August. Cutter died on 20 September, 19 days before the ship arrived at Liverpool. An action by Cutter's widow to recover a proportion of the money failed, as Cutter had not completely performed his obligations under the contract.

---

1 See, for example, s 30(1), Sale of Goods Act (Jamaica); s 31(1), Sale of Goods Act, Ch 337 (The Bahamas); and s 31(1), Sale of Goods Act, Cap 393 (Antigua and Barbuda).

2 See s 30(2), Sale of Goods Act (Jamaica); s 31(2), Sale of Goods Act, Ch 337; and s 31(2), Sale of Goods Act, Cap 393 (Antigua and Barbuda).

3 *Re Moore & Co and Landauer & Co* [1921] 2 KB 519.

4 *Union Eagle Ltd v Golden Achievement Ltd* [1997] 2 All ER 215.

5 See *Sumpter v Hedges* [1898] 1 QB 673; *Bolton v Mahadeva* [1972] 2 All ER 1332.

6 [1775–1802] All ER Rep 159.

Exceptions to the rule of complete performance

Divisible (severable) contracts or obligations

Where the parties intended their contract to be divided into two or more separate parts, each part is a separate contract which can be discharged separately; for example, where there is an agreement for the delivery of goods by instalments, payment is due from the buyer upon delivery of each instalment, and the buyer is not entitled to defer payments until delivery of all the instalments, unless the contract so provides;[7] similarly, in a building contract, where the work and services to be performed by the contractor are itemised, the terms of the contract may show that each service is to be paid for when performed.[8]

Such a divisible contract is to be distinguished from an 'entire' contract, which is

> one in which complete performance by one party is a condition precedent to the liability of the other party. Under such a contract the consideration is usually a lump sum which is payable only upon complete performance by the other party. A partial performance of an entire contract by a party will normally entitle him to nothing, because the payment is not due under the contract, nor is any smaller sum for the value of his partial performance due, since the court has no power to apportion the consideration.[9]

Prevention of performance

Where a party is prevented from completing his part of the bargain by some act or omission of the other party, he may recover payment for the work he has done on a *quantum meruit*, or alternatively he may sue the other party for breach of contract. For example, where P agreed to write a book for D, to be published in a series called 'The Juvenile Library', payment of £100 to be made on completion and, after about half of the book had been written, D abandoned the series, it was held that P could recover £50 as reasonable remuneration on a *quantum meruit.*[10]

Substantial performance

Rigorous application of the rule in *Cutter v Powell*[11] might lead to great injustice if, for instance, in a building contract, a relatively minor defect of workmanship on the part of the contractor entitled the building owner to refuse to make any payment. To avoid such an unfair result, the courts have developed the doctrine of 'substantial performance', which is that if the contract has been substantially, though not completely or precisely performed, the 'injured' party is not discharged from his obligation to pay, though he will be able to counterclaim for damages to remedy any

---

7 *Nigerwest Steel Co Ltd v Eyiowuawi* [1978] NCLR 335. See also *Bolton v Mahadeva*, n 5 above.

8 A Jamaican example is *Madden v PC Reynolds Ltd* (2001) Court of Appeal, Jamaica, Civ App No 21 of 2000, unreported [Carilaw JM 2001 CA 67], where the contract had eight separate and severable portions.

9 *Chitty on Contracts*, Vol 1, 24th edn, para 1278; cited by Langrin JA in *Madden v PC Reynolds Ltd, ibid.*

10 *Planche v Colburn* [1824–34] All ER Rep 94.

11 Above, n 6.

defects. Thus, for example, where C contracts for a lump sum to decorate O's house with three coats of paint throughout, but in one of the rooms only two coats are used, C is entitled to be paid the contract price, but O can counterclaim for compensation sufficient to make good the deficient performance.[12]

This principle has been applied in numerous Caribbean cases in the context of building contracts. A clear example is *Broomes v Morgan*,[13] where the claimant contractor agreed to build a house for the defendant. The building was completed and the defendant went into possession, but he complained of certain defects and refused to pay the balance of the agreed price for the building work. In an action by the claimant to recover this amount, Husbands J found on the evidence that there were defects in the walls, roof, floors, doors and windows, and that these defects were the result of poor building craftsmanship. Nevertheless, he was of the opinion that the work agreed upon had been substantially performed and that the claimant was entitled to the contract price less the estimated cost of remedying the defects; however, since this cost exceeded the balance owing under the contract, the claimant's claim was dismissed.

Acceptance of partial performance

Where the claimant has only partially fulfilled his obligations under the contract, it may be possible to infer from the circumstances a fresh agreement that payment should be made for work already done or goods already supplied. In the case of sale of goods, the legislation provides that, 'where the seller delivers to the buyer a quantity of goods less than he contracted to sell, the buyer may reject them, but if the buyer accepts the goods so delivered, he must pay for them at the contract rate'.[14]

An example of the implication of a fresh agreement to pay is afforded by a Jamaican case, *Charles Gibbs Martin Foster Partnership v Dewar*.[15] Here, the claimants sued to recover an amount due from the defendant as fees for the preparation of architectural drawings relating to office premises in Kingston. According to the evidence, before the drawings were completed, one of the claimant partners, on learning that the defendant was having difficulty in raising finance, advised him to request the suspension of the preparation of the drawings, and the defendant did so request. The claimants then sent him their bill for the value of the work done at that stage. The defendant argued that the claimants had no right to payment until the plans had been completed. Chambers J held, *inter alia*, that when the defendant advised the claimants to stop work, albeit at the suggestion of the claimants, a new contract came into being and the defendant was 'required to pay an amount to satisfy the claimants for the amount of work performed by them to the date of such advice on their presenting their bill'. He continued:

---

12 *Dakin v Lee* [1916] 1 KB 566; *Hoenig v Isaacs* [1952] 2 All ER 176.

13 (1979) High Court, Barbados, No 322 of 1977, unreported [Carilaw BB 1979 HC 33]. See also *Cox v James* (1976) High Court, Trinidad and Tobago, No 757 of 1972, unreported [Carilaw TT 1976 HC 12]; *Baxter v Joseph* (1967) Court of Appeal, Trinidad and Tobago, Civ App No 46 of 1966, unreported [Carilaw TT 1967 CA 26]. Cf *Butler v Ingrahams Auto Electric Supplies Co Ltd* (1991) Supreme Court, The Bahamas, No 90 of 1987, unreported [Carilaw BS 1991 SC 95].

14 Section 30(1), Sale of Goods Act (Jamaica); s 31(1), Sale of Goods Act, Ch 337 (The Bahamas); and s 31(1), Sale of Goods Act, Cap 393 (Antigua and Barbuda).

15 (1977) Supreme Court, Jamaica, No 1336 of 1973, unreported [Carilaw JM 1977 SC 18].

> In requesting a stoppage, there was an implied request by the defendant to the [claimants] to deliver the unfinished work, and for him to pay for the work done so far . . . Put in another way, if the defendant requested the architects not to continue with the drawings, the defendant's undertaking to pay may be inferred, and construed as an agreement to pay the reasonable value for the [claimants' services], even if the original was not completed or even substantially performed.

Tender of performance

In an action for breach of contract, it is a good defence for the defendant to show that he tendered performance, ie that he offered to perform his obligations and that the claimant refused to accept such performance;[16] a further consequence of a refusal of a tender of performance is that the tenderer will be discharged from his obligation and may himself sue the other party for damages. In order for the tenderer to be discharged, the tender must conform exactly to the terms of the contract.[17]

Where the tender is of a money payment, the creditor's refusal to accept the tender does not discharge the tenderer from his obligation to pay the debt; he must remain ready and willing to pay it and, if sued by the creditor, he may pay the money into court.[18]

DISCHARGE BY AGREEMENT

A contractual obligation may be discharged by a subsequent binding agreement between the parties. The following methods are available: (i) rescission; (ii) release by deed; (iii) accord and satisfaction; (iv) variation; and (v) waiver.

Rescission

Where a contract is executory on both sides, that is, where neither party has performed his undertaking, the contract may be rescinded by mutual agreement. Whether such an agreement will have the effect of rescinding the parties' obligations *ab initio*, or of rescinding only those obligations which are unperformed, will depend on the terms of the agreement. The consideration for the discharge is the abandonment by each party of his right to performance.[19] Both contracts made by deed and contracts evidenced in writing may be rescinded (as with all other contracts) by simple writing or orally.[20]

A contract may also be rescinded where the terms of a contract are varied or amended by the parties to such an extent that the court will imply the substitution of a new contract for the original one.[21]

---

16 *Startup v Macdonald* (1843) 134 ER 1029.

17 *Anson's Law of Contract*, 29th edn, p 451.

18 *Ibid.* See CPR, Part 36 (Jam), (ECS).

19 *Mickleton Development Ltd v Bather* (1982) 19 JLR 217 (Court of Appeal, Jamaica).

20 *United Africa Co Ltd v Argo* (1958) 14 NLR 105; *Morris v Baron and Co* [1918] AC 1.

21 *See Morris v Baron and Co, ibid.*

Release by deed

The obligation to perform a contract may be released by deed, which takes effect without the need for consideration.[22]

Accord and satisfaction

Where the party to whom an obligation is owed agrees to accept from the other something different in place of the former obligation, there is 'accord and satisfaction'. 'Accord' is the *agreement* to accept the substituted obligation; 'satisfaction' is the substituted obligation, that is, the *consideration* for the release from the former obligation. In the words of Scrutton LJ:[23]

> Accord and satisfaction is the purchase of a release from an obligation, whether arising under contract or tort, by means of any valuable consideration, not being the actual performance of the obligation itself. The accord is the agreement by which the obligation is discharged. The satisfaction is the consideration which makes the agreement operative.

Satisfaction may be executory (that is, it may consist of a *promise* to do something different from the original obligation), or executed (that is, consisting of the *actual performance* of something different). Where there is accord and satisfaction, the promisor is discharged from his original obligation. If the promisor fails to carry out his promise, he can be sued for breach of the promise, but he cannot be sued on the original obligation, as it has been discharged.[24]

Variation

A contract can be varied by the parties introducing new terms, without intending to rescind the contract or substitute a new one; however, the distinction between a variation and a rescission is not always clear cut, and it is a question of construction as to the intention of the parties.[25] Whereas a rescission may be written or oral in any case, a variation of a contract required to be evidenced in writing can be varied only in writing.[26]

In ascertaining the intention of the parties, it has been suggested that a useful test is whether or not there are any 'executory clauses in the second arrangement as would enable you to sue upon that alone if the first [agreement] did not exist'.[27] If there are such clauses, it may be regarded as a case of rescission and if not, as a variation.

Since a variation involves an alteration of the contractual obligations of the parties, it must be supported by consideration from both sides, whether by way of

---

22 See *BCCI SA v Ali* [2002] 1 AC 251.

23 *British Russian Gazette and Trade Outlook Ltd v Associated Newspapers Ltd* [1933] 2 KB 616, at pp 643, 644.

24 *Ibid.*

25 *Sookraj v Samaroo* (2004) 65 WIR 401 (Privy Council Appeal from the Court of Appeal, Trinidad and Tobago).

26 *Goss v Lord Nugent* [1824–34] All ER Rep 305; *United Africa Co Ltd v Argo* (1958) 14 NLR 105.

27 *Morris v Baron and Co* [1918] AC 1, at 26.

the assumption of fresh obligations or additional detriments, the conferment of new benefits, or the abandonment of existing rights;[28] but it is well settled that the mere performance of existing obligations is not accord and satisfaction.[29] Similarly, the payment of a lesser sum cannot be accord and satisfaction for a debt for a larger amount,[30] though where the sum claimed is unliquidated or disputed, payment of a smaller sum by way of compromise may be a good accord and satisfaction.[31]

Waiver

Where one party to a contract agrees, at the request of the other, not to insist on certain of his strict rights under the agreement, he is said to waive those rights. Waiver does not amount to variation, and the contract itself remains unaffected; for example, where one party orally requests the other for an extension of time for the completion of a building or for the delivery of goods. Unlike in the case of variation, a waiver of a contractual stipulation does not in any case need to be in writing,[32] and will be effective although unsupported by consideration.[33]

The effect of a waiver may be (a) to abrogate a party's right, or (b) to merely suspend it. The distinction is illustrated by two Nigerian cases. In the first, *English Exporters Ltd v Ayanda*,[34] E agreed to ship goods from the United Kingdom to Lagos in January, but the goods did not reach Lagos until March. The evidence showed that A had never complained about the lateness of the arrival of the goods, and he had in fact acquiesced in the postponement of delivery to two later dates. It was held that A, by his conduct, had waived his right to repudiate the goods on the ground of late arrival, nor could he sue E for damages for breach of contract. On the other hand, in *Enavharo v Edosomwa*,[35] D agreed to complete the construction of a building by a certain date, but failed to complete on time. C did not treat this as a breach but continued to urge D to complete as soon as possible. D subsequently abandoned the work, and C sued for breach of contract. It was held that the waiver by C had only suspended his rights under the contract and did not abrogate them, so that he had a good cause of action against D for breach when D abandoned the contract.

DISCHARGE BY FRUSTRATION

The basic rule at common law is that a party is not discharged from his contractual obligations merely because, owing to some uncertain event, the contract has become more burdensome, or even impossible to perform. Contractual obligations are absolute, and if a party wishes to protect himself against possible subsequent difficulties

28 *Alan (WJ) & Co Ltd v EL Nasr Export and Import Co* [1972] 2 QB 189.
29 *Stilk v Myrick* (1809) 170 ER 851.
30 *Pinnel's Case* (1602) 77 ER 237; *Graham and Gillies Ltd v WAATECO Ltd* (1975) (2) ALR Comm 50.
31 *Adekunle v African Continental Bank* 1971 (1) NCLR 202.
32 *Levey and Co v Goldberg* [1922] 1 KB 688.
33 *Bruner v Moore* [1904] 1 Ch 305.
34 (1973) 3 ECSLR 374.
35 [1970] NCLR 65.

in performing them, he should stipulate expressly for that protection in the contract. Under the doctrine of frustration, however, a number of exceptions to the strict rule have been developed; though the courts have shown themselves to be reluctant to expand the doctrine, so that its scope is restricted,[36] and there are relatively few cases in which the plea of frustration has been successful. In the leading case of *National Carriers Ltd v Panalpina (Northern) Ltd*,[37] Lord Simon described the doctrine thus:

> Frustration of a contract takes place when there supervenes an event (without default of either party and for which the contract makes no sufficient provision) which so significantly changes the nature (not merely the expense or onerousness) of the outstanding contractual rights or obligations from what the parties could reasonably have contemplated at the time of its execution, that it would be unjust to hold them to the literal sense of its stipulations in the new circumstances; in such a case the law declares both parties to be discharged from further performance.

A contract may be discharged on the ground of frustration only if the following requirements are present:

(i) The contract does not contain an absolute undertaking, express or implied, which precludes frustration.

(ii) Due to some unforeseen event, the fundamental purpose of the contract has become frustrated, that is, made impossible to perform, so that any attempted performance would amount to something *quite different* from that contemplated by the parties when they entered into the contract. It is not sufficient merely that the subsequent event has made the contract more difficult or expensive to perform.[38]

(iii) The frustrating event could not have been contemplated by the parties at the time the contract was made.[39]

(iv) The frustrating event was not 'self-induced', that is brought about by the default of the party pleading frustration.[40]

Juridical basis of frustration

In the well-known case of *Taylor v Caldwell*,[41] the defendants had agreed to permit the claimants to use a music hall on four days for the purpose of staging a series of concerts. After the making of the agreement but before the date of the first concert, the hall was destroyed by fire, without the fault of either party. It was held that the contract was discharged, on the ground that the court would imply a term in the contract that the parties should be discharged if performance became impossible through the perishing of the subject-matter of the contract.

---

36 *Davis Contractors Ltd v Fareham UDC* [1956] 2 All ER 145.

37 [1981] AC 675, at 700.

38 *Davies Contractors Ltd v Fareham UDC*, above.

39 See *Clacken v Causwell* (2010) Supreme Court, Jamaica, No 1834 of 2008, unreported [Carilaw JM 2010 SC 101], *per* Sykes J.

40 *Maritime National Fish Ltd v Ocean Trawlers Ltd* [1935] AC 524. Impossibility of performance brought about by the conduct of one party may also amount to a breach of contract entitling the other party to damages.

41 (1863) 122 ER 309.

The 'implied term' theory articulated in *Taylor v Caldwell* was much criticised as being artificial and unrealistic, since 'there would seldom be a genuine common intention to terminate the contract upon the occurrence of the particular event in question'; in the normal case, 'the parties have not foreseen the event and, even if they had, they would probably have sought to introduce reservations or qualifications or compensations'.[42] Accordingly, an alternative view is that frustration is based not on the court's implying a term in the contract but rather on its imposition of a just and reasonable solution in the particular case. As Lord Wright explained:[43]

> Where, as generally happens, one party claims that there has been a frustration and the other party contests it, the court decides the issue and decides it *ex post facto* on the actual circumstances of the case. The data for decision are, on the one hand, the terms and construction of the contract, read in the light of the then existing circumstances and, on the other hand, the events which have occurred. It is the court which has to decide what is the true position between the parties.

The 'just and reasonable solution' theory, espoused principally by Lord Wright and Lord Denning, is itself not entirely satisfactory, as it would appear to give the court an open-ended discretion to intervene in order to 'do justice' in the particular case, which would undermine the principle of the sanctity of contracts. This danger was recognised by Viscount Simonds, who opined:[44]

> If the true doctrine rests, not on an implied term of the contract between the parties, but on the impact of the law on a situation in which an unexpected event would make it unjust to hold parties to their bargain, I would emphasise that, in this aspect, the doctrine has been and must be kept within very narrow limits.

The most recent formulation of the juridical basis of the doctrine of frustration is to be found in the *National Carriers* case (above). According to Lord Simon in that case,[45] frustration occurs where a supervening event so changes the nature of the contractual rights and obligations, beyond the contemplation of the parties, that it would be unjust to hold them to the contract. The court is accordingly called upon, first, to construe the contract according to its terms and in the light of the circumstances existing when it was entered into; second, to consider whether, in view of the supervening event which has occurred, there would be a radical change in the obligations of the parties; and third, whether it would be unjust to insist on further performance by the parties.

Frustrating events

There is no finite list of events that can give rise to frustration, but the following types of circumstance have arisen in the case law.

---

42 *Chitty on Contracts*, Vol 1, 23rd edn, para 1269.

43 *Denny, Mott and Dickson Ltd v James Fraser and Co Ltd* [1944] AC 265, at 274, 275.

44 *Davis Contractors Ltd v Fareham UDC, ibid* at 150.

45 [1981] AC 675, at 700.

Physical destruction of the subject-matter of the contract

The destruction by fire of the music hall in *Taylor v Caldwell* (above)[46] is a clear example of this type of frustrating event. Similarly, under the Sale of Goods legislation, where a contract for the sale of goods has been made and, before the risk has passed to the buyer and without any fault on the part of either party, the goods have perished, the contract is avoided.[47]

The plea of frustration was raised in a recent Barbadian case, *Hulse v Knights Ltd.*[48] Here, the defendants entered into a contract with the claimant whereby they agreed to produce an album of recorded music for the claimant. In pursuance of the agreement, the claimant delivered to the defendants, *inter alia*, a digital audio tape (DAT) and a cassette master. While the items were still in their possession, there was a fire at the defendants' premises and the DAT, but not the cassette master, was destroyed. Inniss J held that the contract was not frustrated by the destruction of the DAT, an item that was essential for the production of the music albums, because it was technically possible to reproduce a new DAT from the cassette master. He considered the case to be analogous to *Tsakiroglou & Co Ltd v Noblee Thorl GmbH*,[49] where a contract for the sale of groundnuts, to be shipped from the Sudan to Hamburg, was held not to be frustrated by the closure of the Suez Canal, because it remained possible to ship the nuts via the Cape of Good Hope, an alternative route that was certainly much longer and more expensive, but nevertheless not so different as to alter the foundation of the contract.

Death or incapacity of a party to a contract involving personal services

Where a party to a contract involving the performance of personal services dies or is incapacitated, the contract will be frustrated and both parties discharged from their obligations; as, for example, where an eminent concert pianist took ill before a recital,[50] and where an employee suffered a heart attack and, according to the medical evidence, would be unable to work again.[51]

Non-occurrence of an expected event

This type of circumstance is illustrated by the 'Coronation cases',[52] where rooms had been hired overlooking the route of the anticipated procession for the coronation of King Edward VII in London. When, owing to the sudden illness of the King, the procession was cancelled, the hirers of the rooms claimed that the hire contracts had been frustrated and that they were entitled to be discharged from their obligation to pay the hire fees. It was held that the contracts were indeed frustrated, and the hirers

---

46 (1863) 122 ER 309.

47 Section 8, Sale of Goods Act (Jamaica); s 9, Sale of Goods Act, Ch 337 (The Bahamas); and s 9, Sale of Goods Act, Cap 393 (Antiqua and Barbuda).

48 (2004) High Court, Barbados, No 1972 of 1998, unreported [Carilaw BB 2004 HC 29].

49 [1962] AC 93.

50 (1871) LR 6 Ex 269.

51 *Notcutt v Universal Equipment Co (London) Ltd* [1986] 1 WLR 641.

52 *Krell v Henry* [1903] 2 KB 740; *Chandler v Webster* [1904] 1 KB 493.

were discharged from their obligation; the foundation of the hire agreements was the purpose of viewing the procession, and its cancellation had removed that foundation.

Building contracts

Where, in the course of the performance of a building or construction contract, an unexpected event, such as industrial action, a shortage of labour or materials, or a damaging accident, causes a delay in the completion of the work and consequent financial loss to either party, it may be argued that the contract has been frustrated. In general, however, the courts lean against finding frustration in such circumstances. The leading case is *Davis Contractors Ltd v Fareham UDC*,[53] where the claimants contracted to build 78 houses for the defendant council for a fixed sum of £94,000, completion being expected within eight months. Owing to an unexpected shortage of skilled labour and certain materials, the contract took 22 months to complete, and this increased the cost of completion to £115,000. The claimants contended that the contract had been frustrated and that they were entitled to claim on a *quantum meruit* for the actual cost of completion, but the House of Lords rejected the claim. The fact that a contract had become more onerous or more expensive for one party than was anticipated was not sufficient to bring about frustration, and mere hardship or inconvenience to a party did not justify discharge of the contract; rather, it had to be shown that, 'without fault of either party, the contractual obligation has become incapable of being performed because the circumstances in which performance is called for would render it a thing radically different from that which was undertaken by the contract. *Non haec in foedera veni*: "it was not this that I promised to do".'[54]

This approach was taken by the Bermudian Court of Appeal in *Benevides v Minister of Public Works and Agriculture*,[55] a somewhat unusual case where the issue was whether a contract to demolish hotel premises had been frustrated by the prior destruction by fire of 80 per cent of the building. Perhaps the most unusual feature of the case was that frustration was not pleaded by the contractor, as would normally be the case, but by the employer, the Public Works Department, which sought to avoid payment for the demolition and clearance work by taking advantage of what, according to Blair-Kerr P, they had perceived as 'a golden opportunity to save public money'. In holding that the contract had not been frustrated, Smith JA pointed out that, following the fire, there had been no radical change in the nature of the work to be done, which was to demolish the building and clear away the rubble. Clearing away the rubble was the more time-consuming task and, after the fire, this task had become more onerous; on the other hand, the demolition of the main building had been made easier by the fire, and 'the only fresh element that had emerged as a result of the fire was the hazard to the public from falling masonry, and prompt action was

53 [1956] 2 All ER 145.

54 *Ibid*, at 160, *per* Lord Radcliffe. These principles were recently discussed and applied by Sykes J in *Clacken v Causwell* (2010) Supreme Court, Jamaica, No 1834 of 2008, unreported [Carilaw JM 2010 SC 101].

55 (1981) Court of Appeal, Bermuda, Civ App No 2 of 1981, unreported [Carilaw BM 1981 CA 22].

needed to demolish the walls that were liable to collapse.' Smith JA stated in conclusion that 'this was not a case where the contract was frustrated in law in the sense enunciated by Lord Radcliffe[56] ... After the fire there was no radical change in the nature of the original contractual obligations.'

On the other hand, in *Metropolitan Water Board v Dick, Kerr & Co Ltd*,[57] it was held that there was frustration of a contract to construct a reservoir within six years, where, two years after the commencement of the construction, the Minister of Munitions, under statutory powers, ordered cessation of the work and removal of the contractors' plant. The House of Lords took the view that the effect of the Minister's action was that the contract, if resumed after the interruption, would be fundamentally different in character from that originally contemplated by the parties.

Change in the law, or government intervention

Where a contract, which was initially valid, is rendered illegal by a change in the law or fundamentally affected by government intervention, it will be frustrated, at least where the change had the effect of 'striking at the root of' the contract, rather than merely suspending or hindering its operation.[58]

A Jamaican case in which a plea of frustration through government intervention failed is *Couttes Ltd v Barclays Bank plc*.[59] Here, the applicant and the respondent signed an agreement by which the applicant acquired an option to purchase all the shares in S Ltd (a company which owned all the shares in B Co) for a certain price. The option was exercisable within 45 days of the signing of the contract, and it was also a term of the agreement that within the period and before the option was exercised, the applicant would apply to the Minister of Finance for his approval of the purchase, as required by section 21(1) of the Financial Institutions Act, 1992, and it was a condition to the exercise of the option that the Minister should have approved or should be deemed to have approved the purchase. By section 21(2) of the Act, the Minister was required to give his decision within 21 days, and if he failed to respond within the period he would be 'deemed to have waived the requirement for approval'. The applicant duly applied for permission and, not having received a response from the Minister within 21 days, went ahead and exercised the option. Some 30 months later, the Minister revoked B Co's licence under new legislation, the Financial Institutions (Amendment) Act. The applicant claimed a refund of the sum paid for the shares, contending that the option agreement had been frustrated by the action of the Minister; that there had been a total failure of consideration; and that the respondent had been unjustly enriched as a consequence. James J held that there had been no frustration of the option agreement. On the date when the Minister, under section 21(2) of the Financial Institutions Act, was deemed to have waived the requirement for approval, the contract between the parties was at that moment

56 Above, n 54.
57 [1918] AC 119.
58 *Anson, op cit*, p 483.
59 (2002) Supreme Court, Jamaica, No E–466 of 1999, unreported [Carilaw JM 2002 SC 84].

completely performed; the applicant became legally entitled to be registered as the owner of the shares; the obligations on both applicant and respondent were satisfied, and the parties received all that they had bargained for. The applicant could have called upon the Minister to perform his statutory duty and formally declare him a licensee under section 21(2) but, up to the time of the action, he had not done so. There had accordingly been no frustration.

Frustration must not be self-induced

If the alleged frustration of a contract is brought about by the conduct or election of one of the parties, that party cannot plead frustration as, in Lord Sumner's words, 'Reliance cannot be placed on self-induced frustration'.[60] The classic example is *Maritime National Fish Ltd v Ocean Trawlers Ltd*.[61] Here, M chartered from O a steam trawler which needed to be fitted with an otter trawl, a device which, to the knowledge of the parties, could not be lawfully used without a licence from the Canadian Minister of Fisheries. M, which had four other vessels of its own, applied for five licences, but was informed that only three would be granted. In exercising his right to select the vessels to which the licences should apply, M omitted the ship chartered from O. M's contention that the charterparty had been frustrated, and that it was therefore not liable for the hire charges, was rejected by the Privy Council. It was not the act of the Minister in refusing to grant all five licences applied for which was the cause of the failure of the charterparty, but M's own election, and it was of the essence of frustration that it should not be due to the act or election of the party pleading it.

Frustration of leases and contracts for the sale of land

The question of the application of the doctrine of frustration to leases is a problematic one. The orthodox view was that frustration could never apply to a lease because a lease is not merely a contract but creates an interest in land which, once vested in the lessee, cannot be divested except according to the principles of landlord and tenant law. Accordingly, in *Cricklewood Property and Investment Trust Ltd v Leighton's Investment Trust Ltd*,[62] it was held that a 99-year building lease was not frustrated and rent remained payable when wartime legislation prohibited building. Similarly, it has been held that a tenant remains liable for rent notwithstanding that a building on the demised land is destroyed by fire,[63] or by an enemy bomb,[64] or is requisitioned by the government.[65]

More recently, however, in *National Carriers Ltd v Panalpina Northern Ltd*,[66] the House of Lords accepted that a lease could be frustrated not only by physical

60 *Bank Line Ltd v A Capel and Co* [1919] AC 435, at 452.
61 [1935] AC 524.
62 [1945] AC 221.
63 *Matthey v Curling* [1922] 2 AC 180.
64 *Redmond v Dainton* [1920] 2 KB 256.
65 *Eyre v Johnson* [1946] 1 All ER 719.
66 [1981] All ER 161.

catastrophe, such as where 'some vast convulsion of nature swallowed up the property altogether, or buried it in the depths of the sea',[67] but also by a supervening event so far beyond the contemplation of the parties that it would be unjust to enforce the lease. On the facts of the case itself, in which there was a 10-year lease of a warehouse, it was held that there was no frustration and rent remained payable by the tenant when the local authority closed the only access road to the warehouse, rendering it unusable for a 10-month period in the middle of the 10-year term; though a longer interruption might have frustrated the lease.

The doctrine of frustration has been invoked, without success, in contracts for the sale of land where, for instance, premises which are the subject-matter of the sale are destroyed by fire, or where a building is compulsorily acquired by a local authority. In practice, the purchaser will take out an insurance policy against destruction or damage by fire, as the risk of such damage passes to the purchaser as soon as the contract of sale has been executed and the equitable title in the property has passed to him; and it has been held that where, after 'exchange of contracts', the land agreed to be sold becomes subjected to a compulsory purchase order, there is no frustration of the contract and the purchaser is not entitled to rescind, as he takes the risk that the land may at any time be affected by such orders. This situation arose in *E Johnson & Co (Barbados) Ltd v NSR Ltd*.[68] Here, the respondent paid to the appellant's attorney (as stakeholder) a deposit towards the purchase of certain land, and the parties entered into a contract for the sale of the property, agreeing a completion date. About two months after the conclusion of the contract and before the date fixed for completion, the Barbados Government published a notice in the *Official Gazette* under section 3(1) of the Land Acquisition Act, Cap 228, to the effect that the property contracted to be sold was likely to be needed for the construction of a primary school. One of the issues in the case was whether the respondent was entitled to rescind the contract on the ground of frustration. Both the Barbados Court of Appeal and the Privy Council held that there was no frustration. In the words of Lord Jauncey:[69]

> On the conclusion of a contract for sale of land, the risk passes to the purchaser. It will be presumed, in the absence of specific provision to the contrary, that the purchaser has agreed to accept the normal risks incidental to land ownership. The risk of interference with land-owning rights by the Crown or statutory authorities is always present. The land may be needed for the construction of a road or an airport, way-leaves for power lines or for gas or oil pipes may be required, restrictions may be imposed on the use of the land by planning legislation or the peace and quiet which the owner had hoped to enjoy may be shattered by a noisy local development. These are some of the examples of the ways in which a landowner is at risk of having his rights and enjoyment removed or curtailed. A threat of compulsory purchase, and publication of a section 3 notice can amount to no more than that, does not radically alter the nature of the contract of sale. What it does is simply to increase the likelihood of an existing, albeit remote, risk becoming an eventuality. In *Hillingdon Estates Co v Stonefield Estates Ltd*,[70] Vaisey J, in the context of a notice to treat served by an acquiring authority after conclusion of a contract for sale but before completion, remarked:[71]

67 *Cricklewood Property and Investment Trust Ltd* [1945] AC 221, at 229, *per* Lord Simon.
68 [1997] AC 400.
69 *Ibid*, at 407.
70 [1952] Ch 627.
71 *Ibid*, at 634.

> No doubt these departmental interferences and interventions do make a very great difference to ordinary life in this country, but that does not mean that, whenever such interference or intervention takes place, parties are discharged from bargains solemnly entered into between them. In my judgment, it is the duty of the parties, in such a case as this, to carry out their obligations; and I cannot see that there is in this case any reason at all for supposing that there is either an implied term of this contract that it should be frustrated in the event which has happened, or that there has been such a destruction of the fundamental and underlying circumstances on which the contract is based as to justify my saying that the contract did not exist, or ceased to exist at the date when the notice to treat was served.

Their Lordships consider that these observations are equally applicable to the position in this case after the publication of the section 3 notice. In *Amalgamated Investment and Property Co Ltd v John Walker & Sons Ltd*,[72] a building was entered in the statutory list of buildings of special architectural or historical interest a few days after the date of a contract for its sale. The listing had the effect of dramatically reducing its market value. The Court of Appeal held that the risk of a building being listed was one that every owner and purchaser must recognise that he is subject to, with the result that the contract was not frustrated. It follows that a section 3 notice does not amount to a frustrating event.

The effects of frustration

When a frustrating event occurs, the contract is 'brought to an end forthwith, without more and automatically',[73] so there can be no liability in damages for acts or omissions occurring *after* the date of the frustration. Unlike in the case of contracts vitiated by mistake,[74] a frustrated contract is not void *ab initio*; it begins as a valid contract but ceases to have effect on the occurrence of the frustrating event; the legal consequence is that 'each party must fulfill his contractual obligations so far as they have fallen due before the frustrating event, but he is excused from performing those that fall due later'. Thus, in one of the 'Coronation cases', *Krell v Henry*,[75] since the procession had been cancelled a few hours before the rent became due, it was held that the rent could not be recovered.

The principle that, after the frustrating event, 'the loss lies where it falls', could cause hardship to a party. In another 'Coronation case', *Chandler v Webster*,[76] a room overlooking the procession route had been let for £141, payable immediately. The tenant had paid £100, with £41 outstanding, when the procession was cancelled. It was held that the tenant not only could not recover the £100, but remained liable to pay the balance of £41. The tenant's argument that he was entitled to recover the £100 in quasi-contract on account of a total failure of consideration was rejected by the court, as the contract was not void *ab initio* but only from the moment of the occurrence of the frustrating event, and so there had been no total failure of consideration.

---

72 [1977] 1 WLR 164.

73 *Hirji Mulji v Cheong Yiu Steamship Co* [1926] AC 497, at 505, *per* Lord Sumner.

74 See Chapter 8, above.

75 [1903] 2 KB 740.

76 [1904] 1 KB 493.

The rule in *Chandler* was disapproved by the House of Lords in *Fibrosa Spolka Akcyjna v Fairbairn Lawson Combe Barbour Ltd*,[77] where it was held that money handed over in fulfilment of a contract which was subsequently frustrated could be recovered in quasi-contract on the ground of total failure of consideration, notwithstanding that the contract was not void *ab initio*. However, the law was still considered unsatisfactory in that (i) if the party seeking recovery of his money had received any benefit, however small, from the other party's performance, there would be no total failure of consideration and the money paid would be irrecoverable, and (ii) the party obliged to repay the money might have incurred expenses in performing the contract, and at common law he could not set off those expenses against the money to be repaid.

Accordingly, to cure these defects, the Law Reform (Frustrated Contracts) Act, 1943 was enacted in England, and almost identical legislation has been passed in a number of Commonwealth Caribbean jurisdictions, such as Barbados,[78] Jamaica,[79] Belize[80] and Bermuda.[81] The effect of the Acts is as follows:[82]

(i) money payable before the frustrating event ceases to be payable;
(ii) money paid before the frustrating event is recoverable, whether or not there has been a total failure of consideration;
(iii) any expenses incurred by the party to whom money was paid or payable in performing the contract may be set off against the money to be repaid, at the discretion of the court; and
(iv) where one party has obtained a valuable benefit under the contract, the other party may, at the court's discretion, recover a sum equivalent to that benefit.

DISCHARGE BY BREACH

Breach of contract always entitles the innocent party to sue for damages for the breach; but he will not be entitled to treat the contract as terminated and be discharged from his obligations unless the guilty party has either (a) *repudiated the contract*, or (b) *been guilty of a fundamental breach*. In either of these two instances, the innocent party is entitled to regard himself as discharged from further liability to perform his obligations towards the guilty party, in which case the guilty party will also be discharged, though remaining liable to pay damages.

Repudiation

Where one of the parties to a contract shows, by words or conduct, that he has no intention of carrying out his side of the bargain, he is said to 'repudiate' the

---

77 [1942] 2 All ER 122.
78 Frustrated Contracts Act, Cap 202 (Barbados).
79 Law Reform (Frustrated Contracts) Act (Jamaica).
80 Law of Contract Act, Cap 166 (Belize).
81 Law Reform (Misrepresentation and Frustrated Contracts) Act 1977 (Bermuda).
82 The Acts do not apply to contracts of insurance, carriage of goods by sea, charterparties (except time charterparties and charterparties by demise), and contracts for the sale of specific goods where the goods have perished before the risk passed to the buyer.

agreement. Repudiation may be express, for example, where D wrote a letter to C stating that he did not intend to fulfill his obligations,[83] or where a vendor of land orally refused to proceed with the conveyance following a dispute over the payment of legal fees[84] (in which cases the intention to renounce was clear), or it may be implied from conduct. If implied repudiation is relied upon, there must be sufficient proof of an intention to renounce the contract. In the words of Devlin J:[85]

> A renunciation can be made either by words or by conduct, provided it is clearly made. It is often put that the party renunciating must 'evince an intention not to go on with the contract'. The intention can be evinced either by words or by conduct. The test of whether an intention is sufficiently evinced by conduct is whether the party renunciating has acted in such a way as to lead a reasonable person to the conclusion that he does not intend to fulfil his part of the contract.

On the other hand, a 'mere refusal or omission of one of the contracting parties to do something which he ought to do' will not amount to repudiation ... there must be an absolute refusal to perform his part of the contract'.[86] Thus, if the refusal to perform is not absolute and unqualified, but arises, for instance, from a mistaken belief that there is some legal impediment to performance, there will be no repudiation. A well-known example is *Mersey Steel and Iron Co v Naylor, Benzon & Co*.[87] There, M Co contracted to sell to N Co 5,000 tons of steel, to be delivered at the rate of 1,000 tons monthly, commencing in January 1881, payment to be made within three days of receipt of shipping documents. M Co delivered part of the January instalment, and another in February. Before payment for these deliveries became due, a petition was presented for the winding up of M Co. N Co thereupon refused to make any payments, erroneously believing that in view of the petition, they ought not to do so without an order of the court. M Co informed N Co that they were treating this refusal to pay as a repudiation discharging M Co from all further obligation. N Co continued to express their willingness to accept future deliveries and to make all due payments, if permitted to do so. The House of Lords held that N Co's conduct did not amount to repudiation. It was impossible 'to ascribe to [N Co's] conduct under these circumstances the character of a renunciation of the contract'. It was 'just the reverse; the purchasers were desirous of fulfilling the contract; they were advised that there was a difficulty in the way, and they expressed anxiety that that difficulty should be as soon as possible removed'.[88]

A recent Trinidadian case, in which one of the main issues was whether or not there had been a repudiation, is *Coggins v Garage and Rolling Door Co*.[89] Here, the defendant contracted to supply, install and commission an automatic, remote

83 *Nigerian Supplies Manufacturing Co Ltd v Nigerian Broadcasting Corporation* [1967] 1 All NLR 35.

84 *Turnquest v Von Hamon* (1990) Supreme Court, The Bahamas, No 675 of 1988, unreported [Carilaw BS 1990 SC 31].

85 *Universal Cargo Carriers Corporation v Citati* [1957] 2 QB 401, at 436.

86 *Freeth v Burr* (1874) LR 9 CP 208, at 214, *per* Keating J. For example, where a schoolteacher refused to supervise school meals when required to do so under her contract of employment: *Gorse v Durham County Council* [1971] 2 All ER 666.

87 (1884) 9 App Cas 434.

88 *Ibid*, at 441, *per* Lord Selborne.

89 (2007) High Court, Trinidad and Tobago, No 2550 of 2004, unreported [Carilaw TT 2007 HC 262].

controlled garage door for C. After installation, C complained that the door did not shut properly, there remaining a two-foot space between the door and the garage floor. The defendants insisted that C pay the balance of the purchase price (which, according to the agreement had become due 'on the day of installation and prior to commissioning'), before they attended to the alleged defect in the door and complete the commissioning, while C, for his part, refused to pay the balance of the price. Jamadar J considered that the defendant's refusal to commission the door, which would have completed its obligations under the contract, did not amount to repudiation of the agreement, since it was 'clear that the defendant believed that the door had been installed and that the balance was due at that point, whether or not it had been duly commissioned; and the defendant always maintained its readiness to perform the contract, that is to commission and/or repair the door according to its honest interpretation of the contract.'

Anticipatory breach

Where a party to a contract, *before the date fixed for performance*, makes it clear to the other (the 'innocent party') that he does not intend to carry out his obligations under the agreement, there is said to be 'anticipatory breach', amounting to repudiation, and the innocent party may regard himself as discharged and sue for damages for breach.[90] This principle is founded on the notion that 'the promisee has an inchoate right to the performance of the bargain, which becomes complete when the time for performance has arrived', and 'in the meantime, he has a right to have the contract kept open as a subsisting and effective contract'.[91]

Once the innocent party, C, has accepted the anticipatory breach of the other, D, the latter cannot withdraw his renunciation expressly or by tendering performance on the due date.[92] On the other hand, if C refuses to accept D's repudiation and insists on performance by D, the contract will remain in existence for the benefit of both parties and at their risk, so that D may take advantage of any supervening event that has the effect of discharging the contract. In *Avery v Bowden*,[93] B chartered A's ship, agreeing to sail to a Russian port and there to load the vessel with cargo within 45 days. On arrival at the port, the ship's master demanded the cargo, but B's agent was unable to supply any, and advised the master to leave. The latter, however, decided to remain at the port in the hope that the cargo would be forthcoming. Before the 45 days had elapsed, the Crimean War broke out and rendered further performance illegal. On the assumption that the failure of B to provide a cargo amounted to an anticipatory breach of contract, the supervening outbreak of war had given B a good defence to the breach.

90 *Jemmott v Rodriguez* (2009) High Court, Trinidad and Tobago, No 2888 of 2006, unreported [Carilaw TT 2009 HC 49], *per* Rajnauth-Lee J, citing *Woodar Investment Development Ltd v Wimpey Construction UK Ltd* [1980] 1 WLR 277, at 280, where Lord Wilberforce said that, 'in considering whether there has been a repudiation by one party, it is necessary to look at his conduct as a whole. Does this indicate an intention to abandon and to refuse performance of the contract?'

91 *Frost v Knight* (1872) LR 7 Exch 111, at 114, *per* Cockburn CJ.

92 *Xenos v Danube Rly* (1863) 13 CBNS 824.

93 (1855) 119 ER 647.

Repudiation during the performance of a contract

A repudiation which occurs during the performance of a contract will entitle the innocent party to sue immediately for damages and to be released from all his contractual obligations. In *Cort v Ambergate Railway Co*,[94] C contracted to supply A with a quantity of railway chairs at a certain price and at specified times. After C had delivered about half of the chairs, A informed C that it would not require any more and requested C to stop further delivery. C sued for breach, pleading that it had remained ready and willing to supply more chairs, but had been prevented from doing so by A's conduct. It was held that C's claim succeeded; it was not necessary for C to have actually tendered the chairs.

Failure of performance

Where one party to a contract commits a fundamental breach (that is, a breach which 'goes to the root of the contract' and which has the effect of depriving the innocent party of the main object of the agreement), the latter may repudiate the contract, in which case he will be discharged from his obligations, or he may elect to 'affirm' the contract, in which case the agreement will remain in force.

Independent and interdependent obligations

Not every breach by a contracting party will bring about a discharge. First, where the obligations of each party are *independent* of one another, a breach by one will not affect the obligations of the other, which will continue to be binding. A notable instance of an independent obligation is that of a tenant to pay rent due under a lease. His obligation to pay rent is independent of any obligation on the part of the landlord to repair the premises, so that the latter's failure to repair does not entitle the tenant to withhold payment of rent.[95] Similarly, a covenant in a separation agreement by which a husband agreed to pay maintenance to his wife was held to be independent of the wife's obligation not to molest the husband, so that breach by the wife did not absolve the husband from his liability for maintenance.[96]

On the other hand, many contractual obligations are treated as *interdependent*, so that the obligation of each party to carry out his part of the bargain is dependent or conditional on the other party being ready and willing to perform his obligations. For instance, in contracts for the sale of goods, delivery by the seller and payment by the buyer are usually regarded as simultaneous obligations, and indeed the Sale of Goods Acts[97] provide that:

94 (1851) 17 QB 127.

95 *Taylor v Webb* [1937] KB 283.

96 *Fearon v Earl of Aylesford* (1884) 14 QBD 792, at 800.

97 Section 28, Sale of Goods Act (Jamaica); s 29, Sale of Goods Act, Ch 337 (The Bahamas).

> Unless otherwise agreed, delivery of the goods and payment of the price are concurrent conditions, that is to say, the seller must be ready and willing to give possession of the goods to the buyer in exchange for the price, and the buyer must be ready and willing to pay the price in exchange for possession of the goods.

Divisible contracts

Where the obligations under a contract are 'divisible' (for example in the case of a sale of goods, where the seller contracts to deliver the goods in instalments at specified times, and the buyer agrees to pay for each instalment on delivery), breach of one or more segments of the contract (for example, short delivery of one or more instalments) may not entitle the innocent party to be discharged, though it will entitle him to sue for damages for the breach.

Fundamental breach

Breach of a *condition* in a contract, such as the conditions as to title, fitness for purpose and merchantability in a contract for the sale of goods, will entitle the innocent party to rescind the contract and recover the purchase price, since a condition is regarded as a term of fundamental importance. Similarly, breach of a term which is not a condition but which is regarded as an important one, will entitle the innocent party to rescind, so long as it is shown that the breach 'goes to the root of the contract',[98] or is 'fundamental',[99] 'affecting the very substance of the contract'[100] or 'frustrating the commercial purpose of the venture'.[101] Diplock LJ suggested the following test:[102]

> Does the occurrence of the event deprive the party, who has further undertakings to perform, of substantially the whole benefit which it was the intention of the parties as expressed in the contract that he should obtain, as the consideration for performing those undertakings?

Put another way, 'the right of discharge . . . depends on the answer to this question: Does the breach go so far to the root of the contract as to entitle the injured party to say, "I have lost all that I cared to obtain under this contract: further performance cannot make good the prior default"?'[103]

98 *Federal Commerce and Navigation Co Ltd v Molena Alpha Inc* [1979] 1 All ER 307, at 314, *per* Lord Wilberforce.

99 *Photo Production Ltd v Securicor Transport Ltd* [1980] AC 827, at 849; *Thompson v Corroon* (1993) 42 WIR 157, at 172, 173 (Privy Council Appeal, Antigua and Barbuda), *per* Lord Lowry.

100 *Wallis, Son and Wells v Pratt and Haynes* [1910] 2 KB 1003, at 1012; *Thompson v Corroon, ibid.*

101 *Jackson v Union Marine Insurance Co* (1874) LR 10 CP 125, at 145, 147, 148.

102 *Hongkong Fir Shipping Co Ltd v Kawasaki Kisen Kaisha Ltd.*

103 *Anson's Law of Contract*, 29th edn (2010), p 523.

Consequences of breach

Where the innocent party treats the contract as discharged

Where the innocent party treats the contract as discharged by the other's repudiation or fundamental breach, he is released from further performance of the contract.[104] The guilty party will be liable for damages for the breach and any other breaches occurring before the discharge, but he too will be absolved from *further* performance of the contract. Although both parties are absolved from future performance, any rights which have been acquired unconditionally under the agreement are unaffected.[105] Thus, for example, in a building contract where the contractor's work is to be paid for in instalments, the latter can sue for any instalments due but unpaid at the time of the discharge,[106] whether it was the building owner or the contractor that was in breach; similarly, an employee who is dismissed for breach of his contract of employment can recover any unpaid wages due to him at the date of dismissal.

Where C (the innocent party) decides to treat the contract as discharged, he is said to 'accept' D's (the guilty party's) repudiation, and he must make this acceptance known to D, otherwise the contract will be regarded as continuing in force. As Lord Scott emphasised in the Privy Council in a Trinidadian case, *Sookraj v Samaroo*:[107]

> A repudiation does not itself determine the contract. It gives a right to the innocent party, by accepting the repudiation, to determine the contract. If the innocent party does not accept the repudiation, the contract remains in existence for the benefit of both parties. The acceptance of a repudiation requires no particular form; but it must be unequivocal and it must be communicated to the party in breach. These are all basic and well-known principles.

This principle was applied in a Guyanese case, *Singh v Bacchus*.[108] Here, in September, 1989, the parties entered into a contract for the sale of the respondent's land, and the appellant paid to the respondent 10 per cent of the purchase price.[109] Time was never made of the essence of the contract. In April 1990, the appellant's attorney wrote a letter to the respondent, in which he gave 'notice that the said agreement of sale and purchase be cancelled' and requested a refund of the purchase money paid. There was no reply to this letter until December 1990, when the respondent's attorney

---

104 *Thompson v Corroon* (1993) 42 WIR 157 (Privy Council Appeal, Antigua and Barbuda); *Heyman v Darwins Ltd* [1942] AC 356.

105 *McDonald v Dennys Lascelles Ltd* [1933] 48 CLR 457; applied in *Gibson v Gotts* (2006) Supreme Court, The Bahamas, No 25 of 2000, unreported [Carilaw BS 2006 SC 14].

106 *Hyundai Heavy Industries Co Ltd v Papadopoulos* [1980] 2 All ER 29.

107 (2004) 65 WIR 401, at 407. See also *Bahama Reef Condominium Association v Moss* (2012) Court of Appeal, The Bahamas, Civ App No 30 of 2011, unreported, *per* Allen P.

108 (1996) 54 WIR 246.

109 Kennard C (at 248,249) drew a distinction between money paid as a *deposit*, that is, by way of security for the completion of the contract, which the vendor is entitled to retain if the purchaser fails to complete, and money paid as a *part-payment* of the purchase price which the purchaser is entitled to recover (less any expenses incurred by the vendor) if he fails to complete. This distinction had been made in earlier Guyanese cases: *Smith v Itwaria* [1938]LRBG 61; *Hutchins v Allen* [1931–7] LRBG 46; *Antar v Valverde* [1942] LRBG 443; *Chin v Alli* [1969] Guyana LR 240, where Mitchell J adopted the dictum of Crean CJ in *Smith v Itwaria* that 'The law seems to be quite clear that if payment is made in part payment of the purchase money, it cannot be retained by the vendor of the property'.

wrote to the appellant's attorney stating that, in view of the latter's emphatic cancellation of the agreement, the respondent 'now considers the agreement to have been rescinded absolutely'. Meanwhile, the appellant, assuming that the contract was still subsisting, had taken steps to advertise the property for sale and had in fact entered into an agreement to sell to a third party.

Kennard C, delivering the judgment of the Guyana Court of Appeal, concluded that there had been no repudiation in law, since the respondent, the innocent party, had not 'accepted' the appellant's repudiation by making it known to the appellant, within a reasonable time, that he regarded the contract as at an end and that he considered himself to be discharged from all further obligations. Accordingly, the contract was still subsisting and the appellant was entitled to specific performance of it. He emphasised that where there is an anticipatory breach or the breach of an executory contract, and the innocent party wishes to treat himself as discharged, he must make his decision known to the party in default, and, unless and until this is done, the contract continues in existence; for, in the words of Asquith J, 'an unaccepted repudiation is a thing writ in water and of no value to anybody'.[110] Kennard C said:[111]

> Inactivity, in my view, cannot be construed as an acceptance of a repudiation of a contract. Acceptance of a repudiation comes closer to acceptance of a contractual offer, for what is required is words or conduct which make it plain that the innocent party is responding to the repudiation by treating the contract as at an end. The [innocent] party may rescind the contract or (as it is sometimes expressed) 'accept the repudiation', by so acting as to make it plain that, in view of the wrongful action of the party who has repudiated, he claims to treat the contract as at an end. The respondent took no action whether by words or conduct, to indicate that he was treating the contract as at an end. Accordingly, ... as the contract subsists for the benefit of both parties, the appellant would be entitled to an order of specific performance.

Where the innocent party treats the contract as still in force

Where the innocent party elects not to accept the other's repudiation or decides to 'affirm' the contract, notwithstanding the guilty party's fundamental breach, the effect is that the contract remains in force for both parties. In addition, each party retains the right to sue for past and future breaches and, in particular, the innocent party can recover damages for the other's repudiation or breach of which he complains. Thus, where S delivered to B goods of the wrong size and of an inferior standard to that specified in the contract, and B accepted delivery and later resold the goods, B was taken to have treated the contract as still in force, but he was entitled then to sue for damages for the breach.[112]

Another, somewhat controversial, consequence of the principle that, following affirmation by the innocent party, the contract remains in force, is that in the case of an anticipatory breach, the innocent party may ignore the repudiation, proceed to

---

110 *Howard v Pickford Tool Co* [1951] 1 KB 417, at 421.

111 (1996) 54 WIR 246, at 250.

112 *Modern Publications Ltd v Academy Press Ltd* [1967] NCLR 146.

complete his performance of the contract, and then sue for the contract price. Such a situation arose in *White and Carter (Councils) Ltd v McGregor*[113] where W, an advertising contractor, agreed to display advertisements on M's garage for a period of two years. Before anything had been done by W, M requested cancellation of the contract, which amounted to repudiation. W refused to accept the repudiation and proceeded to perform the contract by displaying advertisements as agreed. W then sued for payment. It was held by a majority of the House of Lords that W's claim succeeded. This decision has been criticised, principally on the ground that such a ruling is inconsistent with a claimant's duty to mitigate his loss, and that it encourages futile and wasteful expenditure. The decision has not been overruled, however, and remains good law, though it seems there will be no right to complete a contract following anticipatory breach if the claimant 'has no legitimate interest, financial or otherwise, in performing the contract rather than claiming damages'.[114]

113 [1962] AC 413.
114 *Ibid*, at 430, 432, 439.

CHAPTER 14

REMEDIES FOR BREACH OF CONTRACT

The appropriate remedy for a particular breach of contract will depend on the subject matter of the contract and the nature of the breach. In some cases, more than one remedy may be available. In all cases, the claimant must state in his pleadings the remedy or remedies he is seeking. The possible remedies are:

(a) Action for unliquidated damages.
(b) Action for liquidated damages.
(c) Action for damages by way of recovery of a specific sum of money owed under a contract, for example for the agreed price of goods or services under sale of goods legislation.[1]
(d) Action for a reasonable price for goods sold, under sale of goods legislation, where the price is not fixed by the contract.[2]
(e) Action on a *quantum meruit.*
(f) Action for specific performance.
(g) Action for an injunction to restrain breach of a negative term in a contract.

UNLIQUIDATED DAMAGES

The purpose of an award of unliquidated damages is primarily to compensate the claimant for the defendant's breach of contract. Such damages are thus known as 'compensatory'. The court may award *substantial* damages, which are intended to place the claimant in the position he would have been in, had the contract been performed by the defendant, or *nominal* damages, that is, a small 'token' award in cases where the defendant is technically in breach but the claimant has suffered no actual loss.

Exemplary (punitive) damages are sometimes available in tort claims, but never for breach of contract.[3]

Measure of damages

Compensatory damages in contract claims are most often referable to financial loss, but they may also include physical damage to the claimant's person or property (for example, where a defective product causes personal injury to a consumer), the loss of comfort or privacy, and (in limited circumstances) inconvenience and mental distress. The purpose of compensatory damages in a claim for breach of contract is to put the claimant in the position he would have been in had the contract been performed properly. Thus, for instance, in a construction contract where the

---

1 Section 48, Sale of Goods Act (Jamaica); s 49, Sale of Goods Act, Ch 337 (The Bahamas); and s 49, Sale of Goods Act, Cap 393 (Antigua and Barbuda).

2 Section 9, Sale of Goods Act (Jamaica); s 10, Sale of Goods Act, Ch 337 (The Bahamas); and s 10, Sale of Goods Act, Cap 393 (Antigua and Barbuda).

3 *Addis v Gramophone Co Ltd* [1909] AC 488.

contractor has produced a defective building, the measure of damages is the cost of repair or reinstatement;[4] in a contract for the sale of goods, if the seller fails to deliver, the buyer's damages will be equivalent to the difference between the market price for goods of that description and the contract price on the day fixed for delivery;[5] and where the goods which the seller fails to deliver are not readily available on the market, the proper measure of damages is the profit the buyer would have made on a resale, if the contract had been carried out.[6] Where the buyer fails to take delivery, the seller may recover as damages the difference between the contract price and the market price at the time when the goods ought to have been accepted;[7] and where the seller is a *dealer* in the particular goods sold and, as a result of the buyer's non-acceptance, he has lost a profit on the sale, he is entitled to be compensated for that loss, even if he has (or could have) succeeded in finding another buyer, for he will have profited from only one sale instead of from two.[8]

Damages for mental distress

Damages for mental distress are recoverable by a claimant where such distress is directly consequential on physical inconvenience caused by a breach of contract; for example, where a contractor failed to build a house properly, so that it could not be lived in or rented out, and the owner's 'whole existence was affected by having this unpleasant episode hanging over her head'.[9] Damages for mental distress are also available in respect of breach of a contract which has as its main purpose the provision of enjoyment or peace of mind. Thus, in *Jarvis v Swans Tours Ltd*,[10] the claimant recovered damages for the disappointment caused to him when a winter sports holiday in Switzerland, advertised in the defendants' brochure as a 'house party' featuring various entertainments and promising a 'great time', utterly failed to live up to expectations. Other instances of recovery of damages under this head were: where a firm of solicitors failed to obtain appropriate financial relief for the claimant in matrimonial proceedings;[11] where a cemetery owner, in breach of contract, failed to provide a burial plot next to the claimants' parents;[12] and where a newspaper was in breach of contract by failing to publish an 'In Memoriam' to the claimant's father.[13]

---

4 *Vaughn v Odle* (1982) High Court, Barbados, No 765 of 1981, unreported [Carilaw BB 1982 HC 44].

5 Section 50, Sale of Goods Act (Jamaica); s 51, Sale of Goods Act, Ch 337 (The Bahamas); and s 50(3), Sale of Goods Act, Cap 393 (Antigua and Barbuda). Where a seller has delivered goods but the buyer has lawfully rejected them, the case becomes in effect one of non-delivery, and the measure of damages is the same as that applicable to non-delivery: *McGregor on Damages*, 14th edn, para 629; *Manning v Neal and Massey Ltd* (1982) High Court, Trinidad and Tobago, No 1210 of 1976, unreported [Carilaw TT 1982 HC 50].

6 *Boshali v Misr (Nigeria) Ltd* 1967 (1) ALR Comm 260.

7 Section 49, Sale of Goods Act (Jamaica); s 50, Sale of Goods Act, Ch 337 (The Bahamas); and s 50(1), Sale of Goods Act, Cap 393 (Antigua and Barbuda).

8 *Thompson Ltd v Robinson (Gunmakers) Ltd* [1955] 1 All ER 154.

9 *Harvey-Ellis v Jones* (1987) High Court, Barbados, No 931 of 1985, unreported [Carilaw BB 1987 HC 82].

10 [1973] 1 All ER 71. See also *Jackson v Horizon Holidays Ltd* [1975] 3 All ER 92 (pp 213–215, above) where the plaintiff contracted with a travel agency for a four-week holiday in Ceylon for himself, his wife and two young children, in 'luxurious accommodation', and what was provided was 'sub-standard and downright disgraceful'. It was held that the plaintiff could recover not only for his own loss and mental distress but also for that suffered by his wife and children.

11 *Dickinson v James Alexander & Co* (1990) 20 FLR 137.

12 *Reed v Madon* [1989] Ch 408.

13 *Eweka v Midwest Newspaper Corp* (1976) 6 ECSLR 280.

A Caribbean example of an award of damages for mental distress and injury to feelings is *Brathwaite v Bayley*.[14] Here, the defendant had contracted with the claimants to take photographs at their wedding, a firm arrangement being agreed as to the number and type of photographs to be taken. The defendant attended and took photographs, but he failed to provide any proofs for the claimants to make a selection, and ultimately delivered an album of photographs which the claimants found to be unsatisfactory. Noting that this was the first case of its kind to come before the courts in Barbados, Chase J held the defendant to be in breach of contract and the claimants to be entitled to damages. He pointed out that a distinction had been drawn by the authorities between, on the one hand, commercial contracts, where damages for mental suffering are unobtainable because such damage would not be in the contemplation of the parties as part of the business risk involved, and, on the other, contracts involving personal, social and family interests, where the court may award damages if it thinks that the parties, in the particular circumstances of the case, would have had such damage in their contemplation. Chase J continued:

> The defendant must reasonably have foreseen that any failure on his part to take and deliver the photographs as agreed would have denied the parties the enjoyment they anticipated and as such would have resulted in injury to their feelings. How should this kind of injury be quantified by way of adequate compensation is undoubtedly a difficult exercise, since the loss to each of the injured parties is essentially one of subjectivity. However, the court has to do the best it can in a matter such as this. In *Jarvis v Swans Tours Ltd*[15] . . . Lord Denning [said]: 'In a proper case, damages for mental distress can be recovered in contract, just as damages for shock can be recovered in tort. One such case is a contract for a holiday, or any other contract to provide entertainment and enjoyment. If the contracting party breaks his contract, damages can be given for the disappointment, the distress, the upset and the frustration caused by the breach. I know that it is difficult to assess in money, but it is no more difficult than the assessment which the courts have to make every day in personal injuries cases for loss of amenities.' This court finds the above passage to be of relevance to the present case. The plaintiffs looked forward to having photographs of their wedding so that they and their relatives and friends could reflect upon them and recall the happy moments of the occasion. Those photographs would also have provided a reference point for any children they may have contemplated. They had looked forward to the enjoyment which the photographs would have provided. All of that is lost by the defendant's breach. I am therefore of the view that the plaintiffs' damages should not be limited to the sum deposited for the photographs, but should include a sum that would compensate for the injury to their feelings resulting from the breach.

In *Jamaica Telephone Co Ltd v Rattray*,[16] the claimant sued the telephone company for damages in respect of the wrongful disconnection of his telephone service for a ten-week period. One of the issues in the case was whether damages could be recovered for 'the disappointment, annoyance and frustration' caused to the claimant by the disconnection. Rowe P, in the Jamaican Court of Appeal, after referring to *dicta* of Lord Denning MR and Stephenson LJ in *Jarvis*,[17] confirming that such damages were

14 (1992) High Court, Barbados, No 755 of 1988, unreported [Carilaw BB 1992 HC 23].

15 [1973] 1 All ER 71.

16 (1993) 30 JLR 62.

17 *Jarvis v Swans Tours Ltd* [1973] 1 All ER 71.

recoverable in a 'failed holiday' case, proceeded to consider whether they should be recoverable in the present case for the deprivation of telephone service. Rowe P pointed out, first of all, that 'the general rule of law is that damages are not recoverable in contract for injury to one's feelings', and that the reason for the rule, as explained in *McGregor on Damages*,[18] is that:

> Contracts normally concern commercial matters, and mental suffering arising from breach is not in the contemplation of the parties as part of the business risk of the transaction. If, however, the contract is not primarily a commercial one, in the sense that it affects not the plaintiff's business interests but his personal, social and family interests, the door should not be closed to awarding damages for mental suffering if the court thinks that, in the particular circumstances, the parties to the contract had such damage in their contemplation.

On the other hand, Bingham LJ, in *Watts v Morrow*,[19] suggested that the availability of damages for mental distress depended not on foreseeability of such harm, but on public policy. He said:

> A contract-breaker is not in general liable for any distress, frustration, anxiety, displeasure, vexation, tension or aggravation which his breach of contract may cause to the innocent party. This rule is not, I think, founded on the assumption that such reactions are not foreseeable, which they surely are or may be, but on considerations of policy. But the rule is not absolute. Where the very object of a contract is to provide pleasure, relaxation, peace of mind or freedom from molestation, damages will be awarded if the fruit of the contract is not provided or if the contrary result is procured instead. If the law did not cater for this exceptional category of case, it would be defective.

In the *Jamaica Telephone Co* case, Rowe P posed the question whether it was the kind of case in which 'the very object of the contract was to provide pleasure, relaxation, peace of mind and freedom from molestation', and concluded that it was not. A telephone when installed was not intended for a temporary or singular purpose like a holiday. However, since the telephone company enjoyed a monopoly in Jamaica, it must have appreciated that any arbitrary disconnection of the service would result in the dislocation of the plaintiff's means of communication, and might expose her to unnecessary risks in the event of an emergency. Since there was no proof of special damage in the case, general damages were to be regarded as nominal but, in view of the seriousness of the breach of contract, the amount of damages 'should not be derisory'. Ultimately, the Court awarded the plaintiff $5,000 damages.

A more recent decision in this area of the law is that of the House of Lords in *Farley v Skinner*.[20] Here, C purchased a house in the vicinity of Gatwick Airport, after receiving a favourable report from D, a surveyor/valuer, regarding aircraft noise. After C had spent about £100,000 on improving the property, he discovered that D's report was erroneous, in that the house was located directly below an early-morning 'stacking point' for aircraft waiting to land, and the noise was considerable at that time of the day. It was held that C had paid no more for the house than would a

18 15th edn, paras 96, 97.

19 [1991] 4 All ER 937, at 959.

20 [2002] 2 AC 732.

reasonable purchaser who was aware of the noise, and so he was not entitled to damages on that basis, but he was entitled to damages for the mental distress caused by his discovery about the aircraft noise.

Date for assessment of damages

The general rule is that damages for tort or for breach of contract are assessed as at the date of the breach,[21] but the rule is subject to exceptions.[22] For instance, as Megaw LJ explained in the leading case of *Dodd Properties (Kent) Ltd v Canterbury City Council*:[23]

> Where there is serious structural damage to a building, it would be patently absurd, and contrary to general principle on which damages fall to be assessed, that a plaintiff, in time of rising prices, should be limited to recovery on the basis of the prices of repair at the time of the wrongdoing; on the facts here, being two years at least before the time when, acting with all reasonable speed, he could first have been able to put the repairs in hand. Once that is accepted, . . . the damages are not required . . . to be assessed as at the date of the breach.

In a Barbadian case, *Harvey-Ellis v Jones*,[24] the claimant sought damages from the defendant for breach of a contract to build a house in a good and workmanlike manner. According to the structural report of a firm of civil engineers, there were many cracks in the building, attributable to inadequate foundation support, and extensive remedial work was required. Williams CJ found that 'in view of the claimant's financial circumstances, she could not, up to the present, reasonably attempt to carry out the remedial work', and he held, following *Dodd Properties*, that the damages should be assessed not at the date when the breach was first discovered, but at the date of the trial (by which time building costs were much higher). The decision was based on the principle that where there was a material difference between (a) the cost of repair at the date of the breach or discovery of the breach and (b) the cost when the repairs could, in the circumstances, reasonably be undertaken, the latter was the appropriate measure of damages.

Remoteness of damage

Damages in any case will be awarded only if the loss suffered by the claimant is not too remote a consequence of the defendant's breach of contract. It was established in the leading case of *Hadley v Baxendale*[25] that damage is not too remote if it is 'such as

---

21 *Johnson v Agnew* [1979] 1 All ER 883, at 896, *per* Lord Wilberforce; *Martin v Harportland* (1988) High Court, Barbados, No 140 of 1987, unreported [Carilaw BB 1988 HC 32]. This rule is also embodied in the Sale of Goods legislation: see, for example, ss 49, 50, Sale of Goods Act (Jamaica); and ss 50, 51, Sale of Goods Act, Ch 337 (The Bahamas)

22 *Johnson v Agnew, ibid.*

23 [1980] 1 All ER 928.

24 (1987) High Court, Barbados, No 931 of 1985, unreported [Carilaw BB 1987 HC 82]. A similar conclusion was reached in *Vaughn v Odle* (1982) High Court, Barbados, No 765 of 1981, unreported [Carilaw BB 1982 HC 44], *per* Douglas CJ.

25 (1854) 156 ER 145.

may fairly and reasonably be considered either arising naturally, that is, according to the usual course of things, from such breach of contract itself, or such as may reasonably be supposed to have been in the contemplation of both parties, at the time they made the contract, as the probable result of the breach of it'. This rule can be seen to consist of two branches:

(i) Damages are recoverable if the claimant can show that he has suffered damage arising *naturally and in the ordinary course of events* from the breach.

(ii) Damages are recoverable where the damage arises from unusual circumstances, if the claimant can show that both parties were aware, when the contract was made, that if the contract were broken, damage of an unusual character would result from the breach.

For example, in *Simpson v London and North Western Railway*,[26] C was accustomed to exhibiting his products at agricultural shows. He delivered certain packets to D's agent for transportation to the showground at Newcastle, writing on the consignment note: 'Must be at Newcastle on Monday certain'. Owing to D's negligence, the packets did not arrive until the show was over. It was held that C could recover the profits he would have earned had the packets arrived at Newcastle in time, as the loss arose 'naturally and in the usual course of things from the breach'.

Another well-known application of the *Hadley v Baxendale* test is *Victoria Laundry Ltd v Newman Industries Ltd.*[27] In this case, V Ltd were launderers and dyers who decided to extend their business. For this purpose, and for the purpose of obtaining certain exceptionally lucrative dyeing contracts, they needed a larger boiler. N Ltd, an engineering firm, contracted to sell and deliver to V Ltd a boiler of the required capacity on June 5. The boiler was damaged in transit and was not delivered until November 8. N Ltd were aware of the nature of V Ltd's business and that V Ltd were 'most anxious' to put the boiler into use 'in the shortest possible space of time'. It was held that N Ltd were liable to V Ltd for the amount of the *normal* profits they would have made, had the boiler been delivered on time, as such loss flowed naturally from the breach, but they were not liable for the loss of the lucrative dyeing contracts, which they could not have known about.

The *Victoria Laundry* case clearly shows that a defendant will be liable under the second branch of the *Hadley v Baxendale* rule only if it knew, at the time the contract was made, of the special circumstances which ultimately gave rise to the damage. Put in another way, a defendant will be liable only where the loss to the claimant was reasonably foreseeable as liable to result from the breach: the principle which, as Asquith LJ pointed out,[28] is the basis of both branches of the *Hadley v Baxendale* rule. However, whereas liability under the first branch is based on 'imputed' knowledge (that is, knowledge which every reasonable person is taken to have in the 'ordinary course of things', including awareness of the loss which would ordinarily result from a breach of contract), liability under the second branch is based on 'actual' knowledge of special circumstances *outside* the 'ordinary course of things', which could result in extra loss in the event of a breach of the contract.

26 (1876) 1 QBD 274.

27 [1949] 2 KB 528.

28 *Ibid*, at 539.

The principles in *Hadley v Baxendale* have been frequently applied in courts in the Caribbean. A recent example is *Frederick v Lee*.[29] This case concerned a contract for the sale of a minibus by L to F for a specified price. After the bus was delivered, F found numerous defects in it and he returned it to L, seeking to rescind the contract and to recover the price on the ground of breach of the implied conditions as to fitness for purpose and merchantability under the sale of goods legislation. In addition, F sought to recover the road tax and insurance premium allegedly paid with respect to the vehicle, and the interest he claimed he had paid on a bank loan to finance the purchase. According to the evidence, L knew that F intended to use the minibus for the transport of passengers for reward, but there was no evidence that L knew of the alleged bank loan. Crane-Scott J explained the legal position thus:

> The court is aware that the appropriate starting point in resolving a problem involving the measure of damages for breach of contract is the general rule that the claimant is entitled to be placed, so far as money can do it, in the same position as he would have been in had the contract been performed. The general rule is, however, not without limits, and the full loss which a claimant may be compensated for under the general rule is liable to be cut down by a variety of factors and considerations, all of which are discussed in numerous decided cases and legal texts. [According to Asquith LJ in the *Victoria Laundry* case[30]], 'the governing purpose of damages is to put the party whose rights have been violated in the same position . . . as if his rights had been observed. This purpose, if relentlessly pursued, would provide him with a complete indemnity for all loss *de facto* resulting from a particular breach, however improbable, however unpredictable. This, in contract at least, is recognised as too harsh a rule. Hence, the aggrieved party is only entitled to recover such part of the loss actually resulting as was at the time of the contract reasonably foreseeable as liable to result from the breach. What was at that time reasonably foreseeable depends on the knowledge then possessed by the parties, or, at all events, by the party who later commits the breach.'

Applying these principles to the facts of the case, Crane-Scott J held that F was entitled to recover the purchase price of the vehicle, but she rejected F's other claims. The road tax and insurance premium would have been recoverable under the first branch of *Hadley v Baxendale* as loss which was 'reasonably foreseeable as liable to result from the breach "in the ordinary course of things"', but there was insufficient evidence that such payments were made. The interest on the bank loan would have been recoverable under the second branch of *Hadley*, if F had been able to establish that, at the time the contract was entered into, L had actual knowledge of the loan and 'would as a reasonable man have foreseen that if the minibus did not meet the required standard of fitness for purpose, there was a serious possibility that the claimant (F) would hold him liable for payment of interest on the bank loan'. There was, however, insufficient evidence concerning the loan.

Mitigation of damage

Where one party has suffered loss as a result of the other's breach of contract, the injured party is under a duty to 'mitigate' his loss, that is, to take reasonable steps to minimise the effects of the breach. Whether a claimant has acted reasonably in a

29 (2007) High Court, Barbados, No 622 of 2006, unreported [Carilaw BB 2007 HC 18].
30 *Victoria Laundry Ltd v Newman Industries Ltd* [1949] 2 KB 528, at 539.

particular case is a question of fact, not of law.[31] Any failure to mitigate will be taken into account by the court in its assessment of the damages, and the injured party will be penalised to that extent. The principle was explained by Lord Haldane in *British Westinghouse Electric and Manufacturing Co Ltd v Underground Electric Railways Co of London Ltd*:[32]

> The fundamental basis [of damages] is compensation for pecuniary loss naturally flowing from the breach; but this first principle is qualified by a second, which imposes on a plaintiff the duty of taking all reasonable steps to mitigate the loss consequent on the breach, and debars him from claiming any part of the damage which is due to his neglect to take such steps. In the words of James LJ in *Dunkirk Colliery Co v Lever*,[33] 'The person who has broken the contract is not to be exposed to additional cost by reason of the plaintiffs' not doing what they ought to have done as reasonable men, and the plaintiffs not being under any obligation to do anything otherwise than in the ordinary course of business.' As James LJ indicates, this second principle does not impose on the plaintiff an obligation to take any step which a reasonable and prudent man would not ordinarily take in the course of his business. But when in the course of his business he has taken action arising out of the transaction, which action has diminished his loss, the effect in actual diminution of the loss he has suffered may be taken into account even though there was no duty on him to act.

Circumstances in which there would be a duty to mitigate

As Morrison JA has recently stated in the Jamaican Court of Appeal,[34] in assessing whether the injured party had fulfilled his duty to mitigate, 'the governing criterion is reasonableness, which is a question of fact dependent upon the particular circumstances of each case, not of law, and the burden of proving that a claimant failed to take reasonable steps in mitigation rests upon the defendant.' Thus, for example:

(a) Where a contractor abandons a building before completion, it is the duty of the building owner to take steps to have the building completed by another contractor as soon as possible, and any increase in the cost of the building brought about by his own delay cannot be recovered from the contractor as damages.[35]

(b) An employee who is wrongfully dismissed from his employment must make reasonable efforts to obtain, and should accept an offer of, suitable alternative employment; failure to do so may result in an award of nominal damages only.[36]

(c) The master of a ship, on failure of the charterer to provide the cargo agreed under the charterparty, should accept freight from other cargo owners at the best rate obtainable.[37]

31 *Moore v DER Ltd* [1971] 3 All ER 517, at 521, *per* Karminski LJ; *Quinland v Harney Motors Ltd* (2008) High Court, St Vincent and the Grenadines, No 0197 of 2007, unreported, *per* Blenman J.

32 [1912] AC 673, at 689.

33 (1878) 9 Ch D 20, at 25.

34 *National Transport Co-operative Society Ltd v Attorney General* (2011) Court of Appeal, Jamaica, Civ App No 117 of 2004, unreported.

35 *Taiwo v Princewell* [1961] All NLR 240.

36 *Shindler v Northern Raincoat Co* [1960] 2 All ER 239; *Brace v Calder* [1895] 2 QB 253.

37 *Harries v Edmonds* (1845) 1 Car & Kir 686.

(d) A person who complains of defective repair work on his car by an incompetent repairman should have the necessary remedial work done by competent vehicle repair specialists as soon as reasonably practicable, and should not wait for several weeks before doing so.[38]

On the other hand, the court will not lose sight of the fact that it is the innocent party who is required to take positive action to minimise his loss, and the burden of proof on the guilty party to show failure to take such action is not a light one. In particular, the innocent party should not be obligated to take steps which are risky or clearly disadvantageous to him. In *Pilkington v Wood*,[39] for example, P purchased a house for £6,000, having been advised by W, his solicitor, that the title was good. When he attempted to sell the house a year later, it was discovered that the title was defective and the property was not saleable. W admitted that he had been negligent in investigating the title, but he argued that P ought to have mitigated his loss by suing the vendor for failing to convey a good title. It was held that it would be unreasonable to have required P to sue the vendor, since litigation on the issue of title would have been complex, involving application of difficult provisions of the Law of Property legislation, and the outcome would have been uncertain. According to Harman J, it would not be reasonable to require P to undertake such a risky venture, simply 'to protect his solicitor from the consequences of his own carelessness'.[40]

The issue of the duty to mitigate in the context of an anticipatory breach was brought to the fore in the well-known and controversial case of *White and Carter (Councils) Ltd v McGregor*.[41] As explained in Chapter 13, where D repudiates the contract by informing C, before the date fixed for performance, that he does not intend to carry out his part of the bargain, C has a choice: he may either accept D's repudiation and sue immediately for damages, in which case he will be under the ordinary duty to mitigate, or he may refuse the repudiation, hold D to the agreement, and await the date for performance. If C chooses the latter course, the contract will remain in full force, no damages will be payable, and there will be no question of mitigation. In the words of Diplock J,[42] 'It cannot be said that there is any duty on the part of the plaintiff to mitigate his damages before there has been any breach *which he has accepted as a breach*.'[43]

In *White and Carter*,[44] W Ltd's business was the supply of refuse bins to local councils. Traders would hire advertising space on the bins. M contracted to hire advertising space for three years, to begin on the date when the first advertisement was displayed, but on the same day, he wrote to cancel the contract. W Ltd refused to accept M's repudiation and proceeded to prepare the advertisements, then to attach them to the bins, and continued to do so for the full three-year period. W Ltd made no attempt to find other advertisers to replace M, and ultimately sued M for

---

38 *Foster v Seerattan* (1996) High Court, Barbados, No 579 of 1989, unreported [Carilaw BB 1996 HC 2].

39 [1953] 2 All ER 810.

40 *Ibid*, at 813.

41 [1961] 3 All ER 1178.

42 *Shindler v Northern Raincoat Co* [1960] 1 WLR 1038, at 1048.

43 Emphasis supplied.

44 [1961] 3 All ER 1178

the agreed price. It was held in the House of Lords, by a majority, that W Ltd succeeded in their claim.

This decision of the House of Lords makes a mockery of the principle of mitigation of damage, and its absurdity was exposed by Lord Keith, who gave the following example:[45]

> It would seem that a man who has contracted to go to Hong Kong at his own expense and to make a report, in return for remuneration of £10,000, and who, before the date fixed for the start of the journey and perhaps before he has incurred any expense, is informed by the other contracting party that he has cancelled or repudiates the contract, is entitled to set off for Hong Kong and produce his report in order to claim in debt the stipulated sum.

It may thus be said that the actions of W Ltd were unreasonable. Although, following the repudiation by M, they undoubtedly had the right to remain inactive and await the time for performance: 'they were not content to remain passive; they embarked upon a course of conduct which cost money, served no useful purpose and was, as they knew, unwanted by the respondent. They had chosen, in other words, to inflate their loss.'[46]

Nevertheless, the *White and Carter* case has not been overturned, and the principle applied therein is still regarded as valid. Fortunately, a dictum of Lord Reid in the case has provided an avenue for escaping the harshest consequences of the decision. He opined that, 'if it can be shown that a person has *no legitimate interest, financial or otherwise, in performing the contract rather than claiming damages*, he ought not to be allowed to saddle the other party with an additional burden with no benefit to himself . . . Just as a party is not allowed to enforce a penalty, so he ought not to be allowed to penalise the other party by taking one course when another is equally advantageous to him.'[47] Subsequent cases have confirmed Lord Reid's approach. It has been said that the rule in *White and Carter* has 'no application whatever in a case where the plaintiff ought, in all reason, to accept the repudiation and sue for damages – provided that damages would provide an adequate remedy for any loss suffered by him';[48] that 'any fetter on the innocent party's right of election whether or not to accept a repudiation will only be applied in extreme cases, *viz* where damages would be an adequate remedy *and* where an election to keep the contract alive would be wholly unreasonable';[49] and 'there comes a point at which the court will cease, on general equitable principles, to allow the innocent party to enforce his contract according to its strict legal terms'.[50]

The issue of mitigation of losses arose and was discussed in the Jamaican Court of Appeal in a recent case, *National Transport Co-operative Society Ltd v Attorney*

---

45 *Ibid*, at 1190.

46 Cheshire, Fifoot & Furmston, *Law of Contract*, 15th edn, 2007, p 783.

47 Emphasis supplied.

48 *Attica Sea Carriers Corporation v Ferrostaal Poseidon Bulk Reederei GMBH* [1976] 1 Lloyd's LR 250, at 255, *per* Lord Denning MR.

49 *Gator Shipping Corporation v Trans-Asiatic Oil Ltd SA* [1978] 2 Lloyd's LR 357, at 374, *per* Kerr J; see also *Ocean Marine Navigation Ltd v Koch Carbon Inc (The Dynamic)* [2003] EWHC 1936, para 23, *per* Simon J.

50 *Clea Shipping Corporation v Bulk Oil International Ltd* [1984] 1 All ER 129, at 136, *per* Lloyd J.

General,[51] where, under two franchise agreements, NTCS had been given exclusive licences by the Government of Jamaica (GOJ) to operate public passenger transport services for a period commencing in March 1995. GOJ impliedly repudiated the agreements in June 1995, and again in September 1998, but NTCS continued to run bus services and ultimately sought to recover the cost from GOJ. One of the issues in the case was whether NTCS was under a duty to mitigate its losses by ceasing to provide the transportation services when it became clear that GOJ had repudiated the agreements. It was held that the actions of NTCS in continuing to run the bus services after the repudiation of the franchise agreements by GOJ were not unreasonable in the circumstances. Morrison JA pointed out that NTCS comprised 350 members who owned and operated 450 buses and employed more than 1500 persons, and it had incurred substantial debt liabilities in connection with the operation of the franchises. It was a large operation, the agreed amount of capital employed by NTCS over the relevant period being $54,560,000, and the scope of the operation had to be kept in mind in determining the reasonableness of NTCS's conduct in the face of the repudiation in June 1995. Further, at least until September 1998, when GOJ gave a licence to JUTC to operate bus services, a withdrawal of services by NTCS would have meant that the public would have been left without transportation. For these reasons, it could not be said that NTSC had failed to take reasonable steps to mitigate its losses. In the view of Morrison JA, a distinction had to be drawn between (i) the proposition that, in deciding whether to rescind or affirm a contract, the innocent party is under no duty to have regard to considerations of mitigation of loss, and (ii) the proposition that, having elected to keep the contract alive, he will be able to recover such loss as was unavoidable following that election, subject to the principle that reasonableness is the touchstone for the assessment of the innocent party's conduct, and that the burden of proving unreasonableness rests on the wrongdoer.

LIQUIDATED DAMAGES

Damages are 'liquidated' when they are agreed between the parties and incorporated in the contract: for example, in a building contract, where the contractor expressly agrees to pay the building owner a certain amount by way of damages if, owing to his default, the work is not completed on time, or, in a contract for the sale of land, where P agrees that, in the event of his inability to make the payments due by a certain date, the vendor should be at liberty to find another purchaser and return the payments to P, less a deduction of 10 per cent by way of damages.[52]

A liquidated damages clause in a contract is binding on the parties. In the event of a breach, the exact sum fixed in the contract can be claimed by the innocent party, no more and no less, and no action for unliquidated damages can be entertained. A liquidated damages clause, which is a genuine pre-estimate of the loss which will be suffered on account of a breach, must be distinguished from a penalty clause, which is not a genuine pre-estimate of loss but a stipulation *in terrorem* (that is, as a

51 (2011) Court of Appeal, Jamaica, Civ App No 117 of 2004, unreported.

52 *Chrysostom v James* (2001) High Court, Trinidad and Tobago, No 197 of 1995, unreported [Carilaw TT 2001 HC 126].

deterrent to breach). Penalty clauses are void so that, in the event of a breach, such a clause will be disregarded and the claimant will be able to sue for unliquidated damages.

Whether a particular clause amounts to liquidated damages or a penalty is a question of construction of the contract and depends upon the intention of the parties as expressed in their agreement. As Lopes J explained:[53]

> The distinction between penalties and liquidated damages depends on the intention of the parties to be gathered from the whole of the contract. If the intention is to secure performance of the contract by the imposition of a fine or penalty, then the sum specified is a penalty, but if, on the other hand, the intention is to assess the damages for breach of the contract, it is liquidated damages.

Where the intention of the parties is unclear, the following guidelines may be applied by the court:[54]

(a) The use by the parties of the words 'penalty' or 'liquidated damages' is not conclusive.[55]
(b) If the amount stipulated is extravagant or unconscionable in comparison with the greatest loss that could conceivably be caused by the breach, it is a penalty.[56]
(c) Where the same amount is payable on the occurrence of one or more of several types of breach, some serious and some trivial, it will be presumed to be a penalty.[57]
(d) If the particular breach consists only of the non-payment of money, and the amount stipulated to be paid in the event of a breach is greater, there is a penalty.
(e) It is no obstacle to the amount stipulated being a genuine pre-estimate of loss that the consequences of the breach are such as to make precise pre-estimation virtually impossible.

Deposits in contracts for the sale of land

Sale of land

In contracts for the sale of land, it is customary for the purchaser, on the signing of

---

53 *Robophone Facilities Ltd v Blank* [1966] 1 WLR 1428, at 1447; *Quality Realty Services Ltd v Peterson* (1982) High Court, Trinidad and Tobago, No 4151 of 1978, unreported [Carilaw TT 1982 HC 84], *per* Narine J.

54 *Dunlop Pneumatic Tyre Co Ltd v New Garage Ltd* [1915] AC 79, at 86, *per* Lord Dunedin.

55 *Wilson v Love* [1896] 1 QB 626, at 630.

56 As in *Furniture Ltd v Clarke* (2004) Court of Appeal, Barbados, Civ App No 21 of 1997, unreported [Carilaw BB 2004 CA 1], where, in a hire-purchase agreement, a clause provided 'a formula for the company's attempt to recover sums which could well exceed the greatest loss flowing from breach of the agreement. The wording of the clause is vague. The clause seeks to secure performance of the contract by the imposition of an open-ended, arbitrary amount in whose computation the hirer has no say. There is no pre-determined, agreed and quantifiable amount, no genuine forecast of the probable loss. The clause seeks to provide for a greater measure of compensation than the ordinary law of damages' – *per* Simmons CJ.

57 As in *Quality Realty Services Ltd v Petersen* (1982) High Court, Trinidad and Tobago, No 4151 of 1978, unreported [Carilaw TT 1982 HC 64], where, in an estate agency agreement, a clause requiring the principal to pay, for every breach of the agreement, 4% of the purchase price of the land being offered for sale, was held to be a penalty, as it was 'a provision *in terrorem* to secure the performance of the contract' – *per* Narine J.

the contract or, in some jurisdictions, on 'exchange of contracts', to hand over to the vendor's attorney or solicitor as 'stakeholder' a deposit, which is customarily 10 per cent of the purchase price; and it will normally be an express term of the contract that, in the event that the purchaser fails to complete the purchase, the vendor may forfeit the deposit. Such a provision for forfeiture of a deposit will not be regarded as a penalty, despite the fact that 10 per cent of the purchase price may not be a genuine pre-estimate of the loss which the vendor would be likely to suffer should the purchaser fail to complete. However, to be forfeitable by the vendor, the amount of the deposit must be 'reasonable', and 10 per cent of the purchase price would satisfy the reasonableness test. These propositions were established by the Privy Council in a well-known Jamaican case, *Workers Trust and Merchant Bank Ltd v Dojap Investments Ltd*,[58] where Lord Browne-Wilkinson, delivering the advice of the Court, said:[59]

> In general, a contractual provision which requires one party, in the event of his breach of the contract, to pay or forfeit a sum of money to the other party, is unlawful as being a penalty, unless such provision can be justified as being a payment of liquidated damages, being a genuine pre-estimate of the loss which the innocent party will incur by reason of the breach. One exception to this general rule is the provision for the payment of a deposit by the purchaser in a contract for the sale of land. Ancient law has established that the forfeiture of such a deposit (customarily 10 per cent of the contract price) does not fall within the general rule and can be validly forfeited, even though the amount of the deposit bears no reference to the anticipated loss to the vendor flowing from the breach of contract.

In the *Workers Trust* case, the Privy Council held that the deposit of 25 per cent required by the vendor bank, being well in excess of the normal 10 per cent figure, was not a true deposit 'by way of earnest'; the provision for its forfeiture was a plain penalty; and the amount had to be repaid in full to the purchaser.

In *Pompey v Mahadeo*,[60] the prospective purchaser of land under an agreement for sale paid $150,000 in accordance with the agreement as 'a deposit and on account of the purchase price'. The agreement expressly made time of the essence, but made no provision as to forfeiture of the deposit in the event of default by the purchaser. The purchaser failed to complete within the time fixed by the contract, and the vendors thereupon gave him written notice that they regarded the agreement as having been repudiated by him and later sued for damages in the Guyana High Court. The trial judge found for the claimant vendors and held that the purchaser's deposit should be forfeited.

On appeal to the Court of Appeal, Bernard C, delivering the judgment of the Court, pointed out first of all that the contract description of the $150,000 payment as 'a deposit and on account of the purchase price' seemed to embrace two principles. On the one hand, if the amount is paid as a *deposit or earnest for the due performance of the contract*, at common it is liable to be forfeited where the purchaser fails to complete, or to go towards part payment of the purchase price where the purchaser does complete. On the other hand, if the amount is paid as *part payment of the purchase*

58 [1993] 2 WLR 702; (1992) 42 WIR 253.

59 *Ibid*, at 705; at 258.

60 (2002) 61 WIR 293.

price, it is recoverable where the contract is rescinded, whether it is the vendor or the purchaser who is at fault. Whether a payment is to be regarded as a deposit or as a part payment of the purchase price depends on the terms of the contract and the intention of the parties.

As Bernard C noted, the present case presented the Court with a dilemma, because the contract referred to the payment as both a deposit and a part payment. In dealing with the issue, the trial judge had referred to both Guyanese and English authorities. In *Chin v Ali*,[61] a Guyanese case, the sum of $600 had been paid by the purchasers under an agreement for sale 'as deposit in part payment', and the contract also provided that the sum represented liquidated damages payable to the vendor, should the purchasers fail to complete by accepting transport within the time specified in the contract. On failure of the purchasers to complete, it was held that the amount had been paid as a deposit and was not recoverable by them. Similarly, in an English case, *Howe v Smith*,[62] where a sum of money was paid 'as a deposit and in part payment of the purchase money', it was held that the deposit, although to be taken as part payment if the contract were completed, was also a guarantee for the performance of the contract and, since the purchaser had failed to complete within a reasonable time, he had no right to recover the amount. Bernard C was of the view that the trial judge's analysis and application of these authorities could not be faulted, and that the $150,000 was to be treated as a deposit and *prima facie* irrecoverable by the purchaser. However, although the instant case fell within the general rule as to retention of a deposit by the vendor when a purchaser is in default, the amount of the deposit in this case exceeded the '10 per cent of purchase price' figure established as in the *Workers Trust* case, and regarded as the normal amount for a deposit in contracts of sale in Guyana, as well as in Jamaica and in England. The deposit in the instant case was in fact 17 per cent of the purchase price and, if the Privy Council's ruling in *Workers Trust*[63] (where the deposit was 25 per cent of the purchase price) were followed, the vendor would be ordered to repay the deposit in full. Bernard C, however, preferred the approach of the Jamaican Court of Appeal in *Workers Trust*, which was to 'adopt a middle course' by ordering retention by the vendor of the 10 per cent and repayment of the balance to the purchaser. The Privy Council had disagreed with the Jamaican Court, on the basis that the bank had contracted for a deposit consisting of one global sum, that is, 25 per cent of the purchase price, and if this was to be regarded as an unreasonable sum and therefore not a true deposit, then it had to be repaid as a whole. Interestingly, Bernard C took the view[64] that, unlike the Jamaican courts, the courts in Guyana were not bound by the decisions of the Privy Council; those decisions were of persuasive authority only. Accordingly, she ordered the vendors to repay to the purchaser $60,000 (7 per cent of the purchase price) and that they were entitled to retain $90,000 (10 per cent of the purchase price).

---

61 [1969] Guyana LR 240.

62 (1884) 27 Ch D 89.

63 [1973] 2 All ER 370.

64 (2002) 61 WIR 293, at 300.

QUANTUM MERUIT CLAIMS

A *quantum meruit* is a claim for an *unliquidated* sum by way of payment for services rendered. The difference between a *quantum meruit* claim and a claim for damages is that the latter is a claim for compensation, while the former is a claim for *reasonable remuneration*.

Quantum meruit claims may arise in the following types of circumstance:

(a) where there is an express or implied agreement to render services, but no agreement as to the amount of remuneration, reasonable remuneration is payable;[65] or

(b) where, from the circumstances of the case, a new contract is implied, taking the place of the original agreement, the party who has performed his obligations under the fresh implied contract can sue on a *quantum meruit*. Thus, where a principal wrongfully revoked his agent's authority before the agent had completed his duties, the agent was held to be entitled to recover on a *quantum meruit* for the work he had done and the expenses he had incurred in the course of his duties.[66]

Quantum meruit claims are frequently encountered in courts in the Caribbean. In *Harrison v Bailey*,[67] for instance, the claimant brought an action against the defendant for damages for breach of contract or, in the alternative,[68] a *quantum meruit* for architectural services performed by him in connection with the construction of a block of apartments. There was evidence of an agreement that the claimant would perform the architectural services without charge, but that in return he would be awarded the contract for the construction of the block. The architectural services were performed, but the claimant was not awarded the construction contract. Regarding the claim for damages for breach of contract, Williams CJ first of all noted that there was no agreement as to the amount which the claimant was to receive under the proposed construction contract and no formula for fixing the level of remuneration, nor was there any evidence of any customary scale of charges operative in Barbados. The claim in contract therefore failed. Williams CJ held, however, that the claimant could recover a reasonable sum for his services, on a *quantum meruit*. He explained:

> I find that the claimant expended much time and effort towards the preparation of the plans. He was preparing the plans in the expectation of being remunerated, not directly by payment for his architectural services, but indirectly out of a contract to construct the apartments. In the end, the contract went to Nord Construction, for one reason or another ... In such circumstances, the claimant is entitled to a *quantum meruit*. Taking into account all the circumstances including the nature of the arrangement between the parties, I allow $12,000 on a *quantum meruit*.

---

65 *De Bernardy v Harding* (1853) 8 Ex Ch 822; *Design Construct Management Associates Ltd v Tobago Race Club Ltd* (1997) High Court, Trinidad and Tobago, No 1808 of 1994, unreported [Carilaw TT 1997 HC 104].

66 *De Bernardy v Harding* (1853) 8 Ex Ch 822.

67 (1979) High Court, Barbados, No 433 of 1978, unreported [Carilaw BB 1979 HC 9].

68 A claimant may, in certain circumstances, claim for work done under a contract whilst at the same time making an alternative claim on a *quantum meruit*: *Jairam v Mootoo* (1975) High Court, Trinidad and Tobago, No 1313 of 1971, unreported [Carilaw TT 1975 HC 29], *per* des Iles J.

Another clear example is the Bahamian case of *Kirk v Hanna*.[69] Here, the claimant had, without remuneration, performed work in connection with the establishing and running of a car rental business, pursuant to a partnership agreement which never became legally binding. Isaacs J held that the claimant was entitled on a *quantum meruit* to $300 for each week that she had worked in the business. He said:

> The final issue is whether or not the claimant ought to be compensated on a *quantum meruit* basis for the value of the work performed for the business. The case of *Craven Ellis v Canons Ltd*[70] provides the principle under which a claimant can recuperate income for services rendered even where no valid contract exists. In that case, an estate agent, having been made a director of a company, successfully claimed payment on a *quantum meruit* basis for services rendered to the company as an estate agent, notwithstanding that the agreement containing the terms on which he was to act as managing director was declared null and void.
>
> In the instant case, this court has determined that the unexecuted partnership agreement does not bind the company, and that it is a meaningless document as against the defendant, who has transferred all of the assets of Tanner's to the company. The claimant however has rendered services to Tanner's, which is the business of the company, and those services have been accepted, placing this case squarely within the principle in *Craven Ellis*, entitling the claimant to recover payment for services rendered on a *quantum meruit* basis . . . In these quasi-contractual cases, the court will look at the true facts and ascertain from them whether or not a promise to pay should be implied, irrespective of the actual views or intentions of the parties at the time the work was done or the services rendered. It seems an unjust result in the circumstances for the claimant not to be compensated for services rendered.

Questions as to the amount to be awarded by the court on a *quantum meruit* claim relating to labour and materials supplied by a contractor arose in a Trinidadian case, *Callender v John*.[71] Here, C had agreed to construct an extension to D's dwelling house. The work was still incomplete when D wrongfully repudiated the agreement. C elected to accept the repudiation and to treat the contract as at an end. He then sued on a *quantum meruit* for the work done. Crane J stated that the question to be decided was 'what value is to be placed on the work done?' He pointed out that it had been held by the Privy Council in *Slowey v Lodder*[72] that the measure of relief in a *quantum meruit* claim is the actual value of the work, which could refer to (a) the amount spent by the innocent party in carrying out the work, or (b) the market value or the value of the work to the defendant in the condition in which it stood at the time of the termination of the agreement, or (c) the actual cost of construction of the work done, determined by an objective valuation of the cost of materials required on site, and the cost of the necessary labour performing in an efficient manner, including a percentage of 20 per cent for the builder's commission, as well as the value of the materials remaining on site. Crane J opined that alternative (c) was the appropriate test, but he proceeded to dismiss the claim, in the absence of a satisfactory valuation.

---

69 (2005) Supreme Court, The Bahamas, No FP/CLS/17 of 1999, unreported [Carilaw BS 2005 SC 44].

70 [1936] 2 All ER 1066.

71 (1984) High Court, Trinidad and Tobago, No 1865 of 1979, unreported [Carilaw TT 1984 HC 85].

72 (1901) 20 NZLR 321.

Specific performance

Specific performance is an equitable remedy whereby the court orders the defendant to carry out his undertaking exactly according to the terms of the contract. The remedy is discretionary and is normally available only where damages would not adequately compensate the claimant.[73] The remedy is most often granted to enforce contracts for the sale or lease of land, since each piece of land is considered to have unique features, and an award of damages would not be a sufficient remedy for the purchaser if the vendor refused to complete. Less commonly, specific performance may be granted to enforce a contract for the sale of property other than land, if it is particularly valuable (such as a particularly rare work of art)[74] or unavailable on the market (such as shares in a private company).[75]

Discretion of the court

The court's discretion regarding an award of specific performance is exercised according to the following principles:

(a) It will not be granted if damages would be a sufficient remedy for the claimant.[76]

(b) It will not be granted if the claimant has not come to court 'with clean hands', that is, if his conduct in the transaction has not been fair and 'above- board', or if he is guilty of conduct which amounts to a breach of the terms of the contract.[77]

(c) It will not be granted if the claimant has been guilty of 'laches', that is, undue delay in bringing his claim.

(d) It will not be granted if it would cause undue hardship to the defendant.[78]

(e) A gratuitous promise, that is, one given for no consideration, is not specifically enforceable.[79]

(f) It will not be granted to enforce a contract for personal services, such as a contract to perform in a theatre.[80]

(g) It will not be granted to enforce a contract that would require the constant supervision of the court.[81]

(h) It will not be granted if the contract lacks 'mutuality', that is, where the contract is not binding on *both* parties (for example, a minor cannot be granted specific performance of a contract which is not binding on *him*).

---

73 *Beswick v Beswick* [1968] AC 58.

74 *Philips v Lamdin* [1949] 2 KB 33.

75 *Oughtred v IRC* [1960] AC 206.

76 *South African Territories Ltd v Wallington* [1898] AC 309.

77 *Coatsworth v Johnson* (1886) 55 LJQB 220.

78 *Malins v Freeman* (1837) 48 ER 537; *Co-op Insurance Society Ltd v Argyll Stores (Holdings) Ltd* [1997] 3 All ER 297.

79 *Jefferys v Jefferys* (1841) 41 ER 443.

80 *Lumley v Wagner* (1852) 42 ER 687. But an injunction may be granted to restrain breach of a negative term in a contract for personal services: *ibid*.

81 *Ryan v Mutual Tontine Westminster Chambers Association* [1893] 1 Ch 116.

APPENDICES

INFANTS ACT

CHAPTER 46:02

Act
28 of 1925
Amended by
33 of 1945
28 of 1973
50 of 1976
45 of 1979
15 of 1981
*20 of 1981

**See* Note on Amendment at page 2

Current Authorised Pages

Pages (inclusive)		*Authorised by L.R.O.*
1– 17	..	*1/2006*

Index of Subsidiary Legislation

Note on Maintenance Orders made under the Act

For Maintenance Orders made under Part I of the Act (which has been repealed)—*See* Section 20 and also Item 9 of the Schedule to Act No. 14 of 1988.

Note on Amendment

This Act has been amended by Act No. 20 of 1981 (Fifth Schedule) but Act No. 20 of 1981 had, not up to the date of the last revision of this Act, been brought into operation.

Note on section 28

For regulating the form and mode of procedure and generally, the practice of the Court in respect of the matters to which this Act relates, *see* Order 86 of the Rules of the Supreme Court (1975) inserted as an Appendix to this Act.

CHAPTER 46:02

INFANTS ACT

ARRANGEMENT OF SECTIONS

CHAPTER 46:02

INFANTS ACT

1950 Ed. Ch. 5. No. 12. 28 of 1925.

An Act relating to the guardianship, custody, and property of infants.

Commencement.

[18TH JUNE 1925]

Short title.

1. This Act may be cited as the Infants Act.

Interpretation.

2. In this Act—

"Court" means the High Court or a Judge thereof;

"lands" includes all lands of any tenure, and all estates or interest in any lands, not being settled estates within the meaning of the Leases and Sales of Settled Estates Ordinance; (Ch. 27. No. 15. [1950 Ed.].)

"parent" includes any person at law liable to maintain a child, or entitled to his custody;

"person" includes any school or institution.

PART I

GUARDIANSHIP AND CUSTODY OF INFANTS

3–18 [Sections 3 to 18 repealed by the Family Law (Guardianship of Minors, Domicile and Maintenance) Act Ch. 46:08)].

PART II

CONTRACTS OF INFANTS

Contracts by infants, except for necessaries, to be void.

19. All contracts, whether by specialty or by simple contract, henceforth entered into by infants for the repayment of money lent or to be lent, or for goods supplied or to be supplied (other than contracts for necessaries), and all accounts stated with infants, shall be absolutely void; but this Act shall not invalidate any contract into which an infant may, by any existing or future written law, or by the Rules of Common Law or equity, enter, except such as now by law are voidable.

20. No action shall be brought whereby to charge any person upon any promise made after full age to pay any debt contracted during infancy, or upon any ratification made after full age of any promise or contract made during infancy, whether there shall or shall not be any new consideration for the promise or ratification after full age.

No action to be brought on ratification of infant's contract.

PART III

INFANTS' SETTLEMENTS

21. (1) Every female infant may upon or in contemplation of her marriage, with the sanction of the Court, make a valid and binding settlement or contract for a settlement of all or any part of her property, or any property over which she has any power of appointment, whether real or personal, and whether in possession, reversion, remainder or expectancy.

Infant may make settlement on marriage. [28 of 1973].

(2) Every conveyance, transfer, appointment, and assignment of such real or personal estate, or contract to make a conveyance, transfer, appointment, or assignment thereof, executed by the infant with the approbation of the Court for the purpose of giving effect to the settlement, shall be as valid and effectual as if the person executing the same were of the full age of eighteen years.

(3) This section shall not extend to powers of which it is expressly declared that they shall not be exercised by an infant.

22. Where any appointment under a power of appointment or any disentailing assurance, is executed by any infant tenant in tail under this Part and the infant afterwards dies under age, the appointment or disentailing assurance shall thereupon become absolutely void.

In case infant dies under age, appointment to be void.

23. (1) The sanction of the Court to any such settlement or contract for a settlement may be given upon petition presented by the infant or her guardian in a summary way, without the institution of a suit.

Sanction of Court to be given on petition.

(2) Where there is no guardian the Court may require a guardian to be appointed or not as the Court thinks fit.

(3) The Court also may, if it thinks fit, require that any persons interested or appearing to be interested in the property should be served with notice of the petition.

PART IV

SALE OF INFANTS' ESTATES

Court to authorise sale of infants' lands.

24. The Court may, on the petition of any infant by his guardian or next friend, if it thinks it proper and for the benefit of the infant, from time to time authorise the sale of any lands of the infant, subject, if the Court so directs, to any charge or encumbrance affecting the same; and every such sale shall be conducted and confirmed in the same manner as, by the Rules and practice of the Court for the time being, is or shall be required in the sale of lands sold under a decree of the Court.

Notice of petitions to be published and persons may be heard.

25. Notice of any petition to the Court under section 24 shall be inserted in such newspapers as the Court directs, and any person, whether interested in the lands or not, may apply to the Court, by motion, for leave to be heard in opposition to or in support of any such petition, and the Court is hereby authorised to permit the person to appear and be heard in opposition to or in support of any such petition on such terms as to costs or otherwise, and in such manner, as it thinks fit.

Moneys to be paid to Comptroller of Accounts and applied to certain purposes.

26. All money to be received on any sale effected under the authority of this Part shall be paid to the Comptroller of Accounts, to the account of the Registrar of the Court *ex parte* the petitioner in the matter of this Act; and the money, after payment of any costs attending the petition which may be allowed by the Court, shall be applied as the Court from time to time directs to some one or more of the following purposes, namely, the discharge or redemption of any encumbrance affecting the lands in respect of which money was paid, or the payment to any person becoming absolutely entitled.

27. Until the money can be applied as under section 26, the same shall be from time to time invested in such securities authorised by the Court Funds Investment Act as the Court thinks fit, and the interest or dividends of the securities, or such parts thereof as the Court may from time to time direct, shall be paid to the guardian for the time being of the infant, or such other person as would have been entitled to the rents and profits of the lands so sold if the same had not been sold. Money to be invested pending application. Ch. 7:06.

PART V

MISCELLANEOUS

***28.** The Rules Committee established by the Supreme Court of Judicature Act may make Rules for carrying the purposes of this Act into effect, and for regulating the form and mode of procedure and, generally, the practice of the Court in respect of the matters to which this Act relates, and for regulating the fees and allowances to all Officers and Attorneys-at-law of the Court in respect of such matters. Rules. Ch. 4:01.

**See* Note on page 2.

SUBSIDIARY LEGISLATION

INFANTS (PETITION) RULES

ARRANGEMENT OF RULES

RULE

[Subsidiary]

INFANTS (PETITION) RULES

R.G. 22.5.1867.

made under section 28

1. These Rules may be cited as the Infants (Petition) Rules. Citation.

2. The Petition shall state— Particulars of Petition.

(*a*) the name, age and residence of the infant;

(*b*) the description, particular local situation, and present condition of the property intended to be sold;

(*c*) the nature and extent of the estate or interest of the infant, and value of the property or of the estate or interest, as the case may be;

(*d*) all the charges and encumbrances affecting the property or the estate or interest, as the case may be; and

(*e*) the circumstances which make it proper or expedient that the property or the estate or interest should be sold.

3. The particulars stated in the Petition must be verified by affidavit. Verification.

4. On the application of the Attorney-at-law for the Petitioner an order will be made by one of the Judges in Chambers appointing a day for the hearing of the Petition, and directing (with reference to the circumstances of the case) in what newspapers, and how often, the notice required by section 25 of the Act is to be published. Day appointed.

5. The notice will be prepared by the Registrar and submitted to the Judge for his approval before it is published. Notice.

6. All Affidavits and Exhibits intended to be used in support of, or in opposition to the Petition must be filed or deposited in the office of the Registrar three clear days before the hearing of the Petition. Filing, etc.

Order of Court.

7. On the hearing of the Petition, and of any party opposing the same, the Court may make an order for the sale of the property, or of the Estate or interest of the infant, with such restrictions as to price, or reserve bidding, or such other conditions as to the Court seems proper, or may refer the matter to one of the Judges in Chambers for such enquiries, and with such powers and directions as to the Court may seem proper.

Guardian.

8. Where it appears to the Court expedient that a Guardian should be appointed to the infant for the protection of his interests in the matter of the Petition, the Court will refer it to one of the Judges in Chambers to appoint the Guardian and to take the proper security.

Fees and allowances.

9. The fees and allowances to the Officers and Attorneys-at-law of the Court, in respect of the matters under the Act, shall be the same as are allowed under the Rules of the Supreme Court.

APPENDIX

ORDER 86

PROCEEDINGS RELATING TO MINORS, MATRIMONIAL STATUS AND SPOUSES

I. MINORS

Interpretation

1. In this Order—

"the Act" means the Infants Act, Ch. 46:02;

"the Family Law Act" means the Family Law (Guardianship of Minors, Domicile and Maintenance) Act, Ch. 46:08.

2. (1) Subject to paragraph (2) an application concerning the maintenance or advancement of minors or made under the Family Law Act or under Part III of the Act shall be made to a Judge in Chambers by an originating summons intituled—

(i) in the case of an application under the Family Law Act—

In the matter of the Minor

and

In the Matter of the Family Law (Guardianship of Minors, Domicile and Maintenance) Act, Ch. 46:08;

(ii) in the case of an application under the Act—

In the matter of the Minor

and

In the matter of the Infants Act, Ch. 46:02.

(2) *(a)* Where any proceedings (including proceedings for divorce or judicial separation) are pending in relation to the minor; or

(*b*) when the minor is a ward of Court or the administration of the estate or the maintenance or advancement of the minor is under the direction of the Court,

the application shall be made by summons.

Power of Judge pending Appeal

3. Where an appeal is entered against a judgment given or order made under rule 2 the Judge by whom the judgment was given or the order was made may make such orders either *ex parte* or otherwise as he may think proper.

Application to make a Minor a Ward of Court

4. (1) An application to make a minor a ward of Court must be made by originating summons.

(2) Where there is no person other than the minor who is a suitable defendant, an application may be made *ex parte* for leave to issue either an *ex parte* originating summons or an originating summons with the minor as defendant thereto; and except where such leave is granted, the minor shall not be made a defendant to an originating summons under this rule in the first instance.

(3) The date of the minor's birth shall, unless otherwise directed, be stated in the summons and the plaintiff shall—

(*a*) on issuing the summons or before or at the first hearing thereof lodge in the appropriate Registry a certified copy of the entry in the Register of Births, or, as the case may be, in the Adopted Children Register relating to the minor; or

(*b*) at the first hearing of the summons apply for directions as to proof of birth of the minor in some other manner.

(4) Unless the Court otherwise directs, the summons shall state the whereabouts of the minor or, as the case may be, that the plaintiff is unaware of the whereabouts.

(5) Every defendant other than the minor shall, forthwith after being served with the summons —

(a) lodge in the appropriate Registry a notice stating the address of the defendant and the whereabouts of the minor, or as the case may be, that the defendant is unaware of his whereabouts; and

(b) unless the Court otherwise directs, serve a copy of the notice on the plaintiff.

(6) Where any party other than the minor changes his address or becomes aware of any change in the whereabouts of the minor after the issue or, as the case may be, service of the summons, he shall, unless the Court otherwise directs, forthwith lodge notice of the change in the appropriate Registry and serve a copy of the notice on every other party.

(7) The summons shall contain a notice to the defendant informing him of the requirements of paragraphs (5) and (6).

(8) In this rule any reference to the whereabouts of a minor is a reference to the address at which and the person with whom he is living and any other information relevant to the question where he may be found.

When Minor ceases to be a Ward of Court

5. (1) A minor who, by virtue of section 35(2) of the Family Law Act, becomes a ward of Court on the issue of a summons under rule 4 shall cease to be a ward of Court— Ch. 46:08.

(a) if an application for an appointment for the hearing of the summons is not made within the period of 21 days after the issue of the summons, at the expiration of that period;

(b) if an application for such an appointment is made within that period, on the determination of the application made by the summons unless the Court hearing it orders that the minor be made a ward of Court.

(2) Nothing in paragraph (1) shall be taken as affecting the power of the Court under section 35(3) of the Family Law Act to order that any minor who is for the time being a ward of Court shall cease to be a ward of Court. Ch. 46:08.

(3) If no application for an appointment for the hearing of a summons under rule 4 is made within the period 21 days after the issue of the summons, a notice stating whether the applicant intends to proceed with the application made by the summons must be left at the appropriate Registry immediately after the expiration of that period.

Application under the Family Law Act, Ch. 46:08

6. Where there is pending any proceeding by reason of which a minor becomes a ward of Court, any application relating to the
Ch. 46:08. guardianship of minors under the Family Law Act with respect to that minor may be made by summons in that proceeding, but except in that case any such application shall be made by originating summons.

Defendants to Guardianship Summons

7. (1) Where the minor with respect to whom an application
Ch. 46:08. under the Family Law Act is made is not the plaintiff, he shall not, unless the Court otherwise directs, be made a defendant to the summons or, if the application is made by ordinary summons, be served with the summons, but subject to paragraph (2) any other person appearing to be interested in, or affected by the application shall be made a defendant or be served with the summons, as the case may be, including, where the application
Ch. 46:08. is made under section 13 of the Family Law Act with respect to a minor who has been received into the care of a certified school
Ch. 46:01. within the meaning of Part III of the Children Act, that school.

(2) The Court may dispense with service of the summons (whether originating or ordinary) on any person and may order it to be served on any person not originally served.

Guardianship Proceedings may be in Chambers

Ch. 46:08. **8.** Applications under the Family Law Act relating to the guardianship of minors may be disposed of in Chambers.

Applications for Paternity Orders under section 10 of the Status of Children Act, Ch. 46:07

9. An application for a paternity order under section 10
Ch. 46:07. of the Status of Children Act, shall be made by originating summons.

Removal of Proceedings from a Magistrate's Court

10. (1) An application for an order under section 46(1) of the Family Law Act for the removal of an application from a Magistrate's Court into the High Court shall be made *ex parte* by an originating summons, but the Court may direct that the summons shall be served on any person. Ch. 46:08.

(2) The application may be heard by the Registrar or by an Assistant Registrar, but, if an order is made for the removal to the High Court of an application to the Magistrate's Court, that application shall be heard by a single Judge of the Court.

(3) Where an order is made under the said section 46(1), the plaintiff shall send a copy of the order to the Clerk of the Peace of the Magistrate's Court from which the proceedings are ordered to be removed.

(4) On receipt of certified copies of all entries in the books of the Magistrate's Court relating to the proceedings together with all documents filed in the proceedings the Registrar shall forthwith file the said documents and give notice to all parties that the application is proceeding in the High Court.

(5) The application so removed shall proceed in the High Court as if it had been made by originating summons.

Application of Matrimonial Causes Rules

11. (1) Rules 68 to 71 (inclusive) of the Matrimonial Causes Rules (which relate to proceedings under section 50 of the Matrimonial Proceedings and Property Act) shall apply, with the necessary modifications, to proceedings under section 13 of the Family Law Act. Ch. 45:51. Ch. 46:08.

(2) Rules 41, 44 and 45 of the Matrimonial Causes Rules (which relate to the drawing up and service of orders) shall apply to proceedings under this Part of this Order as if they were proceedings under those rules.

II. MATRIMONIAL STATUS

Application for Declaration affecting Matrimonial Status

12. (1) Where, apart from costs, the only relief sought in any proceedings is a declaration with respect to the matrimonial status of any person, the proceedings shall be begun by petition.

(2) The petition shall state—

(a) the names of the parties and the residential address of each of them at the date of presentation of the petition;

(b) the place and date of any ceremony of marriage to which the application relates;

(c) whether there have been any previous proceedings between the parties with reference to the marriage or the ceremony of marriage to which the application relates or with respect to the matrimonial status of either of them and, if so, the nature of those proceedings;

(d) all other material facts alleged by the petitioner to justify the making of the declaration and the grounds on which he alleges that the Court has jurisdiction to make it,

and shall conclude with a prayer setting out the declaration sought and any claim for costs.

(3) Nothing in the foregoing provisions shall be construed—

(a) as conferring any jurisdiction to make a declaration in circumstances in which the Court could not otherwise make it; or

(b) as affecting the power of the Court to refuse to make a declaration notwithstanding that it has jurisdiction to make it.

Further Proceedings on Petition under Rule 12

13. Subject to rule 12 the Matrimonial Causes Rules shall apply with the necessary modifications to the petition as if it were a petition in a matrimonial cause.

III. SPOUSES

Provisions as to Actions in Tort

14. (1) This rule applies to any action in tort brought by one of the parties to a marriage against the other during the subsistence of the marriage.

(2) On the first application by summons or motion in an action to which this rule applies, the Court shall consider, if necessary of its own motion, whether the power to stay the action under section 15(2) of the Married Persons Act, should or should not be exercised. Ch. 45:50.

(3) Notwithstanding anything in Order 13 or Order 19 judgment in default of appearance or of defence shall not be entered in an action to which this rule applies except with the leave of the Court.

(4) An application for the grant of leave under paragraph (3) must be made by summons and the summons must, notwithstanding anything in Order 65, rule 9, be served on the defendant.

(5) If the summons is for leave to enter judgment in default of appearance, the summons shall not be issued until after the time limited for appearing.

CHAPTER 337

SALE OF GOODS

ARRANGEMENT OF SECTIONS

Unpaid Seller's Lien

Stoppage in transitu

Re-sale by Buyer or Seller

PART V
ACTIONS FOR BREACH OF THE CONTRACT

Remedies of the Seller

Remedies of the Buyer

PART VI
SUPPLEMENTARY

CHAPTER 337

SALE OF GOODS

An Act relating to the sale of goods. *37 of 1904* *5 of 1987*

[Commencement 9th June, 1904]

1. This Act may be cited as the Sale of Goods Act. Short title.

2. (1) In this Act, unless the context otherwise requires — Interpretation.

"action" includes counterclaim and set off;

"buyer" means a person who buys or agrees to buy goods;

"contract of sale" includes an agreement to sell as well as a sale;

"delivery" means voluntary transfer of possession from one person to another;

"document of title to goods" includes any bill of lading, dock warrant, warehouse-keeper's certificate and warrant or order for the delivery of goods, and any other document used in the ordinary course of business as proof of the possession or control of goods, or authorising or purporting to authorise, either by endorsement or by delivery, the possessor of the document to transfer or receive goods thereby represented;

"fault" means wrongful act or default;

"future goods" means goods to be manufactured or acquired by the seller after the making of the contract of sale;

"goods" include all chattels personal other than things in action and money. The term includes emblements, industrial growing crops and things attached to or forming part of the land which are agreed to be severed before sale or undo the contract of sale;

"mercantile agent" means a mercantile agent having in the customary course of his business as such agent authority either to sell goods or to consign goods for the purpose of sale, or to buy goods or to raise money on the security of goods;

"property" means the general property in goods, and not merely a special property;

"quality of goods" includes their state or condition;

"sale" includes a bargain and sale as well as a sale and delivery;

"seller" means a person who sells or agrees to sell goods;

"specific goods" means goods identified and agreed upon at the time a contract of sale is made;

"warranty" means an agreement with reference to goods which are the subject of a contract of sale, but collateral to the main purpose of such contract, the breach of which gives rise to a claim for damages, but not to a right to reject the goods and treat the contract as repudiated.

(2) A thing is deemed to be done "in good faith" within the meaning of this Act when it is in fact done honestly, whether it be done negligently or not.

(3) A person is deemed to be insolvent within the meaning of this Act who either has ceased to pay his debts in the ordinary course of business, or cannot pay his debts as they become due, whether he has committed an act of bankruptcy or not.

(4) Goods are in a "deliverable state" within the meaning of this Act when they are in such a state that the buyer would under the contract be bound to take delivery of them.

PART I
FORMATION OF THE CONTRACT

Contract of Sale

Sale and agreement to sell.

3. (1) A contract of sale of goods is a contract whereby the seller transfers or agrees to transfer the property in goods to the buyer for a money consideration, called the price. There may be a contract of sale between one part owner and another.

(2) A contract of sale may be absolute or conditional.

(3) Where under a contract of sale the property in the goods is transferred from the seller to the buyer the

contract is called a sale; but where the transfer of the property in goods is to take place at a future time or subject to some condition thereafter to be fulfilled the contract is called an agreement to sell.

(4) An agreement to sell becomes a salc when the time elapses or the conditions are fulfilled subject to which the property in the goods is to be transferred.

Capacity to buy and sell.

4. (1) Capacity to buy and sell is regulated by the general law concerning capacity to contract, and to transfer and acquire property:

Provided that where necessaries are sold and delivered to an infant, or to a person who by reason of mental incapacity or drunkenness is incompetent to contract, he must pay a reasonable price therefor.

(2) Necessaries in this section mean goods suitable to the condition in life of such infant or other person, and to his actual requirements at the time of the sale and delivery.

Formalities of the Contract

Contract of sale, how made.

5. Subject to the provisions of this Act and of any Act in that behalf, a contract of sale may be made in writing (either with or without seal), or by word of mouth, or partly in writing and partly by word of mouth, or may be implied from the conduct of the parties:

Provided that nothing in this section shall affect the law relating to corporations.

Contract of sale for forty dollars and upwards. *5 of 1987, s. 2.*

6. (1) A contract for the sale of any goods of the value of forty dollars or upwards shall not be enforceable by action unless the buyer shall accept part of the goods so sold, and actually receive the same, or give something in earnest to bind the contract, or in part payment, or unless some note or memorandum in writing of the contract be made and signed by the party to be charged or his agent in that behalf.

(2) The provisions of this section apply to every such contract, notwithstanding that the goods may be intended to be delivered at some future time, or may not at the time of such contract be actually made, procured, or provided, or fit or ready for delivery, or some act may be requisite for the making or completing thereof, or rendering the same fit for delivery.

(3) There is an acceptance of goods within the meaning of this section when the buyer does any act in relation to the goods which recognises a pre-existing contract of sale whether there be an acceptance in performance of the contract or not.

Subject Matter of Contract

Existing or future goods.

7. (1) The goods which form the subject of a contract of sale may be either existing goods, owned or possessed by the seller, or goods to be manufactured or acquired by the seller after the making of the contract of sale, in this Act called "future goods."

(2) There may be a contract for the sale of goods, the acquisition of which by the seller depends upon a contingency which may or may not happen.

(3) Where by a contract of sale the seller purports to effect a present sale of future goods, the contract operates as an agreement to sell the goods.

Goods which have perished.

8. Where there is a contract for the sale of specific goods, and the goods without the knowledge of the seller have perished at the time when the contract is made, the contract is void.

Goods perishing before sale but after agreement to sell.

9. Where there is an agreement to sell specific goods, and subsequently the goods, without any fault on the part of the seller or buyer, perish before the risk passes to the buyer, the agreement is thereby avoided.

The Price

Ascertainment of price.

10. (1) The price in a contract of sale may be fixed by the contract, or may be left to be fixed in manner thereby agreed, or may be determined by the course of dealing between the parties.

(2) Where the price is not determined in accordance with the foregoing provisions the buyer must pay a reasonable price. What is a reasonable price is a question of fact dependent on the circumstances of each particular case.

11. (1) Where there is an agreement to sell goods on the terms that the price is to be fixed by the valuation of a third party, and such third party cannot or does not make such valuation, the agreement is avoided: Agreement to sell at valuation.

Provided that if the goods or any part thereof have been delivered to and appropriated by the buyer he must pay a reasonable price therefor.

(2) Where such third party is prevented from making the valuation by the fault of the seller or buyer, the party not in fault may maintain an action for damages against the party in fault.

Conditions and Warranties

12. (1) Unless a different intention appears from the terms of the contract, stipulations as to time of payment are not deemed to be of the essence of a contract of sale. Whether any other stipulation as to time is of the essence of the contract or not depends on the terms of the contract. Stipulations as to time.

(2) In a contract of sale "month" means *prima facie* calendar month.

13. (1) Where a contract of sale is subject to any condition to be fulfilled by the seller, the buyer may waive the condition, or may elect to treat the breach of such condition as a breach of warranty, and not as a ground for treating the contract as repudiated. When condition to be treated as warranty.

(2) Whether a stipulation in a contract of sale is a condition, the breach of which may give rise to a right to treat the contract as repudiated, or a warranty, the breach of which may give rise to a claim for damages, but not to a right to reject the goods and treat the contract as repudiated, depends in each case on the construction of the contract. A stipulation may be a condition, though called a warranty in a contract.

(3) Where a contract of sale is not severable, and the buyer has accepted the goods, or part thereof, or where the contract is for specific goods, the property in which has passed to the buyer, the breach of any condition to be fulfilled by the seller can only be treated as a breach of warranty, and not as a ground for rejecting the goods and treating the contract as repudiated, unless there be a term of the contract express or implied to that effect.

(4) Nothing in this section shall affect the case of any condition or warranty, fulfilment of which is excused by law by reason of impossibility or otherwise.

Implied undertaking as to title, etc.

14. In a contract of sale, unless the circumstances of the contract are such as to show a different intention, there is —

(a) an implied condition on the part of the seller that, in the case of a sale, he has a right to sell the goods, and that, in the case of an agreement to sell, he will have a right to sell the goods at the time when the property is to pass;

(b) an implied warranty that the buyer shall have and enjoy quiet possession of the goods;

(c) an implied warranty that the goods shall be free from any charge or encumbrance in favour of any third party, not declared or known to the buyer before or at the time when the contract is made.

Sale by description.

15. Where there is a contract for the sale of goods by description, there is an implied condition that the goods shall correspond with the description; and if the sale be by sample, as well as by description, it is not sufficient that the bulk of the goods corresponds with the same if the goods do not also correspond with the description.

Implied conditions as to quality or fitness.

16. Subject to the provisions of this Act and of any Act in that behalf, there is no implied warranty or condition as the quality or fitness for any particular purpose of goods supplied under a contract of sale, except as follows —

(a) where the buyer, expressly or by implication, makes known to the seller the particular purpose for which the goods are required, so as to show that the buyer relies on the seller's skill or judgment, and the goods are of a description which it is in the course of the seller's business to supply (whether he be the manufacturer or not), there is an implied condition that the goods shall be reasonably fit for such purpose:

Provided that in the case of a contract for the sale of a specified article under the patent or other trade name, there is no implied condition as to its fitness for any particular purpose;

(b) where goods are bought by description from a seller who deals in goods of that description (whether he be the manufacturer or not), there is an implied condition that the goods shall be of merchantable quality:

Provided that if the buyer has examined the goods, there shall be no implied condition as regards defects which such examination ought to have revealed;

(c) an implied warranty or condition as to quality or fitness for a particular purpose may be annexed by the usage of trade;

(d) an express warranty or condition does not negative a warranty or condition implied by this Act unless inconsistent therewith.

Sale by Sample

17. (1) A contract of sale is a contract for sale by sample where there is a term in the contract, express or implied, to that effect. Sale by sample.

(2) In the case of a contract for sale by sample —

(a) there is an implied condition that the bulk shall correspond with the sample in quality;

(b) there is an implied condition that the buyer shall have a reasonable opportunity of comparing the bulk with the sample;

(c) there is an implied condition that the goods shall be free from any defect, rendering them unmerchantable, which would not be apparent on reasonable examination of the sample.

PART II
EFFECTS OF THE CONTRACT

Transfer of Property as between Seller and Buyer

18. Where there is a contract for the sale of unascertained goods no property in the goods is transferred to the buyer unless and until the goods are ascertained. Goods must be ascertained.

Property passes when intended to pass.

19. (1) Where there is a contract for the sale of specific or ascertained goods the property in them is transferred to the buyer at such time as the parties to the contract intend it to be transferred.

(2) For the purpose of ascertaining the intention of the parties regard shall be had to the terms of the contract, the conduct of the parties, and the circumstances of the case.

Rules for ascertaining intention.

20. Unless a different intention appears, the following are rules for ascertaining the intention of the parties as to the time at which the property in the goods is to pass to the buyer —

(a) where there is an unconditional contract for the sale of specific goods, in a deliverable state, the property in the goods passes to the buyer when the contract is made, and it is immaterial whether the time of payment or the time of delivery, or both, be postponed;

(b) where there is a contract for the sale of specific goods and the seller is bound to do something to the goods, for the purpose of putting them into a deliverable state, the property does not pass until such thing be done, and the buyer has notice thereof;

(c) where there is a contract for the sale of specific goods in a deliverable state, but the seller is bound to weigh, measure, test or do some other act or thing with reference to the goods for the purpose of ascertaining the price, the property does not pass until such act or thing be done, and the buyer has notice thereof;

(d) when goods are delivered to the buyer on approval or "on sale or return" or other similar terms, the property therein passes to the buyer —

(i) when he signifies his approval or acceptance to the seller or does any other act adopting the transaction;

(ii) if he does not signify his approval or acceptance to the seller but retains the goods without giving notice of rejection, then, if a time has been fixed for the return of the goods, on the expiration of such time, and if no time has been fixed, on the expiration of a reasonable time. What is a reasonable time is a question of fact;

(e) where there is a contract for the sale of unascertained or future goods by description, and goods of that description and in a deliverable state are unconditionally appropriated to the contract, either by the seller with the assent of the buyer, or by the buyer with the assent of the seller, the property in the goods thereupon passes to the buyer. Such assent may be express or implied, and may be given either before or after the appropriation is made;

(f) where, in pursuance of the contract, the seller delivers the goods to the buyer or to a carrier or other bailee (whether named by the buyer or not) for the purpose of transmission to the buyer, and does not reserve the right of disposal, he is deemed to have unconditionally appropriated the goods to the contract.

Reservation of right of disposal.

21. (1) Where there is a contract for the sale of specific goods or where goods are subsequently appropriated to the contract, the seller may, by the terms of the contract or appropriation, reserve the right of disposal of the goods until certain conditions are fulfilled. In such case, notwithstanding the delivery of the goods to the buyer or to a carrier or other bailee for the purpose of transmission to the buyer the property in the goods does not pass to the buyer until the conditions imposed by the seller are fulfilled.

(2) Where goods are shipped, and by the bill of lading the goods are deliverable to the order of the seller or his agent, the seller is *prima facie* deemed to reserve the right of disposal.

(3) Where the seller of goods draws on the buyer for the price, and transmits the bill of exchange and bill of lading to the buyer together, to secure acceptance or payment of the bill of exchange, the buyer is bound to return the bill of lading if he does not honour the bill of exchange, and if he wrongfully retains the bill of lading the property in the goods does not pass to him.

Risk *prima facie* passes with property.

22. Unless otherwise agreed, the goods remain at the seller's risk until the property therein is transferred to the buyer, but when the property therein is transferred to the buyer, the goods are at the buyer's risk whether delivery has been made or not:

Provided that where delivery has been delayed through the fault of either buyer or seller the goods are at the risk of the party in fault as regards any loss which might not have occurred but for such fault:

Provided also that nothing in this section shall affect the duties or liabilities of either seller or buyer as a bailee of the goods of the other party.

Transfer of Title

Sale by person not the owner.

23. Subject to the provisions of this Act, where goods are sold by a person who is not the owner thereof, and who does not sell them under the authority or with the consent of the owner, the buyer acquires no better title to the goods than the seller had, unless the owner of the goods is by his conduct precluded from denying the seller's authority to sell:

Provided that nothing in this Act shall affect —

Ch. 333.

(a) the provisions of the Mercantile Agents Act, or any Act enabling the apparent owner of goods to dispose of them as if he were the true owner thereof;

(b) the validity of any contract of sale under any special common law or statutory power of sale or under the order of a court of competent jurisdiction.

Sale under voidable title.

24. When the seller of goods has a voidable title thereto, but his title has not been avoided at the time of the sale, the buyer acquires a good title to the goods, provided he buys them in good faith and without notice of the seller's defect of title.

Reverting of property in stolen goods etc., on conviction of offender.

25. (1) Where goods have been stolen and the offender is prosecuted to conviction, the property in the goods so stolen revests in the person who was the owner of the goods, or his personal representative, notwithstanding any intermediate dealing with them, whether by sale in market overt or otherwise.

(2) Notwithstanding any Act to the contrary, where goods have been obtained by fraud or other wrongful means not amounting to larceny, the property in such goods shall not revest in the person who was the owner of the goods, or his personal representative by reason only of the conviction of the offender.

Seller or buyer in possession after sale.

26. (1) Where a person, having sold goods, continues or is in possession of the goods, or of the documents of title to the goods the delivery or transfer by that person, or by a mercantile agent acting for him, of the goods or documents of title under any sale, pledge or other disposition thereof, to any person receiving the same in good faith and without notice of the previous sale, shall have the same effect as if the person making the delivery or transfer were expressly authorised by the owner of the goods to make the same.

(2) Where a person, having bought or agreed to buy goods, obtains, with the consent of the seller, possession of the goods or the documents of title to the goods, the delivery or transfer by that person, or by a mercantile agent acting for him, of the goods or documents of title, under any sale, pledge or other disposition thereof, to any person receiving the same in good faith and without notice of any lien or other right of the original seller in respect of the goods, shall have the same affect as if the person making the delivery or transfer were a mercantile agent in possession of the goods or documents of title with the consent of the owner.

Effect of writs of execution.

27. A writ of *fieri facias* or other writ of execution against goods shall bind the property in the goods of the execution debtor as from the time when the writ is delivered to the officer charged with the duty of executing it; and, for the better manifestation of such time, it shall be the duty of such officer, without fee, upon the receipt of any such writ to endorse upon the back thereof the hour, day, month and year when he received the same:

Provided that no such writ shall prejudice the title to such goods acquired by any person in good faith and for valuable consideration, unless such person had at the time when he acquired his title notice that such writ or any writ by virtue of which the goods of the execution debtor might be seized or attached had been delivered to and remained unexecuted in the hands of such officer.

PART III
PERFORMANCE OF CONTRACT

Duties of seller and buyer.

28. It is the duty of the seller to deliver the goods, and of the buyer to accept and pay for them, in accordance with the terms of the contract of sale.

Payment and delivery are concurrent conditions.

29. Unless otherwise agreed, delivery of the goods and payment of the price are concurrent conditions, that is to say, the seller must be ready and willing to give possession of the goods to the buyer in exchange for the price, and the buyer must be ready and willing to pay the price in exchange for the possession of the goods.

Rules as to delivery.

30. (1) Whether it is for the buyer to take possession of the goods or for the seller to send them to the buyer is a question depending in each case on the contract, express or implied, between the parties. Apart from any such contract, express or implied, the place of delivery is the seller's place of business, if he has one, and if not, his residence:

Provided that if the contract be for the sale of specific goods, which to the knowledge of the parties when the contract is made are in some other place, then that place is the place of delivery.

(2) Where under the contract of sale the seller is bound to send the goods to the buyer, but no time for sending them is fixed, the seller is bound to send them within a reasonable time.

(3) Where the goods at the time of sale are in the possession of a third person, there is no delivery by seller to buyer unless and until such third person acknowledges to the buyer that he holds the goods on his behalf:

Provided that nothing in this section shall affect the operation of the issue or transfer of any document of title to goods.

(4) Demand or tender of delivery may be treated as ineffectual unless made at a reasonable hour. What is a reasonable hour is a question of fact.

(5) Unless otherwise agreed, the expenses of and incidental to putting the goods in a deliverable state must be borne by the seller.

Delivery of wrong quantity.

31. (1) Where the seller delivers to the buyer a quantity of goods less than he contracted to sell, the buyer may reject them, but if the buyer accepts the goods so delivered he must pay for them at the contract rate.

(2) Where the seller delivers to the buyer a quantity of goods larger than he contracted to sell, the buyer may accept the goods included in the contract and reject the

rest, or he may reject the whole. If the buyer accepts the whole of the goods so delivered he must pay for them at the contract rate.

(3) Where the seller delivers to the buyer the goods he contracted to sell mixed with goods of a different description not included in the contract, the buyer may accept the goods which are in accordance with the contract and reject the rest, or he may reject the whole.

(4) The provisions of this section are subject to any usage of trade, special agreement or course of dealing between the parties.

Instalment deliveries.

32. (1) Unless otherwise agreed, the buyer of goods is not bound to accept delivery thereof by instalments.

(2) Where there is a contract for the sale of goods to be delivered by stated instalments, which are to be separately paid for, and the seller makes defective deliveries in respect of one or more instalments, or the buyer neglects or refuses to take delivery of or pay for one or more instalments, it is a question in each case depending on the terms of the contract and the circumstances of the case, whether the breach of contract is a repudiation of the whole contract or whether it is a severable breach giving rise to a claim for compensation, but not to a right to treat the whole contract as repudiated.

Delivery to carrier.

33. (1) Where in pursuance of a contract of sale, the seller is authorised or required to send the goods to the buyer, delivery of the goods to a carrier whether named by the buyer or not, for the purpose of transmission to the buyer is *prima facie* deemed to be a delivery of the goods to the buyer.

(2) Unless otherwise authorised by the buyer, the seller must make such contract with the carrier on behalf of the buyer as may be reasonable having regard to the nature of the goods and the other circumstances of the case. If the seller omits so to do, and the goods are lost or damaged in course of transit, the buyer may decline to treat the delivery to the carrier as a delivery to himself, or may hold the seller responsible in damages.

(3) Unless otherwise agreed, where goods are sent by the seller to the buyer by a route involving sea transit, under circumstances in which it is usual to insure, the seller must give such notice to the buyer as may enable him to

insure them during their sea transit, and, if the seller fails to do so, the goods shall be deemed to be at his risk during such sea transit.

Risk where goods are delivered at distant place.

34. Where the seller of goods agrees to deliver them at his own risk at a place other than that where they are when sold, the buyer must, nevertheless, unless otherwise agreed, take any risk of deterioration in the goods necessarily incident to the course of transit.

Buyer's right of examining the goods.

35. (1) Where goods are delivered to the buyer, which he has not previously examined, he is not deemed to have accepted them unless and until he has had a reasonable opportunity of examining them for the purpose of ascertaining whether they are in conformity with the contract.

(2) Unless otherwise agreed, when the seller tenders delivery of goods to the buyer, he is bound, on request, to afford the buyer a reasonable opportunity of examining the goods for the purpose of ascertaining whether they are in conformity with the contract.

Acceptance.

36. The buyer is deemed to have accepted the goods when he intimates to the seller that he has accepted them, or when the goods have been delivered to him, and he does any act in relation to them which is inconsistent with the ownership of the seller, or when after the lapse of a reasonable time, he retains the goods without intimating to the seller that he has rejected them.

Buyer not bound to return rejected goods.

37. Unless otherwise agreed, where goods are delivered to the buyer, and he refuses to accept them, having the right so to do, he is not bound to return them to the seller, but it is sufficient if he intimates to the seller that he refuses to accept them.

Liability of buyer for neglecting or refusing delivery of goods.

38. When the seller is ready and willing to deliver the goods, and requests the buyer to take delivery, and the buyer does not within a reasonable time after such request take delivery of the goods, he is liable to the seller for any loss occasioned by his neglect or refusal to take delivery, and also for a reasonable charge for the care and custody of the goods:

Provided that nothing in this section shall affect the rights of the seller where the neglect or refusal of the buyer to take delivery amounts to a repudiation of the contract.

PART IV
RIGHTS OF UNPAID SELLER AGAINST THE GOODS

"Unpaid seller" defined.

39. (1) The seller of goods is deemed to be an "unpaid seller" within the meaning of this Act —

(a) when the whole of the price has not been paid or tendered;

(b) when a bill of exchange or other negotiable instrument has been received as conditional payment, and the condition on which it was received has not been fulfilled by reason of the dishonour of the instrument or otherwise.

(2) In this Part of this Act the term "seller" includes any person who is in the position of a seller, as, for instance, an agent of the seller to whom the bill of lading has been indorsed, or a consignor or agent who has himself paid, or is directly responsible for, the price.

Unpaid seller's rights.

40. (1) Subject to the provisions of this Act, and of any Act in that behalf, notwithstanding that the property in the goods may have passed to the buyer, the unpaid seller of goods, as such, has by implication of law —

(a) a lien on the goods for the price while he is in possession of them;

(b) in the case of the insolvency of the buyer, a right of stopping the goods *in transitu* after he has parted with the possession of them;

(c) a right of re-sale as limited by this Act.

(2) Where the property in goods has not passed to the buyer, the unpaid seller has, in addition to his other remedies, a right of withholding delivery similar to and co-extensive with his rights of lien and stoppage *in transitu* where the property has passed to the buyer.

Unpaid Seller's Lien

Seller's lien.

41. (1) Subject to the provisions of this Act, the unpaid seller of goods who is in possession of them is entitled to retain possession of them until payment or tender of the price in the following cases, namely —

(a) where the goods have been sold without any stipulation as to credit;

(b) where the goods have been sold on credit, but the term of credit has expired;

(c) where the buyer becomes insolvent.

(2) The seller may exercise his right of lien notwithstanding that he is in possession of the goods as agent or bailee for the buyer.

Part delivery.

42. Where an unpaid seller has made part delivery of the goods, he may exercise his right of lien on the remainder, unless such part delivery has been made under such circumstances as to show an agreement to waive the lien.

Termination of lien.

43. (1) The unpaid seller of goods loses his lien thereon —

(a) when he delivers the goods to a carrier or other bailee for the purpose of transmission to the buyer without reserving the right of disposal of the goods;

(b) when the buyer or his agent lawfully obtains possession of the goods;

(c) by waiver thereof.

(2) The unpaid seller of goods, having a lien thereon, does not lose his lien by reason only that he has obtained judgment for the price of the goods.

Stoppage *in Transitu*

Right of stoppage *in transitu*.

44. Subject to the provisions of this Act, when the buyer of goods becomes insolvent, the unpaid seller who has parted with the possession of the goods has the right of stopping them *in transitu*, that is to say, he may resume possession of the goods, as long as they are in course of transit, and may retain them until payment or tender of the price.

45. (1) Goods are deemed to be in course of transit from the time when they are delivered to a carrier by land or water, or other bailee for the purpose of transmission to the buyer, until the buyer, or his agent in that behalf, takes delivery of them from such carrier or other bailee. Duration of transit.

(2) If the buyer or his agent in that behalf obtains delivery of the goods before their arrival at the appointed destination, the transit is at an end.

(3) If, after the arrival of the goods at the appointed destination, the carrier or other bailee acknowledges to the buyer or his agent, that he holds the goods on his behalf, and continues in possession of them as bailee for the buyer or his agent, the transit is at an end, and it is immaterial that a further destination for the goods may have been indicated by the buyer.

(4) If the goods are rejected by the buyer, and the carrier or other bailee continues in possession of them, the transit is not deemed to be at an end, even if the seller has refused to receive them back.

(5) When goods are delivered to a ship chartered by the buyer it is a question depending upon the circumstances of the particular case whether they are in the possession of the master as a carrier or as agent to the buyer.

(6) Where the carrier or other bailee wrongfully refuses to deliver the goods to the buyer, or his agent in that behalf, the transit is deemed to be at an end.

(7) Where part delivery of the goods has been made to the buyer, or his agent in that behalf, the remainder of the goods may be stopped *in transitu*, unless such part delivery has been made under such circumstances as to show an agreement to give up possession of the whole of the goods.

46. (1) The unpaid seller may exercise his right of stoppage *in transitu* either by taking actual possession of the goods, or by giving notice of his claim to the carrier or other bailee in whose possession the goods are. Such notice may be given either to the person in actual possession of the goods, or to his principal. In the latter case the notice, to be effectual, must be given at such time and under such circumstances that the principal, by the exercise of reasonable diligence, may communicate it to his servant or agent in time to prevent a delivery to the buyer. How stoppage *in transitu* is effected.

(2) When notice of stoppage *in transitu* is given by the seller to the carrier, or other bailee in possession of the goods, he must re-deliver the goods to, or according to the directions of, the seller. The expenses of such re-delivery must be borne by the seller.

Re-sale by Buyer or Seller

Effect of sub-sale or pledge by buyer.

47. Subject to the provisions of this Act, the unpaid seller's right of lien or stoppage *in transitu* is not affected by any sale, or other disposition of the goods which the buyer may have made, unless the seller has assented thereto:

Provided that where a document of title to goods has been lawfully transferred to any person as buyer or owner of the goods, and that person transfers the document to a person who takes the document in good faith and for valuable consideration, then, if such last-mentioned transfer was by way of sale, the unpaid seller's right of lien or stoppage *in transitu* is defeated, and if such last-mentioned transfer was by way of pledge, or other disposition for value, the unpaid seller's right of lien or stoppage *in transitu* can only be exercised subject to the rights of the transferee.

Sale not generally rescinded by lien or stoppage *in transitu.*

48. (1) Subject to the provisions of this section, a contract of sale is not rescinded by the mere exercise by an unpaid seller of his right of lien or stoppage *in transitu*.

(2) Where an unpaid seller who has exercised his right of lien or stoppage *in transitu* re-sells the goods, the buyer acquires a good title thereto as against the original buyer.

(3) Where the goods are of a perishable nature, or where the unpaid seller gives notice to the buyer of his intention to re-sell, and the buyer does not within a reasonable time pay or tender the price, the unpaid seller may re-sell the goods and recover from the original buyer damages for any loss occasioned by his breach of contract.

(4) Where the seller expressly reserves a right of resale in case the buyer should make default, and, on the buyer making default, re-sells the goods, the original contract of sale is thereby rescinded, but without prejudice to any claim the seller may have for damages.

PART V
ACTIONS FOR BREACH OF THE CONTRACT

Remedies of the Seller

Action for price.

49. (1) Where, under a contract of sale, the property in the goods has passed to the buyer, and the buyer wrongfully neglects or refuses to pay for the goods according to the terms of the contract, the seller may maintain an action against him for the price of the goods.

(2) Where, under a contract of sale, the price is payable on a day certain irrespective of delivery, and the buyer wrongfully neglects or refuses to pay such price, the seller may maintain an action for the price, although the property in the goods has not passed, and the goods have not been appropriated to the contract.

Damages for non-acceptance.

50. (1) Where the buyer wrongfully neglects or refuses to accept and pay for the goods, the seller may maintain an action against him for damages for non-acceptance.

(2) The measure of damages is the estimated loss directly and naturally resulting, in the ordinary course of events, from the buyer's breach of contract.

(3) Where there is an available market for the goods in question the measure of damages is *prima facie* to be ascertained by the difference between the contract price and the market or current price at the time or times when the goods ought to have been accepted, or, if no time was fixed for acceptance, then at the time of the refusal to accept.

Remedies of the Buyer

Damages for non-delivery.

51. (1) Where the seller wrongfully neglects or refuses to deliver the goods to the buyer, the buyer may maintain an action against the seller for damages for non-delivery.

(2) The measure of damages is the estimated loss directly and naturally resulting, in the ordinary course of events, from the seller's breach of contract.

(3) Where there is an available market for the goods in question the measure of damages is *prima facie* to be ascertained by the difference between the contract price and the market or current price of the goods, at the time or times when they ought to have been delivered, or, if no time was fixed, then at the time of the refusal to deliver.

Specific performance.

52. In any action for breach of contract to deliver specific or ascertained goods the court may, if it thinks fit, on the application of the plaintiff, by its judgment direct that the contract shall be performed specifically, without giving the defendant the option of retaining the goods on payment of damages. The judgment may be unconditional, or upon such terms and conditions as to damages, payment of the price, and otherwise, as to the court may seem just, and the application by the plaintiff may be made at any time before judgment.

Remedy for breach of warranty.

53. (1) Where there is a breach of warranty by the seller, or where the buyer elects, or is compelled, to treat any breach of a condition on the part of the seller as a breach of warranty, the buyer is not by reason only of such breach of warranty entitled to reject the goods; but he may —

(a) set up against the seller the breach of warranty in diminution or extinction of the price; or

(b) maintain an action against the seller for damages for the breach of warranty.

(2) The measure of damages for breach of warranty is the estimated loss directly and naturally resulting, in the ordinary course of events, from the breach of warranty.

(3) In the case of breach of warranty of quality such loss is *prima facie* the difference between the value of the goods at the time of delivery to the buyer and the value they would have had if they had answered to the warranty.

(4) The fact that the buyer has set up the breach of warranty in diminution or extinction of the price does not prevent him from maintaining an action for the same breach of warranty if he has suffered further damage.

Interest and special damages.

54. Nothing in this Act shall affect the right of the buyer or the seller to recover interest or special damages in any case where by law interest or special damages may be recoverable, or to recover money paid where the consideration for the payment of it has failed.

PART VI
SUPPLEMENTARY

Exclusion of implied terms and conditions.

55. Where any right, duty or liability would arise under a contract of sale, by implication of law, it may be negatived or varied by express agreement or by the course of dealing between the parties, or by usage, if the usage be such as to bind both parties to the contract.

Reasonable time a question of fact.

56. Where, by this Act, any reference is made to a reasonable time, the question what is a reasonable time is a question of fact.

Rights, duties and liabilities enforceable by action.

57. Where any right, duty or liability is declared by this Act, it may, unless otherwise by this Act provided, be enforced by action.

Auction sales.

58. In the case of a sale by auction —

(a) where goods are put up for sale by auction in lots, each lot is *prima facie* deemed to be the subject of a separate contract of sale;

(b) a sale by auction is complete when the auctioneer announces its completion by the fall of the hammer, or in other customary manner. Until such announcement is made any bidder may retract his bid;

(c) where a sale by auction is not notified to be subject to a right to bid on behalf of the seller, it shall not be lawful for the seller to bid himself or to employ any person to bid at such sale, or for the auctioneer knowingly to take any bid from the seller or any such person; any sale contravening this rule may be treated as fraudulent by the buyer;

(d) a sale by auction may be notified to be subject to a reserved price, and a right to bid may also be reserved expressly by or on behalf of the seller;

(e) where a right to bid is expressly reserved, but not otherwise, the seller, or any one person on his behalf, may bid at the auction.

Savings.

59. (1) The rules in bankruptcy relating to contracts of sale shall continue to apply thereto, notwithstanding anything in this Act contained.

(2) The rules of the common law, including the law merchant, save in so far as they are inconsistent with the express provisions of this Act, and in particular the rules relating to the law of principal and agent and the effect of fraud, misrepresentation, duress or coercion, mistake or other invalidating cause, shall continue to apply to contracts for the sale of goods.

(3) Nothing in this Act or in any repeal effected thereby shall affect any Act relating to the sale of goods which is not expressly repealed by this Act.

(4) The provisions of this Act relating to contracts of sale do not apply to any transaction in the form of a contract of sale which is intended to operate by way of mortgage, pledge, charge or other security.

CHAPTER 337B

UNFAIR TERMS IN CONSUMER CONTRACTS

LIST OF AUTHORISED PAGES

1 - 10 LRO 1/2008

ARRANGEMENT OF SECTIONS

CHAPTER 337B

UNFAIR TERMS IN CONSUMER CONTRACTS

An Act for the regulation of unfair terms in consumer contracts and related matters. *1 of 2006*

[Assent 6th February, 2006]

[Commencement 19th March 2007] *S.I. 14/2007.*

1. This Act may be cited as the Unfair Terms in Consumer Contracts Act. Short title.

2. (1) In this Act — Interpretation.

"business" includes a trade or profession and the activities of any government department or local or public authority;

"consumer" means a natural person who, in making a contract to which this Act applies, is acting for purposes which are outside his business;

"court" means the Supreme Court;

"Minister" means the Minister responsible for Consumer Protection;

"seller" means a person who sells goods and who, in making a contract to which this Act applies, is acting for purposes relating to his business;

"supplier" means a person who supplies goods or services and who, in making a contract to which this Act applies, is acting for purposes relating to his business.

3. (1) Subject to the provisions of the First Schedule, this Act applies to any term in a contract concluded between a seller or supplier and a consumer where such term has not been individually negotiated. Terms to which this Act applies. First Schedule.

(2) In so far as it is in plain, intelligible language, no assessment shall be made of the fairness of any term which —

(a) defines the main subject matter of the contract; or

(b) concerns the adequacy of the price or remuneration, as against the goods or services sold or supplied.

(3) For the purposes of this Act, a term shall always be regarded as not having been individually negotiated where it has been drafted in advance and the consumer has not been able to influence the substance of the term.

(4) Notwithstanding that a specific term or certain aspects of it in a contract has been individually negotiated, this Act shall apply to the rest of a contract if an overall assessment of the contract indicates that it is a pre-formulated standard contract.

(5) It shall be for any seller or supplier who claims that a term was individually negotiated to show that it was so negotiated.

Unfair terms.

4. (1) In this Act, subject to subsections (2) and (3), "unfair term" means any term which contrary to the requirement of good faith causes a significant imbalance in the parties' rights and obligations under the contract to the detriment of the consumer.

(2) An assessment of the unfair nature of a term shall be made taking into account the nature of the goods or services for which the contract was concluded and referring, as at the time of the conclusion of the contract, to all circumstances attending the conclusion of the contract and to all the other terms of the contract or of another contract on which it is dependent.

Second Schedule.

(3) In determining whether a term satisfies the requirement of good faith, regard shall be had in particular to the matters specified in the Second Schedule.

Third Schedule.

(4) The Third Schedule contains an indicative and non-exhaustive list of the terms which may be regarded as unfair.

Consequence of inclusion of unfair terms in contracts.

5. (1) An unfair term in a contract concluded with a consumer by a seller or supplier shall not be binding on the consumer.

(2) The contract shall continue to bind the parties if it is capable of continuing in existence without the unfair term.

Construction of written contracts.

6. A seller or supplier shall ensure that any written term of a contract is expressed in plain, intelligible language, and if there is doubt about the meaning of a written term, the interpretation most favourable to the consumer shall prevail.

Prevention of continued use of unfair terms.

7. (1) The Minister may consider any complaint made to him that any contract term drawn up for general use is unfair, unless the complaint appears to the Minister to be frivolous or vexatious.

(2) If having considered a complaint about any contract term pursuant to paragraph (1) the Minister considers that the contract term is unfair he may, if he considers it appropriate to do so, refer the matter to the Attorney-General to bring proceedings for an injunction (in which proceedings the Attorney-General may also apply for an interlocutory injunction) against any person appearing to him to be using or recommending use of such a term in contracts concluded with consumers.

(3) The Minister may, if he considers it appropriate to do so, have regard to any undertakings given to him by or on behalf of any person as to the continued use of such a term in contracts concluded with consumers.

(4) The Minister shall give reasons for his decision to apply or not to apply, as the case may be, for an injunction in relation to any complaint which this Act requires him to consider.

(5) The court may, on an application by the Attorney-General grant an injunction on such terms as it thinks fit.

(6) An injunction may relate not only to use of a particular contract term drawn up for general use but to any similar term, or a term having like effect, used or recommended for use by any party to the proceedings.

(7) The Minister may arrange for the dissemination in such form and manner as he considers appropriate of such information and advice concerning the operation of this Act as may appear to him to be expedient to give to the public and to all persons likely to be affected by this Act.

Application.

8. This Act shall apply to contracts entered into before, on or after this Act comes into operation.

FIRST SCHEDULE (Section 3 (1))

Contracts and Particular Terms Excluded from the Scope of this Act

This Act does not apply to —

(a) any contract relating to employment;

(b) any contract relating to succession rights;

(c) any contract relating to rights under family law;

(d) any contract relating to the incorporation and organisation of companies or partnerships;

(e) any term incorporated in order to comply with or which reflects —

  (i) statutory or regulatory provisions of The Bahamas; or

  (ii) the provisions or principles of international conventions to which The Bahamas is a party.

SECOND SCHEDULE (Section 4 (3))

Assessment of Good Faith

In making an assessment of good faith, regard shall be had in particular to —

(a) the strength of the bargaining positions of the parties;

(b) whether the consumer had an inducement to agree to the term;

(c) whether the goods or services were sold or supplied to the special order of the consumer; and

(d) the extent to which the seller or supplier has dealt fairly and equitably with the consumer.

THIRD SCHEDULE (Section 4 (4))

Indicative and Illustrative List of Terms which may be Regarded as Unfair

1. Terms which have the object or effect of —

(a) excluding or limiting the legal liability of a seller or supplier in the event of the death of a consumer or personal injury to the latter resulting from an act or omission of that seller or supplier;

(b) inappropriately excluding or limiting the legal rights of the consumer vis-à-vis the seller or supplier or another party in the event of total or partial non-performance or inadequate performance by the seller or supplier of any of the contractual obligations, including the option of offsetting a debt owed to the seller or supplier against any claim which the consumer may have against him;

(c) making an agreement binding on the consumer whereas provision of services by the seller or supplier is subject to a condition whose realisation depends on his own will alone;

(d) permitting the seller or supplier to retain sums paid by the consumer where the latter decides not to conclude or perform the contract, without providing for the consumer to receive compensation of an equivalent amount from the seller or supplier where the latter is the party cancelling the contract;

(e) requiring any consumer who fails to fulfil his obligation to pay a disproportionately high sum in compensation;

(f) authorising the seller or supplier to dissolve the contract on a discretionary basis where the same facility is not granted to the consumer, or permitting the seller or supplier to retain the sums paid for services not yet supplied by him where it is the seller or supplier himself who dissolves the contract;

(g) enabling the seller or supplier to terminate a contract of indeterminate duration without reasonable notice except where there are serious grounds for doing so;

(h) automatically extending a contract of fixed duration where the consumer does not indicate otherwise, when the deadline fixed for the consumer to express this desire not to extend the contract is unreasonably early;

(i) irrevocably binding the consumer to terms with which he had no real opportunity of becoming acquainted before the conclusion of the contract;

(j) enabling the seller or supplier to alter the terms of the contract unilaterally without a valid reason which is specified in the contract;

(k) enabling the seller or supplier to alter unilaterally without a valid reason any characteristics of the product or service to be provided;

(l) providing for the price of goods to be determined at the time of delivery or allowing a seller of goods or supplier of services to increase their price without in both cases giving the consumer the corresponding right to cancel the contract if the final price is too high in relation to the price agreed when the contract was concluded;

(m) giving the seller or supplier the right to determine whether the goods or services supplied are in conformity with the contract, or giving him the exclusive right to interpret any term of the contract;

(n) limiting the seller's or supplier's obligation to respect commitments undertaken by his agents or making his commitments subject to compliance with a particular formality;

(o) obliging the consumer to fulfil all his obligations where the seller or supplier does not perform his;

(p) giving the seller or supplier the possibility of transferring his rights and obligations under the contract, where this may serve to reduce the guarantees for the consumer, without the latter's agreement;

(q) excluding or hindering the consumer's right to take legal action or exercise any other legal remedy, particularly by requiring the consumer to take disputes exclusively to arbitration not covered by legal provisions, unduly restricting the evidence available to him or imposing on him a burden of proof which, according to the applicable law, should lie with another party to the contract.

2. Scope of sub-paragraphs (g), (j) and (l) of paragraph 1.

(a) Sub-paragraph (g) is without hindrance to terms by which a supplier of financial services reserves the right to terminate unilaterally a contract of indeterminate duration without notice where there is a valid reason, provided that the supplier is required to inform the other contracting party or parties thereof immediately.

(b) Sub-paragraph (j) is without hindrance to terms under which a supplier of financial services reserves the right to alter the rate of interest payable by the consumer or due to the latter, or the amount of other charges for financial services without notice where there is a valid reason, provided that the supplier is required to inform the other contracting party or parties thereof at the earliest opportunity and that the latter are free to dissolve the contract immediately.

Sub-paragraph (j) is also without hindrance to terms under which a seller or supplier reserves the right to alter unilaterally the conditions of a contract of indeterminate duration, provided that he is required to inform the consumer with reasonable notice and that the consumer is free to dissolve the contract.

(c) Sub-paragraphs (g), (j) and (1) do not apply to —

(i) transactions in transferable securities, financial instruments and other products or services where the price is linked to fluctuations in a stock exchange quotation or index or a financial market rate that the seller or supplier does not control; and

(ii) contracts for the purchase or sale of foreign currency, traveller's cheques or international money orders denominated in foreign currency.

(d) Sub-paragraph (1) is without hindrance to price indexation clauses, where lawful, provided that the method by which prices vary is explicitly described.

CHAPTER 201

THE HIRE-PURCHASE ACT

Arrangement of Sections
Section

HIRE-PURCHASE

An Act to provide for the regulation of hire-purchase and sale upon credit of Goods and for matters incidental thereto.

(26th February, 1987.) **7/1987.**

1. (1) This Act may be cited as the Hire-Purchase Act. **Short title.**

2. In this Act— **Interpretation.**

"action" includes counterclaim and set-off;

"buyer" means a person who buys or agrees to buy goods;

"contract of guarantee" means, in relation to a hire-purchase or credit-sale agreement, a contract made at the request, express or implied, of the hirer or buyer to guarantee the performance of the hirer's or buyer's obligations under the hire-purchase agreement or credit-sale agreement, and the expression "guarantor" shall be construed accordingly;

"credit-sale agreement" means an agreement for the sale of goods under which the purchase price is payable by five or more instalments;

"delivery" means voluntary transfer of possession from one person to another;

"goods" includes all chattels personal other than things in action and money; the term includes emblements, industrial growing crops, and things attached to or forming part of the land, which are agreed to be severed before sale or under the contract of sale;

"hire-purchase agreement" means an agreement for the bailment of goods under which the bailee may buy the goods or under which the property in goods will or may pass to the bailee, and where by virtue of two or more agreements, none of which by itself constitutes a hire-purchase agreement, there is a bailment of goods and either the bailee may buy the goods, or the property therein will or may pass to the bailee, the agreements shall be treated for the purposes of this Act as a single agreement made at the time when the last of the agreements was made:

"hire-purchase price" means the total sum payable by the hirer under a hire-purchase agreement in order to complete the purchase of goods to which the agreement relates, exclusive of any sum payable as a penalty or as compensation or damages for a breach of the agreement and includes any sum payable by the hirer under a hire-purchase agreement by way of a deposit or other initial payment or credited or to be credited to him under such an agreement on account of any such deposit or payment, whether that sum is to be or has been paid to the owner or to any other person or is to be or has been discharged by a payment of money or by the transfer or delivery of goods or by any other means;

"hirer" means the person who takes or has taken goods from an owner under a hire-purchase agreement and includes a person to whom the hirer's rights or liabilities under the agreement have passed by assignment or by operation of law;

"owner" means the person who proposes to let, or has let goods to a hirer under a hire-purchase agreement and includes a person to whom the owner's property in the goods or any of the owner's rights or liabilities under the agreement has passed by assignment or by operation of law;

"property" means the general property in goods, and not merely a special property;

"sale" includes a bargain and sale, as well as a sale delivery;

"seller" means a person who sells or agrees to sell goods;

"total purchase price" means the total sum payable by the buyer under a credit-sale agreement, exclusive of any sum payable as a penalty or as compensation or damages for a breach of the agreement;

"warranty" means an agreement with reference to goods which are the subject of a contract of sale, but collateral to the main purpose of such contract, the breach of which gives rise to a claim for damages but not a right to reject the goods and treat the contract as repudiated.

(2) Where an owner has agreed that any part of the hire-purchase price may be discharged otherwise than by the payment of money, such a discharge is deemed for the purpose of sections 6 and 8 to be a payment of that part of the purchase price.

Application of Act.

3. This Act applies to all hire-purchase agreements and credit-sale agreements under which the hire purchase price or total purchase price, does not exceed the sum of twenty thousand dollars.

Requirements relating to hire-purchase agreements.

4. (1) Before a hire-purchase agreement is entered into in respect of any goods, the owner shall state in writing to the prospective hirer, otherwise than in the note or memorandum of the agreement, a price at which the goods may be purchased for cash (in this section referred to as the "cash price").

(2) An owner is deemed to have complied with subsection (1)—

(a) if the hirer has inspected the goods or like goods and at the time of his inspection tickets or labels were attached to or displayed with the goods clearly stating

LAWS OF ANTIGUA AND BARBUDA

CAP. 201) Hire-Purchase

the cash price, either of the goods as a whole or of all the different articles or sets of articles comprised therein; or

(b) if the hirer has selected the goods by reference to a catalogue, price list, or advertisement, which clearly stated the cash price either of the goods as a whole or of all the different articles or sets of articles comprised therein.

(3) An owner is not entitled to enforce a hire-purchase agreement or any contract of guarantee relating thereto or any right to recover the goods from the hirer, and no security given by the hirer in respect of money payable under the hire-purchase agreement or given by a guarantor in respect of money payable under such a contract of guarantee is enforceable against the hirer or guarantor by any holder therof, unless subsection (1) has been complied with, and—

(a) a note or memorandum of the agreement is made and signed by the hirer and by or on behalf of all other parties to the agreement;

(*b*) the note or memorandum contains a statement of the hire-purchase price and of the cash price of the goods to which the agreement relates and of the amount of each of the instalments by which the hire-purchase price is to be paid and of the date, or the mode of determining the date, upon which each instalment is payable, and contains a list of the goods to which the agreement relates sufficient to identify them;

Schedule.

(c) the note or memorandum contains a notice, which is at least as prominent as the rest of the contents of the note or memorandum, in the terms prescribed in the Schedule; and

(d) a copy of the note or memorandum is delivered or sent to the hirer at his address as contained in the agreement within seven days of the making of the agreement.

(4) Where in an action the court is satisfied that a failure to comply with subsection (1) or with paragraph (b), (c) or (*d*) of subsection **(3)** has not prejudiced the hirer; and that it would be just and equitable to dispense with compliance,

the court may, subject to any conditions that it thinks fit to impose, dispense with such compliance for the purpose of the action.

5. (1) Before making a credit-sale agreement under which the total purchase price exceeds two hundred dollars, the seller shall state in writing to the prospective buyer, otherwise than in the note or memorandum of the agreement, a price at which the goods may be purchased for cash (in this section referred to as the "cash price"). **Requirements relating to credit-sale agreements.**

(2) A seller is deemed to have complied with subsection (1)—

(a) if the buyer has inspected the goods or like goods and at the time of his inspection tickets or labels were attached to or displayed with the goods clearly stating the cash price, either of the goods as a whole or of all the different articles or sets of articles comprised therein; or

(b) if the buyer has selected the goods by reference to a catalogue, price list or advertisement which clearly stated the cash price either of the goods as a whole or of all the different articles or sets of articles comprised therein.

(3) A person who has sold goods by a credit-sale agreement under which the total purchase price exceeds two hundred dollars is not entitled to enforce the agreement or any contract of guarantee relating thereto, and no security given by the buyer in respect of money payable under the credit-sale agreement or given by a guarantor in respect of money payable under such a contract of guarantee is enforceable against the buyer or guarantor by any holder thereof, unless subsection (1) has been complied with, and—

(a) a note or memorandum of the agreement is made and signed by the buyer and by or on behalf of all other parties to the agreement;

(b) the note or memorandum contains a statement of the total purchase price and of the cash price of the goods to which the agreement relates and of the amount of each of the instalments by which the total purchase price is to be paid and of the date, or the mode of determining the date, upon which each instalment is payable, and contains a list of the goods to which the agreement relates sufficient to identify them; and

(c) a copy of the note or memorandum is delivered or sent to the buyer at his address as contained in the agreement within seven days of the making of the agreement.

(4) Where in *an* action the court is satisfied that a failure to comply with subsection (1) or with paragraph (*b*) or *(c)* of subsection *(3)* has not prejudiced the buyer and that it would be just and equitable to dispense with compliance, the court may, subject to any conditions that it thinks fit to impose, dispense with such compliance for the purpose of the action.

Right of hirer to determine hire-purchase agreements.

6. (1) A hirer, at any time before the final payment under a hire-purchase agreement falls due, is entitled to determine the agreement by giving notice of termination in writing to any person entitled or authorised to receive the sums payable under the agreement, and at the same time or prior thereto shall deliver the goods to the owner, and, on determining the agreement under this section, is liable, without prejudice to any liability which has accrued before the termination, to pay the amount, if any, due in respect of the hire-purchase price immediately before the termination, or such lesser amount as may be specified in the agreement.

(2) Where a hirer gives notice of termination of a hire-purchase agreement without delivering the goods as required by this section such notice is of no effect and the hire-purchase agreement remains in force.

(3) Where a hire-purchase agreement has been determined under this section, the hirer, if he has failed to take reasonable care of the goods is liable to pay damages for the failure.

(4) Nothing in this section prejudices any right of a hirer to determine a hire-purchase agreement otherwise than by virtue of this section.

Avoidance of certain provisions.

7. Any provision in an agreement—

(a) whereby an owner or any person acting on his behalf is authorised to enter forcibly upon any premises for the purpose of taking possession of goods which have been let under a hire-purchase agreement, or is relieved from liability for any such forcible entry;

(b) whereby the right conferred on a hirer by this Act to determine the hire-purchase agreement is excluded or restricted;

(c) whereby the right conferred on a hirer by this Act to remedy the breach of a hire-purchase agreement in accordance with this Act is excluded or restricted or whereby any liability in addition to any liability imposed by this Act is imposed on a hirer by reason of the continuation of the hire-purchase agreement under this Act;

(d) whereby a hirer, after the determination of the hire-purchase agreement or the bailment in any manner whatsoever, is subject to a liability which exceeds the liabilitv to which he would have been subject if the agreement had been determined by him under this Act;

(e) whereby any person acting on behalf of an owner or seller in connection with the formation or conclusion of a hire-purchase or credit-sale agreement is treated as or deemed to be the agent of the hirer or the buyer; or

(f) whereby an owner or seller is relieved from liability for the acts or defaults of any person acting on his behalf in connection with the formation or conclusion of a hire-purchase agreement or credit-sale agreement,

is void.

Duty of owners and sellers to supply documents and information.

8. (1) At any time before the final payment has been made under a hire-purchase or credit-sale agreement, the owner or seller, within seven days after receiving a request in writing together with the sum of two dollars for expenses from the hirer or buyer shall supply to the hirer or buyer at an address given in the request a copy of any memorandum or note of the agreement, together with a statement signed by the owner or seller or his agent showing—

(a) the amount paid by or on behalf of the hirer or buyer;

(*b*) the amount which has become due under the agreement but remains unpaid, and the date upon which each unpaid instalment became due, and the amount of each such instalment; and

(c) the amount which is to become payable under the agreement, and the date or the mode of determining the date upon which each future instalment is to become payable, and the amount of each such instalment.

(2) The owner or seller is deemed to have complied with subsection (1) if he delivers the copy of the memorandum or note of agreement and the statement, or sends the same by registered post to the hirer or buyer at the address given in the request, and where no address is given, the owner or seller is deemed to have complied with subsection *(1)* if he delivers the copy of the memorandum or note or agreement and the statement, or sends the same by registered post to the hirer or buyer at his address given in the hire-purchase agreement.

(3) Where the owner or seller fails without reasonable cause to comply with subsection (1), then, while the default continues—

(a) no person is entitled to enforce the agreement against the hirer or buyer or to enforce any contract of guarantee relating to the agreement, and, in the case of a hire-purchase agreement, the owner is not entitled to enforce any right to recover the goods from the hirer; and

(*b*) no security given by the hirer or buyer in respect of money payable under the agreement or given by a guarantor in respect of money payable under such a contract of guarantee is enforceable against the hirer or buyer or the guarantor by any holder thereof.

(4) A person who fails without reasonable cause to comply with subsection *(1)* for a period of one month, is liable on summary conviction to a fine of five hundred dollars.

Duty of hirer to give information as to whereabouts of goods.

9. (1) Where under a hire-purchase agreement a hirer has a duty to keep the goods comprised in the agreement in his possession or control, the hirer shall, on receipt of a request in writing from the owner, inform the owner where the goods are at the time when the information is given, or, if it is sent by post, at the time of posting.

(2) A hirer who fails without reasonable cause to give the information required to be given by subsection (1) within fourteen days of the receipt of the notice, or who gives any information for the purposes of subsection (1) which he knows or has reasonable cause to believe is false, is liable on summary conviction to a fine of five hundred dollars.

Conditions and warranties to be implied in hire-purchase agreements.

10. (1) In every hire-purchase agreement there is—

(*a*) an implied warranty that the hirer shall have and enjoy quiet possession of the goods;

(*b*) an implied condition on the part of the owner that he has a right to sell the goods at the time when the property is to pass;

(c) an implied warranty that the goods are free from any charge or encumbrance in favour of any third party at the time when the property is to pass;

(d) except where the goods are let as second hand goods and the note or memorandum of the agreement made in pursuance of section 4 contains a statement to that effect, an implied condition that the goods are of merchantable quality; but no such condition is implied by virtue of this paragraph as regards defects of which the owner could not reasonably have been aware at the time when the agreement was made, or, if the hirer has examined the goods or a sample thereof, as regards defects which the examination ought to have revealed.

(2) Where the hirer expressly or by implication makes known the particular purpose for which the goods are required, there is an implied condition that the goods are reasonably fit for such purpose.

(3) The warranties and conditions set out in subsection (1) are implied notwithstanding any agreement to the

contrary and the owner is not entitled to rely on any provision in the agreement excluding or modifying the condition set out in subsection (2) unless he proves that before the agreement was made the provision was brought to the notice of the hirer and its effect made clear to him.

(4) Nothing in this section prejudices the operation of any other enactment or rule of law whereby a condition or warranty is to be implied in a hire-purchase agreement.

Appropriation of payments made in respect of hire-purchase agreements.

11. A hirer who is liable to make payments in respect of two or more hire-vurchase agreements to the same owner. notwithstanding any agreement to the contrary, is entitled, on making any payment in respect of the agreements which is not sufficient to discharge the total amount then due under all the agreements to appropriate the sum so paid by him in or towards the satisfaction of the sum due under any one of the agreements, or in or towards the satisfaction of the sums due under any two or more of the agreements in such proportions as he thinks fit, and if he fails to make any such appropriation, the payment shall by virtue of this section be appropriated towards the satisfaction of the sums due under the respective hire-purchase agreements in the proportions which those sums bear to one another.

Evidence of adverse detention in actions by owners to recover possession of the goods.

12. (1) Where, in an action by an owner to enforce a right to recover possession of goods which have been let under a hire-purchase agreement the owner proves that before the commencement of the action and after the right to recover possession of the goods accrued the owner made a request in writing to the hirer to surrender the goods, the hirer's possession of the goods is deemed to be adverse to the owner for the purpose of the owner's claim to recover possession.

(2) Nothing in this section affects a claim for damages for conversion.

Owner may only recover goods by action where seventy per cent of hire-puchase price paid.

13. (1) Where goods have been let under a hire-purchase agreement and seventy per cent of the hire-purchase price has been paid, whether in pursuance of a judgment or otherwise, or tendered by or on behalf of the hirer or any guarantor, the owner shall not enforce any right to recover possession of the goods otherwise than by action.

(2) If an owner recovers possession of goods in contravention of subsection (1), the hire-purchase agreement, if not previously determined, shall determine, and—

(a) the hirer is released from all liability under the agreement and is entitled to recover from the owner, in an action for money had and received, all sums paid by the hirer under the agreement or under any security given by him in respect thereof; and

(*b*) any guarantor is entitled to recover from the owner, in an action for money had and received, all sums paid by him under the contract of guarantee or under any security given by him in respect thereof.

(3) This section does not apply where the hirer has determined the agreement or the bailment by virtue of any right vested in him.

Powers of court in certain actions by owners to recover possession of the goods.

14. *(1)* Where, in a case to which section *13* applies, an owner commences an action to enforce a right to recover possession of goods from a hirer after seventy per cent of the hire-purchase price has been paid or tendered, the action shall be commenced in the Magistrate's Court, and after the action has been commenced the owner shall not take any step to enforce payment of any sum due under the hire-purchase agreement or under any contract of guarantee relating thereto, except by claiming the sum in the said action.

(2) Subject to such exceptions as may be provided for by rules made under the Magistrate's Code of Procedure Act, all the parties to the agreement and any guarantor shall be made parties to the action. Cap. 255.

(3) Pending the hearing of the action the court shall have power upon the application of the owner, to make such orders as the court thinks just for the purpose of protecting the goods from damage or depreciation, including orders restricting or prohibiting the user of the goods or giving directions as to their custody.

(4) A person who fails to comply with any requirements of an order under subsection *(3)* is liable on summary conviction of a fine of five hundred dollars.

(5) On the hearing of the action the court may, without prejudice to any other power—

(a) make an order for the specific delivery of all the goods to the owner;

(b) make an order for the specific delivery of all the goods to the owner and postpone the operation of the order on condition that the hirer or any guarantor pays the unpaid balance of the hire-purchase price at such times and in such amounts as the court, having regard to the means of the hirer and of any guarantor, thinks just, and, subject to the fulfilment of such other conditions by the hirer or a guarantor as the court thinks just; or

(c) make *an* order for the specific delivery of a part of the goods to the owner and for the transfer to the hirer of the owner's title to the remainder of the goods.

(6) No order shall be made under subsection (5) (*b*) unless the hirer satisfies the court that the goods are in his possession or control at the time when the order is made.

(7) The court shall not make an order transferring to the hirer the owner's title to a part of the goods unless it is satisfied that the amount which the hirer has paid in respect of the hire-purchase price exceeds the price of that part of the goods by at least one-third of the unpaid balance of the hire-purchase price.

(8) Where in an action under section 13 in accordance with rules of court the hirer makes an offer to repay the unpaid balance of the purchase price on terms and conditions that are accepted by the owner, the court may make an order under subsection (5)(*b*) in accordance with the hirer's offer without hearing evidence as to the matter set out in subsection (5)(*b*) or in subsection (6).

(9) No order under subsection *(8)* shall be made before the date fixed for the hearing of the action where a guarantor is a party to the action.

(10) Where damages have been awarded against the owner in the proceedings the court may treat the hirer as

having paid in respect of the hire-purchase price, in addition to the actual amount paid, the amount of the damages, or such part thereof as the court thinks fit, and thereupon the damages shall accordingly be remitted either in whole or in part.

(11) In this section, the expression—

"order for the specific delivery of the goods to the owner" means an order for delivery of the goods to the owner, without giving the hirer an option to pay their value;

"price" in relation to any goods means such part of the hire-purchase price as is assigned to those goods by the note or memorandum of the hire-purchase agreement, or, if no such assignment is made, such part of the hire-purchase price as the court may determine.

(12) Where before the hearing of an action to which this section applies the owner recovers possession of a part of the goods, the references in subsection (5) to all the goods shall be construed as references to all the goods which the owner has not recovered, and, if the parties have not agreed upon an adjustment of the hire-purchase price in respect of the goods so recovered, the court may for the purposes of subsection (5) (*b*) and *(c)* make such reduction of the hire-purchase price and of the unpaid balance thereof as the court thinks just.

(13) Where an owner recovers a part of the goods let under a hire-purchase agreement, and the recovery was effected in contravention of section 13, this section does not apply in relation to any action by the owner to recover the remainder of the goods.

(14) A Magistrate's Court shall have jurisdiction to hear and determine an action referred to in subsection (1) notwithstanding that the hire-purchase price of the goods claimed in such action exceeds fifteen hundred dollars, and, subject as hereinafter provided, the provisions of the Magistrate's Code of Procedure Act, including the provisions relating to

appeals, and of any rules made thereunder shall apply in respect of every such action as they apply in respect of actions which a Magistrate's Court is authorised to hear and determine under that Act.

(15) The application of the provisions of the Magistrate's Code of Procedure Act and of any rules made thereunder in respect of any action referred to in subsection (1) shall be subject to the provisions of this Act.

Effect of postponement of operation of an order for specific delivery of goods to the owner.

15. (1) While the operation of an order for the specific delivery of goods to the owner is postponed under section 14, the hirer is deemed to be a bailee of the goods under and on the terms of the hire-purchase agreement, and

(a) no further sum is payable by the hirer or a guarantor on account of the unpaid balance of the hire-purchase price, except in accordance with the terms of the order; and

(b) the court may make such further modification of the terms of the hire-purchase agreement and of any contract of guarantee relating thereto as the court consider necessary having regard to the variation of the terms of payment.

(2) Where an order for the specific delivery of the goods to the owner is postponed and the hirer or a guarantor fails to comply with any condition of the postponement, or with any term of the agreement as varied by the court, or wrongfully disposes of the goods, the owner shall take no civil proceedings against the hirer or guarantor other than making an application to the court by which the order was made, except that in the case of a breach of any condition relating to the payment of the unpaid balance of the hire-purchase price, it is not necessary for the owner to apply to the court for leave to execute the order unless the court has so directed.

(3) When the unpaid balance of the hire-purchase price has been paid in accordance with the terms of the order, the owner's title to the goods shall vest in the hirer.

(4) The court may at any time during the postponement of the operation of an order—

(a) vary the conditions of the postponement and make such further modification of the hire-purchase agreement and of any contract of guarantee relating thereto as the court considers necessary having regard to the variation of the conditions of the postponement;

(*b*) revoke the postponement; or

(*c*) make an order, in accordance with section *14,* for the specific delivery of a part of the goods to the owner and for the transfer to the hirer of the owner's title to the remainder of the goods.

(5) Where an order is made under section 14(5) *(b),* the powers of the court under subsection *(4) (a)* and *(c)* of this section may be exercised, notwithstanding that any condition of the postponement has not been complied with, at any time before the goods are delivered to the owner in accordance with a warrant issued in pursuance of the order; and where such a warrant has been issued the court shall—

(a) if the court varies the conditions of the postponement under subsection *(4) (a),* suspend the warrant on the like conditions;

(b) if the court makes an order under subsection (4) (c) for the specific delivery of a part of the goods to the owner and for the transfer to the hirer of the owner's title to the remaining part of the goods, cancel the warrant so far as it provides for the delivery of the last mentioned part of the goods.

(6) Where a warrant referred to in subsection *(5)* has been issued, in so far as it provides for the delivery of the goods the warrant may be discharged at any time before delivery of the goods to the owner, by the payment to the owner by the hirer or guarantor of the whole of the unpaid balance of the hire-purchase price, and the owner's title to the goods shall thereupon vest in the hirer.

Successive hire-purchase agreements between the same parties.

16. Where goods have been let under a hire-purchase agreement and after seventy per cent of the hire-purchase price has been paid or tendered the owner makes a further hire-purchase agreement with the hirer comprising those goods, sections 13 and *14* shall have effect in relation to that further agreement as from the commencement thereof.

Provisions as to bankruptcy of hirer.

17. Where, under the powers conferred by this Act, the court has postponed the operation of an order for the specific delivery of goods to any person, the goods shall not, during the postponement, be treated as goods which are by the consent or permission of that person in the possession, order or disposition of the hirer for the purposes of section 40 of the Bankruptcy Act.

Cap.41.

Where less than seventy per cent of hire-purchase price is paid owner to give notice before enforcing his right to recover possession of goods if failure to pay instalments is only breach.

18. (1) Where, whether in pursuance of a judgment or otherwise, less than seventy per cent of the hire-purchase price has been paid or tendered by or on behalf of the hirer or a guarantor on goods let under a hire-purchase agreement, and the hirer's only breach is failure to pay any instalment of the hire-purchase price which is then due, the owner may not enforce a right to recover possession of the goods without giving to the hirer twenty-one clear days notice of his intention to do so.

(2) The notice referred to in subsection (1) shall be in writing and shall state the amount of the hire-purchase price which is then due and unpaid, and shall further state that it is the intention of the owner, on the expiration of twenty-one clear days after the notice has been given to the hirer, to enforce his right to recover possession of the goods unless the hirer has previously made good his default.

(3) Where within twenty-one clear days after a notice under subsection (1) has been given the hirer pays to the owner all instalments of the hire-purchase price due at the date of the notice the hire-purchase agreement continues in force as if the breach stated in the notice had never occurred.

(4) For the purposes of this section, a notice is deemed to have been given if it is directed to the hirer, and delivered at, or despatched by registered letter to, his address as mentioned in the hire-purchase agreement.

(5) Where an owner recovers possession of goods in contravention of subsection (1), section 13 (2) applies as it applies where an owner recovers possession of goods in contravention of section 13 (1).

(6) This section does not apply where the hirer has determined the agreement or the bailment by virtue of any right vested in him.

19. Where a hirer refuses to give up possession of goods to an owner whose right to recover the goods is subject by virtue of this Act, to any restriction, the hirer is not liable to the owner for conversion of the goods by reason only of such refusal.

Hirer's refusal to surrender goods not to be conversion in certain cases.

20. A hirer who obstructs or attempts to obstruct an owner in the lawful exercise of his right to recover possession of goods when the owner's right to recover possession of the goods is not subject to any restriction imposed by or under this Act, is liable on summary conviction to a' fine of five hundred dollars.

Obstruction.

21. *(1)* Where under a hire-purchase agreement made after the commencement of this Act the owner is required to carry out an installation, and payment is required for such installation the note or memorandum of the agreement shall specify the amount to be paid in respect of the installation but such amount shall not be treated for the purposes of this Act as part of the hire-purchase price.

Installation charges.

(2) For the purposes of this section, the expression "installation" means—

(a) the installing of any electric line as defined in the Public Utilities Act;

(*b*) the fixing of goods to which the agreement relates to the premises where they are to be used, and the alteration of premises to enable any such goods to be used thereon;

(c) where it is reasonably necessary that any such goods should be constructed or erected on the premises where they are to be used, any work carried out for the purpose of such construction or erection.

22. (1) The following sections of this Act apply to the extent specified below, in relation to all hire-purchase agreements whether made before or after the commencement of this Act, that is to say—

Application of Act to existing agreements.

(a) section 11 of this Act, so far as it relates to payments made after the commencement of this Act;

(b) section 12 of this Act, so far as it relates to recovery of possession of goods after the commencement of this Act.

(2) Save as mentioned above, this Act does not apply to any hire-purchase agreement or credit-sale agreement made before the commencement of this Act.

SCHEDULE Section 4 (3) (c)

Notice to be Included in Note or
Memorandum of Hire-Purchase Agreement

Right of Hirer to Terminate Agreement

1. The hirer may put an end to this agreement by giving notice of termination in writing to any person who is entitled to collect or receive the hire-rent and at the same time or prior thereto by delivering the goods to the owner.

2. He must then pay instalments which are in arrear at the time when he gives notice.

3. If the hirer does not deliver the goods to the owner at the time mentioned in paragraph 1 above, the notice of termination will be ineffective and the agreement will remain in force.

4. If the goods have been damaged owing to the hirer having failed to take reasonable care of them, the owner may sue him for the amount of the damage unless that amount can be agreed between the hirer and the owner.

5. The hirer should see whether this agreement contains provisions allowing him to put an end to the agreement on terms more favourable to him than those just mentioned. If it does he may put an end to the agreement on those terms.

Restriction of Owner's Right to recover Goods
where seventy per cent of the Hire-Purchase price has been paid

1. *[After (here insert an amount equal to seventy per cent of the hire-purchase price) has been paid, then] unless the hirer has himself put an end to the agreement, the owner of the goods cannot take them back from the hirer without the hirer's consent unless the owner obtains an order of the court.

2. If the owner applies to the court for such an order, the court may, if the court thinks it just to do so, allow the hirer to keep either—

(a) the whole of the goods, on condition that the hirer pays the balance of the price in the manner ordered by the Court; or

(*b*) a fair proportion of the goods having regard to what the hirer has already paid.

Restriction of Owner's Right to recover Goods where less than seventy per cent of the Hire-Purchase price has been paid

1. Where less than (here insert an amount equal to seventy per cent of the hire-purchase price) has been paid, unless the hirer has himself put an end to the agreement or has committed some breach of the agreement other than failure to pay any instalment of the hire-purchase price, the owner of the goods cannot take them back from the hirer without the hirer's consent unless the owner has given the hirer twenty-one clear days written notice of his intention to do so.

2. If within the said period of twenty-one clear days the hirer pays to the owner all instalments of the hire-purchase price due at the date of the issue of such notice, the agreement will continue in force.

*If the agreement is a "further" agreement within the meaning of section 16 of this Act, the words in square brackets should be omitted.

MISREPRESENTATION ACT

CHAPTER 82:35

Act
12 of 1983

Current Authorised Pages

Pages (inclusive)		*Authorised by L.R.O.*
1–5	..	*1/2006*

Note on Subsidiary Legislation

This Chapter contains no subsidiary legislation.

CHAPTER 82:35

MISREPRESENTATION ACT

ARRANGEMENT OF SECTIONS

CHAPTER 82:35

MISREPRESENTATION ACT

12 of 1983.

An Act to amend the law relating to innocent misrepresentations.

Commencement. [228/1986].

[20TH OCTOBER 1986]

Short title.

1. This Act may be cited as the Misrepresentation Act.

Removal of certain bars to rescission for innocent misrepresentation.

2. Where a person has entered into a contract after a misrepresentation has been made to him, and—

(a) the misrepresentation has become a term of the contract; or

(b) the contract has been performed,

or both, then, if otherwise he would be entitled to rescind the contract without alleging fraud, he shall be so entitled, subject to this Act, notwithstanding the matters mentioned in paragraphs *(a)* and *(b)*.

Damages for misrepresentation.

3. (1) Where a person has entered into a contract after a misrepresentation has been made to him by another party thereto and as a result thereof he has suffered loss, then, if the person making the misrepresentation would be liable to damages in respect thereof had the misrepresentation been made fraudulently, that person shall be so liable notwithstanding that the misrepresentation was not made fraudulently, unless he proves that he had reasonable ground to believe and did believe up to the time the contract was made that the facts represented were true.

(2) Where a person has entered into a contract after a misrepresentation has been made to him otherwise than fraudulently, and he would be entitled, by reason of the misrepresentation, to rescind the contract, then, if it is claimed, in any proceedings arising out of the contract, that the contract ought to be or has been rescinded, the Court or arbitrator may declare the contract subsisting and award damages in lieu of rescission, if of opinion that it would be equitable to do so, having regard to the nature of the misrepresentation and the loss that would be caused by it if the contract were upheld, as well as to the loss that rescission would cause to the other party.

(3) Damages may be awarded against a person under subsection (2) whether or not he is liable to damages under subsection (1), but where he is so liable any award under subsection (2) shall be taken into account in assessing his liability under subsection (1).

Avoidance of provision excluding liability for misrepresentation.

4. If a contract contains a term which would exclude or restrict—

(a) any liability to which a party to a contract may be subject by reason of any misrepresentation made by him before the contract was made; or

(b) any remedy available to another party to the contract by reason of such a misrepresentation,

that term shall be of no effect except in so far as it satisfies the requirement of reasonableness as stated in section 5 and it is for those claiming that the term satisfies that requirement to show that it does.

The "reasonableness" test.

5. (1) In relation to a contract term, the requirement of reasonableness for the purposes of section 4 is that the term shall have been a fair and reasonable one to be included having regard to the circumstances which were or ought reasonably to have been known to or in the contemplation of the parties when the contract was made.

(2) A contract term is to be taken for the purposes of this Act, as satisfying the requirement of reasonableness, if it is incorporated or approved by, or incorporated pursuant to a decision or ruling of, a competent authority acting in the exercise of any statutory jurisdiction or function and is not a term in a contract to which the competent authority is itself a party.

(3) In this section "competent authority" means any Court, arbitrator or arbiter, government department or public authority.

Saving for past transactions.

6. Nothing in this Act shall apply in relation to any misrepresentation or contract of sale which is made before the commencement of this Act.

BERMUDA
1977 : 53

LAW REFORM (MISREPRESENTATION AND FRUSTRATED CONTRACTS) ACT 1977

ARRANGEMENT OF SECTIONS

[29 December 1977]

[preamble and words of enactment omitted]

Interpretation

1 In this Act—

"contract" includes a contract to which the Crown is a party;

"court" means the court or arbitrator by or before whom a matter is brought to be determined;

"discharged" means relieved from further performance of the contract.

Removal of certain bars to recission for innocent misrepresentation

2 Where a person has entered into a contract after a misrepresentation has been made to him, and—

LAW REFORM (MISREPRESENTATION AND FRUSTRATED CONTRACTS) ACT 1977

(a) the misrepresentation has become a term of the contract; or

(b) the contract has been performed,

or both, then, if otherwise he would be entitled to rescind the contract without alleging fraud, he shall be so entitled, subject to the provisions of this Act, notwithstanding the matters mentioned in paragraphs (a) and (b).

Damages for misrepresentation

3 (1) Where a person has entered into a contract after a misrepresentation has been made to him by another party thereto and as a result thereof he has suffered loss, then, if the person making the representation would be liable to damages in respect thereof had the misrepresentation been made fraudulently, that person shall be so liable notwithstanding that the misrepresentation was not made fraudulently, unless he proves that he had reasonable grounds to believe and did believe up to the time the contract was made that the facts represented were true.

(2) Where a person has entered into a contract after a misrepresentation has been made to him otherwise than fraudulently, and he would be entitled, by reason of the misrepresentation, to rescind the contract, then, if it is claimed, in any proceedings arising out of the contract, that the contract ought to be or has been rescinded the court may declare the contract subsisting and award damages in lieu of rescission, if of opinion that it would be equitable to do so, having regard to the nature of the misrepresentation and the loss that would be caused by it if the contract were upheld, as well as to the loss that rescission would cause to the other party.

(3) Damages may be awarded against a person under subsection (2) whether or not he is liable to damages under subsection (1), but where he is so liable any award under subsection (2) shall be taken into account in assessing his liability under subsection (1).

Avoidance of certain provisions excluding liability for misrepresentation

4 If any agreement (whether made before or after 29 December 1977) contains a provision which would exclude or restrict—

(a) any liability to which a party to a contract may be subject by reason of any misrepresentation made by him before the contract was made; or

(b) any remedy available to another party to the contract by reason of such a misrepresentation, that provision shall be of no effect except to the extent (if any) that, in any proceedings arising out of the contract, the court may allow reliance on it as being fair and reasonable in the circumstances of the case.

Application of section 6

5 (1) Section 6 shall apply to a contract that has become impossible of performance or been otherwise frustrated and the parties to which for that reason have been discharged.

(2) The aforementioned section does not apply—

(a) to a charter-party or to a contract for the carriage of goods by sea, except a time charter-party or a charter-party by way of demise; or

(b) to a contract of insurance; or

(c) to a contract for the sale of specific goods where the goods—

(i) without the knowledge of the seller, have perished at the time when the contract is made; or

(ii) without any fault on the part of the seller or buyer, perish before the risk passes to the buyer.

Sums payable before parties discharged

6 (1) The sums paid or payable to a party, in pursuance of a contract before the parties were discharged—

(a) in the case of sums paid, are recoverable from that party as money received by him for the use of the party by whom the sums were paid; and

(b) in the case of sums payable, cease to be payable.

(2) If, before the parties were discharged, the party to whom the sums were paid or payable incurred expenses in connection with the performance of the contract, the court, if it considers it just to do so having regard to all the circumstances, may allow him to retain or to recover, as the case may be, the whole or a part of the sums paid or payable not exceeding the amount of the expenses.

(3) Without restricting the generality of subsection (2), the court, in estimating the amount of the expenses, may include such sum as appears to be reasonable in respect of overhead expenses and in respect of work or services performed personally by the party incurring the expenses.

LAW REFORM (MISREPRESENTATION AND FRUSTRATED CONTRACTS) ACT 1977

(4) If, before the parties were discharged, any of them has, by reason of anything done by another party in connection with the performance of the contract, obtained a valuable benefit other than a payment of money, the court, if it considers it just to do so having regard to all the circumstances, may allow the other party to recover from the party benefited the whole or a part of the value of the benefit.

(5) Where a party has assumed an obligation under the contract in consideration of the conferring of a benefit by another party to the contract upon another person, whether a party to the contract or not, the court if it considers it just to do so having regard to all the circumstances, may for the purposes of subsection (4) treat a benefit so conferred as a benefit obtained by the party who has assumed the obligation.

(6) In considering whether a sum ought to be recovered or retained under this section by a party to the contract, the court shall not take in account a sum that, by reason of the circumstances giving rise to the frustration of the contract, has become payable to that party under a contract of insurance, unless there was an obligation to insure imposed by an express term of the frustrated contract or by or under an enactment.

(7) Where the contract contains a provision that upon the true construction of the contract is intended to have effect—

(a) in the event of circumstances that operate, or but for that provision would operate, to frustrate the contract; or

(b) whether such circumstances arise or not,

the court shall give effect to the provision and shall give effect to this section only to such extent, if any, as appears to the court to be consistent with that provision.

(8) Where it appears to the court that part of the contract can be severed properly from the remainder of the contract, being a part—

(a) wholly performed before the parties were discharged; or

(b) wholly performed except for the payment in respect of that part of the contract of sums that are or can be ascertained under the contract,

the court shall treat that part of the contract as if it were a separate contract that had not been frustrated and shall treat this section as applicable only to the remainder of the contract.

Saving for transactions before 29 December 1977

7 Subject to the provisions of section 4 nothing in this Act shall apply to any contract made before 29 December 1977.

INDEX